A PATTERN OF VIOLENCE

A PATTERN OF **VIOLENCE**

How the Law Classifies Crimes and What It Means for Justice

David Alan Sklansky

THE BELKNAP PRESS *of* HARVARD UNIVERSITY PRESS

Cambridge, Massachusetts · London, England 2021

First printing

Library of Congress Cataloging-in-Publication Data

Names: Sklansky, David A., 1959– author.
Title: A pattern of violence: how the law classifies crimes and what it means for justice /
    David Alan Sklansky.
Description: Cambridge, Massachusetts : The Belknap Press of Harvard University Press,
    2021. | Includes bibliographical references and index.
Identifiers: LCCN 2020036310 | ISBN 9780674248908 (hardcover)
Subjects: LCSH: Violence (Law)—United States. | Violent crimes—Law and legislation—
    United States. | Political violence—United States.
Classification: LCC KF9304 .S55 2021 | DDC 345.73/025—dc23
LC record available at https://lccn.loc.gov/2020036310

to Joe

CONTENTS

A PATTERN OF VIOLENCE

INTRODUCTION

Two stories loom large in the recent history of the American criminal justice system. Both are tragedies.

The first story is the story of mass incarceration. At the beginning of the 1980s, when I enrolled in law school, the percentage of people behind bars in the United States was roughly the same as in the United Kingdom and Western Europe. Those rates had stayed more or less constant for decades. During the 1980s and 1990s, however, the American rate of incarceration skyrocketed, and it is now five or ten times as high as the rates in Britain, in Europe, or in democratic societies elsewhere in the world. The rate of incarceration in the United States has dropped a little in recent years, but we still lock up a far greater share of our people than any other sizeable country on earth. We are not just worse than the United Kingdom and Western Europe; we are worse than Russia or China. We have 5 percent of the world's population and 25 percent of its prisoners. And the people we lock up are disproportionately dark-skinned and poor: people of color are 30 percent of the American population but 60 percent of all prisoners.

Mass incarceration has had devastating consequences in the United States, not just for prisoners but also for their families and their communities. It has ruined lives, sucked state budgets dry, and distorted our politics. It has been a decades-long train wreck.

The second story is the story of police reform. At the dawn of the twenty-first century, police reform seemed like a success story. The entire field of law enforcement had been transformed by the philosophy called "community policing"; the central idea was that police should work hand-in-hand with communities instead of holding themselves apart. Affirmative action programs had radically changed the demographics of agencies that only a few decades before had been nearly all male and all white. Police departments had accepted civilian oversight. A new generation of command officers had brought unprecedented levels of thoughtfulness and sophistication to the profession. The police had learned that they could work with their constituents, open themselves up to outside criticism, and at the same time do something many thoughtful people had believed was beyond the power of the police—namely, reduce crime.

In the early 2000s I sat in a university conference room with a group of very smart, very reflective police chiefs from across the United States. They had been called together to try to figure out what the next big thing in policing should be. Remarkably, almost none of the chiefs thought there was any need for a next big thing. They thought policing had been fixed, and that reformers should turn their attention elsewhere. Many people outside policing thought that, too. It was common at that time for scholars and reformers to talk optimistically about the promise of "new governance," and when they did so, they often pointed approvingly to community policing to illustrate what they had in mind.

Today it is difficult to find any informed observer who believes that law enforcement is fixed and can be left alone. We are back where we were at the very beginning of the 1980s, when there was a widespread sense that American law enforcement was in crisis—or even, perhaps, the late 1960s, when America itself seemed in crisis, in significant part because of the police. In the spring of 2020, when a nationwide wave of protests drew tens of thousands of Americans out of quarantine and into the streets, the principal grievances were, once again, about law enforcement. It is not just past efforts at police reform that have been discredited. By the spring of 2020, the very idea of "reforming" the police had been thrown into question. For many Americans, the police seemed beyond reform; they needed to be abolished, and replaced with something radically different.

To a very great extent, each of these two stories—the train wreck of mass incarceration and the collapse of police reform—is a story about how the law understands and responds to violence.

Mass incarceration has been driven in large part by fears about violent crime. Those fears provided much of the fuel for the explosive growth of prison populations in the 1980s and 1990s, and they are helping to keep our imprisonment rates sky high today. Roughly half of the people currently serving prison sentences in the United States have been convicted of offenses classified as violent. If we let everyone else out, our national incarceration rate would be similar to the rates in Russia, Cuba, and Rwanda. If we want to start looking more like England or Ireland or France or Germany in this respect, we will need to dramatically reduce our punishments for violent crime.[1]

That will be hard, because there is a very widespread assumption that violent crime is the worst kind of crime, and that violent criminals need and deserve long sentences. Several years ago, for example, California voters approved a ballot initiative that made it easier for some prisoners to apply for parole. A huge part of the debate over the initiative had to do with whether or not it applied to violent offenders. The opponents said it did. The supporters said it did not. The shared, unstated assumption was that if we do expand parole, we do not want to expand it for violent offenders. The category of violence does a lot of work in American criminal law. And the story of mass incarceration, it turns out, is in part a story about the growing importance of the category of violence in American criminal law, and about changing understandings of violent crime and violent criminals.

The failure of police reform, on the other hand, is partly a story about a decline in the salience of violence in the rules that govern law enforcement, and in our thinking about the police more broadly. There have been times when police reformers in the United States thought a lot about police violence. But the police chiefs in that university conference room in the early 2000s weren't thinking much about police violence. And the champions of community policing in the 1980s and 1990s had not focused on police violence. It had fallen off the radar screen. Partly as a result, the explosion in the use of military equipment and tactics by American police departments in the 1990s and early 2000s did not receive the attention it deserved. Neither did the pervasive, everyday violence of "stop and frisk"—a tactic which some police departments greatly expanded in the late twentieth century and early twenty-first century, and which they characterized as fully consistent with, and even an instrument of, community policing. Despite the controversy in the 1990s about discriminatory traffic stops, the *violence* associated with those stops, and with investigatory detentions of pedestrians, received comparatively little attention.

The reason American policing today seems once again to be in crisis has a lot to do with violence: the violence of military-style policing, the violence of stop and frisk, and above all else the violence of police shootings. The protests in 2020 were not about "police misconduct." They were not about incivility or haughtiness. They did not focus on invasions of privacy, or the use of informants. Like the demonstrations several years earlier, following the deaths of Eric Garner in Staten Island and Michael Brown in Ferguson, Missouri, the marches in 2020 were a response to police violence, especially the extraordinarily high rate at which American police forces kill young men of color. The spark this time was the killing of an unarmed Black man named George Floyd by police officers in Minneapolis. But the protesters' signs also bore a litany of other Black Americans killed by the police in the preceding years: Eric Garner, Michael Brown, Tamir Rice, Freddie Gray, Breonna Taylor, and many more.

Unfortunately, the police reformers of the late twentieth and early twenty-first centuries largely lacked a vocabulary for the problem of police violence. Violence as a category was not a significant part of how they organized the world of police behavior. Neither was it—or is it today—a significant part of the legal rules regulating American police. William Stuntz, perhaps the most perceptive scholar of American criminal law in the 1990s and early 2000s, marveled at "the chasm between the mass of rules and regulations governing where the police can look and what they can touch when they look there, and the virtual absence of any constitutional constraint on when the police can strike a suspect."[2]

The twin tragedies of contemporary criminal justice in the United States thus both have to do with violence. More precisely, they have to do with *ideas* about violence: how the legal system understands violence and tries, or does not try, to tame it. Those ideas are the focus of this book. This book is about how American law thinks, and sometimes fails to think, about violence. It is about the significance the law gives to the line between violent conduct and nonviolent conduct, where it draws that line, and what assumptions it makes about how violence operates. Is violence always worse than nonviolence? How is violence defined? What causes violence, and how is it best controlled? Is violence rooted in the character of violent people or in the circumstances they confront? The answers that the law gives to these questions are more complicated and more varied than we often imagine. The ideas about violence embedded in the law are deeply entangled with race, with gender, with class, with the pictures we carry in our heads of what America is and what it can be, with our ideas about human nature, and with our aspirations for justice.

I have spent my career thinking about criminal justice, first as a prosecutor and then as a law professor. I wrote this book because I have become increasingly convinced that thinking sensibly about criminal justice requires thinking sensibly about violence, and that thinking sensibly means, first and foremost, thinking clearly: identifying and being explicit about what we usually take for granted. The main themes of this book will be descriptive and analytical, but I will draw some morals, as well, and I might as well flag them at the outset.

Nothing in this book will suggest that the concept of violence is incoherent, or that the law would be better off without it. Violence is an evil—sometimes a necessary evil, and often a great evil. Law should try to minimize it. But this book will show that the term "violence" is vaguer than we typically realize, and that our attitudes toward violence are often inconsistent and poorly thought out. Moreover, the fuzziness of the category, and the slipperiness of the judgments we attach to it, can and often do allow legal rules about violence to mask racial or class prejudices. I will argue that the effort to divide up the world into the violent and the nonviolent, or into any other sharply drawn dichotomous categories, blinds us too often to the gradations that actually characterize our collective life. When embraced uncritically by the law, the binary distinction between violence and nonviolence can therefore stunt our moral judgments. But I will also suggest that we can go astray, and often do go astray, by excusing violence too readily or refusing to name it.

This is not a book about the true nature of violence. I am not a historian, psychologist, or sociologist. Nor is this a book about the law's complicated relationship with violence, the way that law simultaneously opposes and embraces brute force. Those are topics of paramount importance. My focus, though, will be on something equally important: how the law thinks about violence—which is to say, how violence is understood, and how the concept of violence is employed, in legal rules and legal discourse.

Strictly speaking, of course, the "law" doesn't think about violence; the people who make and apply the law do. And they do not always think the same way. The ideas about violence reflected in the law have changed over time, and different areas of law often incorporate different thoughts about violence. Even within a particular field of law at a particular moment in history, there are frequently conflicting ideas about violence. To borrow the phrasing of the anthropologist Mary Douglas, law doesn't itself think, it doesn't itself have a mind, but it does provide "commitments for thinking with."[3] And those commitments are variable and often contradictory.

Moreover, law isn't a closed system. Legal reasoning draws, inevitably, on ideas that aren't themselves jurisprudential: scientific theories, moral beliefs, cultural assumptions, and folk understandings. Beliefs about violence reflected in legal rules and legal debates provide a window into this broader universe of claims and intuitions about how violence should be understood and addressed. But legal ideas about violence are also significant in their own right, despite—and sometimes precisely because of—how varied and contradictory they can be. Ideas about violence embedded within the law shape and justify many of the constraints under which we live: the demands that law makes of us, the protections that law offers, and the often quite dramatic intrusions that legal institutions make into our lives.

Ideas about violence can be found in many areas of law: from tort law and family law to the law of evidence. If there is a jurisprudence of violence, though, its heartland is criminal law. Criminal law is the field of law principally charged with responding to violence. Indeed, responding to violence is often described today as the chief mission, the central justification, of criminal law. This book concentrates, accordingly, on ideas about violence in criminal law and in its adjacent fields: criminal procedure (which contains the most important rules regulating the police), juvenile justice (a separate, parallel set of rules and institutions for addressing misconduct by minors), the operation of jails and prisons, and the intersection of criminal law with the constitutional protections for free speech and the right to bear arms.

My focus will be on *American* law, with some occasional detours into its English antecedents. There would be obvious advantages to a less parochial, more comparative approach. American law is what I know best, however, and tracing how ideas about violence play out in this particular legal system is work enough for one book. So for the most part I will put to the side how the concept of violence is employed in legal systems outside the United States. In this respect, I will try to gain in depth what I sacrifice in breadth.

Staying focused on American law, moreover, will let me take advantage of a different kind of breadth: comparing assumptions about violence in substantive criminal law—the law defining offenses and prescribing punishments—with the corresponding ideas in criminal procedure, juvenile justice, prison law, and the implementation of the First and Second Amendments. These cross comparisons are important, because it turns out that the law thinks very differently about violence in different contexts. We will want to ask whether those differences are justified, or whether instead they reveal inconsistencies and blind spots in how we talk about violence.

Before turning to these comparisons, it will help to lay some groundwork. Chapter 1 will therefore introduce three different sets of ideas about violence—sets of ideas that the rest of the book will then trace through different fields of the law. The three sets of ideas correspond to three sets of questions about violence. First, there are beliefs about the *significance* of violence. How much does it matter, and in what ways, if conduct is violent rather than nonviolent? Second, there are ideas about the *definition* of violence. Where should the line be drawn between the violent and the nonviolent? Third and finally, there are assumptions about the *nature* of violence. How does violence operate? How does it start, and how does it stop? Is violence mainly the product of temperaments, of circumstances—or of something else?

Chapter 1 explains why answering these questions can be surprisingly difficult: why, for example, the definition of violence can prove slippery, and why our assumptions about the nature and the moral significance of violence are more complicated than we often recognize. Some of the explanation, I'll argue, has to do with a couple of rhetorical moves frequently encountered in discussions of violence: tit for tat, and the calling out of hypocrisy. Our side has to be violent, we think, given the violence of our opponents. And, given their violence, their complaints about our violence can't be taken seriously. But Chapter 1 will also explore how beliefs about violence are complicated by ideas about gender, class, and race, and by American exceptionalism.

The remaining chapters of the book track these questions and ideas about violence over various legal domains. Chapter 2 focuses on the law's treatment of violent crime. The idea that violent crimes are the worst kinds of crimes, and that violent criminals are the least sympathetic of criminal offenders, is nearly pervasive in contemporary discussions of crime and punishment. But that idea turns out to be relatively new, dating back roughly half a century. Where did it come from, and what consequences has it had?

Over the past several decades criminal law also has come to reflect, more and more, a view of violence as characterological rather than situational—a property of individuals, not just of actions. The influence of this idea can be seen, for example, in laws prescribing stiff mandatory sentences for repeat violent offenders. Modern criminal law increasingly reflects a particular idea about how violence operates: that it is driven by the dispositions and characteristic behaviors of particular, aberrational individuals; that violence is in perpetrators' hearts, not in the situations in which they find themselves. This is not a new view, obviously, but it is new for criminal law to embrace it so enthusiastically. Chapter 2 will examine why lawmakers have increasingly tended to treat criminal violence as characterological instead of situational, and will pay particular attention to the distressing role that racial bias appears to have played in this development.

Chapter 3 focuses on criminal procedure, the set of rules that govern how the police operate. How do the ideas about violence reflected in those rules compare with the ones that shape substantive criminal law? In some ways, we will see, they differ dramatically. Unlike substantive criminal statutes, which increasingly treat violent crime as a category apart, qualitatively worse than other criminal offending, and deserving of especially harsh punishment, the rules governing the police do not focus much on police violence. There are only slight differences, doctrinally, between a police officer telling me to stop and a police officer grabbing me and forcing me to the ground, or between a police officer demanding entry into my house and a police officer breaking through the window. Few special rules distinguish violent police misconduct from other forms of police misconduct. And criminal procedure is far less thoroughly dominated than substantive criminal law by characterological understandings of violence. Chapter 3 will ask what accounts for these differences, and whether they are connected with the disappointing progress of police reform over the past several decades.

Chapter 4 examines the law's response to the overlapping problems of rape and domestic violence. Both of these crimes are typically committed by men against women, and the legal treatment of each has been shaped by ideas about gender and sexuality as well as by ideas about violence. We will explore how understandings of violence in rape law, and in responses to domestic violence, have been shaped not only by ongoing controversies about the nature and extent of male domination, but also by the long, troubled intersection of race with allegations of sexual assault in American history. We will ask what has been gained, and what has been lost, when reformers have emphasized the violence in rape and in domestic assault—and, conversely, when the defining attributes of these forms of victimization have been found in something other than physical violence, such as patriarchy, or power and control. And we will examine long-standing debates over whether perpetrators of rape and domestic assault should be seen as aberrational or instead as alarmingly normal. What changes when these forms of violence are traced to patriarchy or "rape culture," rather than to the pathological dispositions of individual men?

Chapter 5 focuses on violence by children and teenagers. The legal treatment of juvenile violence, especially adolescent violence, has changed dramatically over the past half century. What do those developments—which include the "superpredator" scare of the 1980s, the "zero tolerance" movement in school discipline, changes in the rules for prosecuting minors as adults, and new constitutional restrictions on the punishment of underage offenders—tell us about shifting understandings of violence, and of adolescence? Sometimes youth violence is attributed in part to the age of the perpetrators, and sometimes it is viewed as particularly shocking given the age of the perpetrators—an indication that the perpetrators, in some sense, are not normal children or adolescents. Sometimes violence by minors is thought to be less serious, or more forgivable, than violence by adults, but sometimes the opposite assumption is made. What accounts for those differing determinations? What role does race, in particular, play in the social construction of juvenile violence? In addition to exploring all of these questions about how the law treats violence *by* minors, Chapter 5 will also explore the law's treatment of violence *against* juveniles. Here, too, we will find conflicting impulses. Family law and child welfare law place great importance on protecting juveniles from violence, and even from the mere exposure to violence. But violence against juveniles is often excused, at least if it stays within bounds. Youth violence and violence against youth are typically treated as two separate problems. But Chapter 5 will ask whether that is itself a mistake, given that children who are treated violently are more likely to be violent against others.

The subject of Chapter 6 is violence in jails and prisons. Not all carceral institutions are as dangerous as we often imagine them to be, but some are, if anything, worse. Violent attacks on inmates from guards or from other inmates often seem tacitly accepted, if not actively encouraged, as part and parcel of a custodial sentence. The cultural understanding of prison rape has changed in recent years; it is not quite the object of mirth in popular culture that it used to be. Nonetheless, sexual assault in prison still tends to be treated far less seriously than sexual assault outside of carceral institutions. And to a large extent this is true of all violence behind bars. Officially, physical assault is as serious a crime in prison as it is in the outside world. Unofficially, though, violent crimes in prison are often treated as though they do not entirely count. Prisons and jails are the starkest and deadliest example of zones of exception: areas where the normal rules and assumptions about violence seem suspended. Chapter 6 will explore the links between reactions to carceral violence and underlying ideas about the nature and origins of that violence, and to assumptions about the purpose of jails and prisons.

The final chapter, Chapter 7, asks how ideas about violence shape legal protections for free expression and for owning, carrying, and using firearms. The legal rules that are the focus of Chapter 7 are partly constitutional—the ways in which the Supreme Court has interpreted and applied the First and Second Amendments—and partly statutory: the "stand your ground" laws that, in most parts of the United States, now encourage gun owners to use their weapons to defend themselves and their property. There are some points of continuity between the ideas about violence underlying these legal doctrines and the ideas underlying criminal law. Most importantly, Second Amendment law is increasingly animated by some of the same ideas about the *nature* of violence that can be found in criminal law, especially the idea that violence tends to be characterological rather than situational, the product of individual dispositions rather than the circumstances in which people find themselves—for example, the presence or absence of guns. But there are also significant respects in which the ideas about violence underlying the legal treatment of speech and guns differ from the ideas encountered in criminal law. Unlike criminal law, First and Second Amendment law doesn't treat violence as highly significant and as categorically worthy of special condemnation. First Amendment law tends to give little importance to violence: speech that threatens violence or seems to celebrate violence generally isn't treated differently from speech that threatens or celebrates any other social ill. As for the legal protections given to the gun owners under Second Amendment law and "stand your ground" laws, these treat the resort to lethal violence as something that, far from being categorically worthy of censure, is often to be welcomed and respected.

If this book has a central lesson, it is that the law should avoid thinking about violence simplistically, as a category wholly apart. The sphere of violence does not have sharp or uncontroversial boundaries. Violent conduct is not always more threatening and less excusable than other forms of victimization. And people who engage in violence are not always fundamentally different from the rest of us; violence can be as much a product of circumstance as of character. None of this is to say, though, that violence is not real, that it is simply a label we put on things we don't like, that we'd be better off discarding the category. There are two terrible costs when the law oversimplifies violence. The first is that we wind up demonizing a category of people who are defined to a large extent arbitrarily and, inevitably, to a large extent by race. The second cost, equally damaging, is that we wind up ignoring violence that doesn't fit our preconceptions.

1 | Violence as a Legal Problem

In the third episode of the television comedy *Cheers,* initially broadcast in October 1982, the irascible, wisecracking cocktail waitress Carla Tortelli jumps on a customer's back and repeatedly slams his head into the bar. Afterward the customer threatens to sue the tavern's owner, Sam Malone, if Carla isn't fired. At Sam's insistence, Carla sees a psychologist. She gets better at controlling her temper. The customer is placated and agrees to drop his claim.

The title of the episode is "The Tortelli Tort." Carla's attack isn't slapstick, or at least it doesn't stay slapstick: it's battery. It's framed that way by the legal system that the assaulted customer threatens to invoke. Nonetheless, the attack doesn't play as terribly frightening. No one even thinks of calling the police. Carla is diminutive and endearing. Plus, she is provoked. The customer is obnoxious. He has been talking trash about the Red Sox—this is in Boston—and mocking Sam, Carla's friend as well as her boss. He was asking for it.

The incident upsets Sam, though, and not just because it could cost him his business. The attack fits into a pattern of behavior on Carla's part. As Sam describes it, the pattern isn't one of violence, per se, but rather of Carla losing her temper and abusing customers. The physicality of Carla's conduct makes it tortious, but it isn't central to what bothers Sam. Carla has an anger problem, not a violence problem. Legalities aside, the violence is incidental.

In the universe of on-screen violence, Carla's assault therefore occupies an intermediate position. It isn't laughed away or fully excused, but neither does it signal the crossing of a moral divide. It's a tort, not a crime. A good deal can be said about the factors that tame the attack and lessen its gravity: the lack of visible injuries; the fact that the victim is much larger than Carla; their respective genders; the rough-and-tumble, working-class backgrounds that Carla and the customer evidently share; and—last but not least—the fact that Carla, like everyone else in the episode, is white. It matters, as well, that *Cheers* is more than three decades old; it's doubtful that the kind of violence Carla visits on the abrasive bar customer would be treated as lightly in a mainstream television comedy today. The most important point, though, isn't where "The Tortelli Tort" falls on the spectrum of fictionalized assaults. It's the existence of the spectrum. Cultural interpretations of violence aren't fixed, and the salience of the line dividing violent from nonviolent behavior isn't preordained.

The location and significance of that line are largely determined by the legal system, and law in turn is itself shaped by how violence is understood. The properties of violence and the proper response to violence are not just legal questions, of course. They are hashed out in political campaigns, in philosophy classes, in television comedies, and in conversations in real-life barrooms. Ideas about violence come from all over. But one place they originate is the law: legal rules, legal decisions, and legal discourse.

Ideas about violence are found throughout the law: not just tort law and criminal law, but constitutional law, family law, immigration law, and countless other fields of legislation and jurisprudence. Some of those ideas are explicit; others are subtextual. Either way they deserve attention, not just because they shape the law but because they reverberate in the ways violence is understood and discussed throughout our culture.

Law has a complicated relationship with violence. Violence is law's great problem: its preoccupation, its enemy, and its ally. "Law is the opposite of violence," notes the philosopher Christoph Menke, but at the same time "law is itself a kind of violence." It is common to think of law and violence as warring contraries, each striving to displace the other—the yin and yang of social ordering. As Menke puts it, "legal forms of decision-making are introduced to interrupt the endless sequence of violence and counterviolence and counter-counterviolence." From this perspective, violence is the antithesis of law. But law also depends on and legitimizes the violence of police officers, prison guards, and executioners. "Legal interpretation takes place in a field of pain and death," the late Yale law professor Robert Cover wrote in a famous article; he meant that judicial decisions not only justify but also "signal and occasion the imposition of violence."[1]

This book is not about the law's thorny relationship with violence. That is already the subject of a large and growing literature, much of it inspired by Cover.[2] Instead of asking how we should think about violence and its connection to the law, this book examines how the law itself thinks about violence. What ideas about violence does the law adopt, rely upon, and reinforce? How do words on paper make sense of and try to subjugate fists, rocks, blades, and bullets?

This chapter will explore three sets of ideas that shape the law's response to violence. First, there are ideas about the *definition* of violence. What does "violence" mean, or what should it mean? Where should the line be drawn between the violent and the nonviolent? Second, there are ideas about the *significance* of violence. However violence is defined, how much should it matter, and in what ways, if conduct is violent rather than nonviolent? Third and finally, there are ideas about the *nature* of violence. How does violence operate? How does it start and stop? Is it the product of temperament or of circumstances? Is violence best understood as a quality of particular persons, of particular situations, or of particular acts? The answers that the law provides, or adopts, to all of these questions are inevitably shaped by culture and by social realities. In particular, we will see, it is impossible to understand violence as a legal concept without addressing the fault lines of race, gender, class, and politics.

Defining Violence

To many people, the meaning of "violence" seems obvious. Steven Pinker, the Harvard psychologist and polymath, wrote close to a thousand pages about violence a decade ago without ever seeing a need to define the term. Pinker appears to have taken violence to mean, more or less, the use of force to cause death or serious bodily injury. That probably is how most people use the term, most of the time.[3]

But the term gets used in other ways as well, and often quite deliberately. "Violence," the critic Raymond Williams pointed out, is a "difficult word" of "longstanding complexity." Death or injury isn't always required for something to be called violent. It seems natural, for example, to talk about someone grabbing another person "violently," even if no one gets hurt. Property destruction, as well, is sometimes categorized as violent. The legal scholar Jerome Skolnick, searching in the late 1960s for a narrow and precise definition of violence, settled upon "the intentional use of force to injure, to kill, or to destroy property." The first meaning of "violence" offered by Merriam-Webster is "the use of physical force so as to injure, abuse, damage, or destroy."[4]

More controversially, the term "violence" is often applied to conduct that doesn't involve the use of physical force. Two intuitions underlie uses of that kind. The first has to do with chains of causation; the second has to do with nonphysical harm.

First, some actions that don't themselves involve the use of force can lead to other actions that do. A burglary, for example, can lead to a violent encounter between the intruder and the person whose home is invaded. That is why burglary is sometimes treated as a "violent" offense. Illegal drugs can make users more aggressive, and rival drug dealers can be prone to gun fights. Those are two of the reasons drug crimes are often grouped with crimes of violence. The line can be particularly fuzzy between actual violence and threats of violence, express or implied, especially when the threat comes from the display of a weapon. The same armed activists described as "peaceful" by people who sympathize with their concerns are labeled "terrorists" by people with opposing goals.

The category of violence, moreover, is often extended well beyond "street crimes" like burglary and drug dealing, and well beyond the open display of weapons. Even "white collar" offenses, like fraud or violations of safety regulations, can be, and have been, called "violent," since they can "have a result that is as physical . . . as any traditional violent crime." Legal judgments, too, bring about the infliction of bodily pain, especially in criminal cases; this is what Robert Cover meant when he wrote about "the violence of the law." Environmental degradation and climate change can be understood as a kind of "slow violence"—"incremental and accretive," with "calamitous repercussions playing out across a range of temporal scales."[5]

Second, nonphysical injuries—for example, emotional assaults, or the cumulative tolls taken by racism or poverty—often can seem as hurtful as bodily damage, if not more so. And the line between physical and emotional injuries isn't perfectly sharp: mental trauma can cause physical harm. Moreover, calling a form of victimization "violence" underscores its seriousness. The term has "emotional power," Raymond Williams noted.

Consequently there have been repeated efforts to extend the concept of violence to include "linguistic violence," "structural violence," "symbolic violence," and "quiet violence," both "personal" and "institutionalized."[6]

Traditionally these arguments have challenged the significance of the line between physical and nonphysical injury. "Words can be like rape," explains the anthropologist Nancy Scheper-Hughes: "they can destroy you." More recently neurological arguments have emerged for treating language as violence. The psychologist Lisa Feldman Barrett says that "speech that bullies or torments . . . is literally a form of violence," because the stress it triggers can damage brain cells. The idea that words can be a form of violence is usually associated with the academics toward the left of the political spectrum, but it is by no means limited to academics, or to the left. The National Rifle Association, for example, produced a recruitment video in 2017 urging Americans to fight the "violence of lies with the clenched fist of truth."[7]

The line between words and violence can often seem hazy. In the lead-up to the American Civil War, for example, when brawls and the brandishing of firearms became common on the floor of Congress, one Massachusetts district sent their representative off to Washington with a revolver inscribed with the words "Free Speech." They weren't equating weaponry with verbal expression; they were suggesting (with some justification) that in order for a member of Congress to speak out against slavery, he would need to be willing to defend himself against physical intimidation from Southern representatives. But the inscription also spoke to a larger truth: free speech and violence in this period seemed thoroughly entangled. For Southerners, antislavery rhetoric amounted to incitement of insurrection. For Northerners, speaking out against "slavocracy" required responding in kind to Southern assaults and threats of violence.[8]

If anything is not violent, you might think, it is words. Even children distinguish words from sticks and stones. There is an important sense, the French philosopher Paul Ricoeur pointed out, in which language and violence are not only distinct categories but formal opposites. Language, like law, is "an attempt to reduce violence." But not all language, Ricoeur clarified. The opposition "is not exactly . . . of language and violence, but . . . rather . . . of discourse and violence, more precisely of coherent discourse and violence." And if violence and coherent discourse are opposites, then there is a certain logic in seeing anything that blocks reasoned discussion as a form of violence. Hence "the violence of sexist language"—violent not just because it is hurtful, but also because it silences. Hence "the violence of lies"—violent, one presumes, not just because lies can lead to bloodshed, but also because they pollute the stream of discourse and make reasoned discussion more difficult. "Falsified words," Ricoeur himself argued, ". . . make language the voice of violence."[9]

The idea that words can be a kind of violence has always had its critics. The critics worry not just about censorship; they worry about the concept of violence losing its analytic utility. That is a concern raised by other extensions of the concept as well, and therefore categories such as "structural violence" and "quiet institutional violence" are also controversial. Many people find these uses of the term "violence" not only strange but perverse—a kind of rhetorical stunt that undermines clear thinking and robs the term of meaning. Randall Collins, a sociologist who has studied violence, complains that the phrase "symbolic violence" is "mere theoretical word play," and that "to take it literally would be to grossly misunderstand the nature of real violence." The legal scholar Alice Ristroph warns that when the concept of violence is "extend[ed] beyond actual bodily injury . . . it becomes an abstraction, and eventually that abstraction may become a repository for all we find repulsive, transgressive, or simply sufficiently annoying."[10]

One response offered by proponents of a broader definition of violence has been that the term still has meaning even when extended beyond "overt physical assault," because at the core of the concept of violence is "violation."[11] But this brings us to another major ambiguity in the definition of violence: In order to qualify as violent, does force (or whatever else we sweep into the category of violence) have to be wrongful or illegitimate? Is there such a thing as justified, legitimate violence, or is that a contradiction in terms?

On the one hand, treating wrongfulness or illegitimacy as part of the definition of violence would prevent us from asking whether particular instances of violence are lawful or justified. Instead we would have to ask something like, "Is this violence at all or is it a legitimate use of force?"—which seems strained and unnatural. We could not speak of the violence carried out in battle, for example, without committing ourselves to the view that the fighting was unjustified. We could not talk about the violence allowed in a boxing match, or the violence that law enforcement officers are permitted to use. (The television drama *Justified*, which ran for six seasons beginning in 2010, focused on a heroic, quick-on-the-trigger deputy United States marshal. The title of the series reflected one of its main themes: the tenuous line separating the protagonist from the criminals he gunned down. There was no question the deputy was violent; the question that *Justified* seemed to ask, over and over, was how different his violence was from the unlicensed violence of his antagonists.) And arguments like Cover's, about the violence of the law, would be incoherent. Cover's argument wasn't that law is violent because particular legal rules or institutions are illegitimate; he wanted us to recognize the violence that is entailed even in legal judgments we think just and proper.[12]

On the other hand, there *is* a connotation of disapproval in most uses of the term "violence." That is what made Cover's argument bracing. When an author writes about "police violence" instead of "uses of force by the police," it generally *does* signal that the author thinks the police are doing something wrong, or at least something that should make us seriously uncomfortable. Alice Ristroph suggests that there is an unavoidable equivocality to the concept of violence: sometimes wrongfulness is part of the definition, sometimes not. Even if we try to define violence in purely descriptive terms, "we soon find ourselves back in the contested territory of the normative." The dualism is inescapable, Ristroph argues, because violence "disturb[s] the settled lines we draw between the categories of fact and value, empirical and normative."[13]

There are thus at least two serious ambiguities associated with the concept of violence. First, there is disagreement regarding how far, if at all, the concept should extend beyond the use of force to inflict immediate physical injury. Second, there is uncertainty regarding whether violence must, by definition, be wrongful.

These ambiguities do not just bedevil scholars. They create practical problems for lawyers, judges, and policymakers trying to address the problem of "violence." In the 1980s, for example, Congress passed a law, the Armed Career Criminal Act, that among other things requires long prison sentences for anyone with three or more "violent felony" convictions who is later found with a gun. For two decades the Supreme Court tried repeatedly to clarify what felonies count as "violent" for purposes of this statute, until finally, in 2015, it gave up and declared that a critical part of the sentencing rule was "void for vagueness"—in other words, so inherently ambiguous that it violated the constitutional guarantee of due process.[14]

Part of the problem arose, ironically, from the efforts Congress appeared to have made to be clear about its intentions. The Armed Career Criminal Act defines a "violent felony" to mean a crime punishable by more than a year in prison, if the crime either:

> (i) has as an element the use, attempted use, or threatened
> use of physical force against the person of another; or (ii) is
> burglary, arson, or extortion, or otherwise involves conduct
> that presents a serious potential risk of physical injury to
> another.[15]

The last part of this definition, beginning with the words "or otherwise involves," is called the "residual clause." It suggests that a crime should count as "violent" if it carries a risk of physical injury comparable in some way to the risks posed by burglary, arson, and extortion. But how should a sentencing court decide whether a particular crime satisfies that test? What *are* the dangers of physical injury presented by burglary, arson, or extortion? And how can a court know whether the defendant's past crimes raised similar risks? Writing for the Supreme Court, Justice Scalia reasoned that the "inclusion of burglary and extortion among the enumerated offenses suggests that a crime may qualify under the residual clause even if the physical injury is remote from the criminal act." But, he asked, "how remote is too remote?"[16]

A portion of Justice Scalia's opinion suggested that Congress might have avoided this difficulty if it had skipped the specific examples—if it had just defined a felony as "violent" when the felony (i) included an element of using, attempting to use, or threatening the use of physical force against another person, or (ii) involved conduct risking serious physical injury. And, in fact, aside from the residual clause, the remainder of the Armed Career Criminal Act remains in force—including the first half of the definition of "violent felony." It was only the residual clause that the Supreme Court found unconstitutionally vague. But there also have been fights about how to interpret the rest of the statutory definition. In 2019, for example, the Supreme Court split 5–4 over whether "overcoming resistance" in snatching a necklace counted as "the use, attempted use, or threatened use of physical force"; the majority said that it did. That same year the Court felt called on to decide whether "burglary" occurs within the meaning of the statute whenever someone enters a building legally, stays after they are required to leave, and then commits a crime; the Court decided that it does. More to the point, it's telling that when drafting the residual clause Congress saw the need to list three specific crimes—burglary, arson, and extortion—that it wanted to classify as "violent." The itemization suggests that Congress recognized the difficulty of defining violence with precision, and also that it was not content to allow certain offenses to fall outside the definition simply because they do not result in immediate injury. The legislative history of the Armed Career Criminal Act, traced in Chapter 2 of this book, bears out these impressions.[17]

And it turns out that even without the list of specific examples, the residual clause would not have withstood constitutional scrutiny. We know this because elsewhere federal law defines the phrase "crime of violence" in a way that looks very similar to the definition of "violent criminal" in the Armed Career Criminal Act, but without the exemplar offenses. A "crime of violence" under section 16 of title 18 of the United States Code is either "an offense that has as an element the use, attempted use, or threatened use of physical force against the person or property of another," or any felony "that, by its nature, involves a substantial risk that physical force against the person or property of another may be used in the course of committing the offense." Crimes that satisfy this definition serve as predicates for a range of legal consequences, including deportation. But in 2018 the Supreme Court found the second part of the definition, the part applying to offenses that necessarily involve a "substantial risk" of physical force, void for vagueness, at least when serving as a predicate for deportation. The Court again noted that the list of exemplar offenses in the Armed Career Criminal Act had driven "many a judge a little batty," but even without that problem, the majority concluded, it was simply too difficult to decide whether a crime "by its nature, involves a substantial risk that physical force . . . may be used." The following year the Supreme Court reached the same conclusion about a separate statute, section 924(c) of title 28 of the United States Code—which mandates extra years of prison time for anyone who uses or carries a firearm "during and in relation to any crime of violence or drug trafficking crime"—because that statute defines "crime of violence" exactly the same as section 16.[18]

The Significance of Violence

Once we draw a line between the violent and the not violent, the next question is what significance should attach to that line. Actually, the two questions are intertwined. It's the high salience of the concept of violence—the widespread sense that violence is an especially serious form of victimization—that motivates many of the efforts to expand the category. And many debates about the definition of violence are, at bottom, debates about how much it should matter whether particular conduct would ordinarily be described as violent. When academics write about "structural violence" or "quiet violence," for example, the point usually is to deny that muggings, say, are categorically worse than entrenched patterns of economic inequality, racial disadvantage, or sexual subordination.[19] But arguments of that kind can be made, and often are made, without redefining violence.

It's not always clear that violent conduct is especially bad, or even bad at all. It seems natural to describe a hard tackle in football as violent, but it also seems natural to many people to treat the tackle as unobjectionable, even praiseworthy. Something similar could be said for the violence of soldiers fighting a just war, or the violence carried out by someone acting in self-defense. We can generalize and say that a good amount of violence is viewed as commendable, or at least not seriously blameworthy, because it is *consensual* (as in boxing, football, and other contact sports), or *official* (as in just wars, or properly constrained policing), or *protective* (as when someone acts in self-defense, or defends someone else from attack). More controversially, violence often is celebrated, or at least condoned, when it seems *deserved*—when the victim had it coming.

The law draws all of these lines. At least, it draws the first three lines, and it flirts with the fourth. Each of the lines is controversial. There are arguments about whether the consent to violence in sports is genuine, how far it extends, whether it really makes the violence okay, and if so, under what circumstances. There are arguments about whether someone can legitimately "consent" to violence *outside* of a sporting event. There are arguments about when soldiers or police officers—or parents, or teachers, or custodial staff—should be authorized to use violence, how bad it is for them to exceed those limits if only slightly, and how comfortable we should be with violence just because it is legally authorized. (The last question, in particular, was a continuing preoccupation of the television show *Justified*.) There are particularly loud arguments about self-defense and "standing your ground": when violence for self-protection should be allowed, and to what extent it should be encouraged and even celebrated.[20]

"He deserved it" generally isn't recognized as a valid legal defense. That's why Carla's battery of the obnoxious bar customer in *Cheers* was a tort. Nonetheless, intuitions about unsympathetic victims help to undergird the legal doctrine of provocation, which can reduce murder to manslaughter. And valorized depictions of violent revenge on evildoers are, of course, a staple of popular entertainment, although even there the implied value judgment is sometimes questioned. "Well, I guess they had it coming," a novice bounty hunter says nervously in Clint Eastwood's revisionist western, *Unforgiven,* trying to calm himself after helping to kill two outlaws. "We *all* got it coming, kid," replies his battle-scarred companion.

This book will explore all of these controversies, but the point for now is simply their existence. The point is that the wrongfulness of violence is not always taken for granted, by popular morality or by the law. In fact, popular morality doesn't always take the wrongfulness of violence for granted even when the law does. There's a long, if contested, American tradition of condoning or even celebrating the violent opposition to unjust laws. Take, for example, Jefferson's famous suggestion that "the tree of liberty must be refreshed from time to time with the blood of patriots & tyrants," or the conflicting assessments of John Brown's raid on Harpers Ferry.[21]

Determining the significance of violence is not simply a matter of deciding when violence is wrong. There is the further question of *how* wrong—the question addressed by legal doctrines like provocation. Provocation distinguishes between grades of homicide—which means, usually, distinguishing between grades of lethal violence. But the law also wrestles with how violence compares in wrongfulness with other kinds of transgressions. We often think of violence as the worst form of misconduct, but not always, and the law reflects the same ambivalence.

Crime statistics commonly distinguish between violent offenses and property offenses, and virtually no one views the property offenses as more serious. Fear of crime, for the most part, is fear of violence. It is no surprise, then, that sentencing rules—like those in the federal Armed Career Criminals Act—typically reserve harsher penalties for violent crimes. Drug offenses, though, are often treated with comparable harshness, not just in the United States but also in many other countries. This turns out to reflect popular intuitions about the comparative severity of different crimes, at least in recent decades. Earlier, though, the intuitions may have been different. The torrent of capital statutes enacted in eighteenth-century England focused almost entirely on property offenses.[22]

Today, committing a violent act is usually thought to be more serious than obtaining property by deception: scarier and more iniquitous. But the opposing view has a long history. In the *Inferno,* Dante puts the violent in the seventh circle of hell, but he puts those guilty of fraud below them, in the eighth circle. Dante has Virgil explain that fraud is "man's peculiar evil" and so "displeases God more"; that is why it is punished more harshly.[23]

Schemes to cheat victims out of their money or property—or related offenses, like embezzlement—have seemed to many people, at many times, to be especially craven and contemptible, precisely because they are not out in the open. Here is the philosopher Gerald Runkle, for example, writing in 1976:

> The art and science of deceit is a major industry in the modern world. Its practitioners, the merchandizers, politicians, and religious leaders, utilizing sophisticated technology, do not beat a man into unconsciousness; they merely destroy his powers of thought and sensibility. These "engineers of the human mind" bombard him with stimuli, emotional appeals, and threats in order to manipulate him. How refreshing a little honest violence would be! It would be easier to recognize and to withstand.[24]

Ideas about the relative iniquity of violence and deceit are wrapped up with ideas about gender and about class. Violence is masculine. In every society, in every era, physical attacks have been carried out disproportionately by men, and more particularly by young men. And the association between violence and masculinity is normative as well as empirical. Fighting like a man has long meant fighting physically and openly, as opposed to acting with subterfuge. Fraud can seem more contemptible than "a little honest violence" in part because it seems more cowardly, which is to say less manly. Men and women also tend to perceive violence differently. Men are more apt to excuse or to celebrate the use of physical force; and the specter of violence—especially sexual violence—can color women's lives, and constrain their choices, more than it does for men.[25]

The relationship between violence and class is complicated. Arrests and convictions for violent offenses are negatively correlated with wealth, and the low-class nature of violence can make it seem both less and more forgivable. Violence is crude and unsophisticated, but there is a long-standing view that the dispossessed use violence because they are deprived of other tools. From this perspective, singling out violence for special condemnation looks like a form of class bias, a way of preserving existing social hierarchies. You can see that idea lurking behind Runkle's comparison of "honest violence" with the "art and science of deceit."

The idea was particularly common in the late 1960s and early 1970s; it became something of a fixture of New Left thinking. Squeamishness about violence came to be seen as an excuse for propping up the status quo. The philosopher Robert Wolff called it a "subjective queasiness having no moral rationale"—a "rhetorical device for proscribing . . . uses of force which one considers inimical to one's central interests."[26]

This kind of full-throated apology for violence is less common today, but for many people the sense lingers that categorical condemnations of violence reflect a kind of class bias, and that working-class violence, even when it is not excusable, can still be admired, at least a little, for being muscular and forthright. There was more than a bit of that in Carla's depiction in *Cheers*. You can see the same ambivalence in J. D. Vance's memoir of growing up poor on the outskirts of Appalachia. Vance doesn't condone the violence of his family and their neighbors; he makes it perfectly clear that he views their culture of honor and retribution as toxic. But the violence is linked to much that he admires: resilience, loyalty, a kind of passion for justice, and the fact that "we hillbillies are the toughest goddamned people on this earth." The stories that Vance heard growing up, about "the kind of violence that should land someone in jail," made him "feel like hillbilly royalty, because these were classic good-versus-evil stories, and my people were on the right side." His people, he explains, "were extreme, but extreme in the service of something."[27]

Feelings about violence are colored not just by whose ox is being gored but by who is doing the goring. We're more likely to excuse violence by people we identify with; often we don't even call it violence. When President Donald Trump's administration overruled its own line prosecutors and recommended a lenient sentence for Trump's friend and former advisor Roger Stone—who among other things had tried to silence a witness by telling him to "prepare to die"—the administration argued in court that Stone deserved a lighter sentence than defendants convicted of "violent offenses, such as armed robbery." Federal sentencing guidelines explicitly called for increasing the sentence of defendants convicted of obstructing justice by threatening physical injury. But the administration suggested those guidelines should be reserved for "gang members" and those associated with "violent criminal organizations."[28]

The racial subtext of that argument was hard to miss. And race plays a particularly strong role in determining how violence is perceived and assessed. Black men carrying guns are perceived differently from white men carrying guns. Kids who are physically aggressive are more likely to be expelled from school, or to wind up in delinquency court, if their skin is dark.[29] The toxic intersection of race with ideas about violence will be a large theme of this book.

But tribalism of all kinds—religious and political as well as racial—can powerfully influence how violence is assessed, or even whether it is labeled as violence to begin with. In October 2016, when Trump's presidential campaign seemed doomed, Sheriff David Clarke of Milwaukee County—an ardent Trump supporter—tweeted a call for "pitchforks and torches," accompanied by a picture of an angry, threatening mob. Government corruption, Clarke suggested, required citizens to do more than simply "bitch." After Trump was elected and protest marches were held around the country, Clarke called the protesters "radical anarchists," whose "temper tantrums" needed to be "quell[ed]." There was "no legitimate reason," he explained, "to protest the will of the people." "Riots," he said, should be stopped with declarations of states of emergency, early curfews, mobilization of the National Guard, tear gas, and authorizing "ALL non lethal force."[30]

Trump's political rise sharpened divisions in how violence is assessed, and not just because it reinforced and capitalized on the polarization of American politics. Trump placed a premium on strength in a way that often verged on, when it didn't cross over into, glorification of violence. As a candidate, Trump spoke of how he would like to punch a protester in the face, how it might be better if protesters at his rallies were "roughed up," how he missed the "old days" when a disruptive protester "would be carried out on a stretcher." He asked his supporters to "knock the crap" out of anyone in the crowd "getting ready to throw a tomato," and he promised to pay the legal fees. His rhetoric didn't change much after he was elected. Six months after taking office, Trump urged police officers not to "be too nice" when putting suspects into a police car.[31] He later complained that referees were "ruining" professional football by penalizing hard tackles; the players, he said, "want to hit" and should be allowed to do so.[32]

Midway through his term, Trump threatened that his supporters would resort to violence if they didn't get their way. "I have the tough people," Trump said, "but they don't play it tough—until they go to a certain point, and then it would be very bad, very bad." Trump returned to this theme repeatedly during his presidency. When protesters interrupted his speech to some supporters in October 2019, Trump warned that "they don't know that they're dealing with very tough people." He told the protesters to "go home to mom," and asked his "very tough" supporters to "make sure you don't hurt them."[33] During the coronavirus pandemic of 2020, when groups of right-wing protesters—some of them armed and threatening violence—gathered to demand an early end to quarantine measures, Trump praised them and egged them on, although he was careful to limit his encouragement to the protests taking place in states with Democratic governors. A month later, when nationwide protests over the police killing of George Floyd led to widespread looting, Trump tweeted a threat that "when the looting starts, the shooting starts." Twitter added a warning label noting that the president's message violated the platform's rules against glorifying violence.[34]

Without wading into questions about Trump's precise relationship to fascism and other modern forms of authoritarianism, it is worth noting that his attraction to violence is a point of continuity with those traditions. The historian Michael Ebner notes that violence was central to twentieth-century European fascism, not just as a tactic but as something approaching an ideology, a form of politics valued for its "'positive' formative power," its capacity to discipline the weak and to "harden the strong." There is more than a hint of that sentiment in Trump's rhetoric, and in the rhetoric of some of his allies and supporters. Writing in 2017, the journalist Jelani Cobb observed that "toughness" for Trump was "not a means to an end" but "an end in itself." In the closing weeks of his 2020 reelection campaign, Trump worked to shift attention from his response to the coronavirus pandemic to the need to crack down on violent protests against racism and police brutality. "These people only know one thing and that is strength," he told his supporters. "That's all they know—strength. And we have strength." [35]

Four months after Trump took office, Greg Gianforte, the pro-Trump Republican candidate in a special congressional election in Montana, responded to a question from a reporter by slamming him to the floor and punching him. Gianforte won the election anyway. He later apologized and pleaded guilty to a misdemeanor assault charge, but not before a good number of commentators rushed to his defense. The general theme of the defenses was that the journalist should have fought like a man instead of complaining. Laura Ingraham, a nationally syndicated radio host, taunted the reporter by asking, "Did anyone get his lunch money stolen today and then run to tell the recess monitor?" Trump himself praised Gianforte: "Any guy that can do a body slam, he is my type!"[36]

For their part, many of Trump's opponents proved perfectly capable of celebrating physical violence directed at a worthy target. On the day of Trump's inauguration, a prominent white supremacist was suckerpunched during an on-camera interview; a fair amount (although certainly not all) of the reaction on the left was gleeful. "Punch a Nazi" quickly became a meme on social media—a point later emphasized by Gianforte's defenders.[37]

That retort—How can you criticize, or even be surprised by, Gianforte's body slamming of a reporter if you called for Nazis to be punched?—illustrates a pair of closely related and nearly ubiquitous

tropes in rhetoric about violence: tit for tat, and the calling out of hypocrisy. Our side has to be violent, given the violence of our opponents.
And, given their violence, their complaints about our violence can't be
taken seriously. When Trump called at his rallies for protesters to be assaulted, or praised those actions after the fact, he sometimes complained that "part of the problem . . . is that nobody wants to hurt each
other anymore," but more often he suggested that the protesters were
themselves violent and that his supporters should "punch back." Similarly, when Trump urged police not to "be too nice" with suspects, he
suggested that the suspects deserved some rough treatment: "Like when
you guys put somebody in the car and you're protecting their head. . . .
Like don't hit their head *and they've just killed somebody*—don't hit their
head. I said, you can take the hand away, okay?"[38]

Trump's rhetoric perversely echoed, in a way, the argument advanced
by the New Left in the late 1960s and early 1970s that the violence worth
talking about was not the violence of political activists, it was the violence exercised against African Americans and other people of color in
the United States, and the massive violence employed in Indochina by
the United States military.[39] Here is Angela Davis, for example, interviewed in prison in 1972 and asked about the use of "confrontation" and
"violence" by the Black Panthers:

> You ask me, you know, whether I approve of violence. I mean,
> that just doesn't make any sense at all. Whether I approve of
> guns. I grew up in Birmingham, Alabama. Some very, very
> good friends of mine were killed by bombs, bombs that were
> planted by racists. I remember, from the time I was very small,
> I remember the sounds of bombs exploding across the street.
> Our house shaking. I remember my father having to have
> guns at his disposal at all times, because of the fact that, at
> any moment, we might expect to be attacked. . . . That's why,
> when someone asks me about violence, I just, I just find it
> incredible. Because what it means is that the person who's
> asking that question has absolutely no idea what black people
> have gone through, what black people have experienced in this

country since the time the first black person was kidnapped from the shores of Africa.[40]

Before and after Trump's election, far-right groups used exaggerated reports of violence by left-wing radicals to justify or excuse right-wing uses of force. In 2017, when white supremacists marched with torches in Charlottesville, Virginia, and a Nazi sympathizer drove his car into a group of counterdemonstrators, killing one and injuring nineteen others, some right-wing commentators suggested that the left shared blame for the bloodshed, because "both sides" had come prepared for a fight. Trump himself echoed this response, suggesting there had been "hatred, bigotry, and violence . . . on many sides." After he was criticized for the weakness of his remarks, he explicitly condemned neo-Nazis and white supremacists, but he never retracted his suggestion that there was blame "on many sides." In a prepared statement, Trump said that "racism is evil," that "those who cause violence in its name are criminals and thugs, including the K.K.K., neo-Nazis, white supremacists and other hate groups." He left hanging the suggestion that "hate groups" *on the left* bore much of the responsibility for the violence in Charlottesville. (The Black Lives Matter movement, which arose from protests against police killings of African Americans, was often described as a "hate group"—and a violent one at that—by conservative commentators and activists, before and after the events in Charlottesville.) And one day later Trump again said that there had been "blame on both sides" in Charlottesville, because "a group on the left" had been "very, very violent."[41]

The point is not that there is some kind of equivalence between, on one hand, Angela Davis truthfully recounting the history of violence against African Americans and, on the other hand, Donald Trump defending a deadly neo-Nazi attack by exaggerating the violence of counterprotesters. There is not. The point, rather, is that the logic of tit for tat is pervasive in discussions about violence and deeply embedded in most people's ideas about violence, no matter where they fall on the political spectrum or how tethered they are to reality. The left-wing protesters in the Trump era who used physical force against their opponents—although far fewer and far less violent than the right-wing groups that Trump encouraged and defended[42]—themselves used the logic of tit for tat to justify their tactics. A counterprotester who fought neo-Nazis told a reporter that when "they started swinging clubs, fists, shields . . . we were not shy in defending ourselves." Another argued that, in the current political environment, "you need violence in order to protect nonviolence."[43]

These were but modern echoes of the arguments made by Republican congressmen in the run-up to the Civil War, explaining their need to respond, forcefully and physically, to bullying by Southern representatives. Southerners, for their part, claimed they were responding to Northern aggression. As one historian of the period notes, "even . . . extremists framed their violence as defensive."[44]

The pervasive, taken-for-granted nature of tit-for-tat justifications for violence is one reason the definition of violence matters so much. If rhetoric can be violent, it seems more justifiable to respond to it with physical force—to answer, as the NRA video put it, the "violence of lies with the clenched fist of truth." In fact, the logic of tit for tat is so powerful that "nonviolence" usually means not simply the avoidance of violence but, more specifically, the renunciation of retaliatory violence. Voter registration campaigns, for example, are not ordinarily described as "nonviolent"—unless there is reason to expect that those involved in the campaign may be physically attacked, and they are trained not to respond in kind.

Some people reject violence across the board, even when it is defensive or retaliatory; that was Gandhi's position. Most of us, though, are not willing to go that far. We do not treat violence as categorically worse than other forms of violation. We do not condemn all violence. We even celebrate some violence. Our feelings about violence are closely tied to our feelings about the perpetrators and the victims of violence. At the same time, most of us believe that the criminality of violence, and how seriously it is punished, shouldn't depend on the offender's politics. We rely on law to sort out good violence from bad violence, and bad violence from worse violence—to determine when it matters that an act is violent, how much it matters, and in what way. The law embodies decisions not just about the definition of violence but also about its significance.

It is possible, of course, that the truly important line is not the one dividing violence from nonviolence but the one dividing violence that is in some sense especially serious from less serious violence. The law sometimes reflects that intuition, as well. Lethal violence, in particular, is often distinguished from other forms of violence. For example, the doctrine of self-defense in criminal law places special restrictions on the use of "deadly force"; so do the constitutional rules the Supreme Court has promulgated under the Fourth Amendment for the use of force in law enforcement. Criminologists Franklin Zimring and Gordon Hawkins suggested two decades ago that lethal violence, not crime in general and not violence in general, was "the most serious social control problem in every developed nation"; fear of crime was, for the most part, fear of "life-threatening, personal violence." They were arguing, in essence, for treating the category of violence as less significant, not because some offenses traditionally considered nonviolent were as evil or as harmful as violent crime, but because the truly important line was the one dividing serious—lethal—violence from less serious violence. They could have cast their argument differently, as a redefinition of violence—just as some arguments about the definition of violence, as we have seen, could be reformulated as arguments about the significance of violence.[45]

"War Minus the Shooting"

Sports violence and its legal treatment warrant a brief digression, because they illustrate several themes encountered in the law's treatment of violence more generally, including the intertwined questions of how violence is defined and how it is assessed. The violence in sports is condoned and rarely even called "violence," in large part because athletes are thought to consent to it. The idea is that violence is part of the game; it is what the contestants signed up for. But it can be hard to say exactly what it is that contestants have consented to. Courts have had persistent problems with cases in which players are charged with assaulting each other during the course of a game of, say, basketball or hockey. The difficulty is that lots of hits, checks, and other assaults that are barred by the rules of sports competitions are nonetheless common and, in a sense, regularized. In games like football, hockey, and basketball, a range of technically forbidden violence is expected; the penalties are so frequent, and so relatively minor, that they become themselves part of the game. Courts have sometimes tried to square the circle by saying that players implicitly consent to "minor assaults" outside the formal rules of the game, but only if the conduct is "ordinary and expected," or "reasonably foreseeable"—part and parcel, tacitly, of the sport in which they have chosen to participate.[46]

But people often disagree about what kind of violence is part and parcel of a game; that is one reason these cases wind up in court. And there plainly are limits to what kinds of assaults can be the subject of valid consent. Even mixed martial arts cannot change their rules to allow gunplay. Judicial decisions about sports violence inevitably reflect, in part, ideas about the social utility of allowing certain kinds of violence within the confines of an athletic contest. Sports that are *too* violent—mixed martial arts with guns, or bare-knuckle boxing— are not condoned; assaults that take place in a contest of that kind are simply treated as assaults. Boxing itself was once in this category. Courts frequently suggest, though, that society benefits from encouraging "free and fierce competition"; this was the instinct that led to the gradual acceptance of boxing. (In contrast, courts have been much less receptive to consent as a defense to assault charges in cases involving BDSM, precisely because judges generally do not believe the underlying practices have social benefits that outweigh their dangers.)[47]

There is a long-standing belief that sports give spectators as well as participants a safe outlet for physical aggression, that they provide a kind of catharsis for violence. Not everyone finds these arguments convincing. George Orwell called sports "war minus the shooting"; he thought organized athletic contests, especially between teams representing nations, whipped up violence rather than taming it. Orwell's views about athletics, though, tend to be written off as the carping of, literally, a spoil-sport: an uncomprehending outsider who did not understand the value of physical competition. And, of course, even if sports *are* "war minus the shooting," displacing more destructive forms of violence may be no small thing. The sociologist Randall Collins, who has studied the pathways of violence in sports and elsewhere, sees sports in part as ways of channeling and taming violence: ways of creating fair fights. The social science evidence on the overall effect of sports on rates of violence is inconclusive, and the effects may vary widely, depending on the sport. It may be misleading, moreover, to lump together effects on participants with effects on spectators, "in game" violence with violence off the field, or lethal with nonlethal violence. Like attitudes toward violence in sports, the actual effects of sports violence may be complicated. The critical point for present purposes, though, is that violence in sports is not excused by the criminal law as a necessary evil, or something that, however undesirable, in the end must be tolerated as a matter of personal choice. It is excused because it is valued.[48]

Moreover, in sports as everywhere, ideas about violence are difficult to extricate from ideas about race. Deterred by the heightened obstacles they face in other fields of achievement, young men of color are overrepresented among professional athletes. Roughly 70 percent of players in the National Football League, for example, are African American. When Trump called for more violence in football games, he was calling—a columnist pointed out—for "more violence against black bodies . . . for the amusement of audiences." And that audience is largely white. Seventy percent of the television viewership for NFL games is white; 80 percent of fans attending the games are white. As evidence mounts that concussions from playing tackle football can cause long-term brain damage, football is increasingly dominated by Black players in schools and colleges as well as at the professional level: poverty and racial discrimination make the college scholarships available to football players especially attractive to Black families. It is increasingly difficult to avoid the conclusion that the toleration and enjoyment of violence in professional football has something to do with the fact that the violence is between young men of color—that the violence inflicted on *their* bodies is treated as less objectionable. The history of race in professional sports is tortuous; disentangling it would take an even longer digression. It further complicates the notion, however, that violence in sports is tolerated because it is "consensual," and it serves as a reminder of how often ideas about violence—its definition and its iniquity—are warped by racial bias.[49]

How Violence Operates

There is a third set of ideas about violence embedded in the law—ideas not about how violence should be defined, or about what kind of significance it should be accorded, but about its nature, about how it should be understood. What causes violence? What kind of phenomenon is it? How does it progress? How can it be controlled?

One key question is whether violence is best understood as a property of individuals or of isolated episodes. Put differently, to what extent is violence determined by a person's predisposition, and to what extent is it situational? Should we be concerned about violent people, or violent acts? And if we are concerned about violent people, what characterizes them as a group? Is it their personalities, their feelings and beliefs, their moral codes, or their brain chemistry? And if violence is largely situational, what are the circumstances likely to produce it?

A vast literature addresses these questions, spanning the fields of psychology, neurobiology, sociology, and history. To a great extent the answers depend on what you choose to emphasize. It is like the story of the blind men and the elephant. In every society and every era, the bulk of violence is carried out by young men; that suggests violence is in large part biological. Rates of violence vary widely by location and over time; that suggests that much of what drives violence is cultural and sociological. People who have been violent in the past are more likely to be violent in the future; that suggests violence is a matter of personal predisposition. People prone to violence often turn out to have distinctive brain structures; that suggests violence is driven to some extent by neurophysiology. Even the most violent people are not violent most of the time; that suggests violence is situational.[50]

Whether to treat violence as situational, sociological, biological, or volitional is not wholly an empirical question. It is in part a question of values and social choice. This is particularly true when questions about the nature of violence are addressed by the law. In criminal law, for example, the centuries-old doctrine of *actus reus* requires that crimes be defined by actions, not by a defendant's character or status. This doesn't reflect an empirical judgment so much as an ethical commitment to punishing people for what they have done, not for who they are. That same commitment helps to motivate the long-standing rules of evidence law that restrict the ability of prosecutors to introduce proof of a defendant's violent character, although these rules also reflect a belief that criminal behavior, including violence, is more situational than jurors are apt to appreciate.[51]

So one set of questions about the nature of violence is whether it is situational or dispositional, and what makes certain situations or certain individuals prone to violence. A related question, also addressed repeatedly in legal doctrine, is whether violence is self-sustaining or self-arresting—whether it tends to build on itself or has the capacity to keep itself in check. Violence, or the threat of violence, is often relied upon to stop or to prevent violence. As we will see in Chapter 7, that reliance underlies the expansive interpretation the Supreme Court gave in 2008 to the constitutional right "to keep and bear arms": this was a right, the Court concluded, not just to participate in a public militia, but to have weapons for self-defense. Doctrines of criminal law explicitly authorize the use of violence in response to illegal assaults. There are long-running arguments about whether expanding that authorization could reduce the overall level of violence, or at least the level of unjustified violence. The legal scholar Mary Anne Franks, for example, calls for "encouraging women's willingness and ability to engage in responsive violence against men, as well as raising the visibility of such responsive violence, in order to drive down the incidence of male violence." Policing, of course, relies heavily on the use of authorized violence to reduce unauthorized violence, and some historians and sociologists suggest that private violence tends to rise when people do not believe they can rely on state violence to protect them from others.[52]

On the other hand, perhaps this is all "one huge mistake," as the forensic psychiatrist James Gilligan concluded in a 2000 article. Gilligan was drawing on the idea that violence is self-perpetuating, that punishing people with violence only makes them more violent. He took that idea particularly far, but it is one that many people share to a greater or lesser extent. Violence by law enforcement officers is often blamed for provoking further violence: the sociologist Nikki Jones, for example, says that violence "travels through the bodies and minds of young people" subjected to police harassment. Corporal punishment of children has grown less popular, at least in the developed world, in part because researchers have concluded it produces violent children who grow into violent adults. A long-standing argument against the death penalty is that it brutalizes society, teaching violence by example. Violence is often thought to be not self-limiting but contagious.[53]

No one thinks, of course, that violence is *always* self-limiting, or that it *always* spins out of control. So the more important question may be under what circumstances violence is apt to build on itself. A closely related question is whether violence comes naturally to people, and avoiding violence is a matter of fragile norms and conscious self-restraint, or whether, on the contrary, violence requires special conditions to commence and to sustain itself, so that violence can be avoided, at least in part, by making those special conditions less likely. We often think of violence as something that arises spontaneously and spreads easily, and there is evidence that, compared to other animals, humans are more instinctively violent toward each other. But sociologist Randall Collins concludes, based on detailed analysis of a large number of violent incidents in a range of social settings, that "violence is difficult to carry out, not easy," because it runs "against the grain of normal interaction rituals." He suggests that this is why most people are not violent, and why even violent people are not violent most of the time. The question for Collins is not what causes violence, but what allows it: violence requires a pathway around "the barrier of tension or fear that rises up whenever people come into antagonistic confrontation," and different pathways need to be defused or redirected in different ways. Collins suggests, for example, that it may often be possible "to replace serious violence with relatively mild and ritualistic forms."[54]

Legal rules in the United States have also been influenced by a third set of questions about the nature of violence: questions not about the situational or dispositional origins of violence, and not about the self-limiting or self-perpetuating logic of violence, but about whether the American experience with violence, or certain kinds of violence, is in some way exceptional, and if so why. Why is there so much violent crime in the United States? Why is the United States alone among industrialized democracies in clinging to the death penalty? Why do police in the United States kill suspects so much more frequently than police in the United Kingdom or Europe do? These questions seem urgent in part because of the sense that if American violence is exceptional, it may not be inevitable. If we could figure out what sets us apart, we could try to correct it. Or perhaps not. If, as H. Rap Brown famously said, violence "is as American as cherry pie," perhaps we are stuck with it and need to learn to live with it. Perhaps violence cannot be separated from something deep in the American character—the nation's culture of rugged independence, or its distrust of government, or its respect for civil liberties. Perhaps, as historian David Courtwright suggests, violence is "the dark reverse" of America's "coin of freedom and abundance."[55]

It's not clear that the United States *is* more violent, across the board. Some scholars have suggested the United States is exceptional only in regard to particular kinds of violence, or only in particular places. Franklin Zimring and Gordon Hawkins, for example, argued that, in comparison with other economically advanced democracies, America does not have a crime problem or a violence problem: where it stands out is in its rate of *lethal* violence. The historian Randolph Roth argues that the United States is distinctive in its high rate of homicide among "friends, acquaintances, and strangers," but resembles other societies with regard to "murders involving lovers, spouses, and other adult relatives." Courtwright himself concludes that the United States as a whole has never been especially violent, but that particular places within the country have been. These have been places, Courtwright suggests, with lots of young, unmarried men, in milieus marked by "sensitivity about honor, racial hostility, heavy drinking, religious indifference, group indulgence in vice, ubiquitous armament, and inadequate law enforcement." These factors were present along much of the western frontier,

Courtwright argues, and for different reasons they are found today in impoverished urban neighborhoods.[56]

One of Courtwright's factors—"ubiquitous armament"—touches on a long-standing, often politicized debate about American violence: to what extent rates of violence in the United States are the consequence of the nation's high rate of gun ownership. Gun manufacturers and the National Rifle Association have long suggested that gun ownership by lawful citizens deters and protects against crime. There are scholars who agree. The majority of careful scholars who have studied the question, though—including Courtwright, and including Zimring and Hawkins— blame guns, in part, for increasing levels of violence in the United States, or at least in particular parts of the United States.[57]

The debate about guns in the United States is not just a debate about a particular consumer product; very often it is a debate about culture. This is partly because owning, carrying, and liking guns serves as a cultural signifier in American politics and a badge of group identity; but it is also partly because violence in the United States is sometimes blamed not just on guns but on the *culture* of guns—on the mythology of the cowboy, for example, and his modern descendant, the "armed citizen."[58]

The prevalence of firearms, though, is only one of the geographically specific drivers of violence that Courtwright identifies, and in this respect he is in accord with Roth, with Zimring and Hawkins, and with many other scholars, all of whom stress the complexity of violence. Violence, these scholars insist, is not all of a kind. It lacks a unified etiology. This appears to be the consensus view of historians and social scientists who study violence. Reviewing the literature, Steven Pinker concludes that "violence does not have a single psychological root but a number of them, working by different principles." Here as elsewhere, we need to be on guard against totalizing explanations.[59]

2 | Violent Crime and Violent Criminals

No distinction plays a larger role in contemporary American criminal law than the line between violent and nonviolent offenses. We take it for granted that violent crimes are the serious crimes, the ones that deserve stiffer sentences. The Uniform Crime Reports (UCR) compiled by the Federal Bureau of Investigation divide the index crimes tracked by the Bureau into two groups—"violent crime" (murder, rape, robbery, and aggravated assault) and "property crime" (burglary, larceny, motor vehicle theft, and arson)—and the composite figure for violent crime gets far more news coverage than the comparable figure for property crime. State and federal laws prescribe especially harsh sentences for violent repeat offenders. Most states also make it harder for persons convicted of violent offenses to be released on parole. They make it more difficult, as well, for violent offenders to avoid incarceration altogether: more often than not, drug courts and other programs aimed at diverting offenders from prison exclude defendants charged with violent crimes. Some states also make violent crimes ineligible for sealing or expungement, no matter how much evidence there is of rehabilitation, and it is common for people convicted of violent crimes to be barred statutorily from particular forms of employment. The special restrictions applied to people convicted of violent crimes create what one legal scholar calls a kind of "third-class citizenship"—a "permanently degraded social status" significantly worse than the consequences following from other criminal convictions. Even before conviction, though, defendants charged with violent offenses are often singled out for harsher treatment. Just to give one example, in Nebraska defendants accused of violent crimes cannot claim the usual evidentiary privileges that protect the confidentiality of spousal communications and prevent spouses from having to testify against each other. The assumption that violent crimes are the most serious crimes, the ones most deserving of harsh punishment, runs throughout our system of criminal law.[1]

Even advocates of reducing prison sentences, and improving the treatment of prisoners after their release, often treat violence as something of a third rail. As one commentator complained, nonviolent offenders "have received almost all of the reform attention"; they have been "separated rhetorically from the 'violent' types who are generally considered beyond redemption or mercy." A 1994 report by the federal Department of Justice on the treatment of "low-level offenses" took it for granted that only "nonviolent" offenses could be considered "low-level," because part of what it *meant* for an offense to be "low-level" was that the perpetrator was not particularly likely to be violent in the future. Critics of "recidivist enhancement" statutes often fault such statutes for targeting offenses that are not necessarily violent, like burglary, and excluding some violent offenses, such as assault. As district attorney of San Francisco in the early 2000s, Kamala Harris argued against overreliance on long prison terms—except for violent crimes. Violent offenders, she explained, "have crossed a line that we simply will not tolerate" and need to be "remove[d] . . . from our midst." In 2015, when there was a bipartisan push for sentencing reform in Congress, a bill to mitigate the effects of federal mandatory minimum sentences drew criticism for benefiting offenders who had been convicted in the past of violent offenses; the bill's sponsors responded by amending the legislation "to ensure violent criminals do not benefit." A report in the year 2020 by the Prison Policy Initiative, an advocacy group opposed to mass incarceration, concluded that "almost all of the major criminal justice reforms passed in the last two decades explicitly exclude people accused and convicted of violent offenses."[2]

The fundamental assumption that only nonviolent offenders deserve lenience was vividly illustrated in 2016 when California voters approved a ballot initiative (Proposition 57) to make it easier for some prisoners to be considered for release on parole. Unsurprisingly, the measure was limited to prisoners convicted of nonviolent crimes, but much of the public debate over the initiative had to do with whether, notwithstanding its language, it might wind up helping violent offenders. Opponents, including most of the state's elected prosecutors, argued in the ballot pamphlet sent to voters that the initiative "APPLIES TO VIOLENT CRIMINALS." Supporters, including California governor Jerry Brown, insisted that the new law would "NOT authorize parole for violent offenders."[3]

Part of the difficulty was that the initiative did not itself define "nonviolent felony." Supporters pointed to California's determinate sentencing law, which imposed stiff sentence enhancements for defendants repeatedly convicted of "violent felonies" and then defined the offenses that qualified—a list that included murder, voluntary manslaughter, rape, sexual assault, robbery, extortion, kidnapping, child molestation, mayhem, burglary of an occupied dwelling, and a range of other felonies. After voters approved the initiative, the California Department of Corrections and Rehabilitation promulgated regulations confirming that "nonviolent felonies" under the new law meant felonies not listed as "violent" in the determinate sentencing law. Opponents complained—before and after the passage of Proposition 57—that this definition left out many violent offenses, including, for example, assault with a deadly weapon, rape by intoxication, hostage taking, and arson. Governor Brown countered during the initiative campaign that the statutory list had been augmented in 2000 by a ballot measure backed by the California District Attorneys Association, and if they thought other crimes should be treated as "violent," they should have added those offenses. The district attorneys had "created the damn violent list," the governor charged. (In 2020 another initiative was placed on the California ballot, this one aimed at restoring some of the severity of the state's sentencing laws: a key part of the measure expanded the list of crimes defined as violent.)[4]

The debate over the 2016 ballot initiative in California offers a helpful reminder that although the definition of "violence" is often taken to be self-evident, the category can be surprisingly difficult to delineate. It highlights, too, the importance of underlying, often unarticulated ideas about the nature of violence—in particular, ideas about whether violence is situational or dispositional. Both supporters and opponents of Proposition 57 frequently elided the distinction between violent offenders and persons convicted of violent offenses. That distinction matters greatly if violence is understood to be situational, but less so if violence is thought to be a property of people and not just of acts. Most of all, though, the debate underscored the broad acceptance of the idea that lenience can be appropriate for nonviolent offenders, but not for the violent.

That idea continues to have great power. In recent years, for example, many states have restored voting rights to people who have completed prison sentences for felonies, but generally only if the felonies were nonviolent. In 2019, Senator Bernie Sanders, campaigning to be the presidential nominee of the Democratic Party, called for restoring voting rights to all former prisoners; he was immediately criticized for including people convicted of violent offenses. Two months later, Mayor Bill de Blasio of New York City took a break from his own presidential campaign to criticize the Brooklyn district attorney's office for allowing some young offenders charged with illegal gun possession to avoid jail time and a criminal record by successfully completing a yearlong diversion program. De Blasio called diversion "a valid tool," but only "for nonviolent offenses." Back in California, Jerry Brown was followed as governor by Gavin Newsom, who campaigned on a platform pledging criminal justice reform and reduced levels of incarceration. But in the midst of the coronavirus pandemic of 2020, with advocates warning that the contagion would spread explosively in the state's overcrowded prisons, Newsom drew a sharp line: "I have no interest," he explained, "and I want to make this crystal clear, in releasing violent prisoners from our system." Faced with similar calls to release prisoners to slow the spread of the virus, officials in other states made the same distinction, as did the United States Department of Justice. The result was that prison populations declined only negligibly, by 1.6 percent, during the first three months of 2020, as the pandemic spread. (Prisons soon became the sites of the worst outbreaks of the virus. By October 2020 more than 150,000 prisoners had contracted the disease, and over 1,200 had died from it.)[5]

For decades, it has been common ground in debates about criminal justice that violent crimes are the most serious crimes, the crimes that deserve the harshest penalties. Even *critics of the critics* of our current punishment practices—people who think the reformers don't go far enough—tend to share that view. Over the last decade, many reformers have begun to push, with some success, for elimination of some of the barriers placed in the path of formerly incarcerated people seeking education or employment. Predictably, the reform efforts have focused on helping those with convictions for nonviolent offenses. That restriction has been criticized. But the criticism, when it is offered, is usually that *even* violent offenders deserve a second chance. It is rare for anyone to question the underlying idea that violent offenders are the worst offenders—the scariest, the most culpable, the least deserving of mercy.[6]

Violence, Infamy, and Moral Turpitude

The distinction between violent and nonviolent crimes is so widespread today in legal codes and debates about the law that it can seem utterly natural. Scholars, legislators, and reformers all tend to treat it as obvious that violent crimes are the most serious and deserve the heaviest penalties. Violent criminals, we think, are why we have prisons; they are what criminal law and criminal punishments are designed, above all, to address.[7] But the sharp distinction between violent and nonviolent crimes, and the great weight placed on that distinction, are modern developments, roughly half a century old. As Figure 1 suggests, references to "violent crime" did not become common in American discourse until the 1970s. Before the late 1960s, in fact, references to "violent crime" were less common than references to "infamous crime"—a legal category that, as we will see, was itself never terribly important, and that in no way tracked the line now drawn between violent and nonviolent offenses.[8]

If you peruse, say, the discussion of criminal law in William Blackstone's *Commentaries on the Laws of England*—by far the most widely

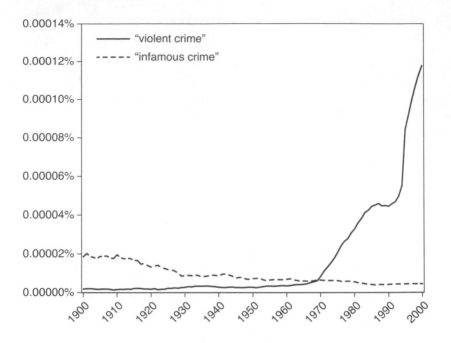

FIG. 1 Frequency of references to "violent crime" in books published in the United States, 1900–2000, compared with references to "infamous crime." The vertical axis measures the occurrences of each phrase as a proportion of all two-word sequences. The lines show seven-year trailing averages. (Data source: Google Books Ngram Viewer.)

read legal treatise in late eighteenth- and early nineteenth-century America—you find few references to violence, and the references you do find cut both ways. Occasionally "violence" is seen as making a crime more serious. Blackstone defines robbery as "open and violent larceny from the person," and he explains that "violence, or putting in fear, is the criterion that distinguishes robbery from other larcenies" and makes it "more atrocious than privately stealing." But Blackstone is just as apt to use the term "violence" to refer to emotions instead of acts, and "violence" of that kind is an extenuating rather than an aggravating factor. Thus, Blackstone notes that "the violence of passion, or temptation, may sometimes alleviate a crime." For example, "to kill a man upon sudden and violent resentment, is less penal than upon cool, deliberate malice." As late as 1935 the American legal scholar Karl Llewellyn thought it obvious that theft, not violence, was "the heart of the really *criminal* Criminal Law."[9]

Historically, the most important distinction drawn among offenses in Anglo-American law has not been between violent and property of-fenses, or between infamous and non-infamous crimes, but between felonies and misdemeanors. This is a very old distinction, dating back perhaps to the twelfth or thirteenth century. Well before the eighteenth century the distinction between felonies and misdemeanors had come to be understood as the distinction between more heinous and less hei-nous offenses, although treason originally was in a special class by itself, even more heinous than felonies, and sometimes the word "crime" was used to refer collectively to treason and to felonies—hence the refer-ences, which used to be common, to "crimes and misdemeanors." Blackstone said that treason was "strictly speaking" a felony, because it met the ancient criterion: it was a crime for which the offender's life and property could be forfeited to the Crown. Later on felonies became, more or less, crimes for which an offender could be executed. Still later, in the United States, felonies were crimes punishable by death or by a term of incarceration in a state prison, which typically meant crimes punishable by a term of a year of more.[10]

By the late nineteenth century, if not earlier, complaints were voiced that the distinction between felonies and misdemeanors was "antiquated and unmeaning," and Great Britain abandoned the distinction in 1967. But the United States has continued to classify crimes as felonies or mis-demeanors. The Supreme Court has called this distinction "minor," "highly technical," and "often arbitrary," but it remains the most perva-sive way that American law distinguishes between more serious and less serious offenses.[11]

The number of crimes classified as felonies has grown dramatically over the centuries, certainly in absolute numbers and possibly also as a proportion of all crimes. Moreover, the precise set of crimes defined as felonies varies from state to state. But "felony" has never meant "violent crime." There have always been nonviolent crimes treated as felonies, and there have always been violent crimes treated as misdemeanors. The original, "common law" felonies, defined not by statute but by judicial decisions, included murder, manslaughter, rape, robbery, and "mayhem" (which meant, roughly, any intentional and disabling maiming). But the list also included arson, burglary, larceny, and sodomy. Assault was not originally a felony—not even assault with a deadly weapon, or assault with intent to kill. Even today, most assaults are misdemeanors rather than felonies.[12]

The law has distinguished among felonies in various ways at various times, but until recently—until, roughly, the last half century—none of these distinctions amounted to separating violent from nonviolent crimes. For example, seventeenth- and eighteenth-century law, both in England and in some of the American colonies, made some felonies but not others eligible for "benefit of clergy," which was a roundabout use of a legal fiction to spare convicted defendants from the death penalty. Originally, benefit of clergy was an actual benefit for actual clergy: it was a rule allowing priests and monks accused of crimes to transfer their cases to ecclesiastical courts. By the seventeenth century, though, the rule had been changed to call for a substitution of lesser punishment, not a transfer to ecclesiastical courts, and it could be invoked by anyone who could read; by the eighteenth century it applied to the illiterate as well. Violent offenses could be "clergyable," and some nonviolent offenses, at least originally, were not. For example, all aggravated forms of theft, including larceny from a dwelling house and larceny of property worth more than a certain amount, were initially exempted from benefit of clergy.[13]

Anglo-American law also distinguished for centuries—and for some purposes, in some places, still distinguishes—between "infamous" crimes and other, lesser offenses. The common-law judges declared anyone who had been convicted of an "infamous" crime incompetent to testify as a witness, and the category gradually became meaningful for other purposes as well. The Fifth Amendment to the United States Constitution, for example, requires a charge from a grand jury before anyone is tried for a capital "or otherwise infamous" crime. In many states, conviction for an infamous crime was held to be grounds for divorce. "Infamous" never meant "violent." The infamous crimes that made a witness incompetent at common law included not just all felonies but all *"crimen falsi"*: crimes involving fraud or misrepresentation. Later, "infamous crimes" came to be understood as crimes punishable by incarceration in a state prison or other stigmatizing penalties, such as hard labor or the loss of the right to vote and to run for office. This has meant that, for the most part, the category of infamous crimes largely tracks the category of felonies.[14]

Yet another distinction drawn by American law, since the early nineteenth century, is between crimes that involve "moral turpitude" and those that do not. The "moral turpitude" standard was initially used to identify "slander per se": statements so obviously harmful to reputation that a plaintiff suing for defamation would not need to offer proof of damages. Beginning in the early 1800s, American courts limited the category of slander per se to accusations that, if true, would make out either "a crime of moral turpitude" or a crime carrying "an infamous punishment." Later the standard of "moral turpitude" was exported to evidence law, where it determined which crimes could be used to impeach the credibility of a witness; to immigration law, where it controlled which misdemeanor convictions would bar an immigrant from entering the United States or justify deportation; and to rules of professional licensing, voter eligibility, and juror selection, where it governed which criminal convictions were disqualifying. Federal evidence law, and the evidence codes of most states, have now abandoned the "moral turpitude" standard for regulating the impeachment of witnesses, but California and Texas still use the standard for those purposes, and crimes involving "moral turpitude" still have special status in defamation law, immigration law, rules of professional licensing, and rules of voter and juror eligibility.[15]

The standard even shows up in some employment contracts. In 2011, when Warner Brothers fired the television actor Charlie Sheen from his lead role in the situation comedy *Two and a Half Men,* the studio justified its action in part based on a contractual provision allowing it to deem Sheen in default if it reasonably believed that (a) he had committed "a felony offense involving moral turpitude," and (b) the conduct interfered with his ability to carry out his side of the agreement. Warner Brothers said this provision had been triggered by Sheen's "furnishing of cocaine to others as part of [his] self-destructive lifestyle."[16]

In *none* of these contexts—defamation, evidence, immigration, licensing, or voter and juror eligibility—have crimes of "moral turpitude" ever been equated, even loosely, with crimes of violence. On the contrary, courts have repeatedly said that violent offenses do not necessarily involve moral turpitude, whereas almost all crimes involving fraud or sexual misconduct do fall within the category.[17] In determining whether a crime that doesn't involve fraud or sexual misconduct nonetheless shows moral turpitude, courts have sometimes asked whether the crime is *malum in se* rather than *malum prohibitum*—that is, whether it involves conduct that would be wrongful even if it were not legally prohibited—or whether it requires *scienter,* a level of conscious intent. They have never asked whether it was violent.

In fact, there is a long history of courts refusing to treat violent offenses as crimes of moral turpitude. Moral turpitude has typically been defined as "conduct that is inherently base, vile, or depraved," and courts have been clear that violence, even homicide, is not necessarily that kind of conduct. Law professor Julia Simon-Kerr, who has studied the history of the moral turpitude standard, points to an illustrative nineteenth-century decision by the Iowa Supreme Court reasoning that it was slander per se to say that someone had poisoned a neighbor's cow, even though an accusation of homicide would *not* have been slander per se. "Homicide may be committed in the heat of sudden passion," the court explained, ". . . but no circumstances can possibly extenuate the moral turpitude of that wretch who will poison his neighbor's horse or cow."[18]

Simon-Kerr notes that decisions of this kind were especially common in the nineteenth century, and she traces them to the gendered honor codes from which courts in that century drew the term and the concept of "moral turpitude." But throughout the twentieth century and into the twenty-first century, crimes of dishonesty or sexual misconduct were, and remain, more likely to be treated as involving moral turpitude than crimes of violence. In 1926, for example, a federal judge in Massachusetts blocked the deportation of a noncitizen who had attacked a police officer with a razor, reasoning that the crime of conviction, assault and battery of a police officer, did not necessarily involve moral turpitude. "If one ordinarily law-abiding, in the heat of anger, strikes another," the judge explained, "that act would not reveal such inherent baseness or depravity as to suggest the idea of moral turpitude." Relying in part on the authority of that decision, courts today continue to hold that simple assault, or even "aggravated assault where the defendant knows that the person he is assaulting is a law enforcement officer and causes bodily injury," is not a crime of moral turpitude for immigration purposes.[19]

Codes and Classifications

The categories of felonies, misdemeanors, infamous crimes, and crimes of moral turpitude all emerged from common-law adjudication: the gradual, case-by-case accumulation of judicial decisions that then served as precedents for later decisions. But since the eighteenth century there have been repeated attempts, some more successful than others, to codify and systematize the criminal law, both in England and later in the United States. Each of these efforts grappled with the question of how best to categorize crimes—what made some kinds of offenses more serious, or deserving of greater punishment. It is striking that until recently none of these schemes placed much, if any, weight on the distinction between violent and nonviolent crimes.[20]

The point of departure for many of these efforts to codify and classify criminal prohibitions was Montesquieu's *Spirit of the Laws,* widely influential in England and in the American colonies. Montesquieu divided crimes into four classes, depending on whether they ran "counter to religion . . . to mores . . . to tranquility . . . [or] to the security of the citizens." The fourth category included physical attacks, like intentional killings, but also violations of "security with respect to goods." In general, Montesquieu thought the penalty for a crime should "be drawn from the nature of the thing," so the death penalty was the proper sanction for homicide, and violations of "security with respect to goods" should preferably be punished with fines or other deprivations of property. But because fines might not deter those of little means, Montesquieu concluded that "the corporal penalty has to replace the pecuniary penalty," even for property offenses. He drew no sharp line—no explicit distinction at all, really—between violent and nonviolent crimes.[21]

Neither did Jeremy Bentham, writing a few decades later. Bentham's classification scheme divided crimes into five categories: (1) "PRIVATE offences, or offences against assignable *individuals*"; (2) "SEMI-PUBLIC offences, or offences affecting a whole subordinate *class* of persons"; (3) "SELF-REGARDING offences: offences against *one's self*"; (4) "PUBLIC offences, or offences against *the state* in general"; and (5) "MULTIFORM or ANOMALOUS offences; . . . containing offences by FALSEHOOD, and offences concerning TRUST." It did not occur to Bentham, as it did not occur to Montesquieu, to treat violent crime as a separate, especially serious category.[22]

Nor did it occur to any of the major codifiers of Anglo-American criminal law: Edward Livingston, who submitted a proposed penal code for Louisiana in 1826; Thomas Macaulay, drafter of the proposed Indian Penal Code of 1837; David Dudley Field and his collaborators, who completed their proposed penal code for New York in 1865; James FitzJames Stephen, who in 1878 made the first serious effort to codify English criminal law; or Herbert Wechsler, architect of the Model Penal Code, which was finalized in 1962. Livingston, for example, sorted crimes into twenty-one categories: fifteen categories of "public offenses which principally affect the state or its government," and six categories of "private offenses which principally affect individuals." One of the latter six categories—"offenses affecting the persons of individuals"—included homicide, rape, assault, abduction, and false imprisonment, but it also included abortion, and it excluded robbery, whether armed or unarmed. Robbery was grouped with arson, burglary, theft, and fraud; these were all categorized as "offenses against private property." Rioting—assembling "with intent to aid each other by violence" either to commit an offense or to violate rights—was classified as a "public offense" and placed in the category of "crimes against public tranquility," a category that also included nonviolent "public disturbances." Livingston's code did not separate out violent crimes.[23]

Neither did the prominent codes that came afterward. Macaulay's Indian Penal Code classified homicide, rape, assault, abduction, and wrongful confinement as "offenses affecting the human body," a category that also included abortion and any touching of a person or an animal "to gratify unnatural lust." Like Livingston, Macaulay treated robberies as "offences against property" and riots as "offences against the public tranquility." New York's Field Code classified riots (along with unlawful assemblies and prize fights) as "crimes against the public peace"; treated homicides, suicides, maimings, robberies, kidnappings, assaults, and duels (along with libels) as "crimes against the person"; and cataloged rapes (along with abortion, child abandonment, bigamy, indecent exposure, and lotteries) as "crimes against the person and against public decency and good morals." Stephen's proposed codification of English criminal law grouped riots together with unlawful assemblies, duels, prize fights, and breaches of the peace; Stephen categorized homicide, assault, rape, abortion, bigamy, child neglect, and defamation as "offenses against the person and reputation"; and he put robbery and burglary, along with theft, fraud, forgery, counterfeiting, arson, and vandalism, under the heading "offenses against rights of property or rights arising out of contracts."[24]

These were the prior efforts at codification that the criminal law scholar Herbert Wechsler and his collaborators drew upon when they compiled the Model Penal Code for the American Law Institute (ALI) in the mid-twentieth century. This massive project began in the early 1950s and reached fruition in 1962, when the ALI formally adopted Wechsler's Code. The Model Penal Code groups felonies into three groups according to their perceived seriousness: first degree, second degree, and third degree. First-degree felonies are supposed to incur the heaviest penalties; third-degree felonies are to be punished the least severely. Violent crimes are distributed throughout these three categories: some forms of aggravated assault, for example, are treated as third-degree felonies, and so are "terroristic threats." Some nonviolent offenses, on the other hand, are categorized as second-degree felonies. These include forgery, arson, abortion, and aggravated forms of burglary.

The Model Penal Code does, however, limit the category of first-degree felonies to violent offenses—at least if robbery is treated as a violent offense, and not, as earlier codifiers typically suggested, as an offense against property. And robbery is a first-degree felony under the Model Penal Code only if the robber tries to kill someone or to cause serious bodily harm. So we can see in the Model Penal Code the beginnings, but only the beginnings, of the idea that later came to seem obvious to scholars and reformers: that violent crimes were the most serious crimes and the crimes that, generally speaking, should trigger the harshest penalties.[25]

The first federal criminal statute referring explicitly to "violent crimes" or "crimes of violence" appears to have been enacted in 1961—the year before the promulgation of the Model Penal Code. For the next twenty years, there was exactly one such reference in all of the federal criminal code. Ten more federal criminal statutes referring to "violent crimes" or "crimes of violence" were added in 1994. By 1996 there were twenty such statutes, and a decade later there were twenty-eight. Today so many federal statutes use the phrase "crime of violence," and employ similar definitions of the term, that the Supreme Court has declared that failing to interpret the phrase consistently "would make a hash of the federal criminal code."[26]

From There to Here

As early as 1978 the journalist Charles Silberman could claim without fear of contradiction that few social problems were as important, as permanent, or as inflammatory as violent crime. "All over the United States," he observed, "people worry about criminal violence." By 1994, President Bill Clinton was warning in his State of the Union Address that "violent crime and the fear that it provokes are crippling our society" and "fraying the ties that bind us." Not crime in general: violent crime. The omnibus federal crime law enacted that year was called the Violent Crime Control and Law Enforcement Act; among other things, it required any state seeking federal funding for prison construction to prove that it had increased both the percentage of violent offenders sentenced to prison and the average time they spent in prison. By 2007 the legal scholar Jonathan Simon was arguing that the United States had "built a new civil and political order structured around the problem of violent crime." Simon thought the country had come to be "governed through crime," that crime was "legitimizing" and "providing context for the exercise of power."[27]

Simon could take for granted in 2007 that his readers would understand that "crime" in this context meant "violent crime." Writing four years later, law professor Alice Ristroph noted that "from the general public to the specialists, everyone seems to think of crime in terms of violence"; everyone seems to believe that "the primary reason to have criminal laws, police forces, and prisons is to address the problem of violent crime." Incarceration, says the criminal justice reformer Danielle Sered, owes its standing in society largely to "its role in protecting people from violence and those who commit it." But how did violence come to be understood as the crux of the crime problem? How did violent crime become a synonym for serious crime?[28]

Part of the answer is that violent crime ballooned in the 1960s and 1970s. Between 1960 and 1980 the annual murder rate doubled in the United States, from 5 per 100,000 people to 10 per 100,000 people. The "violent crime rate" computed each year by the Federal Bureau of Investigation—a figure that adds together murders, rapes, robberies, and aggravated assaults—more than tripled, rising from 161 per 100,000 in 1960 to 597 in 1980. The increases in major cities were even steeper. The annual murder rate in New York City went from 5 per 100,000 in 1960 to 26 per 100,000 in 1980; in Detroit during the same period the figure rose from 9 to 46. One reason people worried more about violent crime in 1980 than in 1960 was that there was more violent crime to worry about.[29]

But that explanation has limited power. To begin with, crime *in general* increased in the 1960s and 1970s, and the increases in nonviolent crime were, if anything, sharper than the increases in violent offending. Figure 2 tracks annual rates of violent crime and property crime in the United States from 1960 through 2014. Both sets of numbers come from the Uniform Crime Reports compiled by the FBI. Throughout the 1960s and 1970s, property crime—combining burglary, larceny, and vehicle theft—rose virtually in lockstep with violent crime.

It was not until the late 1980s that violent crime began to rise more sharply than property crime, and even that divergence may be a statistical artifact. The Uniform Crime Reports rely on data submitted by local police departments, and those numbers suffer from well-known deficiencies: many crimes are never reported to the police, and when a crime is reported, the police often exercise discretion in whether and how to record it. The two kinds of crimes for which the UCR statistics are probably most reliable are murder and vehicle theft: murder because deaths are hard to overlook, and vehicle theft because insurance companies will not reimburse for a stolen car unless the policyholder files a police report.[30] Figure 3 tracks annual changes in the rates of murder and vehicle theft from 1960 to 2014, drawing on the UCR statistics compiled by the FBI. Again, the figures rise pretty much in unison in the 1960s and 1970s. The trends begin to diverge in the mid-1980s, but that is because at that point vehicle theft starts to rise more rapidly than homicide, not the other way around.

By historical standards, the crime increase in the 1960s was unusually steep, and it lasted unusually long. But it wasn't the first time that crime, including violent crime, had risen steeply in American cities. It may have been the first time, though, that violent crime was singled out as an issue of special concern. Homicides spiked in New York City and in Boston in the decades leading up to the Civil War, for example, but violent crime never became, then, the kind of issue that it became in the last part of the twentieth century, and the kind of issue that it remains to this day. Crime and disorder *were* major issues in the nineteenth century; there were arguments in Massachusetts, for example, that Boston should cede some of its municipal autonomy, given the city's failure to control its "dangerous classes." But according to Roger Lane, a pioneering historian of crime and policing in America, "mob action was the only form of violence which generally figured in these complaints, and 'crime' was used typically as a synonym for vice." Lane points out that in this period "the laws concerning drink . . . were subject to constant revision, but except for a reduction in the number of cases involving the death penalty, the general criminal code was not." He concludes that "as the sons and daughters of Massachusetts migrated to the metropolis, the image con-

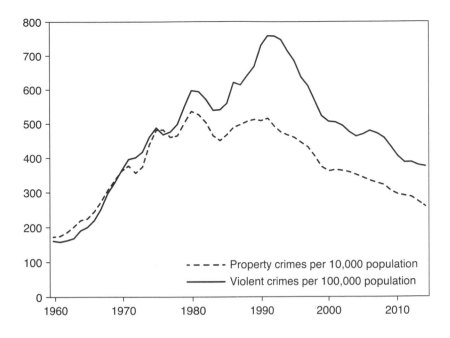

FIG. 2 Property crime and violent crime rates in the United States, 1960–2014. (Data source: Uniform Crime Reporting Statistics compiled by the Federal Bureau of Investigation.)

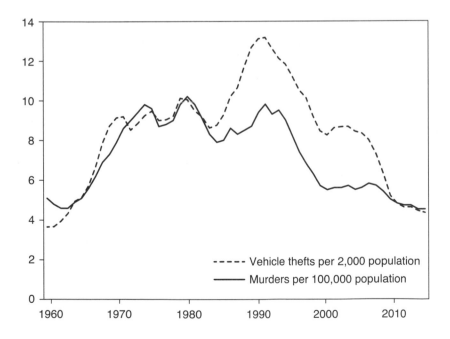

FIG. 3 Murder and vehicle theft rates in the United States, 1960–2014. (Data source: Uniform Crime Reporting Statistics compiled by the Federal Bureau of Investigation.)

jured by the fearful was the rake or the tempter, not the robber or rapist."
Well into the twentieth century, vice—not violence—was the most
common synecdoche for urban crime, in Massachusetts and elsewhere
in the United States.[31]

So crime trends in the 1960s and 1970s do not, by themselves, explain
the focus on violent crime that has come to seem natural in criminal law
over the past half century. Other factors were at work. One, perhaps, was
a global, centuries-long decline in violence, fueled by and in turn rein-
forcing a gradual change in sensibilities—the "civilizing process" described by the twentieth-century German sociologist Norbert Elias.
Steven Pinker's long 2011 book about violence argued that violence has
gradually declined for centuries around the world, albeit unevenly and
in fits and starts. Pinker credited not just changes in manners, which
were Elias's focus, but also widening compassion and the increased application of reason: the Enlightenment writ large.[32]

The rise in violent crime in the 1960s and 1970s—a trend seen
throughout the West but especially pronounced in the United States—
represented a kind of backsliding. It may have been particularly alarming
precisely for that reason. Roger Lane, writing in the late 1960s, concluded that "heightening . . . standards of propriety" had sharply reduced serious crime since the nineteenth century, but that the process
did not proceed without interruption. "There are times," he noted,
"when for various reasons the level of violence overbalances current expectations," and "in such situations the social pressure to maintain and
extend high standards, and to enforce them universally, may result in
frustration," and "the frustration may translate into fear."[33] Charles Silberman offered much the same diagnosis a decade later:

> For people over the age of thirty-five . . . the upsurge in crime
> that began in the early 1960s appeared to be a radical depar-
> ture from the norm, a departure that shattered their expecta-
> tions of what urban and suburban life was like. The trauma
> was exacerbated by the growing sense that the whole world
> was getting out of joint, for the explosive increase in crime
> was accompanied by a number of other disorienting social

changes—for example, a general decline in civility, in deference to authority, and in religious and patriotic observance.[34]

Silberman wasn't alone in connecting concerns about crime in the
1960s and 1970s with concerns about "other disorienting social changes."
And we can go further. Rising concerns about violent crime in the late
twentieth century may have been fueled, in part, by a whole series of
historical developments that made violence seem more frightening—
official as well as unlawful violence, overseas as well as domestic violence.
Those developments included, but were hardly limited to (1) the massive
casualties of the first and second world wars; (2) the rise of modern to-
talitarianism, and the horrific uses of violence by Nazi Germany and
Stalinist Russia; (3) the assassination of President John F. Kennedy, the
later assassinations of Malcolm X, Martin Luther King Jr., and Senator
Robert Kennedy, and the still later attempts on the lives of President
Gerald Ford and President Ronald Reagan; (4) the urban riots of the late
1960s; (5) the televised carnage of the Vietnam War, and the revelation
of the massacre by American troops at My Lai; (6) the wave of bombings,
abductions, armed robberies, and murders carried out by radical groups
in the United States and Europe; (7) the police riot outside the 1968
Democratic Convention in Chicago and the fatal shootings of student
protesters by National Guard troops at Kent State two years later; (8)
the gruesome murders by Charles Manson and his "family," and the
connection those crimes seemed to have with the counterculture and
with a general social unraveling; and (9) the wave of riots and violent
uprisings in prisons across the country in the early 1970s.[35]

All of these developments contributed to a sense that the twentieth
century had taken bloodshed to unprecedented levels, and that—in the
words of psychiatrist James Gilligan—Americans were witnessing "a
continuing and ever-accelerating escalation of the scale of human violence." That wasn't the consensus view of historians, then or now, but it
was and remains a widespread view. It may well have contributed both
to an increased revulsion from violence and to the growing salience of
violence in criminal law.[36] Following the assassinations of Martin Luther King Jr. and Robert Kennedy in 1968, President Johnson appointed

a National Commission on the Causes and Prevention of Violence—which carried out its work in the wake of other presidential commissions, all appointed between the years of 1965 and 1967, on (1) Law Enforcement and the Administration of Justice, (2) Civil Disorders, and (3) Crime in the District of Columbia. In 1970, following the fatal shootings of student demonstrators by National Guard troops at Kent State, President Nixon established yet another presidential commission, this one focused on "campus unrest."

The growing importance of violence in criminal law may have owed something not just to increasing concerns about violence but also to rising interest in nonviolence as a political method and a moral principle. That increased interest was itself a reaction, in part, to the appalling turns that violence took in the twentieth century, but it owed a great deal as well to the celebrated campaigns of civil disobedience led in colonial India by Mahatma Gandhi and then in the American South by the Southern Christian Leadership Conference and the Student Nonviolent Coordinating Committee. The strikes and boycotts organized by the United Farm Workers further burnished the luster of nonviolence for many Americans, particularly on the left. By the 1970s, nonviolent protest had become part of the American civic religion; pictures of Martin Luther King Jr., Cesar Chavez, and Delores Huerta went up alongside George Washington and Harriet Tubman in many public school classrooms. Despite the turn toward violence at many protests in the Trump era, the strategic and moral superiority of nonviolence remained utterly obvious to many activists in the United States. Following "Antifa" attacks on right-wing protesters in Berkeley in 2017, a liberal activist expressed bewilderment. "We're just puzzled," she told a reporter, "as to why people consider violence a valid tactic." Five years later, when police killings sparked protests and lootings across the United States, a city council member in Louisville, supportive of police reform, warned that "we have to be careful to control our message, and violence changes that message." Even a former New Left radical like Mark Rudd, active in the Weather Underground in the late 1960s and early 1970s, now calls nonviolence "the one essential strategy to achieve positive social change."[37]

By the mid-1990s, when mass incarceration started to become a priority issue for criminal justice reformers, it seemed natural to focus on "nonviolent" drug offenders. Nonviolent offenses were the least serious, and nonviolent offenders were the least threatening. Writing in 2010, James Forman Jr. lamented that "since it is especially difficult to suspend moral judgment when the discussion turns to violent crime, progressives tend to avoid or change the subject." Forman warned that targeting reform efforts at nonviolent offenders did not just respond to prevalent ideas about the relative severity of offenses; it reinforced those ideas. The more that reformers highlighted the plight of nonviolent offenders, the more they argued that people who hadn't been violent deserved leniency, the more they suggested by implication that people who *had* been convicted of violent offenses *didn't* deserve leniency.[38]

Rising rates of violent crime, growing revulsion from violence, the veneration of nonviolent protest, and the tactics of criminal justice reformers may all have contributed to the increasing significance of violence in criminal law over the past half century. But it is impossible to understand this or any other development in American criminal justice without taking account of race. The rise in violent crime in the 1960s and 1970s was disproportionately a rise in urban crime, and the rise in urban crime was disproportionately a rise in crimes committed by African Americans. It was also disproportionately a rise in crimes committed *against* African Americans; most violent crime, then as now, was intra-racial. But it was the disproportionate representation of Blacks among offenders, not the disproportionate victimization of Blacks, that became a critical part of the politics of crime in the late twentieth century. "Violent crime rates in the nation's biggest cities," notes the historian Khalil Gibran Muhammad, have come to be "generally understood as a reflection of the presence and behavior of the Black men, women, and children who live there." That understanding, combined with the association of violence with masculinity, and the pervasive focus on violent crime as the kind of crime most worth worrying about, explains why law professor Paul Butler can argue plausibly that "American criminal justice today is premised on controlling African American men."[39]

There is reason to suspect that the association of violent crime with Blackness has influenced the theories that the law has come to embody about how violence operates: the racialization of violent crime has likely had more than a little to do with the increasing tendency to understand criminal violence as a product of offenders' characters, not of the situations in which they find themselves. We will return to this connection later in the chapter. For now, I want to note that the racial tilt in patterns of offending—and, more importantly, in popular understandings of offending—may have played a role not just in legal theories about the *nature* of violence but also in the growing *significance* of violence in criminal law.

The nature of that role isn't completely clear. The tendency of white Americans to associate Blacks with criminality dates back to the nineteenth century, but Muhammad's work suggests that the racial tropes of the late nineteenth and early twentieth centuries emphasized the supposed immorality, dissolution, and sexual rapaciousness of African Americans as much as or more than any across-the-board tendency toward violence.[40] With one arguable exception, discussions of Black criminality in the early twentieth century—like discussions then of crime more generally—appear to have focused more on vice than on violence.

The exception was the fear of Black men sexually assaulting white women—a terror, an obsession, and a rage that helped drive the campaign of terror that lynch mobs waged against African Americans from the end of the Civil War well into the twentieth century. Roughly a quarter of the more than 4,000 African Americans murdered in lynchings during the Jim Crow era—from 1880 through 1940—were accused of sexual assault, but "assault" here must be understood loosely. The Equal Justice Initiative, which has been working to inventory and document America's legacy of lynchings, notes that "the definition of black-on-white 'rape' in the South was incredibly broad and required no allegation of force," because "white institutions . . . and most white people rejected the idea that a white woman could or would willingly consent to sex with an African American man." African American men were lynched for merely coming into contact with, writing to, or "associating with" white women. (This was true as well in the immediate aftermath of the Civil War. The Equal Justice Initiative concludes that at least 2,000 African Americans were lynched from 1865 through 1877, many of them men accused of seeking romantic or sexual intimacy with white women.) Roughly 30 percent of lynching victims in the Jim Crow South were accused of murder, but hundreds, if not thousands, of African Americans were lynched before and during Jim Crow based on accusations of far less serious crimes, including vagrancy, or social transgressions such as "speaking disrespectfully, refusing to step off the sidewalk, using profane language, using an improper title for a white person, suing a white man, arguing with a white man, bumping into a white woman, [or] insulting a white person."[41] As an institution, lynching was not chiefly a response to violence; it was a deployment of violence—deadly, horrific violence—to enforce a social code. The constellation of Black transgressions, real and imagined, that loomed large in white minds in the late nineteenth and early twentieth centuries included, but was not centered around, violent crime.

Nonetheless, when crime rates began to soar in the 1960s and 1970s, the concentration of violent crimes in heavily Black, urban neighborhoods may have made those crimes especially frightening to white Americans, and may therefore have contributed to the rising salience of violence in criminal law. That dynamic may have been fueled by specific, psychological pathways of racial prejudice. For example, white Americans have long associated Blacks with animals, and more particularly with apes—sometimes consciously and sometimes unconsciously. Those associations remain strong today; they show up explicitly in racist tweets and implicitly in unconscious processes studied by psychologists and media scholars. It therefore seemed all the more natural in the 1960s and 1970s to refer to America's increasingly violent urban neighborhoods as "jungles" and to urban criminals as "animals." That imagery, in turn, helped to make violence increasingly central to the American understanding of criminality. The peril of the jungle is not indolence or immorality, but "Nature, red in tooth and claw."[42]

The War on Drugs and Its Aftermath

The increasing significance of violence in criminal law may have yet another cause: it may be, in part, a lingering reaction to the late twentieth-century "war on drugs." After staying stable for decades, incarceration rates in America began to climb in the 1980s, and a large part of the explanation was new, tougher sentences for drug crimes. Historically, drug policies in the United States have gone back and forth between laxity and harshness, and during the Reagan era the pendulum swung very far in the direction of harshness. Statutes mandating long sentences for narcotics offenders were adopted at both the federal and the state level. The federal sentences, required by a statute enacted in 1986, were especially draconian, and they had an especially disproportionate impact on minority defendants. The new federal drug sentences were adopted at the same time that the federal government was implementing a new regime of presumptive sentencing guidelines that heavily restricted the discretion of sentencing judges, and those guidelines wound up following the lead of, and extending the reach of, the mandatory minimum sentences prescribed by the 1986 drug law.[43]

By the early 1990s there was a growing sense among many Americans that the war on drugs had gone too far: that too many people, especially people of color, were being locked up on drug charges for too long. At the same time, politicians were feeling ever-escalating pressure to appear "tough on crime." Democrats had watched Richard Nixon win the presidency in 1968 and 1972 as the candidate of "law and order." They saw George H. W. Bush defeat Michael Dukakis in 1988 by highlighting Dukakis's opposition to the death penalty and his furloughing of a convicted African American murderer, William Horton, who had then absconded, kidnapped a man and a woman, stabbed the man, and raped the woman. In a now-infamous television ad, a political action committee with ties to the Bush campaign showed pictures of Horton, renamed him "Willie," and described the crimes he committed after escaping while on a "weekend pass." The lesson Democrats learned was that they could call for moderation of drug punishments but they could not allow themselves to be out-toughed on "violent crime."[44] The Democratic Party platform in 1992 called for fighting drug addiction with counseling, treatment, and education. It also singled out the rise of "violent crimes" as an "alarming" threat to America's communities and called for "put[ting] more police on the streets" to restore "law and order" in "crime-ravaged communities." Arkansas governor Bill Clinton, who won the Democratic nomination and the presidency in 1992, established his credentials early on the issue of violent crime: in January 1992 Clinton took a break from campaigning in New Hampshire and flew home to oversee the execution of Ricky Ray Rector, a convicted murderer so intellectually disabled he asked to save the dessert from his last meal "for later." Two years after Clinton's election, Congress passed the largest crime bill in American history; it was titled the "Violent Crime Control and Law Enforcement Act of 1994" and contained, among other things, funding for 100,000 new police officers.[45]

Clinton's successful campaign for the presidency in 1992 encapsulated what became the center-left position on criminal justice throughout the 1990s and early 2000s: de-escalate the war on drugs, but give no quarter to violent crime. Politicians and activists opposed to harsh drug sentences almost always talked about "nonviolent" drug offenses; they took care not to call for leniency for violent offenders. This was true of policymakers as well. A 1994 report by the US Department of Justice reconsidered the treatment of "low-level drug law violators," by which the Department meant *nonviolent* drug offenders with little or no criminal history.[46]

That was also the population targeted by drug courts, the cornerstone of liberal efforts to reform drug prosecutions in the 1990s. Drug courts divert offenders from prison and send them instead into treatment programs; typically the threat of a prison sentence hangs over the defendant's head until the treatment program is successfully completed. The first drug treatment court opened in Miami in 1999, and the idea quickly spread across the country, becoming "the generic policy response of choice to dissatisfaction with the war on drugs." From the start, drug courts largely excluded violent offenders: not just defendants currently facing a charge of a violent crime, but also defendants who had been convicted of a violent crime at any point in the past. The 1994 crime bill provided federal funding for drug courts, but mandated the exclusion of any defendant with a current or prior violent offense. By the end of the 1990s, many drug courts had loosened their eligibility criteria, but the vast majority continued to exclude defendants with current or prior convictions for any violent crime.[47]

Drug courts soon provided the template for other kinds of "therapeutic" or "problem-solving" courts, all of which aim to divert certain classes of offenders from prison, as long as they attend and successfully complete treatment programs. Many states now have "mental health courts" and "veterans courts." These programs, too, often exclude violent offenders. This is true even of veterans courts, despite the fact that a large share of the cases that bring veterans into court involve assaults or hit-and-run collisions. In the words of one advocate, excluding violent offenders can mean having "a Veterans Court without veterans." Nonetheless, most veterans courts "focus on non-violent crimes"; some address "low-level domestic violence charges," but that has proven controversial. Kamala Harris, then district attorney of San Francisco, championed diversion courts but not for violent offenders. "Violent offenders," she explained, "have crossed a line that reduces our confidence that we can redirect them." And, as we have seen, Mayor Bill de Blasio of New York City argued as recently as 2019 that diversion programs were a good idea, but only for nonviolent offenses.[48]

Therapeutic courts began to spread across the country at exactly the same time that states and the federal government were adopting new, extraordinarily harsh penalties for violent crime. The most important of these penalties were contained in a wave of "Three Strikes" laws, statutes that mandated long sentences for repeat offenders. These laws sought to put those offenders on notice that "three strikes and you're out," and they zeroed in, generally, on repeat *violent* offenders. Laws authorizing or requiring stiffer sentences for recidivists have a long history, but until the early 1990s these statutes did not use the language of baseball, and—what matters more—they did not focus on violent offenses, or on any other category of crime deemed especially serious.[49] Since their inception, Three Strikes laws have taken aim at violent crime. Sometimes the target offenses have also included narcotics trafficking and / or sex offenses, but violent offenses have always been at the core, not just in the coverage of the statutes but in the rhetoric supporting their adoption.

The first Three Strikes law was adopted in the state of Washington by voter initiative in 1993. It required a life sentence for anyone convicted three times of offenses designated by statute as "most serious"; these included murder, manslaughter, kidnapping, rape, sexual assault, first- and second-degree assault, first-degree burglary, and narcotics trafficking. The federal government followed suit the following year: the Violent Crime Control and Law Enforcement Act of 1994—the same law that provided federal funding for 100,000 new police officers, and for drug courts that excluded violent offenders—mandated life imprisonment for anyone who (a) was convicted in federal court of a "serious violent" felony, and (b) had previously been convicted in federal or state court of either two "serious violent" felonies, or one "serious violent" felony and one "serious drug offense." The law defined "serious violent felony" to include, in general, murder, manslaughter, rape or sexual assault, armed or aggravated robbery—and any other offense, punishable by ten years or more in prison, that involved either the actual, attempted, or threatened "use of physical force against the person of another" or "a substantial risk of physical force against the person of another." The 1994 federal crime bill also required any state that wanted federal funding for prison construction to demonstrate that it had increased both the percentage of violent offenders sentenced to prison and the average prison time served by violent offenders.[50]

The year 1994 also saw the adoption of California's Three Strikes law, which reached further and was considerably more punitive than the federal and Washington State versions. Like its Washington State counterpart, the California law was adopted by voter initiative. The California measure passed in the wake of the highly publicized abduction, sexual assault, and murder of a 12-year-old girl, Polly Klaas, by a repeat violent offender on parole. The California Three Strikes law prescribed long, mandatory sentences for convicted felons with two previous convictions for "violent" or otherwise "serious" felonies. There were also somewhat shorter, but still quite harsh, mandatory sentences for "second strikers": convicted felons with a single previous conviction for a "violent" or "serious" felony. By the end of 1995, twenty-four states had enacted Three Strikes laws. Today, almost every state has laws mandating long, additional sentences, often called "sentencing enhancements," for repeat violent offenders. These laws—particularly California's, which remained the most draconian—helped to ensure that incarceration rates continued to climb in the United States throughout the 1990s, even as crime rates, including rates of violent crime, plummeted. Roughly a quarter of all California prisoners today were sentenced under the Three Strikes law, and that has been true for over ten years.[51]

Even more than the harsh penalties the Three Strikes laws imposed on violent offenders, the politics and debates surrounding these laws demonstrated the extraordinary role that violence had come to play in criminal law by the early 2000s. Polly Klaas was one of a series of victims of violent crime—most of them young, female, and white—who were invoked repeatedly by advocates of tougher sentences for repeat offenders. Victims of violent crime became, as Jonathan Simon has written, "the idealized subject of the law." Even skeptics of Three Strikes laws often reinforced the idea that the criminal justice system should focus its energies and its harshest penalties on violent offenders. Three Strikes laws were criticized for counting, as "strikes," crimes like burglary that were not truly violent. Opponents warned that the laws might even force the release of "violent pretrial felons," by crowding jails and prisons with nonviolent offenders.[52]

The "violent felon" had become the polar opposite of the "low-level drug offender." The latter deserved mercy and understanding; the former needed and deserved carceral containment. That dichotomous view of criminal justice has proven remarkably durable. In 2019, in his first term on the Supreme Court, Justice Kavanaugh dissented at length from the Supreme Court's invalidation of a federal statute mandating extra prison time for offenders who use or carry a firearm while committing a "crime of violence." The Court said the statutory definition of "crime of violence" was unconstitutionally vague. Justice Kavanaugh disagreed, and he added this warning about the implications of the Court's decision: "The inmates who will be released are not nonviolent offenders. They are not drug offenders. They are offenders who committed violent crimes with firearms, often brutally violent crimes."[53]

What Is a "Violent" Crime?

The more that violence matters in criminal law, the more it matters how violence is defined: which crimes are categorized as violent and which are left out of that category. That turns out to be complicated. Most states, and the federal government, have statutes specifying which offenses count as "violent" for purposes of recidivist sentence enhancements, and the list varies from jurisdiction to jurisdiction. Louisiana considers purse snatching to be violent; most other states do not. Arkansas and Rhode Island treat larceny as a violent offense. Mississippi categorizes statutory rape as violent. Delaware and Oklahoma treat dealing in child pornography as a violent offense; New Hampshire classifies *possession* of child pornography as violent. In many states the "violent" offenses that trigger sentence enhancements are the same ones that restrict eligibility for parole, but other states have two separate lists. Sometimes the "violent" crimes addressed by repeat offender statutes are the same ones that make a defendant ineligible for drug court or veterans court, but frequently they are not. In Louisiana and Oklahoma, for example, the same list of violent offenses governs sentence enhancements, restrictions on parole, and disqualification for therapeutic courts. Mississippi uses a single list of "crimes of violence" to determine sentence enhancements, restrictions on parole, and eligibility for drug court, but a narrower list for purposes of restricting access to veterans court. Connecticut uses a different list of violent crimes for sentence enhancements than for parole eligibility. California, as we have seen, uses the same list.[54]

Still, it is possible to generalize. Every statute mandating longer sentences for violent recidivists classifies murder and rape as violent, but almost every one of these statutes also includes some crimes that are not obviously violent—like purse snatching, larceny, statutory rape, or child pornography—and each of these statutes also excludes a wide range of criminal conduct that would satisfy almost any nonlegal definition of "violent." Most states treat arson as a violent offense, even if no one is endangered. It is also common for states to include child molestation and related offenses in the list of crimes that serve as predicates for recidivist sentence enhancements; sometimes this is done simply by labeling these crimes as "violent," and sometimes the statutory category itself is relabeled to include sexual as well as violent offenders.

A wide range of sexual offenses tend more and more to be treated as "violent," either by definition or in effect. As we have seen, many Three Strikes laws treat sexual offenses, even when nonviolent, as predicates for recidivist sentence enhancements; the predicates include, for example, distribution or possession of child pornography. Similarly, the federal "First Step" Act—a relatively modest effort at decreasing rates of imprisonment, enacted with bipartisan support in 2018—expanded eligibility for compassionate release, but excluded prisoners convicted of either violent crimes or sexual offenses, including offenses involving child pornography. And an initiative approved by Florida voters that same year re-enfranchised offenders who had completed their sentences, except for those convicted of murder or any "felony sexual offense"; the latter category, again, includes possession of child pornography. One could say that the Florida law treats consumers of child pornography as being more "violent" than armed robbers, but the initiative—which does not use the term "violent"—might be more accurately described as stepping away from the prevailing modern focus on violent offenders as the most blameworthy and the hardest to forgive. It is a return in a way to the emphasis on sexual offenses, rather than violent offenses, in defining crimes of "moral turpitude." And it is in keeping with the trend over the past two decades to direct greater police and prosecutorial attention to all sexual offenders and to subject them to significantly harsher sentences. (During the coronavirus pandemic of 2020, when many prisoners were granted early release in order to reduce the spread of the virus, prisoners convicted of sex offenses, like those convicted of violent crimes, were often deemed ineligible.) It is consistent, too, with the increasingly frequent identification of "sexually violent predators" as the worst of violent offenders, a category apart within a category apart.[55]

Violence remains the central preoccupation of American criminal law, however, and so the definition of violence remains critical. A key part of that definition, in practice, has to do with burglary. Most states treat at least some forms of burglary as violent; so does the federal government, as we will see. Sometimes burglary has to be aggravated to count as violent. That can mean that only nighttime burglaries are classified as violent, or only residential burglaries, or only burglaries when someone is home. In some states, a burglary counts as violent only if the burglar carries a deadly weapon. What is almost never required, though, is that the burglar actually attack or physically threaten someone.[56]

Burglary is the largest and most important statutory addition to the category of violence. The largest and most important statutory subtraction from that category is simple assault. Most sentencing statutes targeting violent recidivists include aggravated assault as a violent offense, but none include ordinary assault. In most, if not all, jurisdictions, simple assault is not just excluded from the category of violent felonies; it isn't a felony at all. That makes the difference between aggravated and simple assault of very great consequence. In Wyoming, for example, simple assault is punishable only by a fine of up to $750, or, if the victim is harmed, by up to six months in jail. (Following older, common-law usage, Wyoming calls an assault that succeeds in injuring the victim a battery.) Aggravated assault, on the other hand, carries a maximum sentence of ten years, even for a first offense, and it serves as a trigger for Wyoming's recidivist enhancements. Wyoming is utterly typical in this regard: virtually every jurisdiction treats simple assault as a misdemeanor, and often as a low-grade misdemeanor at that, and virtually every jurisdiction treats aggravated assault as a serious felony, punishable by a long term of imprisonment and providing the basis for recidivist sentence enhancements.[57]

The line between simple assault and aggravated assault is hazy, though. In Wyoming, as in most states, an assault can be aggravated by the use of a dangerous or deadly weapon, or by causing "serious bodily injury," intentionally or with great recklessness. (An assault and battery is also aggravated in Wyoming if the offender knows the victim is pregnant;

Florida has a similar provision.) The FBI uses a similar rule for deciding whether an assault reported to the police should be viewed as "aggravated" and therefore included in the violent crime statistics produced by its Uniform Crime Reports program. The FBI calls an assault aggravated if it involves a weapon or causes "obvious severe or aggravated bodily injury."[58]

The trick is defining a "weapon," or a "dangerous" or "deadly" weapon, and deciding what injuries count as "serious." In some states, hands and other body parts can be "deadly weapons"; in other states they cannot. Sometimes dogs are classified as "deadly weapons"; sometimes they are categorically excluded. Ditto for canes, walking sticks, and other everyday objects used as bludgeons. The rapper and music producer Sean "P. Diddy" Combs was arrested in 2015 for aggravated assault after angrily waving a kettlebell during an argument in a college gym, although the charges were dropped. Some courts say that bare feet cannot be classified as "deadly" or "dangerous weapons," but that kicking or stomping can qualify as aggravated assault if the assailant is wearing shoes or sneakers.[59]

There is even more ambiguity about what constitutes a "serious bodily injury." For purposes of the Uniform Crime Reports, the FBI says that injury cannot count as "severe or aggravated" unless it involves "broken bones, loss of teeth, possible internal injury, severe laceration, or loss of consciousness." But the courts of some states define "serious bodily injury" to mean any injury that is "graver and more serious . . . than an ordinary battery." In other states, "serious bodily injury" is defined by judicial decisions, or in some cases legislation, to mean injury that gives rise, or could reasonably give rise, to "substantial risk of death" or "apprehension of danger to life, health, or limb." A Wyoming statute sets forth a particularly elaborate test for "serious bodily injury," requiring a "bodily injury which: (A) Creates a substantial risk of death; (B) Causes severe protracted physical pain; (C) Causes severe disfigurement or protracted loss or impairment of a bodily function; (D) Causes unconsciousness or a concussion resulting in protracted loss or impairment of the function of a bodily member, organ or mental faculty; (E) Causes burns of the second or third degree over a significant portion of the body; or (F) Causes a significant fracture or break of a bone."[60]

The Wyoming Supreme Court has applied this definition strictly. For example, the court overturned a conviction for aggravated assault in a case where the defendant beat the victim with his fists and struck him on the head with an iron stove grate, "causing profuse bleeding and permanent scarring," and an accomplice hit the victim with a baseball bat. The victim was treated at an emergency room but did not require "stitches, inpatient hospitalization, surgery or follow-up medical treatment." The Wyoming Supreme Court held that these facts supported a conviction only for simple assault, not for aggravated assault.[61] This decision is not an outlier. A New Jersey court, for example, found that a broken nose was not "serious bodily injury," because there was no evidence that "the victim suffered a 'loss or impairment' of a bodily function," let alone that the condition was "protracted, prolonged, or extended in time."[62] Another Wyoming decision reversed an aggravated assault conviction in a case where the defendant punched and kicked his girlfriend for an hour and a half and tried to stuff his hands down her throat. The victim lost consciousness, could not eat for five days, suffered facial fractures, and required twenty stitches, but the Wyoming Supreme Court concluded that "the legislature intended that the crime of aggravated assault be based upon injuries significantly more serious."[63]

There are decisions from other jurisdictions taking a more expansive view of what constitutes a serious bodily injury. The courts in several states, for example, have held that losing all or part of a tooth can constitute "serious bodily injury" and therefore turn a simple assault into an aggravated assault.[64] It is clear, though, that many physical attacks, even "brutal" attacks, fall outside the realm of "violent" criminal conduct that can trigger recidivist enhancements.[65] At the same time, in virtually every jurisdiction, defendants can be convicted of "violent" felonies that trigger recidivist enhancements without ever attacking anyone or even threatening anyone. In Wyoming, for example, a burglar who carries a simulated pistol is guilty of aggravated burglary, which is a "violent felony" for purposes of the state's "habitual criminal" law. In several states, any residential burglary counts as a "violent felony," even if the burglar is unarmed and no one is at home; in all of these states, though, an unarmed, nonsexual assault generally is not even a felony, let alone a violent felony, unless it results in, is aimed at causing, or is likely to cause serious bodily injury.[66]

In practice, concludes the legal scholar Franklin Zimring, "aggravated assaults range in seriousness from menacing gestures to attempted murder," and how the assaults are charged and classified is typically a matter of official discretion. Arrest rates for simple and aggravated assault soared in the late 1980s and 1990s, for example, but this does not appear to have reflected any actual increase in violent attacks. It appears instead to have been the result of changes in the standards that police departments applied in deciding when to treat an attack as an assault, and where to draw the line between simple and aggravated assaults. When Mayor Pete Buttigieg of South Bend, Indiana, ran for the Democratic presidential nomination in 2019, critics noted that the FBI's Uniform Crime Reports showed a rise in violent crime in South Bend during his time in office. But that appears to have been a statistical artifact, resulting from a change in the way the South Bend Police Department determined whether to classify an assault as "aggravated," and therefore count it as a violent offense.[67]

The category of violent crime is thus very much a social and legal construct, varying from state to state, from statute to statute, and from case to case. It reflects a series of many small judgments about which kinds of conduct are serious enough to deserve the legal consequences prescribed for violent crimes—particularly the stiff mandatory sentences, exclusion from therapeutic courts, and restrictions on parole. It never includes all criminal conduct that would satisfy ordinary, everyday understandings of the word "violent," and it frequently includes a good deal of conduct falling outside those understandings. That does not mean the category should be abandoned or that its use is a mere pretext; it is in the nature of legal categories to give rise to ambiguities that invite ad hoc redefinitions. But the artificiality and variability of the legal category of violent crime should remind us that there is nothing natural or inevitable about the category: it does not describe a clear, ready-made distinction between offenders who deserve sympathy and those who do not.

Burglary, Career Criminals, and Violence

The rising salience of violent crime, the difficulty defining violent crime, the peculiar role played by burglary in the construction of the category of violent crime, and the hydraulic pressure exerted on penalties for violent crime by the pushback against the war on drugs—all of this can be seen in a nutshell in the story of the Armed Career Criminal Act (ACCA) of 1984, probably the most consequential of the many federal criminal statutes now targeting violent crime. The story of the ACCA is long and convoluted. It begins in 1981, with anticrime legislation focused not on violent crime but on robberies and burglaries committed by "career criminals."

The principal sponsor of the 1981 legislation, and of the 1984 bill that grew out of it, was Senator Arlen Specter of Pennsylvania, a Yale Law School graduate who had previously served for thirty years as the Philadelphia district attorney. In 1981 Specter began a multiyear effort to mandate long federal sentences for recidivist robbers and burglars. Specter's first proposal was to mandate a life sentence for anyone convicted in federal court of robbery or burglary while armed with a gun, if the defendant had twice previously been convicted of robbery or burglary. That proposal ultimately became part of an omnibus crime bill sent to President Reagan in December 1982, but along the way the sentence was changed to a minimum of fifteen years and a maximum of life, and use of the statute was conditioned on the approval of state prosecutors. Reagan pocket vetoed the 1982 crime bill, in part because he objected to this grant of authority to local officials over federal prosecutions. Following the veto, Specter immediately reintroduced his career offender proposal, but moved the discretion whether to file charges back to federal prosecutors, and Representative Ron Wyden of Oregon introduced similar legislation in the House of Representatives. Concerns were again raised about federalism, this time by the American Bar Association and the National District Attorneys Association, and as a result the House bill was amended so that rather than creating a new federal offense, it simply mandated a longer, fifteen-year sentence for defendants with three prior convictions for burglary or robbery who were subsequently convicted of the venerable federal law prohibiting convicted felons from possessing firearms. In this form the ACCA passed both the House and Senate and was signed into law as part of the Comprehensive Crime Control Act (CCCA) of 1984.[68]

Specter's concerns, the concerns that motivated and shaped the ACCA as originally adopted, had less to do with criminal violence than with criminal livelihoods. That was why the statute focused on robberies and burglaries, not on murders, rapes, or aggravated assaults. Specter thought robberies and burglaries were "the most damaging crimes to society," because they were so common and caused such large collective losses. "A person is 40 times more likely to be a victim of robbery than of rape," he pointed out. And, crucially for Specter, robberies and burglaries tended to be committed by "career criminals": people who often had "no lawful employment" and who made "crime for profit" their "full-time occupation." They robbed and burglarized "interchangeably," and "often on a daily basis." Specter repeatedly referred to academic research showing that a small number of offenders committed a disproportionate share of robberies and burglaries, and he had some of the researchers testify in committee hearings. Specter's focus was on "professional predators," people who made their living from crime.[69]

Specter did talk about violent crime, and so did others involved in the passage of the ACCA. Specter said that career robbers and burglars were "at the core of the violent street crime problem tormenting this country today." In "the fight against violent crime," he suggested, nothing exceeded the importance of "the repeat robber and burglar who has committed four, six, eight, a dozen or a dozen and a half such felonies." He contrasted robberies and burglaries with "other violent felonies," which occurred less frequently. Assistant Attorney General Lowell Jensen, testifying for the Department of Justice, praised Specter's 1981 bill as an effort "to assist the national effort to combat the rising incidence of violent crime." Representative William Hughes, who chaired the House

Subcommittee on Crime, said the bill aimed to help federal prosecutors deal with "habitual violent offenders."[70]

But Specter focused on recidivism, not violence. The stated purpose of Specter's original bill was to combat not violent crime but "violent *and major* crime." Robberies were serious because they involved "physical violence or the threat thereof," but burglaries were serious for other reasons: they involved invasions of homes or workplaces, violations of privacy, and property loss.[71] And when the witnesses who testified for or against the ACCA spoke of "violent crime," they almost always used that phrase not in juxtaposition to property crime but as a loose synonym for street crime. This was in keeping with an established practice. President Gerald Ford had told Congress in 1975 that "the sort of crime that obsesses America day and night" was "street crime, crime that invades our neighborhoods and our homes—murders, robberies, rapes, muggings, holdups, break-ins—the kind of brutal violence that makes us fearful of strangers and afraid to go out at night." (Ford, too, had stressed that "most serious crimes are committed by repeaters.") Assistant Attorney General Jensen, testifying in favor of the ACCA, similarly seemed to equate violent crime with street crime, saying it was important to address "violent crime" in order to protect "the property and safety of innocent victims." A representative of the National District Attorneys Association, opposing the ACCA on federalism grounds, argued that federal prosecutors already had more work than they could handle, and he listed automobile theft, cargo theft, and "drug-related prosecutions" as examples of the kinds of "violence-related cases" that federal prosecutors were already declining too often. A survey of local prosecutors, submitted to the House Subcommittee on Crime, reported that the prosecutors opposed the use of federal resources to fight "non-violent offenses"; the examples given were "check cases and fraud."[72]

Still, it seems that no one argued explicitly, before the passage of the ACCA in 1984, that burglary was a "violent crime." When a representative of the ACLU, testifying in opposition to the law, pointed out that a defendant with two burglary convictions might never have committed a "violent crime," no one bothered to contradict her.[73] It didn't really matter. When initially enacted, the ACCA wasn't aimed at violent crime, at least not directly. It was aimed at career offenders.

But other parts of the Comprehensive Crime Control Act of 1984 *did* directly target violent crime, usually along with major drug-trafficking offenses. For example, Chapter I of the CCCA, the Bail Reform Act of 1984, provided for pretrial detention of a defendant charged with a "crime of violence," a drug-trafficking offense punishable by ten years or more of imprisonment, or various other offenses deemed sufficiently serious. Chapter II of the CCCA, the Sentencing Reform Act of 1984, created the United States Sentencing Commission and charged it with promulgating the United States Sentencing Guidelines. The commission was instructed to ensure that a defendant who committed a "crime of violence" or a drug-trafficking offense, and had two previous convictions for such crimes, would receive a sentence "at or near the maximum term"; conversely, the Sentencing Guidelines were to "reflect the general appropriateness" of a noncustodial sentence for a first offender not "convicted of a crime of violence or an otherwise serious offense." Until the Sentencing Commission could promulgate its new guidelines, Congress urged federal judges to reserve prison, in general, for "violent and otherwise serious offenders who pose the most dangerous threat to society," and to give "nonviolent and nonserious offenders . . . alternative sentences, such as restitution and community service." A separate portion of the CCCA created a Bureau of Justice Programs within the Department of Justice and instructed it to, among other things, "encourage the targeting of State and local resources on efforts to reduce the incidence of violent crime and on programs relating to the apprehension and prosecution of repeat offenders."

The CCCA also established several new federal offenses that incorporated references to "crimes of violence." These included "violent crimes in aid of racketeering activity," "solicitation to commit a crime of violence," and—of greatest significance—"us[ing] or carr[ying] a firearm during and in relation to a crime of violence," a new felony punishable by a mandatory sentence of five years of imprisonment for a first offense and ten years for a subsequent offense. And the CCCA included, for the first time, a federal statutory definition of "crime of violence," now codified in section 16 of title 18 of the United States Code: either "an offense that has as an element the use, attempted use, or threatened use of physical force against the person or property of another" or a felony "that, by its nature, involves a substantial risk that physical force against the person or property of another may be used in the course of committing the offense." By 1984 the category of violent crime had emerged as a chief focus, along with narcotics trafficking, of federal crime legislation. In this respect the ACCA, with its narrow focus on "career" robbers and burglars, was a little behind the times.[74]

It caught up two years later. In 1986 Congress amended the ACCA to allow "violent felonies" and "serious drug offenses," not just burglaries and robberies, to serve as predicate offenses. There was broad support for the expansion. Representative Hughes, opening the House hearings, noted that the ACCA had "been used sparingly," with only thirteen defendants indicted under the law in 1985. The low number of charges might have been thought a sign that the law was operating properly, since the premise of the 1984 legislation was that a small number of career offenders were responsible for an outsized share of crime, and since much of the point of the law had been to allow local prosecutors to use the threat of a federal referral to coerce guilty pleas in state court. But in the mid-1980s the politics of crime was operating as a one-way ratchet: more punishment was almost always better. And expanding the set of predicate offenses to include violent crime and drug trafficking seemed to make obvious sense. As Representative Wyden explained, it was "simple logic to include crimes of violence as potential predicate offenses." Why should a referral for federal prosecution be authorized "for a three-time bank robber but not an habitual offender with prior convictions for rape or murder"?[75]

The only disagreement was over which "crimes of violence" should be included. Wyden proposed expanding the ACCA to apply to drug offenses carrying maximum prison terms of ten years or more, and to "crimes of violence" as defined in section 16 of title 18 of the United States Code, the definition Congress had added in 1984. Representative Hughes proposed, instead, that the trigger should be either a ten-year drug-trafficking offense, just as Wyden suggested, or a "violent felony"—defined as "any

State or Federal felony that has as an element the use, attempted use, or threatened use of physical force against the person of another." Wyden characterized the difference between the two bills as "modest," but said that he hoped that the final legislation would include "at least some violent felonies against property," such as arson. The real issue, though—the most important subject of debate in the House hearings on the two bills—had to do with burglary.[76]

It wasn't clear in 1986 how burglary should be thought about, and whether, in particular, it was a "violent" offense. California had included burglary as a predicate crime in the Three Strikes law it adopted in 1984. The following year, though, in a case involving a fatal police shooting of a fleeing, unarmed burglar, the Supreme Court held that the Fourth Amendment did not permit police officers to use deadly force against an escaping suspect without probable cause to believe the suspect "pose[d] a threat of serious physical harm, either to the officer or to others." The mere fact that the suspect had broken into a house at night wasn't enough. The Supreme Court pointed out that the FBI classified burglary as a property crime, not a violent crime, and that, in practice, "burglaries only rarely involve physical violence." In fact, the Justices noted, "only 3.8% of all burglaries involved violent crime." But three dissenting justices suggested that figure would provide "little consolation" to "victims of a forcible intrusion into their home by a nighttime prowler": in absolute numbers, "2.8 million . . . violent crimes were committed in the course of burglaries" over a ten-year period.[77]

Against this background, Representative Hughes questioned in 1986 whether burglary should continue to be a predicate offense for the ACCA, given that "most of our concern today deals with drug offenses and violent crime." In the end, there was a broad consensus in favor of including burglary, but the rationale kept changing. Wyden said burglary should be retained as a predicate offense because it was "part of the original career criminal legislation," and prosecutors were using that authorization with great discretion, "going after people . . . with astronomical numbers of burglaries." A representative of the Department of Justice argued in favor of retaining burglary, both because it was "probably the No. 1 professional crime" and because "it is potentially a very dangerous offense," in that "many crimes of violence do occur in the course of committing a robbery." The district attorney for Philadelphia, testifying on behalf of the National District Attorneys Association, argued that burglary should be kept as a predicate offense because habitual offenders didn't "specialize" but instead "vacillate[d] between committing violent *and* property crimes." An "overwhelming number of victims," he explained, were "raped, robbed or killed by offenders with extensive criminal records which included the crime of burglary." A representative of the National Association of Criminal Defense Attorneys voiced concern about extending the ACCA to crimes like "rape, murder, or assault" that had "nothing to do with profit" and therefore were "unlikely to be repeated with the degree of frequency and regularity which [had] goaded Congress into action" two years earlier. He had "no problem with burglary as a predicate offense," though, because it was true to the original purpose of the ACCA. Even Representative Hughes mused that because the ACCA applied only if the new offense involves the use or possession of a gun, "you could argue that . . . we are talking about a burglar who potentially is carrying a weapon," and perhaps that was enough to classify the defendant as violent.[78]

The bottom line was that the bar for keeping burglary as a predicate offense was very low; when it came to punishment, more was better. As a result, when Congress amended the ACCA in 1986 to include "serious drug offenses" and "violent felonies" as predicate offenses, it defined "violent felony" to mean a felony that *either* (a) "has as an element the use, attempted use, or threatened use of physical force against the person of another," *or* (b) "is burglary, arson, or extortion, involves the use of explosives, or otherwise involves conduct that presents a serious potential risk of physical injury to another."[79]

Congress also settled on an explanation for keeping burglary as a predicate offense. The explanation was not that burglary was the paradigmatic "professional crime." It was that burglary was a crime of violence. The House report explained that the definition of "violent felony" was designed to ensure the inclusion of "crimes against property such as burglary, arson, extortion, use of explosives and similar crimes . . . where the conduct involved presents a serious risk of injury to a person."

Reflecting the new understanding of the ACCA's focus, subsequent court decisions reasoned that both of the original ACCA predicates, burglary and robbery, had been selected because they posed high risks of violence.[80]

The last part of the ACCA definition of "violent felony"—the "residual clause," referencing felonies that "otherwise involve conduct that presents a serious potential risk of physical injury to another"—proved extraordinarily difficult for the federal courts to interpret and apply, until, as discussed in Chapter 1, the Supreme Court finally in 2015 invalidated the clause as unconstitutionally vague. In the meantime, though, the ACCA definition of "violent crime" had been adopted and repurposed by the United States Sentencing Commission—the agency created by the Sentencing Reform Act of 1984, part of the same, omnibus 1984 crime bill that contained the original version of the ACCA. The Sentencing Commission promulgated its initial set of sentencing guidelines in 1987. These included a provision mandating additional prison time for "career offenders," who were defined as adults convicted of a third "crime of violence or controlled substance offense." Initially, "crime of violence" was in turn defined the same, expansive way Congress had defined the term in 18 US Code § 16: an offense that either involved force or the threat of force against persons or property, or that created a risk of such a use of force. In 1989, though, the Sentencing Commission amended the "career offender" guideline and redefined "crime of violence" so that it tracked the definition of "violent felony" in the ACCA. The new guidelines defined "crime of violence" as a crime punishable by imprisonment for a year or more that either (a) "has as an element the use, attempted use, or threatened use of physical force against the *person* of another," or (b) "is burglary of a dwelling, arson, or extortion, involves use of explosives, or otherwise involves conduct that presents a serious potential risk of physical *injury* to another." Like the ACCA, the revised guideline focused on crimes involving actual or potential force against a person, and—again like the ACCA—the guidelines grandfathered in burglary.[81]

Despite their name, the Sentencing Guidelines were initially binding on federal trial courts; they were rules, not just guidelines. In 2005, though, the Supreme Court rendered them "effectively advisory," in order to cure what the Justices thought would otherwise be fatal constitutional flaws in the Sentencing Reform Act. Nonetheless, as the Supreme Court itself has recognized, the guidelines continue to provide "not only the starting point for most federal sentencing proceedings but also the lodestar." Except in cases where the prosecutors ask courts to "depart downward," most federal defendants receive sentences within the guidelines.[82]

So it was no surprise in 2009 when a man named Travis Beckles, who had been caught with a sawed-off shotgun, was sentenced in federal court to thirty years in prison. The Sentencing Commission had made it clear in its official commentary to the Sentencing Guidelines that possession of an illegal firearm was a "crime of violence," and Beckles had earlier, qualifying convictions for narcotics offenses. That brought him within the ambit of the "career offender" guidelines, which called in his case for a sentence ranging from thirty years to life. Beckles argued that the guidelines were void for vagueness for the same reason the Supreme Court had found the residual clause of the ACCA void for vagueness: it is too hard to decide whether a crime creates "a serious potential risk of physical injury to another," particularly when burglary is declared to satisfy that standard by legislative fiat. But the Justices disagreed. Ruling on Beckles's case in 2017, the Supreme Court reasoned that because the Sentencing Guidelines were no longer binding, there was no harm in them being vague.[83]

The Sentencing Commission, though, had already decided otherwise. In 2016 the commission amended the career offender guidelines and narrowed the definition of "crime of violence." The new definition applied only to murder, voluntary manslaughter, kidnapping, aggravated assault, forcible sex offenses, robbery, arson, extortion, possession of banned firearms and explosives, and felonies that involved the use, attempted use, or threatened use of force against the person of another. The residual clause was eliminated "as a matter of policy," for the same reasons the Supreme Court in 2015 had found the parallel clause in the ACCA void for vagueness. Burglary was no longer grandfathered in as a "crime of violence," in part for the same reasons the Supreme Court in 1985 had restricted the use of deadly force against fleeing burglars: the FBI classified burglary as a "property crime," and "most burglaries do not involve physical violence."[84]

The Sentencing Commission also recommended to Congress in 2016 that the Sentencing Reform Act be amended to focus the "career offenders" sentence enhancements on offenders who have committed a "crime of violence," and to allow greater lenience for "career offenders" who have committed only narcotics offenses. And, understandably, the commission lamented the contradictory "patchwork" of federal laws "attempting to specify which prior offenses are crimes of violence or violent felonies for purposes of recidivist enhancements." The commission urged Congress to reduce the "inconsistency and complexity" by "adopting a single, uniform definition of 'crime of violence' for all federal criminal law purposes."[85]

Congress has not yet responded to those suggestions. The result is that federal law, like state law in the United States, defines violent crime inconsistently. For example, burglary remains, by explicit legislative direction, a "violent felony" for purposes of the ACCA, although it now no longer counts as a "crime of violence" under the federal Sentencing Guidelines. More generally, a "violent felony" under the ACCA need not involve any actual use of force or even a threat to use force: a "serious potential risk" of physical injury to someone other than the offender can suffice.[86] That is no longer true of a "crime of violence" under the career offender provisions of the Sentencing Guidelines.

The long, convoluted history of the career offender provisions of the ACCA and the Sentencing Guidelines thus serves to illustrate not only the increasing significance of violence in criminal law, but also the difficulty of pinning down what counts as a violent crime. It illustrates, as well, the manner in which a pushback against the war on drugs has given the category of violence, no matter how indistinct, an even greater role in identifying the offenders for whom long terms of incarceration seem most suitable. And it shows something else: the strong connection between the category of violence in contemporary criminal law and the category of recidivism. Crimes of violence play a large role in "career offender" laws; those laws have been the most important statutory manifestation of the increased significance of violence in criminal law.

The tight connection between the categories of violence and recidivism in modern criminal statutes reflects a particular set of ideas about the nature of violence, and those ideas are worth unpacking.

Career Offender Laws and the Nature of Violence

As violence has become increasingly important in criminal law over the past half century, criminal law has also come to embrace, more and more, an implicit and sometimes explicit understanding of violence as more *characterological* than *situational*. Criminal violence is increasingly understood as a property of *individuals,* not just of *actions.* The most prominent way in which violence figures in modern criminal law is as the predicate for the sentencing enhancements imposed under Three Strikes statutes and other "career criminal" laws. The premise of these laws is that violent crime is largely a problem of violent criminals: repeat offenders who engage in criminal violence again and again, because it is in their nature.

Everyone knows that there are some people who are off-the-charts violent. Even a sociologist like Randall Collins, who insists that violence is difficult, not easy, and that it is overwhelmingly the product of particular kinds of interactions, not particular kinds of individuals, acknowledges that there is a subset of violence carried out by "specialists"—people who are particularly skillful at being violent, and who tend to do it especially often.[87] Part of what is noteworthy about modern recidivist statutes, though, is how few episodes of violence resulting in criminal convictions are required in order to label someone as a "career" or "habitual" offender: it takes only "three strikes," or in many cases only two. Likewise, a single conviction for a violent felony— or even an arrest for a violent felony in the case under adjudication—is often enough to disqualify a defendant from diversion to a therapeutic court. The theory of violence implicitly underlying modern recidivist enhancements, and the eligibility restrictions imposed by many drug courts and veterans courts, is not that a small subset of murders, rapes, robberies, and aggravated assaults is carried out by people who commit violent offenses again and again and again; it is that someone who commits two or three violent crimes is likely to be characteristically and predictably violent. Or that this is likely to be true of at least some significant proportion of two- or three-time violent offenders, and that prosecutors will be able to tell which ones they are. Either way, modern criminal law increasingly reflects a particular idea about how violence operates: that it is driven by the dispositions and characteristic behaviors of particular, aberrational individuals. Violence is in perpetrators' hearts, not in the situations in which they find themselves.

This isn't a new view, obviously, but it is new for criminal law to embrace it so enthusiastically. Anglo-American criminal law has historically been committed to punishing offenders for their acts, not their natures, and especially not their proclivity toward violence. There is a very old idea that every crime must include an "actus reus," a wrongful act, and at least since the nineteenth century criminal law has resisted punishing someone for being a particular sort of person. Rules of evidence prohibit prosecutors from convicting a defendant with evidence of his criminal proclivities, and the paradigmatic example of what the rules disallow is evidence of a defendant's violent character, introduced to show that he is likely to have committed a particular act of violence. This ban on "character evidence" has been justified by arguments that jurors will be too apt to misuse the evidence—too apt to conclude that a defendant's past conduct reliably predicts his future conduct, and too apt to want to punish a defendant for who he is, rather than for what he does.[88]

Recidivist sentencing laws have a long history, but until the late twentieth century they were never targeted, in particular, at violent crimes. In fact, the "habitual criminals" that received the most attention from reformers were thieves and violators of morals laws: pickpockets, dissolutes, and vagrants. Violence tended to be understood as something that flared up and passed, something that overcame rather than expressed a person's true nature. That was why the worst murders, the ones most deserving of condemnation, were the ones that were premeditated—planned with cool deliberation. Under the wrong circumstances, even a usually law-abiding person could be expected to lash out with violence. That was why provocation could reduce the grade of a homicide from murder to manslaughter. "To kill a man upon sudden and violent resentment," Blackstone explained, "is less penal than upon cool, deliberate malice."[89]

It isn't clear why lawmakers have increasingly tended to treat criminal violence as characterological instead of situational, but race may be part of the answer. The historian Khalil Gibran Muhammad has documented a sharp difference between the way early twentieth-century reformers in the United States addressed criminality among European immigrants and the way they addressed it among African Americans. High rates of criminal offending by Irish, Italian, and Eastern European immigrants tended to be seen as the result of the situations in which those immigrants were placed, whereas Black criminality was seen as reflecting something more intrinsic. As summarized by the historian David Levering Lewis, Muhammad's work shows the enduring operation of an unstated conceptual divide: "Whites commit crimes, but black males are criminals." This racialized understanding of offending predated the late twentieth-century rise in the importance of violence in criminal law. But it meant that when violent crime became increasingly associated with Black men—both as a sociological reality and, even more importantly, as a widespread set of cultural understandings—it became easier and more natural to see violent crime as the expression of offenders' fundamental nature.[90]

When the law students that I teach visit prisons, what tends to surprise them most is that the correctional staff view murderers as model inmates. This surprises my students because they had assumed, without giving it much thought, that criminal violence is carried out by hardened, incorrigible offenders, and that the more violent the crime, the less redeemable the offender. The same idea about the origins of violence underlies much of how criminal law now addresses the problem of violence. It is an idea that makes the significance of violence in sorting and responding to criminal behavior seem obvious. But it is a historically contingent idea, and, as we will see, it is not an idea that has shaped other parts of the law nearly so strongly. The contrast is particularly striking with criminal procedure, the set of legal rules governing the police.

3 | Police Violence

On a Thursday afternoon in late May 1957, police in Cleveland, Ohio, broke into the home of a young African American woman named Dollree Mapp. The officers thought Mapp might be running a numbers racket. They also had spotted the car of a man named Virgil Ogletree outside Mapp's house, and they suspected that Ogletree had been involved in the recent bombing of the home of another numbers operator—Don King, the future boxing promoter. Mapp refused to let the police in without a warrant. When they returned with what they said was a warrant, she did not come to the door. So the officers tried kicking in her back door, and when that didn't work they smashed a window and let themselves in. They met Mapp in her hallway and showed her the "warrant." She grabbed the document and stashed it inside her dress. The police wrestled the document back from her, twisting her hand until she cried out in pain, and then handcuffed her and forced her to accompany them while they searched the house. They found some pornographic books and pictures, for which Mapp was subsequently prosecuted. In a basement apartment that Mapp rented out, they also found Virgil Ogletree.

Mapp was convicted and sentenced to prison for possession of obscene materials, but the United States Supreme Court threw the conviction out. It took the Court some time to figure out what bothered it most about Mapp's treatment. Initially the Justices took the case to examine whether the prosecution infringed unconstitutionally on free expression, but ultimately they reversed Mapp's conviction on a different ground: searching Mapp's house without a warrant had violated her Fourth Amendment right against "unreasonable searches and seizures." No warrant for the search was ever produced in court, and the trial judge questioned whether it had ever existed. Law students today still read the Supreme Court's decision in *Mapp v. Ohio,* because it

established the Fourth Amendment "exclusionary rule" for state criminal prosecutions—the rule that evidence obtained through an unconstitutional search or seizure generally cannot be introduced at trial
against a criminal defendant.[1]

Equally significant, though, is what the Supreme Court's decision
in *Mapp v. Ohio* is *not* about. It is not about violence. It is not about the
police breaking into Mapp's house, grabbing her, wrestling with her,
twisting her hand, and handcuffing her. The Justices took note of all of
that, but ultimately it was irrelevant to their decision. At first they
thought the case was about free expression, and then they thought it was
about warrants. They never thought it was about violence—despite the
fact that the Ohio Supreme Court had concluded that the evidence
found in the search was admissible because the police hadn't used "brutal
or offensive physical force." Instead of rejecting that conclusion, the
United States Supreme Court simply ignored it. Brutality and "offensive
physical force" were beside the point.[2]

In this respect *Mapp v. Ohio* is emblematic. There is a long history of
concern with police violence—typically called "police brutality" when it
is thought unjustified, and "use of force" when it is thought legitimate.
Complaints about police violence are as old as the nightstick.[3] Recently
the issue of police violence has received new attention, largely due to the
Black Lives Matter movement and, in particular, the wave of nationwide
protests following the death of George Floyd at the hands of the Minneapolis police in May 2020. But whereas violence became increasingly
significant in substantive criminal law during the second half of the
twentieth century and the first two decades of the twenty-first century,
the story was very different in criminal procedure—the rules governing
what the police can and cannot do. There, over decades, violence became
progressively *less* consequential.

The moment of inflection in both stories was roughly the same: the
early 1960s. The Supreme Court decided *Mapp* in 1961, one year before
the appearance of the Model Penal Code, the first major codification of
criminal prohibitions to treat violence as a significant dividing line. Just
at the point when violence was beginning to emerge as the criminal law's
most important category for sorting serious from forgivable offenses, the

law of criminal procedure, along with the instincts about policing it embodies, was moving in the opposite direction.

The two developments were related. One reason criminal procedure focuses so little on violence is that concerns about violent crime have made police violence seem more necessary and less troubling. As Figure 4 suggests, popular discussion of police violence and "police brutality" rose sharply in the 1960s. In the 1970s and early 1980s, however, when concerns about violent crime skyrocketed, discussions of police violence and police brutality waned. This happened even as discussions of other kinds of controversial police practices—most notably, warrantless searches and seizures—continued to rise.[4] Part of the explanation is that when violent crime seems out of control, physical force by the police seems more legitimate and is less likely to be called "brutality." It is a version of the tit-for-tat logic that was discussed in Chapter 1, the sentiment that President Trump invoked when he urged police officers to stop protecting suspects' heads when putting them into patrol cars: "Like when you guys put somebody in the car and you're protecting their head . . . and they've just killed somebody. . . . [Y]ou can take the hand away, okay?" Trump doubled down on this kind of rhetoric during the nationwide wave of protests and lootings in the spring of 2020. Beyond threatening that "when the looting starts, the shooting starts"—the message that prompted a warning label from Twitter—Trump boasted about the force that Secret Service agents quickly used against protesters near the White House who "got too frisky or out of line": "They didn't know what hit them." He repeatedly urged state and local law enforcement agencies to be "tougher" on looters and vandals, to "fight back," to "do retribution," and not to be "too careful."[5] Trump hardly invented this way of thinking. Here is Manhattan prosecutor Thomas Kane in the 1930s, for example, defending the use of "third degree" to get witnesses to talk: "What are we to do—give our baby killers ice cream?"[6]

But the low salience of violence in the modern law of criminal procedure is not entirely a by-product of the high salience of violence in criminal law, nor does it reflect an indifference to how the police use coercive force. The "third degree," a pervasive feature of policing in the 1930s, became rare by the late twentieth century, and it has stayed rare. It was

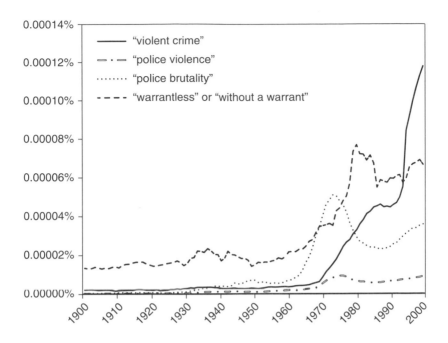

FIG. 4 Frequency of references to "police brutality" and "police violence" in books published in the United States, 1900–2000, compared with references to "violent crime" and to "warrantless" or "without a warrant." The vertical axis measures the occurrences of each phrase as a proportion of all sequences with the same number of words. The lines show seven-year trailing averages. (Data source: Google Books Ngram Viewer.)

eradicated primarily by a wave of public outrage and elite condemnation.[7] Moreover, concerns about police brutality never disappeared in the 1970s and 1980s, and by the end of the 1980s discussions of the topic were once again growing more common. This happened while the focus on violent crime in popular discourse continued its steep upward climb, and while the line between violent and nonviolent offenses grew more consequential than ever in criminal sentencing schemes and criminal justice reform proposals. The last decade and a half of the twentieth century, remember, was the era of Three Strikes laws; it was also the era of diversion programs narrowly targeted at "nonviolent" offenders. It was not an era, though, in which violence became significantly more important in the legal rules governing the police. That is partly because by the late 1980s the Supreme Court had become far less interested in placing new legal constraints on the police, but it is also partly because, as we will see, the framework the Supreme Court constructed in the mid-twentieth century for regulation of the police—the framework erected in cases like *Mapp v. Ohio*—focused much less on violence than on violations of privacy.

The relative unimportance of violence in criminal procedure, therefore, is not simply the flip side of the heavy emphasis placed on violence in criminal law; it has its own history and its own drivers. One of those drivers has been the very idea of the police: our underlying notions about what the police are for and our expectations about how they should operate. There is a long-standing sense, particularly strong in the United States, that the fundamental point of the police is to enforce the law and maintain order through the actual or threatened use of physical force. The police themselves have embraced this idea for most of their history. Line officers have long prized their ability to "take care" of themselves on the street, and that is the quality that, more than any other, has gained them respect among their fellow officers.[8] The notion that violence is inherent to the very idea of the police was a large part of the reason that many of the participants in the nationwide protests in 2020 called, not for the reform of the police, but for their defunding or abolition.

"Police brutality" is often described as the illegal exercise of violence by law enforcement officers, but the line between authorized and unauthorized uses of force by the police has always been hazy. The police have frequently understood their role to include the use of unofficial, "extralegal" force; they have assumed, usually with justification, that this is what the public expected of them. The New York Police Department, with the support of local newspapers, encouraged "nightstick rule" in the early twentieth century, and in the 1930s the department's commissioner, Lewis Valentine, explicitly called on officers to "muss up" gangsters. As late as 1947, then-commissioner Arthur Wallander instructed NYPD detectives to give "the proper treatment" to "hoodlums," "loafers," and "easy money men." In the early 1950s the pioneering police ethnographer William Westley found that officers in Gary, Indiana, understood that local residents wanted them to give "extremely rough treatment" to homosexuals and other "deviants," but to do so unofficially and out of view. Complying with those expectations, Westley argued, accustomed the police "to use violence as a general resource." And then there is Trump.[9]

None of this is to suggest that attitudes about police violence have stayed constant, either among the public or among officers themselves. The third degree was once widely accepted; by the closing decades of the twentieth century it was not. Police violence in response to "contempt of cop" remains widespread, but departments are less likely today than they once were to wink at street justice meted out to idlers or suspected sexual offenders. In the 1960s few police departments had written policies regarding the use of force; by the end of the century most did. It became common in the 1990s and early 2000s for police officers to study "verbal judo" and other techniques of de-escalation. Brawling skills became less central to an officer's reputation within a department. Many departments began providing officers with "crisis intervention" training, to help them avoid violence in encounters with people suffering from flare-ups of mental illness. Finally—and most consequentially—cellphone videos and the Black Lives Matter movement brought new scrutiny to police violence. The nationwide protests in the wake of the 2020 killing of George Floyd were direct outgrowths of that scrutiny.[10]

Those protests also highlighted, though, the degree to which the licit and illicit use of force in law enforcement remained widespread, even routine. The protests responded not just to Floyd's death but to a string of other police killings of African Americans. To a scandalous extent, police violence remained lightly regulated, a peripheral topic in the law of criminal procedure. This chapter will explore why that was, and whether and how it should change. The legal rules governing police conduct, like the rules of substantive criminal law, reflect ideas about the significance of violence, the definition of violence, and the workings of violence. The relative unimportance of violence in the rules of criminal procedure provides a telling contrast with the prominent role violence plays in modern sentencing codes and punishment schemes.

Because criminal procedure doctrines place little emphasis on violence, the definition of violence—or of "brutality" or "force"—matters much less than in substantive criminal law. But in ways that this chapter will explore, language and definitions matter here as well. The term "police brutality," for example, has important and unfortunate overtones, suggesting that police violence is a form of animalism, driven by individual or group character rather than training, protocols, and workplace culture. It can lead to understandings of police violence that overemphasize the significance of "bad apples" or the otherness of police officers as a whole.

The terminology we use to describe police violence therefore reflects and helps to shape our ideas about how violence operates in policing. And just as in substantive criminal law, ideas about how violence operates matter a great deal in regulation of the police. It matters whether violence is understood to be characterological or situational—and, if it is situational, which aspects of an officer's situation are thought to be most important in leading the officer to use force. It matters, too, whether violence is thought to be self-limiting or self-reinforcing: whether tit for tat is understood to be the best way to keep violence in check, or a dynamic that is apt to spin out of control. Police violence has been defended since the nineteenth century, by officers and others, as a necessary corrective to private violence. But there is also a long tradition of worrying that police violence breeds further violence: that official lawlessness encourages private lawlessness, and that violent policing produces more, not less, violent crime.[11]

In criminal procedure, as in substantive criminal law, it is impossible to unravel these various ideas about violence without taking account of race, gender, and class. Race plays a particularly large role here, as in discussions of substantive criminal law. The Black Lives Matter movement, and the nationwide protests in May and June 2020, were responses to the dramatically disproportionate rate at which people of color, particularly young men of color, are victims of police violence. Because of that disparity, the problem of police violence has long been understood differently in minority communities than in white communities. Gender is important, too: excessive violence by police officers has often been blamed on the heavily masculine culture of law enforcement, and—on the other side—tough tactics by the police have been defended and celebrated as a form of manliness. Class figures also, not just because the victims of police violence are disproportionately poor or working class, but because the police themselves are viewed as working class, by officers themselves and by the public. The association of the police with the working class has influenced how police violence is understood and how the law approaches it; it has lent credence, for example, to the notion that police are violent because of the kind of people they are, not because of how they are trained or deployed.

The Insignificance of Violence in Criminal Procedure

To get some perspective on the role that violence now plays in substantive criminal law, we turned to history. We traced how ideas about the relative gravity of criminal offenses have evolved since the eighteenth century. It is harder to do with that criminal procedure, the set of rules governing the police, because those rules are largely a twentieth-century invention. Modern police forces themselves date back only to the middle of the nineteenth century, and constitutional criminal procedure did not develop in earnest until the middle of the twentieth century, when federal law enforcement agencies began to assume significant responsibilities and the Supreme Court began to regulate state law enforcement officers. There is no real analog to our current law of criminal procedure before the 1930s.

Still, criminal procedure has a kind of prehistory: the ragtag collection of statutory restrictions, judicial pronouncements, and received understandings about criminal investigations that served as a background to, and helped to motivate, the Fourth, Fifth, and Sixth Amendments to the United States Constitution. Calling this miscellany "common law," as the Supreme Court often does, suggests that it had more cohesion and consistency than it actually did.[12] Nonetheless, some generalizations are possible, and they are instructive. Eighteenth- and early nineteenth-century limitations on law enforcement did not categorize official conduct based on whether or not it was violent, but it did focus particular attention on conduct that was violent—similar to the way substantive criminal law focused particular attention on violent offenses like murder, rape, mayhem, and assault. That focus was sharper with regard to police conduct, though, than it was for private behavior.

The common-law crime of burglary, for example, did require a kind of violence—a "breaking" of a house. But the breaking could consist simply of opening a door or window; any use of force sufficed. From a very early date, moreover, common-law authorities recognized "constructive" breaking of houses, involving no use of force whatsoever: when entry was obtained by fraud, for example, or by persuasion of a child or other innocent agent. The restrictions on criminal investigations, however, focused more heavily on actions that could be characterized as violent, such as arrests of suspected criminals, which typically involved physical capture, and forcible entries into homes. Searches of homes, for offenders or for evidence, received significantly greater scrutiny when they involved breaking doors open. The influential early nineteenth-century treatise by the English lawyer Joseph Chitty, for example, stressed that although officers seeking to take an offender into custody could break into a house without a warrant, this was "so violent, obnoxious, and dangerous a proceeding" that "it should be adopted only in extreme cases, where an immediate arrest is requisite." Even with an arrest warrant, doors could be broken open only "if admittance cannot otherwise be obtained," and probably only in cases of "treason, felony, or breach of the peace." "In all cases whatever," Chitty emphasized, "it is absolutely necessary that a demand of admittance should be made, and be refused, before outer doors can be broken."[13]

Two decades ago the US Supreme Court concluded that this "knock-and-announce principle" was such a basic part of the common-law restrictions on law enforcement that violating it could make a search or seizure "unreasonable" and hence unconstitutional under the Fourth Amendment. The Supreme Court explained that the rule served three purposes: it avoided unnecessary damage to property, it safeguarded the "privacy and dignity" of residents, and, perhaps most important, it protected "human life and limb"—"because an unannounced entry may provoke violence in supposed self-defense by the surprised resident."

Because the rule was not aimed at helping to hide evidence, though, the Court concluded that the exclusionary rule would not be triggered by its violation. And the Supreme Court made it clear that there would be no violation to begin with if the officers had a good reason not to wait before entering: if, for example, the officers "reasonably believed that a prior announcement would [place] them in peril," or if they had "reason to believe that evidence would likely be destroyed if advance notice were given."[14]

The knock-and-announce principle thus survives in modern search-and-seizure law, but only vestigially. And the rest of search-and-seizure law places little weight on violence in sorting permissible from impermissible police conduct. That wasn't always the case. When the Supreme Court first began to regulate evidence gathering by state law enforcement officers, in 1952, violence was very much on its mind. The case was *Rochin v. California,* and it involved three Los Angeles deputy sheriffs who broke into the bedroom of a suspected drug dealer. The suspect, Antonio Rochin, swallowed what the deputies assumed were illegal pills, so they jumped on him, "squeeze[ed] his throat," and stuck their fingers in his mouth in an effort to recover the contraband. When those efforts failed, the deputies handcuffed Rochin, took him to an emergency room, strapped him to an operating table, and had his stomach pumped against his will. The capsules were recovered; they turned out to contain morphine. Rochin was convicted of drug possession, but the Supreme Court reversed. The Justices reasoned that the force used against Rochin was "so brutal and so offensive to human dignity" as to violate the constitutional guarantee of due process. It was "too close to the rack and the screw." Sanctioning this kind of police violence, the Court said, would "brutalize the temper of [our] society."[15]

The Supreme Court analogized the forcible pumping of Rochin's stomach to coercing a confession, an investigative tactic the Justices had earlier found to violate due process. That conclusion, too, was first reached in a case involving police violence. The violence in *Brown v. Mississippi*—the first case ever in which the Supreme Court found that the Constitution had been violated by state law enforcement officers— was horrifyingly worse than in *Rochin v. California.* Ed Brown and his

two codefendants were Black tenant farmers convicted in 1934 of mur-
dering a white planter. They were convicted based entirely on confessions that had been obtained from them by torture: all three defendants had been whipped, and one had been strung up from a tree by his
neck. The deputy sheriffs who had carried out the torture freely admitted it in court. When asked how badly one of the defendants had
been whipped, one of the deputies testified, "Not too much for a
negro; not as much as I would have done if it were left to me." The Supreme Court had never before reversed a state criminal conviction
because of the actions taken by law enforcement personnel, but it unan-
imously concluded in 1936 that "brutal treatment" of Brown and his codefendants, and the use of the resulting confessions in court, violated
due process. "It would be difficult," the Justices said, "to conceive of
methods more revolting to the sense of justice."[16]

At its origins, then, the Supreme Court's regulation of state law enforcement tactics focused explicitly on police "brutality." This was true
when the Supreme Court first applied the Constitution to state interrogation practices in 1936, and it was true in 1952 when the Justices began
to review searches and seizures by state law enforcement officers. The
attention the Justices paid to police violence in *Brown v. Mississippi* and
Rochin v. California reflected attention the issue received outside of the
courts in the first half of the twentieth century. Most famously, the
Wickersham Commission on Law Observance and Enforcement—a
blue-ribbon panel assembled by President Herbert Hoover, which con-
ducted the first-ever federal review of policing and prosecution in the
United States—strongly condemned the use of the "third degree" in interrogation rooms, a practice the commission made clear was common
throughout the country. The commission's report, "Lawlessness in Law
Enforcement," issued in 1931, helped solidify public opposition to coerced confessions in the years leading up to the Supreme Court's 1936
decision in *Brown v. Mississippi*. The commission paid less attention to
police violence outside of the interrogation room, but it didn't ignore that
problem, either. In fact, the commission blamed gun violence by police
officers for much of the unpopularity of Prohibition, which the commission concluded had gotten off to a "bad start" in part because "high-

handed methods, shootings and killings, even when justified, alienated thoughtful citizens, believers in law and order." The Wickersham Commission itself was the product of growing concerns about law enforcement in the early twentieth century, concerns that were amplified by Prohibition and that often centered around police violence. Even before the Supreme Court overturned the convictions in *Brown v. Mississippi,* state courts had repeatedly complained about the "third degree," although they still allowed prosecutors to use any confessions that seemed reliable, no matter how they had been obtained.[17]

The focus on violence in *Brown* and *Rochin* didn't last. The Supreme Court repeatedly reaffirmed the central holding of *Brown,* that prosecutors could not rely on coerced confessions, but it did so in cases involving haranguing rather than physical torture. The central question was whether the defendant's "will was overborne by official pressure." When the Court decided *Miranda v. Arizona* in 1966, it replaced that amorphous standard with a set of bright-line rules requiring police to advise suspects of their rights, offer to provide them with lawyers, and stop questioning whenever the suspect requested. By then the focus had shifted entirely away from violence in interrogation rooms to the "inherently compelling pressures" of "a police dominated atmosphere." Although the "third degree" had not been eradicated, the Court stressed that it was now the exception rather than the norm, and interrogation practices had become "psychologically rather than physically oriented." The *Miranda* rules were intended to counteract "the compulsion inherent in custodial surroundings."[18]

The shift in focus in interrogation cases, away from violence and toward psychological pressure, partly reflects the striking success the Wickersham Commission and other early twentieth-century reformers achieved in combatting use of the third degree. But the focus has also shifted away from violence in the law of search and seizure, where there is much less reason to believe that the underlying problem of violence has been tamed. In interpreting and applying the Fourth Amendment to the US Constitution, which bans "unreasonable searches and seizures," the Supreme Court has concentrated heavily on protecting informational privacy, the ability to keep secrets from the police. That is why the Supreme Court ultimately ignored the violence in *Mapp v. Ohio* and hinged its decision on the fact that the police had entered Dollree Mapp's house without a warrant. Most of Fourth Amendment law is about where the police can look and what they can monitor. The late legal scholar William Stuntz complained with justification that "we have a large and detailed body of law to tell police when they may open paper bags or the trunks of cars," but "the law speaks softly (or not at all) when it come to the level of force that may be used in making an arrest or conducting a search."[19]

Stuntz traced this emphasis on privacy to *Boyd v. United States,* a late nineteenth-century decision by the Supreme Court, which ruled that a company could not constitutionally be forced to turn over documents showing its failure to pay import duties. The Court later abandoned that holding, along with much of the reasoning in *Boyd*. *Boyd* relied both on the Fourth Amendment and on the Fifth Amendment privilege against compelled self-incrimination, but the Supreme Court has since ruled that businesses don't have a Fifth Amendment privilege, and that a subpoena for documents is not equivalent to a "search" under the Fourth Amendment. Another part of the reasoning in *Boyd* proved ahead of its time, though. The essence of an unconstitutional search, the Supreme Court suggested in *Boyd,* was "not the breaking of . . . doors and the rummaging of . . . drawers," but violating "the sanctity of a man's home and the privacies of life."[20]

Justice Brandeis leaned heavily on *Boyd* when he dissented from the Supreme Court's decision in 1928 that wiretapping was not a "search" or "seizure" regulated by the Constitution. Brandeis argued that the Fourth Amendment should be read to prohibit "every unjustifiable intrusion by the government upon the privacy of the individual." Four decades later a majority of the Supreme Court took essentially the same view. In *Katz v. United States,* decided in 1967, the Supreme Court reversed itself and concluded that the Fourth Amendment did in fact regulate electronic eavesdropping on telephone conversations. Although the Court in *Katz* continued to deny that the Fourth Amendment created any "general constitutional 'right to privacy,'" it stressed that what an individual "seeks to preserve as private, even in an area accessible to the public, may be constitutionally protected." In subsequent decisions the Court clarified that under *Katz* the Fourth Amendment regulated any government infringement of "reasonable expectations of privacy."[21]

Ever since *Katz* the jurisprudence of the Fourth Amendment has focused overwhelmingly on protecting privacy. And in this respect *Katz* was prefigured by a series of decisions earlier in the 1960s—including, as we have seen, the case of Dollree Mapp. The facts of *Mapp v. Ohio* "seemed to cry out for limitation on police force," points out the legal historian Wesley Oliver, but the Supreme Court reversed Mapp's conviction only because the police appeared to have lacked a warrant to enter her house.[22]

It is no accident that the defendants in *Brown v. Mississippi, Rochin v. California,* and *Mapp v. Ohio* all were nonwhite. Police violence has always been directed overwhelmingly at marginalized groups—especially people of color, but also poor whites, political dissidents, and violators of prevailing sexual norms. The restrictions the Supreme Court imposed on state and local law enforcement in the twentieth century were plainly motivated in large part by concerns about how the police treated marginalized groups, particularly African Americans in the states of the former Confederacy. But the Court almost never placed legal significance on the race of the defendants in criminal procedure cases, and it rarely dwelled on the nexus between race and police brutality. *Brown, Rochin,* and *Mapp* were typical in this regard.

If the Court placed little weight on race in criminal procedure, it had nothing at all to say about the policing of sexuality. When William Westley carried out his pioneering ethnography of policing in Middle America, he found that the officers thought it was part of their job to beat up "deviants," a category in which he lumped together homosexuals, exhibitionists, peeping toms, and rapists. Westley wrote in the early 1950s, in the middle of a nationwide panic over "perverts" and "sexual psychopaths," labels that in practice often wound up serving as code for homosexual. The "extralegal" violence that police visited on homosexuals was an open secret in the middle decades of the twentieth century, but it was rarely viewed as an important part of the broader problem of police brutality. Westley was unusual in suggesting that the experience of the police in sex cases helped teach them to view violence as a "general resource." The Supreme Court, in particular, never talked this way. When the Court talked about police violence, it rarely touched on the connection with race, and it never mentioned the connection with sexuality. And as the constitutional rules regulating law enforcement proliferated in the second half of the twentieth century, few of them focused on violence. They focused on privacy. The *Katz* test for what counts as a "search" was a particularly important example, but far from unique.[23]

In recent years the Supreme Court has slightly modified the *Katz* rule regarding the scope of the Fourth Amendment. The amendment applies, the Court now says, if there is either an invasion of a "reasonable expectation of privacy"—the test derived from *Katz*—or a trespass on a suspect's person or his house, papers, or effects. By its terms, the Fourth Amendment bars only "unreasonable searches and seizures" of "persons, houses, papers, and effects," and when the Supreme Court decided in 1928 that wiretapping wasn't regulated by the Fourth Amendment, it did so largely because there had been no physical trespass on anything falling within these four categories. For decades *Katz* was understood to have supplanted the so-called trespass test for whether there had been a search or seizure, but the Court now says that *Katz* simply "*added to*" the earlier test, rather than replacing it. As a consequence, Fourth Amendment law focuses somewhat less relentlessly on privacy than it did until recently. The focus on privacy has been supplemented with attention to trespasses, and violence is of course a kind of trespass on a person. But privacy remains by far the dominant focus. Moreover, the trespasses that have caught the Supreme Court's eye have been trespasses on property—the undercarriage of a car, and the area around a house—not trespasses on persons. Violence remains a peripheral topic in the law of search and seizure.[24]

Part of the reason may be precisely that police violence is heavily targeted at people on the margins: poor people, nonconformists, and people of color. Invasions of privacy are also experienced disproportionately by people on the margins. All kinds of policing are. But the invasions of privacy associated with policing are at least somewhat more widely shared.

Everyone gets pulled over for traffic violations; everyone has their bags searched at sporting events. But most upper- or middle-class white Americans have never been struck by a police officer, and they may not know anyone who has. The lack of firsthand experience may explain, for example, the insignificance of violence in the legal treatment of "stop and frisk," a mainstay of urban policing since the 1960s.[25]

Stop and Frisk, Police Shootings, and the Continuum of Force

Here is how the legal scholar Paul Butler describes the stop-and-frisk tactic, as experienced by young African American men: Police jump out of a car with their guns drawn and order you to face the wall with your hands up, then "they put their hands roughly all over your body." Or "they kick your feet to spread your legs wider" and then "pat you up and down" and "touch your private parts." Here are a few examples collected by law professor Kami Chavis: an officer shoves a suspect against a wall when he reaches for identification; an officer pulls a suspect's arm behind his back and threatens to punch him in the face; an officer smashes a suspect's head into a wall, leaving a gash that requires stitches. These are extreme examples, but they are not outliers. Chavis notes that nearly half of young people surveyed in an intensively patrolled area of New York City said a police officer had used force against them, and the New York Police Department's own statistics show that a decade ago force was being used in tens of thousands of stop-and-frisk encounters every year. Since then, police in New York City have dramatically reduced their use of stop and frisk, largely in response to complaints about, and court challenges to, its disproportionate use against young men of color. But the tactic still is used hundreds of times a day.[26]

The tactic is inherently violent, as Chavis points out: it isn't like having a wand passed over your body at the airport. Butler likens stop and frisk to sexual assault. He calls it a low-grade, sexualized form of police brutality. Butler is neither the first nor the last scholar to notice the sexual overtones of stop and frisk. Seth Stoughton, once a police officer and now a law professor, had a standard phrase he used during a stop and frisk: "I don't mean to feel you up or nothing, but I'm about to." He explains, "I may have had to grope people, but I didn't want to be unprofessional about it."[27]

Very little of this makes it into judicial discussions of stop and frisk, and it doesn't shape how the law treats the tactic. Courts treat "frisks"— like the "stops" that accompany them—as "brief," "slight," "narrowly circumscribed intrusions." It is true that the Supreme Court has required more justification for a frisk than for a stop: a stop requires "reasonable articulable suspicion" that a suspect has committed or is about to commit a crime, whereas a frisk requires both a lawful stop and "reasonable articulable suspicion" that the suspect is "armed and dangerous." *Terry v. Ohio,* the 1967 Supreme Court decision that is the source for these requirements, stressed that a frisk "is a serious intrusion upon the sanctity of the person, which may inflict great indignity and arouse strong resentment." Three years earlier, New York's highest court had called a frisk "a minor inconvenience and petty indignity," which police were justified in carrying out whenever they lawfully stopped someone for questioning. But Chief Justice Earl Warren, who wrote the majority opinion for the Supreme Court in *Terry,* called that suggestion "simply fantastic." He said the very term "stop and frisk" was a euphemism.[28]

Still, what Warren emphasized about "frisks" in *Terry* was the toll they could take on dignity: the demeaning, disrespectful nature of "a careful exploration of the outer surfaces of a person's clothing all over his or her body in an attempt to find weapons." He didn't describe the procedure as violent, or discuss how it could be violent. John Terry, the lead defendant in the case, hadn't just been patted down; the officer had "grabbed" him and "spun him around." But Warren made nothing of that; it was mentioned but then ignored, like the police "running roughshod" over Dollree Mapp. Nor did he address the ways in which frisks could involve considerably more force than what Terry had experienced.[29]

Ever since *Terry,* courts have largely read violence out of the stop and frisk. More precisely, they have read violence out of the *execution* of a stop and frisk. In judicial parlance, "frisk" is more or less a synonym for "patdown," and that is how the procedure is typically envisioned. On the other hand, violence is very much part of the *justification* for stop and frisk. The deadly violence that threatens law enforcement officers, the danger that "the answer to the question propounded by the policeman may be a bullet," is the reason the frisk is permitted, and the reason the Supreme Court conditioned its legality on an officer's articulable basis for worrying that a suspect is armed and dangerous. But the complete absence of violence from the other side of the ledger may be part of the reason that in practice this legal standard has proven undemanding—why anything beyond a bare intuition of danger, or an uncorroborated anonymous tip that a suspect has a gun, usually suffices to justify a frisk.[30]

Violence isn't *entirely* absent from the law of criminal procedure. The Supreme Court ruled in 1985 that the Fourth Amendment imposes special limitations on the use of deadly force: stopping a fleeing suspect by shooting him, or using any other kind of deadly force, is an "unreasonable" and hence unconstitutional seizure unless the police have probable cause to believe the suspect poses a risk of death or serious bodily harm to officers or the public. In addition, some lower courts have established loose requirements for using "severe" or "intermediate" force, like a Taser. One federal court of appeals has said that force of this kind requires an "immediate safety risk"; another had said that it is inappropriate when a suspect has been detained for a "minor infraction" and "clearly poses no risk to the officer or to public safety." Usually, though, the only constitutional standard governing police violence is the general, open-ended rule that the police must act reasonably, under all circumstances. Recently, in fact, the Supreme Court warned against imposing "rigid preconditions" even on uses of deadly force, beyond the general requirement of "reasonableness." The vagueness of that standard, combined with judicial reluctance to second-guess the police, has meant that almost any violence that police employ—grabbing, shoving, tackling, or striking people, brandishing weapons, using Tasers, breaking down doors, running cars off the road—is lawful as long as the officers could plausibly think it was necessary.[31]

In practice, judicial assessments of police violence have long been even more deferential than that. Unlike an illegal search, uses of force by law enforcement typically do not produce evidence that can be suppressed in a criminal trial, so the main way to challenge them in court is through a civil lawsuit seeking a monetary award. But the Supreme Court has held that police officers can't be sued for violating constitutional rights unless it was crystal clear that what they did was forbidden. The Justices have said that this rule of "qualified immunity" is "particularly important in excessive force cases," precisely because liability for excessive force depends so heavily on the particular facts of each individual case. A civil suit against an officer for using excessive force therefore cannot proceed unless, as the Court puts it, "existing precedent 'squarely governs' the specific facts at issue." Generally that means there must have been a previous court decision condemning very similar police conduct in very similar circumstances.[32]

We really do not have rules for police uses of nondeadly force; instead we mostly have highly deferential, after-the-fact, case-by-case review, allowing a finding of liability only if prior decisions in cases with similar facts made it crystal clear that the force used was unconstitutional. The nationwide protests against police violence in 2020 prompted renewed scrutiny of qualified immunity, and the Democratic leadership in the House of Representatives introduced legislation to abolish it. Even if legislation of this kind proves successful, however, the legal standards that govern the use of force by law enforcement officers will remain remarkably minimal. We emphatically do not have, in criminal procedure, what we have in substantive criminal law: an understanding of violent conduct as a category apart, deserving of an especially aggressive legal response.[33]

I have been focusing on judicial decisions, and especially on rulings of the Supreme Court, but the insignificance of violence in criminal procedure is a broader phenomenon. It is a feature of the legal system as a whole, an aspect of contemporary legal consciousness. It is reflected and reinforced, for example, in how police departments themselves regulate the use of force by their officers. Police departments *do* regulate violence by police officers, and they pay a good deal more attention to it than they did, say, in the 1950s and early 1960s. Furthermore, many departments tightened their rules, if only by degrees, in response to the nationwide protests against police violence in 2020.

Most departments approach the issue of police violence through a "use of force continuum." The details vary, but every use-of-force continuum arranges force along a spectrum, starting with mere presence, and then progressing through verbal instructions and steadily increasing degrees of physical coercion. The continuum ends with deadly force. Officers are supposed to start at the bottom of the continuum and work their way upward, going only as far as necessary to get compliance.[34]

The most important feature of a use-of-force continuum is not the substitution of "force" for "violence," although this nomenclature certainly matters. Actually, some departments even avoid the language "use of force," preferring the still more euphemistic phrase "response to resistance."[35] I will return to questions of terminology later in this chapter. The most important thing about a use-of-force continuum, however, is that it is a *continuum*. When it comes to police tactics, there is no sharp line dividing violence from nonviolence. There are more forceful tactics and less forceful tactics, but they are arranged on a continuous scale. The whole point of a continuum is that we are dealing with differences of degree, not of kind. It is the opposite of the categorical distinction drawn in substantive criminal law between crimes of violence and nonviolent offenses.

The "continuum" approach is reflected in legal scholarship, as well. Stuntz was unusual in arguing for more rules addressing police violence. Most legal scholarship on policing focuses on what the Supreme Court has focused on: invasions of privacy. In recent years a few scholars have placed the issue of police violence front and center, but even they, often as not, share the central idea of the use-of-force continuum. Rather than treat violence as a special category of police conduct deserving special rules, they stress the need to regulate and restrict low-level interventions by law enforcement, the entry points of the continuum, in order to minimize the opportunities for the use of force to escalate.[36]

The Ebb and Flow of Public Concern about Police Violence

Part of the reason criminal procedure pays so little attention to violence is that it focuses on privacy instead. Another part of the reason, though, is that the level of public concern about police violence has fluctuated. As Figure 4 suggests, concerns about police violence soared in the 1960s but receded in the 1970s and 1980s. In recent decades the issue of police violence has once again started to receive increased attention, but the trend has been slow and uneven, reflecting the conflicting intuitions Americans have about uses of force by law enforcement.

There is a long history of complaints about police brutality and efforts to rein in violence by the police, but there is also a long history of looking the other way, and of vocal defenses of tough, aggressive police tactics. Progressive reformers of the late nineteenth century and early twentieth century, for example, took aim at police corruption but often saw nothing wrong with encouraging officers to use their nightsticks liberally against criminals and reprobates. Newspapers praised "beneficial clubbing" by the police. Many reformers linked police corruption with toleration of vice; they *wanted* the police to get tough with lawbreakers. This was notably true of Theodore Roosevelt during his tenure on the New York City Police Commission; "speak softly but carry a big stick" wasn't just a figure of speech. Roosevelt opposed restrictions on the use of nightsticks, and under his leadership the Police Commission gave police officers new, more powerful weaponry, and plenty of leeway to use it.[37]

Outside of New York, as well, early twentieth-century Americans often explicitly called for "pugilistic police." Wesley Oliver notes that reformers of the time tended to champion "*appropriate* violence" in law enforcement. They took the view "that police violence was not necessarily a bad thing so long as it was directed against the criminal element." This was a common opinion during Prohibition, as well, when there were explicit calls for the police to "muss up" gangsters. The approach always had critics, and the Wickersham Commission, with its attacks on the "third degree," reflected and strengthened public opposition to illegal— or "extralegal"—police violence. But support for "strong-arm" tactics by the police never went away. That is why, for example, William Westley found in the early 1950s that police officers in Gary, Indiana, believed that the public expected and wanted them to beat up sex offenders.[38]

Police violence attracted lots of attention in the 1960s, in part because violence in general attracted lots of attention in the 1960s, and in part because of the role the police played in the era's distinctive politics. Law enforcement was the face of the state. For student protesters and other

left-wing activists, police officers personified the Establishment, and police violence was simply the domestic manifestation of the violence the
United States government was carrying out in Indochina. So, too, for
African Americans in the impoverished neighborhoods of America's
inner cities, the police often seemed, as James Baldwin put it, like "oc-
cupying soldier[s] . . . at the very center of the revolution now occurring
in the world."[39]

Police officers in the United States in the 1960s were overwhelmingly
white, overwhelmingly male, and overwhelmingly conservative, cultur-
ally as well as politically. These demographics heightened the insularity
of the police, pushed them toward reactionary politics, and made it
easier for minorities and antiwar activists to see the police as the enemy.
Furthermore, the police often reacted clumsily and heavy-handedly to
political protests and the wave of urban riots in the late 1960s, which reinforced the perception that they were violent and out of control. More
and more people were afraid of the police, and what they feared mostly
was police brutality: "the gun in the holster, and the swinging club."
When Baldwin wrote that he knew from firsthand experience how it felt
to be "at the mercy of the cops," he meant that in a very tangible, bodily
sense: he knew "the thunder and fire of the billy club, the paralyzing
shock of spittle in the face, and . . . what it is to find oneself blinded, on
one's hands and knees, at the bottom of the flight of steps down which
one has just been hurled." When antiwar protesters chanted "the whole
world is watching" outside the 1968 Democratic Convention in Chicago,
what the world was watching was the protesters getting pummeled and
teargassed by the police. There were echoes of that chant fifty-two years
later, during the protests over police killings in 2020. Once again, moreover, heavy-handed treatment of protesters by the police reinforced
many of the concerns that had motivated the protests in the first place.[40]

Unsurprisingly, then, much of the criticism of the police in the 1960s,
and much of the energy of police reformers at the time, focused on limiting and controlling police violence. When civilian oversight boards for
law enforcement agencies began to appear in the 1960s and 1970s, they
were aimed, above all else, at the problem of police brutality. Scholars
who wrote about policing focused on violence, too. The criminologist

Jerome Skolnick called his widely influential 1966 study on the police *Justice without Trial,* placing at the very center of his account the ability of the police to inflict punishment outside of any legal process. William Muir, a political scientist who published a celebrated analysis of policing in 1977, thought the central challenge of law enforcement was to be wise and humane when employing coercive force—that is, when resorting to or threatening the use of violence. Contemporary with Muir's research, a team of academics led by the criminologist Hans Toch explored the possibilities for involving rank-and-file officers in the design and implementation of police reform; the problem the group chose to attack, naturally enough, was violence between officers and civilians.[41]

But public attention to police violence waned in the 1970s and 1980s, for several reasons. First and foremost was the growing concern about violent crime, which made many people tolerant of, or even eager for, "rough tactics" by the police. Just as in earlier eras, there was a growing sentiment that it was time for the police to take their gloves off. Gun violence associated with Prohibition Era gangsters led prosecutors like Thomas Kane to defend the use of the "third degree" during interrogations. The spiraling crime rates of the 1970s and 1980s made a box-office hero of Dirty Harry Callahan, the rogue, gun-happy officer played by Clint Eastwood in five movies between 1971 and 1988. The Dirty Harry movies were part of a whole wave of escapist entertainment in the 1970s and 1980s that celebrated vigilantism, sometimes by rule-bending police officers and sometimes by crime victims who had been pushed too far. These on-screen stories reflected a broad appreciation for fighting fire with fire: using justified violence, whether legal or illegal, to avenge unjustified violence and to bring it under control.[42]

Rising crime rates were not the only reason concerns about police violence receded in the 1970s and 1980s. The police themselves became less frightening to many Americans. Litigation over hiring and promotion policies forced many metropolitan police forces to become less monolithically white and male during this period. The number of minority officers and female officers rose dramatically. So did the number of minority and female police chiefs, albeit more slowly. Civilian oversight boards, which police departments initially fought tooth and nail, gradually became commonplace. And the community policing movement changed the way police departments all across the country thought about and talked about themselves. Rhetoric about the "thin blue line" gave way to calls for partnership with the community. Police departments grew less insular, less defensive, and more sophisticated about and responsive to the diverse communities they served.[43]

In the process, the police also became better at controlling crime. But crime rates did not begin to drop until the 1990s, and it was even longer before *fear* of crime began to recede. In the mid to late 1970s and throughout the 1980s, public attitudes toward the police were shaped both by a sense that crime, and particularly violent crime, was getting worse and worse, and by a sense that the police were getting smarter, fairer, more open, and more diverse. These perceptions were based in reality. Crime, including violent crime, really did spiral upward in the 1970s and 1980s, and there were important respects in which the police really did improve.

By the 1990s and early 2000s, all of this had led in many quarters, particularly outside minority communities, to a certain degree of complacency about the police. There was a sense that law enforcement had been broken but it was now largely fixed, or at least that we knew how to fix it. The problem of police brutality, in particular, dropped off many radar screens. That issue periodically reemerged as a focus of national debate, after events like the beating of an African American motorist named Rodney King by Los Angeles police officers in 1991 and the fatal shooting of a Guinean immigrant named Amadou Diallo by New York City police officers in 1999. Increasingly, though, progressive police executives tended to think that the problem of policing had been solved, that all that remained was implementation. Plenty of people outside policing thought that, too. It was common for scholars of law and public policy, for example, to use the reformed police departments of the 1990s and early 2000s as models for how other governmental agencies should be overhauled. Scholarly criticism of the police never disappeared, of course, but a remarkably broad consensus emerged that, by and large, law enforcement agencies were on the right course.

Today it's difficult to find scholars, reformers—or, for that matter, police chiefs—who are so sanguine about the state of American policing. The bleaker outlook is largely the result of three controversies that have dogged police departments over the past decade. The first has to do with complaints about stop and frisk, particularly in New York City, complaints that have belatedly brought attention to the violence often associated with "frisks," particularly when the suspects are young men of color. The second has to with the militarization of policing: the increased use of military-style equipment and tactics by police departments. The third, and most important, is the renewed concern that the Black Lives Matter movement brought to the issue of police killings, the concern that exploded across the country in 2020. What all three of these issues have in common is that they sit at the intersection of concerns about racial bias in policing and concerns about violence in policing. And all three received relatively little notice until the second decade of the new millennium.

This is particularly true of the latter two issues, law enforcement militarization and police killings. The militarization of policing over the past half century began with SWAT—"special weapons and tactics"—teams, which large departments began forming in the 1970s. Initially these units were reserved for rare but highly volatile situations: riots, hostage takings, barricaded suspects, and so on. Over time, though, SWAT teams began to be used heavily in drug searches, and they became something that even smaller departments thought they needed. The "war on drugs" in the 1980s accelerated the expansion and repurposing of SWAT teams, and it gave new plausibility to the idea that police should look and act like warriors. Then the federal government got involved, donating surplus military equipment to police departments and, especially after the terrorist attacks of September 11, 2001, giving them money to buy advanced weaponry and other battlefield equipment. The Obama administration imposed some restrictions on the use of federal funds to supply local police departments with certain kinds of military equipment. The restrictions were mild: they applied largely to categories of equipment that police departments had not been receiving. But the Trump administration rescinded them anyway. Military-style police equipment was prominently employed during the protests and looting in the spring of 2020, including an infamous use of tear gas against protesters near the White House so that the president could pose with a bible in front of a damaged church.[44]

SWAT teams and other militarized forms of policing have always been used disproportionately in communities of color, which is one reason the violence associated with them often went under the radar. This was true, as well, of police killings. In the 1990s and early 2000s, few scholars or reformers concentrated on the use of deadly force by the police. Even Paul Chevigny, a stalwart campaigner against police brutality in New York City since the 1960s, believed by the 1990s that "the principal problem of police violence for the present day" was *nondeadly* force. Throughout the first decade of the twenty-first century, police shootings received far less press coverage and far less scholarly attention than official executions, even though statistics maintained by the federal government indicated that more than ten times as many people were killed each year by police than by applications of the death penalty. And the official statistics, it turns out, undercounted police killings and downplayed the reasons to worry about them—omitting more than half of the deaths, and classifying all of the rest as "justifiable homicide." About a thousand people are killed by police every year in the United States, vastly more than in any country to which we would care to compare ourselves. This is true even after adjusting for population: the odds of getting killed by the police are roughly five times higher in the United States than, for example, in Canada, Australia, England, Italy, or Germany.[45]

The victims of police shootings, moreover, are disproportionately African American. Blacks comprise roughly 12 percent of the American population, but more than a quarter of all people killed by the police. As with the use of military equipment and tactics by the police, it is hard to escape the conclusion that the problem of police killings received relatively little attention throughout the 1990s and early 2000s in part because the problem was experienced disproportionately by people of color. Police killings did not become a subject of national discussion until late 2014, and what brought attention to the issue then, more than anything else, was the Black Lives Matter movement and especially the protests held in the wake of the deaths of Michael Brown, who was shot by a police officer in Ferguson, Missouri, and Eric Garner, who was suffocated by a police officer on Staten Island. The protests turned police killings from a largely forgotten issue into what the Associated Press called "the top news story of 2014."[46]

The Black Lives Matter movement didn't come out of nowhere. It was made possible by two technological developments: cellphones with video cameras, and social media. But it also was the product of political and intellectual developments. It was the coming of age of a new generation of racial justice activists, and—more importantly for our purposes—it reflected a reorientation of thinking about race, a renewed focus on the tangible, corporal complaints of people of color, the way that racism operated not just as a system of abstract advantages and disadvantages, not just as a demeaning series of insults to status, but as a history of violence, a history of assaults and trespasses on physical bodies, often at the hands of the police. This is why Paul Butler, for example, argues that the damage done by stop and frisk is "more like police brutality than racial microaggression." It is why the sociologist Nikki Jones emphasizes how police violence shapes the lived experience and the outlook of minority youth. And it is why Ta-Nehisi Coates stresses the "visceral experience" of racialized policing and of racism more broadly, the way that it "dislodges brains, blocks airways, rips muscle, extracts organs, cracks bones, breaks teeth."[47]

Force, Brutality, and Theories of Police Violence

Police violence usually isn't called violence. It is usually called either "use of force" (the phrasing employed by the police and those sympathetic to them) or "police brutality" (the language used by their critics). Both terms are worth unpacking, because they can influence how people think about police violence: how much to worry about it, the pathways that produce it, and the best ways to control it.

The reason the police don't describe what they do as "violence" is that the term has a pejorative connotation. It usually, although not always, is understood to refer to the *illegitimate* or *unjustified* use of force. So describing police conduct as "violent" can suggest that it is necessarily wrongful. As I suggested in Chapter 1, this is the strongest argument for defining violence differently: for keeping the concept of violence value-neutral. Making wrongfulness part of the definition of violence makes it impossible to discuss, for example, whether and when the violence of war is justified—or about the circumstances under which we want the police to be violent.

That difficulty is averted by using the term "use of force" rather than the term "violence" to describe what the police do when they tackle a suspect, break through a door, or fire their weapons. But "use of force" has a euphemistic quality. It sounds measured and methodical, rather than explosive and hard to control. It downplays the elements of danger and destruction, the "thunder and fire." "Use of force" is not by definition legitimate and justified; no one thinks that "wrongful use of force" is a contradiction in terms. But the language of "force" does tend to make police violence seem less frightening and troubling than it otherwise might be. This is even truer of the phrase that some departments now prefer, "response to resistance."

"Police brutality," a term that opponents of police violence have used since the mid-nineteenth century, has different problems. It is unmistakably pejorative: no one talks about "legitimate" or "justified" brutality. In fact, police brutality is usually defined as the use of *unlawful* violence by law enforcement officers. The bigger problem with the phrase "police brutality" is the suggestion it conveys that violent officers are acting not as human beings but as beasts. It is similar in this way to calling violent criminals "animals" or calling an impoverished urban neighborhood a "jungle." Historian Marilynn Johnson points out that "in highlighting the animal-like traits of policemen—most of whom came from working-class backgrounds"—Progressive Era critics of "police brutality" tapped into and reinforced elites' long-standing tendencies to think of laborers as "bestial or subhuman." She notes that this kind of thinking proved remarkably persistent, "with middle-class radicals of the 1960s casting police as 'pigs' and 'brutes.'"[48]

Class bias is a long and troubling feature of criminal procedure law, and it is not restricted to discussions of police violence. Complaints about government searches in the Colonial Era, for example, routinely appealed to class privilege; officers were denounced as "dirty," "insolent," "impertinent," "rude," and so on.[49] But the rhetoric of "police brutality," like the wider practice of comparing police to animals, does not just encode class prejudice. It also may subtly shape how the legal system thinks about the origins of police violence and the best ways to control it.

Describing violence as brutality, or describing police as "brutes" or "pigs," reinforces a view of police violence as characterological rather than situational: the consequence of individual officers' dispositions rather than the circumstances in which they find themselves. And that is a deeply entrenched tendency. It has long been common to trace all forms of police illegality, not just unlawful violence, to rogue officers— "bad apples" that spoil the barrel. That intuition helps to explain the Supreme Court's strong reluctance to penalize officers for "good faith" violations of the law, either with evidence suppression or with money damages. The Justices have steadily expanded the "good faith" exception to the rule calling for suppression of evidence obtained in violation of the Fourth Amendment—the principal means of enforcing constitutional restrictions on the search-and-seizure powers of the police. And, as we have seen, the Court has immunized police officers from civil suits based on constitutional violations, as long as they acted in the reasonable, good-faith belief that their actions were lawful. Part of the rationale for the good-faith exception to the exclusionary rule has been skepticism that "innocent" mistakes by the police can be deterred. But the Court has also reasoned that the exclusionary rule should be reserved for "flagrant" violations, and shouldn't be something that "conscientious . . . responsible law enforcement officers" need to worry about.[50] Similar considerations lie behind the rule that officers cannot be sued for constitutional violations if they acted in reasonable good faith, a rule that the Supreme Court has stressed is "particularly important in excessive force cases."[51]

Police departments and local governments do not enjoy this kind of immunity. They can be sued for constitutional violations by the officers they employ, even when the officers acted in good faith, if the violations can be traced to an official policy or established custom.[52] Likewise, the federal government can sue local police departments that have a "pattern or practice" of violating constitutional rights.[53] That statutory authority—created by Congress in 1994—has been used against excessively violent departments, but only sparingly, and the Trump administration all but renounced it. Moreover, the pervasive understanding of unlawful police violence as "brutality" colors even efforts to hold departments and local governments liable for condoning excessive violence, and it has shaped the kinds of structural reform sought by private plaintiffs and, occasionally, by the federal Department of Justice. Those lawsuits have sometimes faulted how officers are trained regarding the use of force, but they have placed much greater emphasis on systems for identifying and tracking "problem officers." The goal has been to get police departments to do a better job identifying their bad apples—and then either rehabilitating them or taking them off the streets.

Activists and scholars have often criticized this focus on bad apples. The problem, they have argued, is not isolated officers but the occupational culture of law enforcement—a culture of paranoia, intolerance, and above all *toughness*. Police brutality, these critics have suggested, is the product not of violent officers but of a violent system, a violent mentality. Sometimes that mentality is blamed on what working as a police officer does to a person; sometimes it is blamed on the kinds of people who become police officers. Either way, blaming the mentality or culture of law enforcement for police brutality is itself a kind of characterological explanation. It replaces rogue officers with rogue forces, or a rogue profession, but it still finds the root of police violence in the police themselves, in their dispositions and proclivities, not in the circumstances in which they find themselves.[54]

Still, characterological understandings of violence have not dominated recent criminal procedure law and discussions of police violence in the way they have increasingly dominated substantive criminal law and discussions of violent crime. Police departments and their defenders have focused very much on circumstances in their discussions of police violence. They have identified the origins of police violence in the dangers and difficulties that officers face. Much of an officer's day may be filled with tedium, but the stresses of the job are undeniable. And those stresses are greater in the United States than in Europe, or in Britain or Canada or Australia, if only because there are so many more guns in the United States. American officers are much more likely to get shot. And even when suspects do not fire at the police, even when they are unarmed and do not appear threatening, the danger of gunplay lurks in the background of every encounter officers have when patrolling or responding to a call.

Policing in the United States is less dangerous than it used to be. The death rate of officers on the job fell by roughly two-thirds in the last quarter of the twentieth century, partly because of the widespread adoption of Kevlar. But the odds of suffering a lethal assault on the job still are more than ten times higher for police officers in this country than in, for example, England or Germany.[55]

Here, as elsewhere, rival theories of violence capture separate, partial truths. It is a question of what you want to emphasize, and for what purpose. Some officers *are* more violent than others. Some departments are more violent than others. Programs targeting problem officers, and problem departments, are sometimes effective in reducing violence. So there is in fact a characterological side to police violence. But there is a situational side, too. That is one reason why even officers caught on video beating up or shooting a suspect can often defend themselves successfully against charges of brutality: the circumstances in which the police operate do help to explain at least some police violence, regardless of whether they excuse it.

There has been a missing piece, though, in many discussions of police violence. Critics of police brutality have emphasized the characterological explanations of violence; the police and their defenders have traced police violence to the circumstances that officers encounter. The missing piece has to do with the responsibility of the police for the situations in which they find themselves: the tactics that place officers in positions where they feel called upon to use force. Good police tactics help officers avoid those positions and give them time to reflect. Good police departments train their personnel in those tactics and require their use. But many departments have not trained their officers in these tactics, and even more departments have lacked policies requiring their use.[56]

A good deal of police violence can be attributed in part to the training that officers receive, and the tactics they employ in the hours, minutes, and seconds leading up to the use of force. But courts—including the US Supreme Court—generally do not hold officers or their departments accountable for the tactics that put officers in situations where they are called upon to use force. Fourth Amendment law, as interpreted by the Supreme Court and as applied by lower courts, focuses instead almost exclusively on the moment in which an individual officer employs violence, and courts routinely declare their reluctance to second-guess the "split-second" decisions officers make "in circumstances that are tense, uncertain, and rapidly evolving."[57]

When courts assess the "reasonableness" of police violence, why do they place so little weight on the training officers receive, and on the tactics an officer employs early in an encounter? Part of the reason is a series of procedural rules the Supreme Court has established for civil rights lawsuits, which make it easier for plaintiffs to focus their arguments on the actions of individual officers rather than on a department's policies or general practices, not just in cases alleging brutality, but in all cases challenging the constitutionality of police conduct. Liability can be based on poor training, for example, only if the defendant can be shown to have been "deliberately indifferent" to constitutional rights, and courts typically will not even take up the issue of departmental or municipal liability until an underlying constitutional violation by an individual officer has been shown. Another part of the reason, though, is the ingrained habit of looking only at the moment in which force is used: what law professors Brandon Garrett and Seth Stoughton call the "'split second' theory of policing." And that theory, in turn, can be traced partly to the nature of the debate over the causes of police violence. One camp has emphasized characterological explanations, focusing on either occupational culture or problem officers; the other camp has emphasized the circumstances that lead officers to use force. Too often what has been crowded out is attention to how police get themselves into those circumstances, and the training and tactics that could help officers avoid them—or, as a last resort, navigate them with less risk to life or limb.[58]

Here is an example of the kind of issue that gets crowded out. Most of the roughly one thousand people shot to death by the police in the United States each year are carrying guns, but roughly 15 percent—about 150 a year—are armed only with knives. Police officers are almost never killed with knives. Moreover, police in England or Europe almost never shoot anyone armed only with a knife. The reason so many people armed only with knives are killed by the police in the United States comes down to training and tactics. Police overseas are trained to "contain and negotiate" when facing suspects armed with knives. In the United States, in contrast, police officers have been told for years about a "21-foot rule": once a suspect with a knife is within 21 feet of you, you won't have time to draw and fire your gun before you are stabbed.

There is zero science behind this "rule." It was devised by a police trainer who timed how long it took officers to unholster and shoot their weapons (one and a half seconds, he concluded), and how fast a typical man can run in that time (21 feet, he found). He published his results in a trade magazine, and they quickly became part of the lore of American policing. Criminologists and police executives have repeatedly dismissed the 21-foot rule as a poor guide for officers in the field. Even the trainer who came up with the rule has disavowed it as anything more than a rough heuristic. Nonetheless, belief in the rule remains common among officers, and the rule is still often taught in police academies. Moreover, no police department has been found liable for failing to disabuse its officers of the rule, partly because of the high bar set by the "deliberate indifference" standard, partly because of the requirement that plaintiffs first prove a constitutional violation by an individual officer, and partly because the very fact that the rule is so widely relied upon makes it seem "reasonable" to many courts.[59]

Comparing Ideas about Violence in Criminal Law and Criminal Procedure

Substantive criminal law and criminal procedure law have both been shaped by ideas about what causes violence. As we saw in Chapter 2, modern criminal law takes a strongly characterological view of violence: it reflects the assumption that violence is driven more by individual proclivities than by circumstances, that violent offenses are committed mostly by violent people. That is why a person needs to commit so few violent offenses—often one will suffice, and two or three is almost always enough—to be branded as a violent offender for purposes of sentencing enhancements, restrictions on parole eligibility, and exclusion from drug courts, veterans courts, and similar diversion programs. The strongly characterological focus of modern criminal statutes is something of a break with tradition. Two signal features of Anglo-American criminal law—the *actus reus* requirement, and the rule against character evidence—reflect a long-standing wariness about characterological explanations of criminality. There are few traces of that wariness in modern criminal statutes targeting violent crime.

Modern criminal procedure law is also shaped by ideas about the nature of violence, but the commitment to characterological explanations here is far less complete—partly, perhaps, because the image of police brutality is less racialized than the image of violent crime. In the public mind, the face of violent crime is the face of a young man of color, and offending by members of racial minorities is more readily attributed to character rather than circumstances. But most police officers are white. Law enforcement is far more integrated than it was half a century ago, but minorities remain underrepresented.[60] *Class* prejudice does shape the public perception of police officers—and, even more so, of violent police officers. That kind of prejudice also lends credence to characterological explanations of violence, but it doesn't operate as strongly as racial bias.

That may be one reason there is a powerful counter-narrative to accounts that tie police brutality to the character of individual officers, to the culture of particular departments, or to the occupational mind-set of law enforcement. The counter-narrative traces police violence to the circumstances in which officers find themselves. Because this counter-narrative is generally advanced by the police themselves or by their defenders, it tends to gloss over the responsibility of the police themselves for the circumstances in which they find themselves—which is to say, it downplays the importance of police training and tactics. For their part, campaigners against police brutality also often slight those factors, because their attention is focused on matters of individual character, departmental culture, and occupational mind-set.

That is not the sharpest contrast, however, between how ideas about violence operate today in criminal law and in criminal procedure. The sharpest contrast has to do with the significance of violence. Until the early 1960s, criminal statutes placed little weight on the distinction between violent and nonviolent offenses. Since then, though, that distinction has become criminal law's master divide, the most common proxy for identifying the worst offenses and the defendants least deserving of mercy. Nothing like that has happened in criminal procedure, or in our thinking more generally about the police. If anything, violence matters less in criminal procedure today than it used to. Some of that can be traced to the way in which privacy has crowded out other values in criminal procedure, some of it to the idea that the police need to be violent to combat violent crime, and some of it, perhaps, to the habit of referring to police violence simply as "force" or "response to resistance." It is a mistake to make too much of violence, but it may be worse to fail to even name it.

4 | Rape and Domestic Assault

In 1969 the Scottish writer George MacDonald Fraser published a novel titled *Flashman*. It was the initial installment of what proved to be a wildly popular series. The narrator and protagonist of the books is Harry Flashman, a Victorian soldier and adventurer. Early in the first novel Flashman tries to rape his father's mistress. Furious at being fought off, he hits her twice in the face and knocks her to the floor. "I looked round for something to go after her with," he tells the reader, "a cane or a whip, for I was in a frenzy and would have cut her to bits if I could." A little later he is stationed in India, where he buys himself a 16-year-old mistress and then, peeved because he is being transferred to Afghanistan, gives her "the soundest thrashing of her pampered life."

This is all presented as picaresque, and by and large that is how the book and its sequels were received. Flashman was an "anti-hero," not a villain. Reviewers called the series "marvelously funny"—"one of the bright gems of the English comic novel." Nor was the appeal limited to Britain. By the time Fraser died in 2008, Flashman had fans all over the world, including in the United States. John Updike, the late twentieth-century American man of letters *par excellence,* was an enthusiast.

If any female critic ever wrote fondly about the books, though, I have yet to locate her. And notwithstanding its continued popularity, it's doubtful that *Flashman* would be greeted as warmly if the novel were written today. Harry Flashman was racist in a way that was supposed to be funny but seems even less amusing today than it did in the 1970s. The deeper problem, though, is his habit of beating up women, which no longer reads as simply "caddish."[1]

Modern readers are apt to have two different reactions to scenes of Flashman slapping women around. On the one hand, it seems like violence, pure and simple, and it is not any more entertaining because its victims are female. On the other hand, the fact that the violence is directed at women does seem to matter. It's not just violence, it's sexual violence; and it is wrapped up in the intended appeal of the books. The various editions of *Flashman* all have similar cover art: they all depict the central character standing in dress uniform, hand on his sword, with a loosely clothed, dark-skinned woman seated submissively at his feet. Flashman was something of a sadist, even outside of a sexual context: he liked to see "a good flogging," and took pleasure in placing bets "on whether the man would cry out before the tenth stroke, or whether he would faint."[2] But violence toward men was never as central to his character or to his story as his sexual conquests.

There is some tension between the two reactions a reader today is apt to have to Flashman's assaults on women. One reaction is: this is just *violence*. The other is: this is a special *kind* of violence. It's fully consistent to say both that it's important to recognize the violence in sexual violence, and that it's important to recognize the ways in which sexual violence can differ from other kinds of violence. Still, there's a tension between emphasizing the *violence* in sexual violence and the *sexual* in sexual violence. The same tension has run through the debates over the past half century about the law's response to rape and sexual assault, and to the closely related problem of domestic violence. Rape law reform since 1970 has been driven, first, by an insistence that rape is a crime of violence, and second, by a widespread belief that the crime of rape, or sexual assault, should not be defined by or require the use of physical force. There have been parallel debates about how to think about and respond to domestic violence. The feminist movement of the 1970s and 1980s, which lay behind the wave of rape law reforms during that decade, also sparked a new focus on domestic violence, and new demands that violence within intimate relationships be treated as criminal—that the perpetrators be arrested, prosecuted, and locked up. In subsequent decades, though, there were increasing calls to recognize the ways in which domestic violence differs from other forms of violence, and calls for different responses. There has also been a growing sense that violence is too narrow a lens for understanding victimization within intimate relationships: that domestic violence has to be understood as just one part of the broader problem of domestic abuse, and that the problem at the heart of domestic abuse is not violence, per se, but power, domination, and coercive control.

All of this is to say that ideas about violence have played an important role in shaping legal responses to rape, sexual assault, and domestic violence. And not just ideas about the significance of violence, about how much it matters whether or not particular conduct is violent. Debates about rape and domestic violence have often taken the form of disagreements about how violence should be defined—what should count as violence—and, even more so, about the nature of violence, and sexual violence in particular. To what extent are sexual assault and domestic violence the products of culture—of patriarchy, of misogyny, or of social patterns of power and domination? To what extent are they manifestations, instead, of individual character? And to what extent should they be understood as the product of circumstances? Different answers to these questions have shaped legal responses to rape and domestic violence at different times.

Here as elsewhere, ideas about violence intersect, often in explosive ways, with ideas about race and class. But gender is the demographic fault line that has most powerfully shaped these areas of the law, and most powerfully shaped arguments about how they should change. The perpetrators are most often—but certainly not always—male, and the victims are generally—but far from universally—female. Questions endure about whether and how rape, sexual assault, and domestic violence should be understood as *sexual* offenses, but there is no question that they are gendered.

Rape and domestic violence are overlapping but separate problems. Most sexual assaults are committed by perpetrators who know their victims, but some, obviously, are carried out by strangers. Much domestic violence consists of sexual assaults, but most does not. The problems also follow different patterns and present different challenges. By most measures, sexual assault is less common than domestic violence—not just because more men commit domestic violence than commit sexual assault, but also because domestic violence tends to become part of the ongoing, day-to-day life of a household or an intimate relationship in a

way that sexual assault usually does not. Nonetheless, there are important similarities in how ideas about violence have played out in both of
these areas, especially with regard to how they have intersected with
ideas about race, class, and above all gender.

Rape as Violence

It may seem odd that feminists in the 1970s and 1980s felt the need to
insist that rape is violence. After all, rape had long been defined as a
crime involving, as an essential element, the actual or threatened use of
physical force. William Blackstone's eighteenth-century formulation,
which became canonical, described rape as "carnal knowledge of a
woman forcibly and against her will." And rape had long been understood as a particularly serious felony. It remained a capital offense in a
handful of American states until 1977, when the US Supreme Court ruled
that executing a defendant for rape was "cruel and unusual" in violation
of the Eighth Amendment. The Court reasoned that rape was not comparable to murder "in terms of moral depravity and . . . injury to the
person and the public," although it was "without a doubt deserving of
serious punishment."[3]

The problem was that although rape was, in theory, an especially serious offense, in practice it was notoriously difficult for women who were
raped to seek redress through the criminal justice system. Rape prosecutions encountered a series of special challenges, and those challenges
were linked to another way in which the reality of rape law differed from
the theory. In theory, rape required violence, but in practice, the legal
system seemed to treat the essential harm of rape as something other
than the violence inflicted on the victim. Rape law, as actually adminis-
tered, seemed to protect, first and foremost, the interest of men—
fathers and husbands—in the sexual purity of women. The law did not
recognize forced intercourse between a husband and wife as rape; "marital rape" was, formally, a contradiction in terms. Prosecutors rarely
brought rape charges when the victims departed from the ideal of a
white, upper- or middle-class, "virtuous" woman—either a faithful wife
or a virgin. And when, contrary to usual practice, prosecutors did bring

charges in cases involving working-class women, women of color, or sexually active women, juries typically refused to convict. Rules of evidence allowed defense attorneys in rape trials to introduce evidence of the alleged victim's reputation for promiscuity, and the attacks of this kind frequently became the principal focus of the proceeding. Victims felt that they rather than the defendants were on trial, and the trauma of the proceedings discouraged women from pressing charges. All of this was consistent with the idea that rape was akin to wrongful seduction, and rapists were often described as sexual offenders, grouped together with exhibitionists, peeping toms, and homosexuals.[4]

The legal treatment of rape changed significantly in the 1970s and 1980s, at least on paper. The marital exception was substantially eliminated, evidence about the victim's sexual history was greatly restricted, corroboration requirements were dropped, and the common requirement that prosecutors prove the victim had exhibited "utmost resistance" was weakened or abandoned. The driving force behind all of these changes was feminism. More precisely, the reforms were brought about by anti-rape organizing that was itself part of the broader, late twentieth-century movement for women's liberation—a movement now commonly referred to as "second-wave feminism," to distinguish it from early twentieth-century feminism, which had focused on getting women the right to vote.[5]

Legal reform was not the sole aim of the anti-rape movement in the 1970s and 1980s, or even, initially, the movement's principal focus. Feminists in the early 1970s saw rape as a cultural problem: a key component of women's oppression. Writing in 1971, Susan Griffin called rape "the All-American crime." Fear of rape, Griffin said, was a "daily part of every woman's consciousness" but was cloaked by a "conspiracy of silence." Rape was "not an isolated act"; it was "a form of mass terrorism" and "the quintessential act of our civilization." The "basic elements of rape" were "involved in all heterosexual relationships," and therefore could not be eliminated with "simple reforms." Attacking rape required attacking "patriarchy itself." That same year Susan Brownmiller put the rapist at one end of a spectrum, adjacent to the "gooser . . . the ogler, the lip-smacker, the animal-noise maker, and the verbal abuser." Rape, she suggested, was "a metaphor for all male-female relations." Four years later Brownmiller elaborated on these ideas in her influential book *Against Our Will.* Rape, she argued, needed to be understood as the ultimate instrument of patriarchy. Rape wasn't just a crime, it was the linchpin of a whole culture of misogyny and male domination—what feminists came to call "rape culture." In 1970 Kate Millett had sounded a similar theme, if only in passing, in her book *Sexual Politics,* one of the foundational texts of second-wave feminism. "Patriarchal force," Millett wrote, ". . . relies on a form of violence particularly sexual in character and realized most completely in the act of rape. . . . In rape, the emotions of aggression, hatred, contempt, and the desire to break or violate personality, take a form consummately appropriate to sexual politics."[6]

"A form of violence particularly sexual in character"—like many feminists in the early 1970s, Millett insisted that rape was both violent *and* sexual. Griffin, too, called rape "the perfect combination of sex and violence"; it showed how tightly "in our culture male eroticism is wedded to power." For many feminists in the early 1970s, a historian of the movement has noted, rape "represented the perverse combination of pleasure and violence (and pleasure *in* violence) that was elemental to patriarchy." But the violence was the part that seemed to need emphasis. "We are not accustomed to associate patriarchy with force," Millett noted. But rape, she insisted, was precisely male domination through violence. By the end of the 1970s the core claim of the anti-rape movement, or at least the mainstream of that movement, was that "rape is violence, not sex."[7]

Stressing the violence of rape accomplished several things. It deromanticized rape, categorizing it with murder and assault instead of with carnality and seduction.[8] It pushed back against the notion—still common in the mid-twentieth century—that rape, although illegal, was a natural and understandable expression of the male sex drive.[9] It served as a reminder that rape was a *crime,* and a particularly serious one; it therefore gave rhetorical support to efforts to make the criminal process tougher on rapists and more welcoming to their victims.

Calling rape "violence" also did some work in widening what counted as rape. If violence was what counted, and not the damage to chastity, to honor, or to the interests of the victim's husband or father, then it was harder to ignore rapes within marriage, rapes of working-class and minority women, rapes of sexually active women, and rapes of men. And if rape was the ultimate manifestation of a culture of sexism and misogyny—of "rape culture"—then insisting on the violence of rape was a way of underscoring the seriousness of more prosaic forms of patriarchy, like sidewalk ogling, workplace harassment, and pornography. Feminist attacks on pornography in the 1970s and 1980s relied especially heavily on the link between pornography and rape—on the idea that, as Robin Morgan famously put it, "pornography is the theory, and rape the practice"—and on the understanding of rape as violence first and foremost. The feminist critics of pornography emphasized the ways in which pornography glorified, fetishized, and encouraged violence; going further, they insisted that pornography *was itself* "violence," because it debased and violated women.[10]

The drive for restrictions on pornography failed. It ran aground because of strong resistance from civil libertarians, including many feminists, and because of technological changes that made the very idea of regulating access to sexual content seem increasingly quixotic. By many measures, though, the anti-rape movement of the 1970s and 1980s was a success. Rape laws were reformed to loosen restrictions on prosecution, reduce requirements that victims try to fight off their attackers, and curb attacks on the character of testifying victims. Rape crisis centers, which provide hotlines, counseling, and other support for victims of sexual assault, were established in communities across the United States; by the end of the 1970s there were more than a thousand of these organizations. At the federal level, the Violence Against Women Act (VAWA) of 1994, which significantly increased federal financial support for rape crisis centers, also recognized gender-motivated violence as a civil rights violation and, in the very title of the legislation, reinforced the understanding of rape as first and foremost a crime of violence.[11]

Accompanying these legal and institutional changes was a shift in the cultural understanding of rape. (At least that is true of heterosexual rape outside of prisons. Prison rape—and in particular the rape of male prisoners—is another story, which will have to wait for Chapter 6.) It is

rare today to hear rape described as natural, understandable male behavior. Rape is beyond the pale. A sense of shame still attaches to rape
victims, and partly as a result the crime often goes unreported. But the
cloak of silence around rape has become thinner and thinner over the
past half century, as more and more victims have stepped forward.
There was a particularly sharp rise in the number of rapes reported in
2017 and 2018 in the wake of the "#MeToo" movement, which encouraged women to go public with their experiences of sexual assault and
sexual harassment.[12]

The greatest achievement of the anti-rape movement of the 1970s and
1980s may be that rape appears to have become less common. It is hard
to tell for sure, because rape statistics are notoriously hard to interpret.
The first problem is that many rapes go unreported, and the extent of
the underreporting has varied over time. The second complication is
that the meaning of the term "rape" has varied over time as well. The
legal definition of rape has been altered by the wide-scale repeal of the
marital rape exception, the trend away from requiring "utmost resistance" from victims, and, in many places, the reinterpretation or elimination of the requirement that rape be accomplished by "force." Equally
important, the lay understanding of rape, at least among many people,
has expanded to include coerced sex between acquaintances, even when
it does not result in visible injuries and may not seem "violent" in some
conventional senses of that word. All of these factors make it difficult
to compare rape statistics from different years.

Since 1973, however, the National Crime Victimization Survey con-
ducted by the US Department of Justice has estimated the incidence of
rape based on responses collected from a random sample of the population, rather than relying on reports to the police. The survey was overhauled in the early 1990s, and direct questions about rape and sexual assault were added for the first time, so data collected in the 1970s and
1980s cannot easily be compared with data collected in later years. Moreover, the old form of the survey plainly resulted in rape being drastically underreported, and the new survey, although a clear improvement,
may still undercount the crime. Still, it is encouraging that the trend in

rapes reported by victims, both before and after the survey redesign, is sharply downward.[13]

Nonetheless, the success of the anti-rape movement has been limited, and some of its failures may be attributable, ironically, to part of what helped the movement succeed: defining rape as violence. Even as legal restrictions on rape prosecutions have diminished and the support provided to rape victims has improved, the changes have been most dramatic in the treatment of cases involving rapes that are "violent" in the narrowest sense: forced sex with a stranger, accomplished by the threat of deadly force, or an assault leaving serious physical injuries. The idea has lingered that this is "real rape" or "legitimate rape"; for all the attention paid to "date rape," women who are coerced to have sex with partners or acquaintances still find it difficult to get what they have experienced labeled and treated as a crime. That has changed, somewhat, in the wake of the #MeToo movement, but in general police and prosecutors remain suspicious of rape allegations in "non-stereotypical" cases, and in most parts of the United States these cases are still rarely prosecuted.[14]

Until recently the FBI continued to define rape, for purposes of the crime statistics it collected, the same way Blackstone had defined the crime: as "the carnal knowledge of a female, *forcibly* and against her will." In 2012 the Bureau changed its definition to include any forced sexual penetration, as well as "nonforcible" rape. That same year, though, a senatorial candidate argued that abortion should be flatly banned, even for rape victims, because "legitimate rape" could not result in pregnancy. ("If it's a legitimate rape," he explained, "the female body has ways to try to shut that whole thing down.") President Obama responded that "rape is rape," but even today, in the day-to-day operation of the criminal justice system, it frequently remains true that "rape is violence"—and if not violent, it is not a crime at all.[15]

Feminists themselves have recognized that equating rape with violence has costs, and they have long been divided, as a group and sometimes as individuals, about whether those costs are worth paying. Writing in the mid-1980s, Susan Estrich described "a debate of some vigor as to whether rape should be thought about as sex or violence," with the first position—"rape as sex"—advocated by "feminist theoreticians who argue for a more expansive understanding of coerced sex," and the second position—"rape as violence"—attributed to "'liberal' (as opposed to radical) feminists." Millett's perspective in the early 1970s, that rape should be understood as both violent *and* sexual, that it was "a form of violence particularly sexual in character," had given way to a polarized contest between two mutually inconsistent ways of understanding the offense.[16]

Estrich herself found it difficult to pick a side in the contest between "rape as sex" and "rape as violence." She bemoaned the idea that rape was "real" only when it involved the kind of force that schoolboys use on the playground; she wanted rape law to recognize "that power can be exercised without violence." So while she recognized that "the 'rape as violence' approach may strengthen the case for punishing violently coerced sex," Estrich worried that "it may do so at the cost of obscuring the case for punishing forced sex in the absence of physical violence." On the other hand, Estrich thought, "[focusing] on the violent aspects of rape makes clear that you are not trying to prohibit all sex and that violent men . . . must not only be treated as sexually aberrant, but also be incapacitated as dangerous to the community." And calling rape violence would help to underscore that sex *shouldn't* be violence: it would push back against the long-standing view that violence in sex was "normal." On balance, therefore, Estrich suggested that "rape as violence" was "the better approach both theoretically and strategically." Thirty pages later, though, Estrich argued that "rape was about sex and sexual violation." What made a "violent rape different—and more serious—than an aggravated assault" was "the injury to personal integrity involved in forced sex," and the same injury was present when sex was coerced without a weapon or a beating.[17]

That view—that rape was sex obtained though the exercise of power or domination, with or without violence—became the consensus view of anti-rape activists. Catharine MacKinnon, the feminist scholar generally credited with having invented the legal category of "sexual harassment," argues that rape should be defined as any "physical invasion of a sexual nature under circumstances of threat or use of force, fraud, co-ercion, abduction, or the abuse of power, trust, or a position of dependency or vulnerability."[18] There have been qualms within the movement about widening the category of rape this far. Even the term "date rape" has been criticized by some feminists, partly on the ground that it infantilizes women by treating them as "passive victims" who lack the ability to say no. For similar reasons, some feminists worried about the creation of sexual harassment law: they were concerned that it trivialized and diverted attention from the true horror of violent sexual assault. Those apprehensions continue to be raised, but among feminists and anti-rape activists the argument has been lost. Sexual harassment training has become a pervasive fixture of American workplaces, even if it does less to change behavior than to insulate employers from liability. The remedies for sexual harassment are civil and administrative, not criminal. But particularly in the wake of the #MeToo movement, reformers increasingly group rape together with other forms of criminal sexual predation or "abuse," the common element of which is sex that is coerced or otherwise involuntary. The American Law Institute, for example, has been working for years on a revision of the sexual assault provisions of the Model Penal Code. The new rules, still in draft form, criminalize all sex that the perpetrator should know is nonconsensual. Violence—"physical force"—is relevant only as one way to prove lack of consent, as an "aggravating element," separating more serious from less serious versions of the offense. Estrich, too, had suggested that coerced sex without violence should be treated as rape, but a less serious form of rape.[19]

Meanwhile there is renewed interest in the decades-old work of Andrea Dworkin, one of the "radical" feminists most prominently associated with what Estrich called the "rape as sex" view. During her lifetime, Dworkin's influence seemed to fizzle along with the anti-pornography campaign she helped to lead, without success, in the 1970s and 1980s. But in the #MeToo era, a new generation of feminists has found itself drawn to Dworkin's understanding of rape as "our primary model for heterosexual relating." Like most rape law reformers today, Dworkin insisted that "*any* forced sexual act must be considered rape." In fact, she went further and suggested that a kind of "presumptive rape" takes place whenever social circumstances make a woman's consent to sex less than fully voluntary. She didn't actually say that "all sex is rape," but it is easy to see why that idea became widely attributed to her. She repeatedly denied that any sharp line—and certainly not the presence of "violence" as it is generally understood—separated rape from "normal" sex in a society structured by male domination.[20]

So the resurgent interest in Dworkin is yet another sign of mounting dissatisfaction with "rape as violence." It is consistent with the growing tendency to categorize rape together with other forms of "sexual abuse," defined in terms of power of domination (although Dworkin would not have thought that even that category had sharp boundaries under conditions of patriarchy). It resonates, as well, with a development we encountered in Chapter 2: the trend over the last couple of decades to treat "sex offenses" as a category apart in criminal law, especially serious and especially deserving punishment, much as violence has been treated as a category apart. Some states in fact define violence—for purposes of sentencing enhancements, eligibility for parole and probation, and access to therapeutic courts—to include some sex offenses not actually involving force. Other states simply extend to sex offenses, or at least some of them, the same treatment given to crimes of violence.[21]

The reduced salience of violence in defining rape, the growing support for "rape as abusive sex" instead of "rape as violence," has encountered significant resistance, including from some feminists. Much of the opposition stems from concerns about widening the net of criminal law. It grows out of many feminists' long-standing uneasiness about the anti-rape movement's embrace of criminal sanctions, the movement's transformation into a form of what has been pejoratively called "carceral feminism."[22]

In the 1980s some feminists found common cause with law-and-order conservatives. They joined together to press for more vigorous policing and prosecution of sexual assault, as well as for stronger legal restrictions on pornography. Other feminists resisted this alliance, and the result was a fracturing of the anti-rape movement that persists to this day. Many activists and scholars worry that combatting sexual assault by ramping up arrests and prosecutions has exacerbated the explosive growth in US prison populations. They want to attack rape without fueling mass incarceration.[23]

Race and the Nature of Sexual Violence

Concerns about "carceral feminism" intersect powerfully with concerns about race. Members of racial minorities, especially African Americans, are dramatically overrepresented in US prisons, and mass incarceration has been famously called the "new Jim Crow." And, of course, there are special reasons to worry about the racialized use of rape laws. Most rape, like most violent crime, is intra-racial, but fears of Black men sexually assaulting white women have always played an outsized role in the public imagination. Of the close to 4,000 Black men lynched in the United States from the end of Reconstruction through the mid-twentieth century, roughly a quarter had been accused of sexual assaults against white women. Today African Americans are overrepresented among rape defendants, as they are overrepresented among violent crime defendants in general.[24]

Black women active in the civil rights movement led protests in the late 1950s and in the 1960s against the failure to prosecute white men who raped Black women, and Black feminists in the 1970s wrote about and organized around the issue of sexual assault of Black women. It was an issue with a long and horrific history: enslaved Black women were routinely raped by their white "owners," and sexual assaults on African American women were an important part of the regime of racial terror that continued in the South following the end of the Civil War. The legal system's failure to protect Black women from sexual assault was not limited to the South, and it did not stop when Jim Crow ended. But the dominant voices in the anti-rape movement of the 1970s, as in second-wave feminism more broadly, were the voices of white women. This made race a complicated territory for the anti-rape movement to navigate, and it was not always navigated skillfully.[25]

Susan Brownmiller's handling of race in *Against Our Will* was a particularly divisive case in point. Brownmiller devoted a chapter of her book to the racial politics of rape. She acknowledged the long history of "the white man [using] the rape of 'his' women as an excuse to act against black men," but she also insisted that African American men themselves, acting in the name of their manhood, bore some of the responsibility for the persistent image of "the black man as rapist." She pointed in particular to *Soul on Ice,* the celebrated collection of prison essays by the Black Panther leader Eldridge Cleaver. Cleaver wrote that raping white women had been, for him, "an insurrectionary act," a way to get revenge on the white man by flouting his laws and despoiling his women. Cleaver said he later realized he had "gone astray," and that he "could not approve the act of rape." Brownmiller understandably found this a weak apology, especially because after Cleaver's release from prison he told an interviewer that rape had been "simply one of the weird forms my rebellion had taken." And Brownmiller was appalled by the failure of writers on the left to hold Cleaver accountable, at what she called their "rush to accept the Cleaver rationale for rape."

Unfortunately Brownmiller linked these points to a much wider argument about the racial politics of rape. There was too much excusing, she suggested, of actual rapes carried out by African American men, because misplaced guilt had made interracial rape a "huge political embarrassment for liberals," and it had become "unfashionable in extreme white radical circles to question *any* misguided aspiration articulated by blacks." Furthermore she argued that the long association of rape accusations with lynchings and executions of African American men in the South needed to be reinterpreted and qualified. This was even true, Brownmiller suggested, of the brutal murder and mutilation of Emmett Till in 1955, a pivotal event in the prehistory of the civil rights movement. Till was fourteen years old when he was killed for allegedly whistling at a white woman; he had been visiting family in Mississippi. Yes, Brownmiller wrote, Till's murder was ghastly and unforgivable, but "we must also accept" that the whistle, in context, "was a deliberate insult just short of physical assault."

Brownmiller's broadsides about racial politics, her insistence that African American men themselves were partly responsible for the stereotype of the Black rapist, and above all her effort to reframe the story of Emmett Till as partly about the victimization of white women—all of this drew strong criticism from African American readers, including many African American women, and it contributed to a growing schism between white feminists and feminists of color. "The crossroads of racism and sexism had to be a violent meeting place," Brownmiller wrote, and there was "no use pretending it doesn't exist." Her critics didn't deny the reality of that "violent meeting place," but they disagreed about what occurred there and what kind of pretending needed to end. Angela Davis spoke for many Black feminists when she charged that Brownmiller and white feminists like her were recycling racist tropes, apologizing for racial terror, and marginalizing the victimization of Black women. "The black woman is getting raped while the white woman is doing the screaming," complained the sociologist Nathan Hare.[26]

The racial politics of rape are less divisive today. There is still disagreement about whether systemic racism within the criminal justice system—in general, and specifically with regard to sex crimes—is reason enough not to expand the scope of rape laws. But the nature of the "crossroads of racism and sexism" is less controversial than it used to be. There is broad understanding, at least among reformers, that most sexual assaults are intra-racial, and it is far rarer to hear worries about racial sensitivity obstructing anti-rape work.

Another dispute about the nature of sexual violence continues to shape rape law and anti-rape policy, though. It has to do with the origins of sexual violence: whether sexual assaults are caused by the warped psychology of individual offenders, or instead by patterns of male domination and misogyny running throughout our society—"rape culture." On the second view, rapists aren't monsters, or, for that matter, truly deviant; they are just men who—because of the circumstances in which they happen to find themselves—act out, and make physically manifest, a script that lies latent in most men, or at least a very large number of them. This is a version, of course, of the character-versus-circumstances debate about violence more generally, the debate that has also left marks on modern sentencing statutes, on therapeutic courts and other penal diversion programs, and on efforts to address police brutality. We will see in later chapters that this debate has inflected juvenile justice, prison policies, and constitutional law as well.

In the area of sexual violence, as in substantive criminal law more generally, the trend over the past several decades has been toward thinking about violence as dispositional rather than situational. The women who started the anti-rape movement in the 1970s took the opposite position. Rape is "normal," argued Susan Griffin; it is "encouraged as part of our culture." Rape wasn't committed by "psychopaths," Andrea Dworkin wrote, but by "normal men"; other than a criminal conviction, there was "nothing . . . to distinguish the rapist from nonrapist." Many feminists today take a similar view, arguing that rape lies latent in our culture. We can't make progress against rape, they suggest, if we continue to see rapists as monsters; on the contrary, rapists are "all too human."[27]

Nonetheless, the understanding of rape that informs contemporary rape laws is strongly characterological. The legal system treats rape as a crime that tends to be committed by a particular kind of person: a sexual predator. Evidence that a defendant committed other offenses in the past generally is excluded from trials as unduly prejudicial; in cases of sexual assault, however, evidence of this kind is explicitly allowed by federal evidence law, and some states admit the evidence as well. It is thought to be more probative in these cases. As we have seen, recidivist statutes often group sex crimes together with violent offenses as the categories of prior convictions that will trigger sentence enhancements, or single out "sexually violent predators" for particularly harsh sentences. Moreover, statutes enacted by every state and the federal government require sex offenders to register with local law enforcement officials, and provide for notice to community members whenever someone convicted of a sex offense moves into their neighborhood. No pattern of offending is required to trigger these requirements; one conviction is enough. These registration and notification laws typically apply in theory to all sex offenders, not just violent sex offenders. But the degree of required notification depends on the perceived likelihood that an individual will reoffend, and in most states that assessment relies first and foremost on whether the defendant was convicted of an offense involving physical violence, and if so, how much. Since 2006, federal law has encouraged this approach by withholding some grant funds from states that do not follow it.[28]

The harsh sentences and the registration and notification requirements imposed on "sexually violent predators"—and even the statutory language itself of "sexually violent predators"—stand in contrast to the arguments about the nature of rape advanced by feminists and anti-rape activists in the 1970s. The severity and the focus of rape laws draws on a strongly characterological understanding of sexual assault, and in turn reinforces that view. This is one reason some feminists remain critical of the way in which the anti-rape movement allied itself with groups advocating tough-on-crime policies, and uncomfortable with the dominant role that criminal prosecutions have come to play in the anti-rape agenda. There are other reasons, as well. One is the persistence of racial biases in rape prosecutions: not only the disproportionate rate at which men of color are prosecuted and the disproportionately heavy sentences they receive, but also the tendency of the system, even today, to respond more forcefully when rape victims are white. There is evidence, as well, that draconian penalties for sexual assault, together with registration and notification requirements, can make prosecutors more reluctant to charge "non-stereotypical" rape cases—cases not involving a physically violent attack by a stranger—and juries less willing to return guilty verdicts in such cases.[29] And there has always been a strand of feminist thinking that is skeptical of coercive state power in general; part of the point of feminism, from this perspective, is precisely to imagine more cooperative modes of social organization, including different ways of responding to violence.

Understanding rape as violence was key to the achievements of the anti-rape movement. But the latter history of the anti-rape movement is partly a history of increasing worries about the role that ideas about violence have come to play in rape law: ideas about the significance of violence in identifying and understanding rape; related ideas about how to define violence, or "force," in the definition of rape; and ideas about the nature of sexual violence, whether to see it as dispositional or cultural. The history of domestic violence law has followed a similar pattern: an early insistence of the *violent* nature of domestic abuse, followed by later worries about making violence too significant or defining it too narrowly. And in the areas of domestic violence, too, there has been a swing toward understanding violence as strongly rooted in the character of offenders.

The Violence in Domestic Violence

Domestic violence, as a conceptual category and an object of legal reform, emerged in the 1970s. Like the anti-rape movement, which in many ways served as its model, the domestic violence movement grew out of second-wave feminism.[30] Feminists in the 1970s saw rape as a manifestation of the same culture of patriarchy that let men hit their wives with impunity. Legally, assaults within the home were criminal; unlike rape laws, assault laws had no spousal exception. The old common-law rule allowing husbands to physically discipline their wives was abolished by the early twentieth century. But practice differed from theory. Police were reluctant to intervene in domestic disputes, beyond separating the parties to allow tempers to cool, and prosecutors rarely filed criminal charges for spousal assaults that weren't fatal.[31]

As with rape, the early responses by second-wave feminists to domestic violence did not primarily take the form of efforts at law reform. In the late 1960s and early 1970s, feminists who focused on domestic violence created shelters for abused women and mounted public education campaigns, often through consciousness-raising groups housed in the shelters. The efforts in this period were aimed at bodies and minds: providing sanctuary to women fleeing abusive home lives, and changing the way assaults on women inside the home were understood, including by the victims themselves. In the words of one activist, the movement sought "to name the hidden and private violence in women's lives, declare it in public, and provide safe havens and support." The very use of the term "domestic violence" served to identify physical assaults on women inside the home as *violence*, and to connect them conceptually with assaults outside the home. (Until the 1970s the phrase "domestic violence" had referred to violence that was "domestic" as opposed to international: riots or insurrection within the boundaries of the United States.)[32]

Stressing the violence in domestic violence suggested inescapably that it should be treated more like assaults by strangers: treated, in other words, like a crime. And like the anti-rape movement, the domestic violence movement in the 1980s found itself in uneasy alliance with law enforcement agencies and "tough on crime" conservatives, calling for more arrests, more prosecutions, and more punishment of men who assaulted their wives and girlfriends. The calls were successful. Many jurisdictions around the country mandated arrest in domestic violence cases, barred prosecutors from dropping the cases, authorized longer sentences, and loosened rules of evidence to make convictions easier to obtain, even when victims declined to testify.[33] States and localities also made it easier for women to obtain civil protection orders, requiring abusers to stay away from their victims. If the abuser and the victim lived together, the protection order required the abuser to move out. Even when the victim did not seek a protection order, courts began to issue them in criminal cases, as conditions of a defendant's pretrial release. Violations of protection orders—both civil protective orders, sought by victims, and criminal protective orders, sought by prosecutors—were themselves prosecuted as crimes, typically as misdemeanors.[34] At the federal level, the Violence Against Women Act of 1994 provided funding for battered women's shelters and established a National Domestic Violence Hotline, but it also established new federal crimes and higher penalties for intimate assaults, and grants to support state and local prosecution of domestic violence cases.[35]

Domestic violence appears to have declined since the 1980s, despite an upturn during the 2020 coronavirus pandemic when many victims found themselves isolated at home with their abusers. But it is unclear how much of the credit for the long decline, if any, should be given to the increase in arrests and prosecution, as opposed to the aging of the American population—older women are assaulted less often—and to improvements in legal services provided to victims.[36] The more aggressive use of arrests and prosecutions in domestic violence cases has been controversial from the start, including and maybe particularly among feminists. The turn toward criminal law has been criticized for taking agency away from victims of domestic violence, including in ways that may endanger them. Mandatory arrest policies have often resulted in both parties to domestic disputes being arrested. An influential study in the early 1980s, which suggested that mandatory arrest policies decreased reoffending by perpetrators of domestic violence, proved difficult to replicate; later studies suggested that arrests might actually increase recidivism. "No drop" policies, requiring prosecutors to move forward with domestic violence cases even over victims' objections, can coerce victims into providing evidence against their abusers even when it may provoke further violence, and may discourage some victims from reporting their abuse in the first place. Mandatory arrest policies can have these effects, too. Protection orders, and their criminal enforcement, have been called a form of "state-imposed de facto divorce." And both the victims and the offenders entangled in the criminal justice system by virtue of all of these policies tend disproportionately to be poor and members of racial minorities. The criminalization of domestic violence has therefore been criticized, including by some feminists, for worsening the racial inequity of the criminal justice system more broadly.[37]

Not all critics of "carceral feminism" object to emphasizing the *violence* in domestic violence; some, as we will see, value the focus on violence as a way to *limit* the criminalization of domestic abuse. Conversely, many supporters of more aggressive use of arrests and prosecutions for victimization within intimate relationships have had their own second thoughts about the term "domestic violence" and the focus of attention on physical attacks. Researchers and activists increasingly suggest that focusing on violence is reductive. The central problem in abusive relationships, they argue, is domination and exploitation; physical assaults are just one way that control is exercised, and not necessarily the most harmful way. There is an increasing focus on psychological forms of abuse, which sometimes, but not always, are linked to the threat of physical violence.[38]

This has led to suggestions that the concept of violence should be broadened to include "emotional violence," and accordingly that laws and programs targeting domestic violence should be broadened to address psychological as well as physical abuse. In the United Kingdom and in Ireland, "controlling or coercive" conduct by a spouse or intimate is now a separate crime. There have been calls, largely unsuccessful so far, for similar legislation in the United States.[39]

Just as some feminists and domestic violence activists in the 1980s entered into an uneasy alliance with law enforcement groups and "tough on crime" conservatives, opposition to expansive criminalization of domestic abuse now draws together an awkward coalition of decarceration advocates and cultural conservatives. In 2018 the US Department of Justice changed the definition of "domestic violence" on its website, eliminating language that included "emotional," "economic," or "psychological abuse" aimed at controlling an intimate partner. The new definition limited the category of domestic violence to "felony or misdemeanor crimes of violence" committed within a household, family, or intimate relationship. The Trump Justice Department's new, narrow definition of "domestic violence" did not reflect uneasiness with mass incarceration or with racial inequities in arrests and prosecutions. It reflected uneasiness with feminism, or perhaps with government bureaucracy, or with government bureaucracy in the service of feminism.[40]

Understanding Domestic Violence

The domestic violence movement did not simply name and publicize the violence women experienced from intimate partners; it provided a set of ideas about how to understand that violence and respond to it. The ideas came in two packages: the cycle of violence, and the power and control wheel. Both sets of ideas have been widely and lastingly influential.

The cycle of violence (Figure 5) was proposed by psychologist Lenore Walker at the end of the 1970s. Her idea was that the marriages and

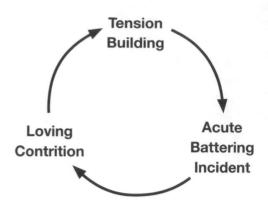

FIG. 5 A representation of Lenore Walker's "cycle of violence" theory.

intimate relationships within which domestic violence occurs have a particular, repeated dynamic. An explosion of violence is followed by a period of contrition and displays of affection, during which the abuser apologizes and reconciles with the victim; the contrition phase is followed by a tension-building stage, in which the abuser becomes angry and the victim tries to avoid provoking him; the escalating tension eventually triggers another explosion of violence; and the cycle repeats itself. Walker thought that women stay in relationships of this kind because the cycle of violence creates a form of learned helplessness. She called the problem "battered woman syndrome."[41]

Beginning in the 1980s, expert testimony about battered woman syndrome, often from Walker herself, began to be offered in criminal trials in support of self-defense claims raised by women who had killed their abusive husbands. The point of the testimony was to explain why the women didn't leave their partners while they had a chance. Some defendants also relied on Walker's theory to explain why their attacks on their abusers should be deemed justified or excusable, even if the next explosion of violence directed at the defendant might not seem to have been "imminent," in the sense that the legal doctrine of self-defense traditionally required. Courts were initially hostile to admitting expert testimony about battered woman syndrome, but that soon changed, in some states by judicial decree, in others by virtue of statutory enactment. Some courts also began to instruct juries that they should assess the reasonableness of the defendant's actions from the vantage point of a "reasonable battered woman," not a "reasonable person" in the abstract. Later, evidence about Walker's cycle of violence was admitted in support of duress claims advanced by women who testified that they had been battered. Prosecutors themselves began to introduce expert evidence about battered woman syndrome in cases against men accused of domestic violence.[42]

Despite the wide influence it continues to exert, the theory of battered woman syndrome has been heavily criticized, including by some feminists. Some of the criticism has to do with perceived weaknesses in the evidence supporting the theory. Some has to do with Walker's language: describing victims of domestic violence as passive and "helpless," and using the term "syndrome" to describe what some argue is a set of circumstances, not a psychological condition. Some of the criticism has to do with the claimed universality of the theory: even if it accurately describes some abusive relationships, it may not offer insight into all of them. This is true even if domestic violence is understood, as it traditionally has been understood, as mainly a problem about women victimized by men. But battered woman syndrome, and the law of domestic violence more generally, has also been faulted for ignoring the dynamics of battering in same-sex relationships, and the experiences of men abused by women.[43]

Moreover, whatever its merits, battered woman syndrome is a theory about abusive relationships and why battered women stay in them. It is not a theory about where violence comes from: what drives men to be batterers, and how they can be reformed. Walker's focus was the women in abusive relationships, not the men who abused them.

In this respect the cycle of violence is perfectly complemented by the power and control wheel (Figure 6), the central component of the Domestic Abuse Intervention Project developed in the early 1980s in Duluth, Minnesota. The "Duluth Model" is a treatment program for batterers, the most widely emulated program of its kind. When courts order men who have battered their spouses or girlfriends to participate in a violence prevention program, more often than not it follows the approach of the Duluth Model. The heart of the curriculum is the power

FIG. 6 The Duluth Model's "power and control wheel." (Reprinted with permission of Domestic Abuse Intervention Programs.)

and control wheel, a diagram summarizing the theory of domestic violence on which the Duluth Model is based.[44]

Despite its circular form, the power and control wheel does not describe a cycle. It is meant to be read from the outside in. The most basic feature of domestic abuse is physical and sexual violence, represented by the outer band of the power and control wheel. The hub of the wheel is power and control: what batterers use physical and sexual violence to obtain. And between the outer band and the hub of the wheel is a series of spokes representing tactics that abusers combine with physical and sexual violence to maintain power and control: coercion and threats, intimidation, economic abuse, emotional abuse, isolation, strategic use of the couple's children, male privilege, and "minimizing, denying and blaming."[45]

The Duluth Model thus understands domestic violence as an instrument of male domination, and it is consistent with the idea that domestic violence is fundamentally about power. The United States doesn't have a freestanding crime of coercive control in intimate relationships, but the prevailing approach to treating the perpetrators of domestic violence in the United States is predicated on the understanding that domination is at the heart of the offense.

Like Walker's cycle of violence, the Duluth Model has its critics. As with battered woman syndrome, some of the criticism of the Duluth Model pertains to its empirical support. Experimental proof of the program's effectiveness is thin. Beyond its evidentiary basis, the model's emphasis on male domination has struck some critics as heavy-handed and bullying. The curriculum has been accused of stereotyping and vilifying offenders: treating "all domestic violence misdemeanants . . . as potential O. J. Simpsons—purposeful, controlling, strategic, and ultimately murderous in their use of violence." Part of the point of the Duluth Model is to contextualize domestic violence by situating it in the general culture, but in practice, its critics say, it has demonized offenders instead, reverting to a dispositional rather than situational understanding of intimate abuse. (Many states have evidentiary rules that make it easier to introduce evidence of a defendant's prior wrongdoing in domestic violence cases than in other criminal cases—something that a range of jurisdictions, including the federal courts, also do for sexual assault and child molestation. Those rules, too, have been criticized for taking an excessively dispositional view of domestic violence.)[46]

Like Walker's cycle of violence, the Duluth Model has also been called essentializing and reductive. Critics complain that it treats all domestic violence as heterosexual, with male perpetrators and female victims, and that it treats all male-on-female domestic violence as having the same logic. (That charge has been made, as well, against rules allowing liberal use of propensity evidence against defendants charged with domestic violence.) One issue that has always hovered in the background of domestic violence law is to what extent domestic violence should be understood as *violence,* plain and simple. That issue winds up having several different strands. One is how *central* violence is to domestic violence: whether emotional and psychological abuse is as damaging and deserves as much attention as physical assaults. A second question is to what extent the violence in domestic violence has its own distinctive profile—whether, like rape, domestic violence is "particularly sexual in character." A third question is whether, if domestic violence *is* distinctive, what makes it distinctive is patriarchy—and if so, how we should think about violence within same-sex relationships, or violence inflicted by women on their husbands or partners. A fourth question is how important it is to make distinctions within the category of domestic violence—between heterosexual and same-sex relationships, between male violence and female violence, or between other subcategories that differ in fundamental ways. A fifth and final question is the inverse of the first one: not how central violence is to domestic violence, but how central domestic violence is to violence more generally.[47]

Violence, Domestic and Otherwise

It may be a mistake to see domestic violence as just one particular kind of violence. Instead, perhaps, we should see the problem of domestic violence as the problem of violence, full stop, but viewed from a particular angle, with home and intimate partnerships in the foreground. A very large percentage of violence is "domestic": nearly half of all women killed annually in the United States are killed by husbands, boyfriends, and former husbands and boyfriends; and most sexual assaults are committed by perpetrators who know their victims. Furthermore, domestic violence is often closely linked with forms of violence we do not ordinarily think of as domestic. More than half of all mass shootings, for example, begin with the killing of a partner, former partner, or family member. It is possible that police violence, too, is linked with domestic violence: rates of spousal and partner abuse are unusually high among police officers.[48]

Even aside from these chains of causation, the lessons learned about domestic violence, like those learned about sexual assault, may be applicable to violence more generally. If substantive criminal law has erred by placing too much weight on the category of violence, and criminal procedure has erred in the opposite direction, the legal treatment of domestic violence, like the policing and prosecution of rape, illustrates both dangers. The violence inside households and intimate relationships was long overlooked; it wasn't treated as real violence. The first task of domestic violence activists, like the first task of rape law reformers, therefore was—and remains—to make a particular form of violence more visible, to insist that it be treated as *violence*. But just as with rape, an excessive emphasis on the *violence* in domestic violence proved limiting. Focusing only on physical assaults can mean ignoring related forms of abuse within households and relationships.

The emphasis that the Duluth Model places on power and control is one way to avoid this second kind of myopia. That focus resonates with the increasingly influential feminist understanding of rape culture as a dimension of patriarchal authority and dominance. And this is a perspective that some feminists have long suggested should be applied to violence more broadly. The feminist scholar Gloria Watkins, publishing under the name bell hooks, has been particularly emphatic on this score. She has argued that all violence is linked to domination, and that anti-rape activism and domestic violence activism should be viewed as just one part of a larger movement against all violence. And once you start looking, it is not difficult to see the theme of power and control in other forms of violence. In 2020, for example, when President Trump urged state and local law enforcement agencies to use more force—including deadly force—in response to the unrest triggered by recent police killings, he said it was necessary to "dominate" protesters, because "if you don't dominate, you're wasting your time." (In the following days several commentators noted that "dominate" seemed to have become the president's favorite word.) It may be too sweeping to treat *all* violence as being about power and control, but that lens might still help us understand a good deal about violence outside the context of households and intimate partnerships.[49]

Domestic violence also offers lessons for the debate between characterological and situational understandings of violence. The most widely used tool for estimating the risk that a victim of domestic violence will be killed by her partner, the Danger Assessment, takes into account some of the partner's general characteristics—for example, whether he abuses drugs or alcohol—but focuses most attention on the history of his interactions with the victim, and on a range of situational factors, such as whether he owns a gun, whether he is out of work, and whether the victim has a child that is not the child of her partner. The Danger Assessment thus serves as a warning against understanding violence as being wholly a matter of individual disposition or wholly a matter of circumstances. And downplaying situational factors can make it harder, not just to evaluate the risk that domestic violence will turn lethal, but to recognize domestic violence in the first place. Like rapists, perpetrators of domestic violence can escape detection when they seem too normal and do not match preconceptions of what a violator will look like.[50]

While it can therefore be a mistake to distinguish too sharply between domestic violence and other forms of violence, we can err, as well, by failing to draw distinctions within the category of domestic violence. There are particular forms of physical assaults on wives and girlfriends that appear to be especially predictive of later lethal attacks—including, possibly, mass shootings. This appears to be true, notably, of strangulation. And researchers increasingly emphasize that not all domestic violence follows the same patterns: some domestic violence fits the coercion and control narrative at the heart of the Duluth Model, whereas other domestic violence (particularly, in many cases, violence by women) is more episodic and circumstantial, reflecting a loss of control rather than bullying and domination. Domestic violence intervention programs may be more effective if they are more tailored.[51]

Legal scholars, like naturalists, historians, and linguists, like to talk about "lumping" and "splitting," two complementary tools for organizing the world. Lumping involves grouping together things that might otherwise seem unrelated; splitting involves drawing distinctions within a category that might otherwise appear uniform. Both tools are indispensable. The trick is to use them wisely and deliberately.

Debates about rape and domestic violence over the past few decades have been, to a significant extent, debates about lumping and splitting. The insistence that rape is a crime of violence, and the creation of the category of domestic violence, were exercises in lumping: necessary, overdue recognition of the terror and physical brutality that links sexual and domestic assaults with other acts of violence. But the "particularly sexual" nature of rape matters, too, and so does the intimate context of domestic violence. Rape and domestic violence are in some ways just like other physical attacks, and in some ways different. We need to hold both truths in our heads at the same time.

Lumping rape and domestic assaults into the category of violence splits them off from coerced sex and forms of intimate abuse that are not violent, or that are violent only if we expand the definition of that term to include psychological, emotional, and economic persecution. That expansion can be helpful. It allows us to see the degree to which forms of rape and domestic abuse that are not conventionally "violent" can nonetheless share some of the evil of violent sexual assaults and domestic violence as it has more conventionally been understood. It can also allow us to appreciate the ways in which violent and nonviolent forms of victimization can feed off each other—for example, how physical assaults, emotional manipulation, and economic pressure can work together in an abusive relationship.

For other purposes, though, it still can be important to distinguish domestic abuse that takes the form of violence, in the traditional sense of physical assault, actual or threatened. The line isn't always sharp. Sometimes what is called "psychological violence" involves explicit or implied threats of physical force—pointedly cleaning a gun, for example, to establish an atmosphere of intimidation. Still, it may be worth preserving a distinction between domestic violence, actual or threatened, and other forms of relationship abuse. One reason to preserve that distinction is precisely that it sharpens the connection between rape and domestic violence, on the one hand, and other forms of violence, on the other.

5 | Violence and Youth

Lord of the Flies—that massively influential staple of high school English classes—concludes with a scene of mutual incomprehension. When the schoolboys are finally rescued from the island where they have been marooned, the naval officer who discovers them can't fathom how they descended to fratricide. It seems to him that they had a great adventure. Meanwhile one of the boys, Ralph, weeps for "the end of innocence" and "the darkness of man's heart." He can't see the glamour in any part of what he and the other boys have been through. The reader is on Ralph's side, of course; the naval officer's perplexity underscores the book's central lesson. Exactly what that lesson is remains controversial, but it plainly has something to do with violence and how a group of children— or at least a group of boys—can turn savage. The officer's bafflement is connected to the novel's perennial appeal. It's not incidental that the castaways are young people. There is something about violence among juveniles that seems particularly shocking, or particularly telling, or both.[1]

Just as the legal response to rape and domestic assault reflects ideas about violence as well as ideas about sex and gender, the legal response to youth violence has been shaped both by beliefs about children and adolescence and by ideas about the nature, significance, and definition of violence. The legal response to youth violence, and to juvenile offending more generally, has changed significantly over the past several decades. Those changes and the lessons they offer are the subjects of this chapter.

For most of the twentieth century, minors who committed crimes were tried and sentenced not in regular criminal courts but in separate juvenile courts, and they were incarcerated, if at all, not in regular prisons but in separate juvenile facilities, and typically for less time than adult offenders. Juvenile courts were invented in Illinois at the close of the nineteenth century, and the innovation soon spread not only throughout the United States but around the world. These courts aimed not at retribution but at rehabilitation, or at least at giving young offenders a chance to mature out of delinquency. In the 1980s and 1990s, though, many juvenile offenders, especially those who had committed "violent" crimes, were prosecuted as adults and sent to adult prisons, for decades or for the rest of their lives. At the same time, schools around the country announced "zero tolerance" for violations of disciplinary rules, particularly rules against violence. Instances of physical bullying that were once dismissed as age appropriate, at least for boys, now became grounds for suspension. Like the prosecution and punishment of minors as adults, the more aggressive use of school disciplinary sanctions was part of what law professor Barry Feld calls the "Get Tough Era" of juvenile justice. The policies implemented in that period were fueled in large part by an increase in violent crimes carried out by minors, and by the fears this fed of "superpredators" and a coming "bloodbath of violence."[2]

In one sense that era has never really ended: many of the policies enacted in the 1980s and 1990s are still on the books. But beginning in the early 2000s, courts and legislatures began to sour on the get-tough approach to juvenile offending. This happened for several reasons. First, and probably most important, rates of youth violence declined sharply; the generation of superpredators never materialized. Second, advocacy groups brought increasing attention, not just to the harshness of the new policies, but to the glaring racial disparities they had produced. The tougher sanctions were imposed disproportionately on minority boys, and to a lesser extent on minority girls. Zero-tolerance polices had created a "school-to-prison pipeline," and the children and adolescents sent into the pipeline were, again, disproportionately students of color, particularly boys. Third, scientists found new evidence that human brains are not fully developed until early adulthood, and that the parts of the brain responsible for higher-order thinking and self-control are the last to conclude their maturation. Fourth, partly relying on these developments in brain science, the Supreme Court ruled in a series of cases that the Constitution did not allow the imposition of the death penalty for juvenile offenses, did not permit sentences of life without possibility of parole for non-homicide crimes committed by juveniles, and prohibited the mandatory sentencing of juveniles convicted of homicide to life without possibility of parole. Feld and other scholars of juvenile justice credit these decisions with sparking a renewed appreciation, at the state and local levels, that juvenile offenders are kids, and that "kids are different."[3]

The embrace of get-tough policies for juvenile offenders in the 1980s and 1990s, and the partial retreat from those policies in the years since, is partly a story of ideas about children and adolescents. The super-predator scare fed on anxieties about monstrous children, long a staple of popular entertainment. Later, scientific research about changeable adolescent brains rang true with courts and legislatures because it reso-nated with common experience. When, for example, the Supreme Court was considering the constitutionality of the death penalty for juvenile offenses, Justice Breyer asked at oral argument whether the new scien-tific evidence "simply corroborated something that every parent al-ready knows"—namely, that teenagers' personalities are not yet "fully formed." Solicitor General Seth Waxman agreed that the research "ex-plains, corroborates, and validates what we sort of intuitively" knew about adolescents.[4]

But if the shifting responses to juvenile offending have been shaped by ideas about childhood and adolescence, they also have reflected and reinforced particular beliefs about violence. The get-tough era was fueled in part by the notion that violence changes everything: that the juvenile justice system was designed for "truants, vandals, and petty thieves" and was not suited for "the violent juvenile offenders of today." There was a sense, too, that "the violent juvenile offenders of today" weren't really juveniles, or at least they weren't children, regardless of their age. Defending the decision to prosecute an 11-year-old murder de-fendant as an adult, a Chicago prosecutor explained in 1977 that "he may be 11 chronologically," but "he's a violent, violent person." That idea—that violent crimes should be handled in criminal court, not in ju-venile court—remains common, although not as common as it once was. In 2019, Oregon made it easier for juvenile court judges to keep juris-diction over teenagers charged with violent crimes, instead of sending them to the adult system. Prosecutors opposed the reform, asking rhetorically—in the words of one district attorney—"which murder, which violent rapist, which violent robber should be dealt with in the juvenile system"?[5]

As elsewhere in the law, the more significant violence becomes, the more it matters how violence is defined. In the same way that the stiff mandatory sentences targeted at adult offenders gradually expanded their footprint as more and more crimes were labeled violent, there was a steady expansion of laws allowing minors to be prosecuted and punished as adults as mounting categories of juvenile offending were moved into the "violence" box from the "truancy, vandalism, and petty thievery" box. Something similar happened, too, with disciplinary codes in schools, as the scope of zero-tolerance policies expanded.

Changes in approaches to juvenile offending have also reflected changes in ideas about the *nature* of violence, and in particular the nature of juvenile violence. The superpredator scare of the 1980s and 1990s was an extreme example of a theory of violence as dispositional rather than situational. The retreat from get-tough policies in juvenile justice has been driven in part by renewed appreciation for the ways in which adolescent violence, like all adolescent offending, can reflect circumstances rather than deep-seated character. The impulsivity of teenagers, and their susceptibility to peer influence, make situational explanations for violence more plausible, as does the fact that so many kids age out of offending.[6]

Race, ever present in discussions about violence, has played a particularly large role in the shifting understandings of youth violence. Children and adolescents of color, particularly when they are implicated in acts of violence, are far more likely than white youth to forfeit their status as minors. This happens in a literal, legal sense when juvenile offenders are prosecuted and punished as adults—something that happens much more often to minority youth. But it also happens at a more fundamental, psychological level. Race plays a troubling, outsized role in determining whether a minor who commits an act of violence is seen first and foremost as a *minor* or as a *violent offender:* as a child or as a superpredator. And on a larger scale, the degree to which juvenile violence is understood as a Black or brown problem has strongly influenced when the problem has been seen as a societal failing, and when as a threat to be contained. In the 1950s, for example, when four white teenagers in Brooklyn were prosecuted for a series of shockingly brutal crimes—which including killing two men for the thrill of it, and kidnapping and whipping two girls—the predominant public reaction was to wonder about the social roots of youth violence. As we will see, attacks attributed to Black teenagers in later decades elicited a very different reaction.[7]

This chapter will focus largely on the legal response to violence committed by minors, but we will give attention as well to ideas about violence *against* minors. Corporal punishment of children, at home and at school, is less common than it used to be. The tide of opinion, both popular and elite, is running against these practices. But physical beatings of children, whether by their parents or by school officials, are hardly things of the past. Corporal punishment in public schools remains legal in a significant minority of states. Every year tens of thousands of children are paddled or beaten by educators, with the full sanction of the law. The subjects of these beatings are disproportionately minority or disabled or both. And while more than sixty countries have outlawed spanking by parents, no American jurisdiction has followed suit, and none appears likely to do so. As a rule, only the gravest assaults on children by their parents or guardians—assaults that result in death or serious bodily harm, assaults that appear sadistic in their infliction of pain or degradation, or assaults that are sexual in nature—are treated as crimes in the United States.[8]

Police officers, in contrast, have no special dispensation to use force against children and adolescents. But neither are there any targeted legal restrictions on officers grabbing, striking, or otherwise assaulting minors. The only rule, for the most part, is the general constitutional ban on seizures that seem under all the circumstances to be "unreasonable." As we saw in Chapter 3, the law of criminal procedure does not distinguish, in general, between violent and nonviolent forms of police misconduct; violence does not have the same significance here that it does in substantive criminal law. One could imagine treating violence against children as different, either for humanitarian reasons or to avoid turning the children themselves violent. But just as the law draws no general distinction between violent and nonviolent police conduct, law enforcement officers who use physical force against minors are not subject to any special rules or any heightened scrutiny. If anything, physical force against minors is likely to be more readily approved by reviewing courts, partly because young people can seem more threatening—stronger and less restrained—than their elders, and partly because of the centuries-old assumption that children and adolescents often need physical discipline.

Youth violence and violence against youth are typically treated as two separate problems, but that may be a mistake. One of the reasons spanking at home and at school has become less popular around the globe is the strong consensus that has emerged among experts on child development that children who are physically disciplined are more likely later to be violent themselves. Scholars have warned that police violence directed at minors can operate similarly—that young people who are physically assaulted by law enforcement officers are more likely to use violence against others.[9] That is one reason to study, side by side, the way the law thinks about violence *by* young people and the way it thinks about violence *against* young people. The other reason is more basic, and it is a set of beliefs that runs throughout this book: that ideas about violence are more complicated and more contingent than we often realize; that ideas about violence, when employed inconsistently, can mask racism and other toxic biases; and that it therefore behooves us to be as thoughtful and reflective as we can be when we talk about violence.

"Old Enough to Do the Crime"

Juvenile justice, as a separate field of jurisprudence and a separate system of social institutions, is more than a century old. It was invented, more or less, at the close of the nineteenth century when progressive reformers opened the Cook County Juvenile Court, directly across the street from Hull House, Chicago's first and most influential settlement home. There had long been correctional institutions designed especially for minors, but the juvenile court was something new; it reflected the belief that children and adolescents who violated the law should be held to different standards and be handled with different procedures than adult offenders. The creators of juvenile courts couched the mission of the new institution in the language of rehabilitation. Instead of punishment, juvenile justice would aim at "saving" children and "making them honest citizens" instead of criminals—or, as Judge Julian Mack put it in an early manifesto for the new courts, "not so much to punish as to reform, not to degrade but to uplift, not to crush but to develop." The law professor and criminologist Franklin Zimring argues that, in practice, juvenile courts rarely placed much emphasis on rehabilitation, in the sense of affirmative efforts to improve an offender's character. Instead, he suggests, the raison d'être of juvenile courts has always been simpler: to keep juvenile defendants out of the adult criminal justice system, where they would likely harden into more serious offenders.[10]

Either way, the notion that juvenile offenders should be adjudicated by separate courts applying separate standards proved remarkably popular. It quickly spread across the United States and around the world. Zimring claims plausibly that no American legal innovation has achieved greater global popularity.[11]

In the last decades of the twentieth century, however, the United States dialed back its commitment to this innovation. Juvenile courts were never abolished, but they were given less to do; many of the cases they previously would have handled were sent instead to regular criminal courts. From their inception, juvenile courts always had the ability to send particular cases to the adult system. This authority typically was reserved for extreme cases, involving especially serious crimes committed by adolescents on the threshold of adulthood. Most violent crimes did not qualify. In the early twentieth century, even homicides were often handled in juvenile courts, at least in some jurisdictions.[12]

This changed in the closing decades of the twentieth century, particularly in the 1980s and 1990s. New laws throughout the United States made it easier to transfer juvenile offenders to regular criminal court, or to handle them there from the outset. Some states lowered the age at which juveniles could be transferred to the adult system, some states—a majority, eventually—mandated transfer for certain offenses, and some states adopted "direct file" laws giving prosecutors the discretion whether to charge certain crimes in juvenile court or adult court. Furthermore, some states—again, eventually a majority—declared that once a juvenile had been convicted in adult court, any future charges against that defendant would also be handled in adult court. Partly as a result of these changes, the number of offenders under age 18 admitted to state prison more than doubled between 1985 and 1997. The rate at which arrestees under 18 wound up being sent to state prison also nearly doubled. And many of the juveniles tried in adult court were punished pursuant to harsh new sentencing laws adopted in the 1980s and 1990s, the laws we examined in Chapter 2.[13]

The major impetus for redirecting so many juvenile offenders to adult court at the end of the twentieth century, and for the mandatory sentencing laws enacted during the same period, was nationwide alarm about increases in violent crime, and youth violence in particular. In the late 1980s, rates of adolescent homicide in urban areas skyrocketed, at a time when homicide rates among Americans aged 25 and older were declining and the number of older adolescents in the United States was also declining. Several academics concluded that a new kind of juvenile offender had materialized and that the situation was likely to get much worse as the aging of the "echo boom"—the children of baby boomers—increased the raw number of adolescents in the United States. The political scientist John DiIulio warned in an influential article that we were about to see an explosion of "juvenile super-predators": "super crime-prone young males," "remorseless" and "radically self-regarding," who "place zero value on the lives of their victims" and who, "as long as their youthful energies hold out" will "murder, rape, rob, assault, burglarize, deal deadly drugs, and get high." The criminologist James Fox predicted that when the young children of the 1990s became adolescents, the United States could face "a bloodbath." Americans, he said, were "sitting atop a demographic time bomb."[14]

Politicians latched onto these fears. Florida congressman Bill Mc-Collum, for example, warned in 1996 that the "predators out there" weren't "children anymore"; they were "the most violent criminals on the face of the earth." Campaigning for her husband's reelection that same year, Hillary Clinton said—in remarks that later came back to haunt her—that "the kinds of kids that are called super predators" had "no conscience" and "no empathy," and that before worrying about "why they ended up that way . . . we have to bring them to heel."[15]

By 1996, though, rates of youth homicide actually had begun to decline, and the rates continued to plummet without interruption for the next ten years, falling by roughly 75 percent. The time bomb never went off. In 2001 a report by the US surgeon general called superpredators a "myth" and concluded that "there is no evidence that young people involved in violence during the peak years of the early 1990s were more frequent or more vicious offenders than youths in earlier years." DiIulio confessed error and regretted that the superpredator theory had proven difficult to retract. "Once it was out there," he lamented, "there was no reeling it in."[16]

How had the predictions been so wrong? Part of the story might be changed circumstances: scholars have variously credited the end of the crack epidemic and its notoriously violent turf battles between rival dealers, the success of environmental regulations that lowered levels of lead in the environment, and the decline in unwanted births that followed the legalization of abortion. Another part of the story, though, was sloppy statistics in the first place. DiIulio and Fox ignored reasons to suspect that the abnormally high rates of youth homicide witnessed in the early 1990s did not, in fact, reflect any underlying change in the characteristics of young offenders, and were likely to regress to historical averages. One of those hints was that the increase in youth homicide in the 1980s and 1990s was not accompanied by rises in other measures of youth violence, and it was entirely an increase in gun homicides. Rates of youth homicide by other means stayed relatively constant, and so did juvenile arrest rates for rape and robbery. Juvenile arrest rates for assault *did* increase in the late 1980s and early 1990s, but so did the corresponding arrest rates for adults, and in both cases the change appeared to be a statistical artifact: police departments appear to have lowered the thresholds for what counted as simple or aggravated assault.[17]

The superpredator theory proved so popular, and so difficult to reel in, because it resonated with what people were ready to believe. It felt right. Rates of juvenile homicide had, in fact, soared in the 1980s and early 1990s, and as always the killings that received the most attention were the most sensational. It was easy to believe that the killers, regardless of their chronological age, were not really "kids." Doubtless this was all the easier because the spike in juvenile homicide, as DiIulio and Fox pointed out, was particularly dramatic in Black, inner-city neighborhoods. Calling the perpetrators "superpredators" turned them into— as Zimring puts it in his retrospective critique of this period—"a separate (and essentially nonadolescent) species." There is something of a tradition of this kind of linguistic transformation. As the criminologist John Laub has pointed out, it is unclear how, if at all, the "superpredators" of the 1990s differed from "the 'serious, violent juvenile offenders' of the 1970s and 1980s and the 'chronic offenders' of the 1960s and 1970s." Zimring agrees. Whenever youth violence appears to be increasing, he concludes, "there is worry that a new, more vicious type of juvenile offender is the cause."[18]

In effect, the superpredator theory distinguished violent juvenile offenders taxonomically, not just from normal children and adolescents, but from juvenile offenders of the past. We were dealing, explained a Chicago prosecutor in 1994, with "a whole new breed." The case for taking them out of juvenile court seemed obvious. Governor Pete Wilson of California voiced the new common sense in 1997: "Juvenile court was not designed to deal with youths who commit serious and violent crime, gang murderers, rapists, carjackers, or kids who carry assault weapons."[19]

"Adult crime, adult time" went one popular slogan; another formulation was "old enough to do the crime, old enough to do the time." Jerome Irons was tried as an adult in Missouri in 1998 and sentenced to fifty years for a burglary and armed assault committed when he was 16; the prosecutor said he wanted to "send a message . . . that if you are going to act like somebody old, you are going to be treated like someone old." The following year Anthony Laster, a mentally disabled 15-year-old, was charged as an adult in Florida for grabbing $2 of lunch money from a classmate; the state attorney defended the decision on the ground that any "violent juvenile crime" should be treated as an "adult crime committed by a juvenile."[20]

"Adult" crime thus was often understood to mean "violent" crime. A spokesman for the state attorney who charged Anthony Laster made this explicit: the office drew the line, he said, "where there is a threat of physical violence." The following year, when the same state attorney charged a 13-year-old with first-degree murder, he defended his decision on the ground that "murder is an adult crime just being committed by someone in a 13-year-old body." Similarly, when legislators in the 1980s and 1990s began to make it easier, and in some cases mandatory, to prosecute juveniles as adults, the principal focus was on violent crimes. Inevitably, though, the category of "adult" crimes expanded, and by the end of the 1990s many states had either categorically removed from juvenile court any minors charged with certain property and drug offenses or had given prosecutors discretion to charge these cases in criminal court. Nearly 40 percent of all juveniles tried as adults in the nation's largest counties in 1998 were charged with property, drug, or public order offenses. More than three-quarters were Black or Latino.[21]

The understanding of children and adolescents as superpredators did not only provide the basis for prosecuting minors as adults; it also influenced the sentences handed down. Moving minors to adult court exposed them to adult sanctions, including, in some cases, long mandatory minimum terms, life sentences without possibility of parole, and the death penalty. Judges typically had discretion in sentencing juveniles who had been charged and convicted as adults, and it might be expected that youth would be treated as a mitigating factor. That undoubtedly happened in many cases. Overall, though, there is considerable evidence that in the last decades of the twentieth century, youth became an *aggravating* factor in criminal sentencing. Juveniles tried as adults received, on average, significantly longer sentences than older defendants convicted of similar offenses.

Some of this may have been due to a selection effect: when judges or prosecutors had discretion whether to keep a case in juvenile court or transfer it to adult court, the cases transferred tended to be the ones that elicited less sympathy and more outrage. But even after controlling for case characteristics, social scientists found that juveniles tried as adults in the 1980s and 1990s received harsher sentences than older defendants. "By the mid-1990s," conclude two legal scholars who have studied juvenile homicide prosecutions in this period, "youth had ceased to be a mitigating factor in adult court, and instead had become a liability."[22]

Youthful defendants were, and often still are, treated more harshly for at least three reasons. The first reason is actuarial: young offenders simply have more years of potential offending ahead of them. This is why the sentencing guidelines in some states assign young offenders extra points toward the scores that are then used to calculate their presumptive sentences.[23]

The second reason is that when adolescents commit crimes, they tend do so in groups, not acting alone. That can be taken as a mitigating factor. In fact, when the Supreme Court decided in the early twenty-first century that crimes by adolescents called for special treatment under the Constitution, part of the Court's reasoning was that because teenagers were more susceptible to peer pressure, especially harsh sentences made less sense for them. Not coincidentally, the three cases in which the Supreme Court drew this distinction all involved crimes committed by more than one offender. (More about these cases later.) But criminal law has a long tradition of treating groups of offenders acting together as especially threatening and warranting special sanctions. Moreover, much of the panic about youth violence in the 1980s and 1990s focused on frightening combinations of teenagers: either organized gangs, or "wolf packs" engaged in chaotic "wilding." Kamala Harris, then district attorney of San Francisco, spoke for a generation of law enforcement officials in 2009 when she called gangs "our most serious threats": a "ruthless, toxic . . . form of social cancer."[24]

There is reason to doubt whether many gangs were as organized or as powerful as law enforcement—and often gang members themselves—made them out to be. It is hard here to separate myth from reality, and hard to know when "gang related" crimes were actually *caused* by gangs—when, for example, gangs were making their members violent, as opposed to attracting members who were already violent. Nonetheless, in the closing decades of the twentieth century, anti-gang legislation was passed in all fifty states and at the federal level. Led by California, most states adopted special, heightened penalties for crimes committed by gang members or affiliates—who were, disproportionately, adolescents or young adults. Many, if not most, of those laws are still on the books. In addition to the formal sentencing enhancements available in gang cases, the mere introduction of evidence that the defendant was associated with a gang biased juries in favor of conviction, and may have biased sentencing judges as well. That, too, remains true today. Furthermore, when juveniles convicted of gang crimes, or suspected of gang affiliation, were released on probation or parole, they often were barred from associating with gang members or affiliates; violating those rules could send them back to jail. Again, release conditions of this kind are still commonplace.[25]

There is a final reason youth has been and often still is an aggravating factor in criminal sanctioning. It is the same intuition that made the superpredator theory seem so plausible: the idea that minors who commit serious acts of violence must have something fundamentally wrong with them, that youth violence is particularly likely to be characterological rather than situational. It was clear to Governor Wilson that juveniles responsible for "serious and violent crime" weren't just making mistakes, they were "mak[ing] mistakes a lifestyle." When the state of Missouri sought the death penalty in 1994 against 18-year-old Christopher Simmons for a murder he had committed when he was 17, the prosecutor scorned the suggestion that youth was a reason to spare the defendant's life. "Think about age," he urged the jury. "Seventeen years old. Isn't that scary? Doesn't that scare you? Mitigating? Quite the contrary I submit. Quite the contrary."[26]

The jury may have agreed: Simmons was sentenced to death. A decade later the Supreme Court invalidated his sentence on the grounds that capital punishment for offenses committed by juveniles, even for murder committed by juveniles, was unconstitutionally "cruel and unusual." That decision, as we will see, reflected a significant shift in the understanding of juvenile violence—a return, in a way, to older ideas. Why did it take so long to arrive? One reason is school shootings.

School Shootings, Zero Tolerance, and the School-to-Prison Pipeline

In the middle of the 1990s—right around 1994 or 1995—rates of youth violence in the United States began to decline sharply. By the end of the decade they had returned to the levels of the early 1980s. During the same period, though, there was an increase in what the FBI calls "active shooter" incidents at elementary and secondary schools: episodes in which someone with a gun fires indiscriminately in a populated area in an effort to kill people. Most of the shooters were students or former students at the schools in which the rampages took place. Incidents of this kind remained relatively uncommon, and they were a very small fraction of juvenile homicides, but they received a great deal of media attention—partly because the school setting and the mass, indiscriminate nature of the killings were particularly horrifying, and partly because the rampages occurred in places, and among populations of young people, not usually victimized by gun violence. All of this was true of the most notorious school shooting of the 1990s, the 1999 massacre of twelve students and a teacher at Columbine High School, in the suburban, middle-class, largely white community of Littleton, Colorado. At the time, Columbine was the deadliest school shooting in the nation's history.[27]

One thing the school shootings of the late 1990s did have in common with the surge in youth homicide in the late 1980s and early 1990s was the involvement of guns. Virtually all of the increase in juvenile homicide in the 1980s and 1990s, and virtually the entire drop in juvenile homicide in the late 1990s, involved gun homicides. The killings at Columbine sparked a nationwide debate about gun control, but no major legislation emerged from that debate. Instead, the largest impact that school shootings had on public policy in the late 1990s and early 2000s was to reinforce the kinds of concerns that characterized the superpredator scare: concerns that there was something new and different about contemporary adolescents, that we were seeing a new, more violent breed of juveniles. As a result, the drive to prosecute more minors as adults continued well into the 2000s, long after rates of juvenile violence had plummeted and the superpredator theory had been discredited.[28]

The school shootings of the 1990s also prompted new worries about the physical safety of schools. Those worries, in turn, were addressed in two main ways. The first was a "hardening" of schools: new metal detectors, armed guards, security cameras, and locked gates.[29] The second was a crackdown on violations of school disciplinary rules, including bullying.

There is a very long tradition of treating assaults and physical threats among schoolchildren and adolescents, particularly boys, as an inevitable part of growing up, and possibly even salutary. Part of growing up was learning to take care of yourself, learning not to be a sissy. (That is the idea that the radio host Laura Ingraham was invoking when she taunted a reporter who had complained about being slammed to the floor and punched by a Republican congressional candidate: "Did anyone get his lunch money stolen today and then run to tell the recess monitor?"[30]) Beginning in the 1980s, though, researchers and policymakers began to take bullying seriously. They began to treat it as harmful—among other things, bullied children have higher rates of suicide and a range of mental and emotional disorders—and as a problem to be controlled. These research and policy initiatives began in Scandinavia and were slow, initially, to reach the United States. But concerns about school bullying in the United States rose sharply after Columbine, driven by widespread reports (later contested) that the killers had been bullied.[31]

Not all bullying involves violence. Researchers and policymakers also apply the term to patterns of verbal or "relational" aggression among children or adolescents, in person or over the internet. Physical bullying is more common among boys; girls are more likely to engage in verbal or relational bullying. The good news is that all forms of bullying have decreased over the past twenty years, in the United States and overseas. Much of the success may be attributable to anti-bullying curricula and targeted counseling strategies that have been widely adopted in schools.[32]

Concerns about bullying in the wake of the Columbine shootings also led, though, to policies that proved less successful and in many ways counterproductive: zero-tolerance approaches to school discipline. The language of zero tolerance was first applied to narcotics enforcement strategies in the 1980s, in schools and elsewhere. The idea was that any violation of drug laws, no matter how minor, would be punished. Depending on the context, the punishment could take the form of criminal prosecution, impoundment of sea vessels, or suspension or expulsion of students. Federal legislation in 1994 borrowed the concept of zero tolerance and applied it to school violence, presumptively requiring schools to adopt policies calling for the automatic expulsion of any student found with a gun on campus. By the early 2000s, schools throughout the United States had committed themselves to automatically expelling or suspending students who violated a significantly broader range of disciplinary rules, often including bullying and physical aggression in addition to possession of guns or drugs. Once tolerated as something of a rite of passage, physical fights could now be grounds for mandatory suspension.[33]

Some of these disciplinary policies are still in place, but many have been repealed. Beginning sometime around 2010, a consensus began to form among educators and policymakers that zero-tolerance policies were a mistake. These measures had caused suspensions and expulsions to surge without any detectable effect on school safety. And once students were removed from class, even temporarily, their chances of graduating plunged and the odds dramatically increased that they would find themselves entangled in the criminal justice system. Zero-tolerance policies helped to create, in effect, a school-to-prison pipeline, and a heavily disproportionate number of the students sent into the pipeline were Black or Latino.[34] In 2011 the Obama administration launched a "Supportive School Discipline Initiative," explicitly aimed at disrupting the school-to-prison pipeline by addressing "inappropriate school discipline." In 2014 the US Department of Education directed schools to suspend or expel students only as a last resort, and to guard against racial discrimination in the use of those measures. By then there was a broad, nationwide trend toward reducing the number of suspensions and expulsions, with only a few jurisdictions moving in the opposite direction. Even charter schools—many of which had made zero tolerance for disciplinary violations part of their brand—began to abandon that approach.[35]

That trend appears likely to continue, notwithstanding the political developments of the past several years. In 2018 the Department of Education under President Trump repudiated the guidance it had provided to schools in 2014. The new administration suggested that lax school discipline and excessive concerns about avoiding racial discrimination might be responsible for school shootings, including the massacre of seventeen students and staff members at Marjory Stoneman Douglas High School in Parkland, Florida, in February 2018—even though most school shooters are white, and the shooter in Parkland was a white student who had been expelled. The Trump administration's position underscores the continuing draw of a characterological focus in understanding violence, including juvenile violence. The administration's interdepartmental report in response to the Parkland shooting stressed the importance of "maintaining order in schools" and recommended relying on teachers to watch the "behavioral patterns" of their students and "correct—and where necessary, discipline—those behaviors that are unwelcome or unsafe for the school community." Notably, though, the report did not so much as mention "zero tolerance," nor did it call for greater use of suspensions and expulsions. There is no indication that zero-tolerance policies for school discipline will regain popularity, and most states and localities remain committed to minimizing suspensions and expulsions.[36]

Girls and Violence

Juvenile violence, like adult violence, is largely committed by boys. The superpredator scare was largely about boys, and the overwhelming majority of school shooters are boys. But since the early 1990s, girls have constituted a rising proportion of juveniles arrested for violent crime, and this is particularly true for assaults. In 2015 girls accounted for more than a quarter of all youth arrests for aggravated assault and close to 40 percent for simple assault. The figures in 1990 were considerably lower: close to 15 percent for aggravated assault and 25 percent for simple assault. Most of this change occurred between 1990 and 2005; since then the percentages have stayed roughly constant. Driven largely by changes in arrest rates for assault, the female share of arrests for crimes included in the FBI's Violent Crime Index—homicide, rape, robbery, and aggravated assault—roughly doubled between 1980 and 2005, from close to 10 percent to close to 20 percent.[37]

The growth in the female proportion of juvenile arrests for violent crimes, and for assault in particular, does not appear to reflect any actual increase in violence by girls. It is entirely explained by two other factors: the plunge in the corresponding arrest rates for boys, and a lowering of the threshold for arresting and charging girls with assault. The lowered threshold, in turn, appears to be partly a reflection of the reduced tolerance in general, across genders, for physical bullying and other low-level violence between minors, and partly an unanticipated consequence of efforts to treat domestic violence more seriously. Mandatory arrest policies for domestic violence were adopted largely to protect women from violent partners, but there is evidence that these policies have also resulted in more arrests of girls who get into physical altercations with their parents or siblings. There is no evidence, though, that girls actually became more violent at any point over the past several decades, either inside or outside the home.[38]

Nonetheless, the story about girls' arrest rates for violent offenses offers some important lessons, and those lessons reinforce themes we have encountered repeatedly in this book. The first lesson has to do with the magnetic pull of certain narratives about violence, and particularly, in the modern era, narratives that emphasize characterological explanations of violence and resonate with fears of moral decline. Just as the superpredator narrative spread and proved difficult to dislodge in the 1990s because it seemed so plausible, so did a similar narrative about violent girls in the early years of the twenty-first century. When the arrests of girls for assault began to climb, a good number of observers took this as confirmation of what they already believed: that violence committed by girls was "a burgeoning national crisis." "The change in girls' behavior is overwhelming," said one expert, the author of a book entitled *Sugar and Spice and No Longer Nice*. Girls today, he warned, "are not what people think they are." A decade later—long after girls' arrest rates for violent crimes had begun to fall at the same rate as the corresponding rates for boys—a columnist, voicing what still passed for conventional wisdom in many quarters, claimed without evident fear of contradiction that "female violence is on the rise in a big way," and that "there's something wrong with America's girls."[39]

A second lesson has to do with the slippery definition of violent crime. We often tend to think of violent crime as though it is a category with sharp boundaries; this is part of why it can seem plausible that people who commit violent crimes are themselves in a category apart, that they have something fundamentally wrong with them. As we saw in Chapter 2, though, what counts as a violent crime is often fairly arbitrary. One reason for that is the open-ended ways in which the law defines simple and aggravated assault. Many, probably most, physical attacks aren't charged as assault, and they therefore are not treated as crimes. Furthermore, most attacks that *are* charged as assaults are charged as simple assaults, not aggravated assaults, which means that they do not count as felonies, let alone "violent felonies," and they are not included in the annual FBI Index of Violent Crimes. Police, prosecutors, and juries typically have great discretion in deciding whether something should be treated as a simple assault, an aggravated assault, or not an assault at all. That is why arrests for simple and aggravated assault could spike in the late 1980s and 1990s, even though the number of physical attacks does not appear to have increased. And that is why there could be a surge in the number of girls arrested for assault in the 1990s and early 2000s, without any rise whatsoever in the underlying incidence of violent behavior among girls.

"Children Are Different"

In a series of three cases decided between 2005 and 2012, the Supreme Court ruled that the Fifth Amendment ban on "cruel and unusual punishments" places special limitations on the sentences that can be imposed for offenses committed by juveniles. The number of defendants directly impacted by these decisions is relatively small, but the decisions may be more important for their reasoning than for their holdings. Collectively, they have helped steer the legal treatment of youthful offenders away from the excesses of the get-tough era and back toward the traditional values and assumptions of the juvenile justice system, even in cases of violent crime.

The first of these cases, *Roper v. Simmons,* was decided in 2005. The defendant, Christopher Simmons, was convicted and sentenced to death for a brutal, senseless killing he had carried out with a friend when he was 17. We encountered *Roper v. Simmons* earlier. This was the case in which the prosecutor urged the jury at the sentencing phase of the trial to treat the defendant's youth as an aggravating rather than a mitigating factor. The Supreme Court viewed that argument as obviously improper, but the Justices went considerably further: they used this case as the opportunity to declare that executing a defendant for any crime committed before the defendant reached the age of 18 was "cruel and unusual" and therefore unconstitutional. Five years later, in *Graham v. Florida,* the Court said that a life sentence without possibility of parole was similarly "cruel and unusual," and therefore similarly unconstitutional, when it was imposed for a non-homicide offense committed as a juvenile. Finally, in 2012, the Justices decided in *Miller v. Alabama* that the reasoning of *Graham* applied in homicide cases as well: the Constitution barred a sentence of life without possibility of parole for any offense committed as a juvenile, just as it barred a death sentence for any offense committed as a juvenile.[40]

The direct reach of these three decisions was significant but limited. When the Supreme Court decided *Simmons,* seventy-one convicted defendants—about 2 percent of the death row population nationwide—were awaiting execution for crimes they had committed as juveniles. The Court's decision granted them a reprieve, and it prevented any new death sentences for crimes committed by juveniles. It had no direct application, though, to noncapital cases. For their part, *Graham* and *Miller* mandated only the *possibility* of parole. States were required to provide defendants convicted for juvenile offenses with "some meaningful opportunity" to seek eventual release, but they didn't need to actually let anyone out. By their terms, moreover, *Graham* and *Miller* applied only to a *life* sentence, not to a sentence of years, no matter how long.[41]

The reasoning of these three decisions, though, swept wider than their holdings. All three rested on the idea that, for purposes of criminal punishment, youth mattered. As Justice Kagan put it in her majority opinion in *Miller,* "children are different." Justice Kennedy, who wrote for the Court in *Simmons* and then again in *Graham,* emphasized three particular differences: the impulsivity and poor judgment often shown by juveniles; their greater susceptibility to peer pressure and outside influences; and the fact that their personalities were not yet fully formed. In combination, Justice Kennedy wrote, these factors weighed strongly against any conclusion that a crime committed by a juvenile, no matter how heinous, was proof of an "irretrievably depraved character." In *Graham* Justice Kennedy quoted with approval the conclusion of a lower court that "incorrigibility is inconsistent with youth," and Justice Kagan relied on the same reasoning when she wrote for the Court in *Miller.* In *Simmons* the Court treated the differences between adolescents and adults as largely a matter of common sense, something that "any parent knows." But Justice Kennedy noted in *Simmons* that new research by scientists and sociologists provided additional support for those impressions, and in *Graham* and *Miller* the Court placed even more weight on that research, especially on the findings by psychologists and neuroscientists.[42]

The Supreme Court was sharply divided in *Simmons, Graham,* and *Miller. Simmons* and *Miller* were 5–4 decisions. The vote in *Graham* was 6–3, but one of the six was Chief Justice Roberts, who concurred in the judgment without joining the majority opinion. All three decisions triggered angry dissents. Among other things, the dissenters accused the Court of imposing its own value judgments, and they stressed the artificiality of the cutoff at age 18, or any other sharp line between adolescence and adulthood. They complained, too, about the use of the word "children" to describe older adolescents, especially older adolescents who committed serious crimes.[43]

There was force to some of the objections. It is plainly true that young people mature in different ways and at different rates; even Justice Kennedy's majority opinion in *Simmons* acknowledged that any categorical age threshold would be imprecise. And even some scholars who applauded the Court's decisions in *Miller* objected to Justice Kagan's use of the term "children" to describe older adolescents. Some of those scholars also warned about the hazards of trying to draw normative conclusions from the scientific research highlighted by the Court in *Simmons, Graham,* and *Miller.* Nonetheless, there is broad support among legal scholars and criminologists for the reasoning at the heart of these decisions: the idea that the impetuosity, suggestibility, and incomplete maturation of adolescents calls for treating them differently when they commit crimes, even serious crimes. This was the basis for creating a separate juvenile justice system in the first place, and there is broad support for these ideas, once again, among judges and policymakers. One sign of that support is that several state legislatures and lower courts have extended the reasoning of *Simmons, Graham,* and *Miller* beyond their strict holdings, giving all juveniles with long custodial terms a right to periodic reconsideration of their sentences, or invalidating the application of mandatory minimum sentences to young offenders.[44]

If *Simmons, Graham,* and *Miller* stand for the proposition that "kids are different," they also stand for the position that violence *isn't* different, or at least that it isn't as significant as youth when the two categories overlap. *Simmons* and *Miller* were murder cases, and the defendant in *Graham* was convicted of armed robbery and then had his probation revoked because of his involvement in a home invasion robbery. The Supreme Court concluded, in essence, that when a minor commits a violent crime, even murder, it is still first and foremost a crime committed by a juvenile, and it needs to be treated that way. This was part of what the dissenters found so wrong with these decisions. For dissenters, violence could trump youth. It could even cancel out youth. The dissenters in *Simmons* argued, in part, that at least near the boundary between adolescence and adulthood, an especially brutal crime can justify the conclusion that the defendant had acted with "sufficient moral culpability" to justify execution. Some murders by juveniles, Justice Scalia argued, "are not just the acts of happy-go-lucky teenagers." The dissenters in *Graham* and *Miller* made essentially the same argument about life without possibility of parole. Justice Alito, dissenting in *Miller,* mocked the suggestion that "a 17½-year-old who sets off a bomb in a crowded mall or guns down a dozen students and teachers is a 'child' and must be given a chance to persuade a judge to permit his release into society." Seventeen-year-olds commit lots of murders, he pointed out, and "some of these crimes are incredibly brutal." It just stood to reason, then, that "many of these murderers are at least as mature as the average 18-year-old." Justice Alito was appealing to the same intuition that had led to sending so many juvenile offenders to regular criminal courts beginning in the 1980s and 1990s: serious violence is inconsistent with true juvenility, and therefore juveniles who commit serious violence should be treated the same as adults.[45]

There is some basis for the view that violent juvenile offending differs from other forms of juvenile offending, at least if we reserve the label "violent" for homicide, aggravated assault, and rape. Age-specific rates of arrest for robbery, burglary, theft, and arson all peak somewhere between ages 13 and 18, and they decline rapidly after that. Arrest rates for homicide, aggravated assault, and rape follow a different trajectory: they peak in very late adolescence or early adulthood—the late teens or early twenties—and then decline more slowly. These patterns are consistent with the view that juveniles who commit property offenses are more likely to age out of criminality than those who commit violent crimes. But other evidence suggests that it is artificial to distinguish between violent and nonviolent juvenile offenders, because although some juvenile offenders "specialize" in this way, most do not. Overall, the major connections between juvenile and adult offending are twofold: the vast majority of adult offenders begin offending as juveniles, but the majority of juvenile offenders do not continue to offend as adults. Furthermore, aggravated assaults and homicides by adolescents show the same distinctive pattern as other adolescent crimes: they are committed predominantly by groups of adolescents, not by offenders acting alone. This was true, notably, of the crimes committed by the defendants in *Simmons, Graham,* and *Miller.* That suggests that at least some of the observations the Supreme Court made in *Simmons, Graham,* and *Miller*—the observations about the suggestibility of adolescents and their susceptibility to peer pressure—are no less applicable to violent juvenile offenders, or even to juveniles who commit particularly brutal crimes. And there is no reason to think that the other distinctive characteristics of adolescents stressed by the Court in these cases—their impulsivity and poor judgment, and their unfinished maturation—are any less applicable to violent juvenile offenders.[46]

Violence against Juveniles

The law's ambivalence about violence by juveniles—whether it is ordinary or pathological, whether it is more forgivable than violence by adults or less so—is matched by an ambivalence about violence *against* juveniles. On the one hand, protecting juveniles from violence—even from being *exposed* to violence—is sometimes treated as being of paramount importance, not just because children are "innocents," but because there is good reason to think that children who live with violence are more likely to grow into violent adults. On the other hand, violence against juveniles, at least if it stays within bounds, is often treated as fully excusable, if not actually laudatory. "He that spareth his rod hateth his son," as the Bible has it.[47]

Physical punishment of children is less popular than it used to be, partly because there is mounting evidence that it does little or nothing to improve children's behavior and, over the long run, is apt to make them more aggressive, more antisocial, and more violent. Whipping children and beating them with sticks has long been out of fashion, and elite views have turned against milder forms of physical discipline as well. Expert opinion is solidly against spanking; the American Academy of Pediatrics, for example, recommends against any physical punishment of children. More than sixty countries around the world have outlawed the practice.[48]

No American jurisdiction has followed suit, however, and none appears likely to do so. The Model Penal Code excuses parental assaults on children, no matter how young, as long as there is no substantial risk of "death, serious bodily injury, disfigurement, extreme pain or mental distress or gross degradation." Many state laws go further and allow parents to beat their children as long as there is no danger of grave physical injury or death. (Sexual assaults against children are, of course, a different matter. They are treated as serious crimes. But that is because of their sexual nature, not because of the violence involved.)[49]

Around 70 percent of American adults agree that "it is sometimes necessary to discipline a child with a good, hard spanking." That figure is down from over 80 percent in the mid-1980s, but it has held steady for the past decade. Slightly over half of American parents claim that they never spank their own children, and 28 percent say they do so only "rarely." But fewer than one in five American adults favor outlawing physical punishment of children. And views about spanking vary according to geographical region, educational background, and race. African American parents, in particular, are more likely to report that they spank their children, and more likely to defend physical punishment, even serious beatings, as a form of "tough love," necessary in particular for African American children for whom straying from the straight and narrow, or disrespecting authority figures, can mean winding up dead. Now himself a parent, Ta-Nehisi Coates remembers and understands his father repeating "the old mantra—'Either I can beat him or the police.'" (This is a reminder of the ways different forms of violence that seem unrelated—like police violence and corporal punishment—can in fact be linked; one form of violence can prompt and help to justify another.) Addressing the NAACP in 2009, and receiving a warm response, President Obama spoke fondly of the days when, if parents "saw some kid fooling around and—it wasn't your child, but they'll whup you anyway. Or at least they'll tell your parents [and] the parents will. . . . That's the meaning of community."[50]

There is considerably less support in the United States today for corporal punishment inflicted by teachers and school officials, a form of discipline that is rarer than it was a generation ago. More than seven out of ten Americans oppose allowing teachers and school administrators to inflict corporal punishment on students, and most states have banned the practice in public schools. In private schools, though, the practice remains legal everywhere but in Iowa and New Jersey. Moreover, corporal punishment in public schools is still lawful in nineteen states, and more than 106,000 students were paddled, swatted, or otherwise physically punished in American public schools during the 2013–2014 academic year, the last year for which statistics are available. That was a dramatic decline from a decade earlier, though, when the annual figure was more than twice that high.[51]

Whether the figure will continue to decline so sharply is unclear. The trend toward state bans on corporal punishment in public schools has slowed in the past two decades; no state has outlawed the practice since New Mexico did so in 2011. At this point corporal punishment in public schools is very much a regional practice. Over 96 percent of all children in public schools who were spanked or paddled during the 2013–2014 school year lived in one of nine states: Alabama, Arkansas, Florida, Georgia, Louisiana, Mississippi, Oklahoma, Tennessee, or Texas. Half of all children in Alabama, Arkansas, and Mississippi attend schools that use corporal punishment. Mississippi is the most enthusiastic user of the practice. In 2013–2014, close to 25,000 schoolchildren received corporal punishment in Mississippi: a quarter of the national total, and about one in twenty students statewide.[52]

The Supreme Court last considered the legality of corporal punishment in public schools in 1977, when it decided *Ingraham v. Wright.* James Wright was an eighth-grader in Miami, Florida, who was paddled so hard by his middle school principal that he missed half a month of school and had to make two trips to the hospital. Many observers expected the Supreme Court to use his case to ban corporal punishment in public schools. Instead the Supreme Court upheld the practice, ruling that the Eighth Amendment ban on "cruel and unusual punishments" applied only to *criminal* punishments, and that the due process interests of students were fully protected by the rule, long imposed by common law, that corporal punishment could not go beyond what was "reasonably necessary." The Court was influenced, in part, by the absence of any emerging consensus against corporal punishment in schools. At the time only two states had banned the practice, and polls indicated that most adults supported it. The Justices could "discern no trend toward its elimination."[53]

That trend is more apparent today, but in the intervening decades the Supreme Court has become a much more conservative institution, and it has lost whatever appetite it had for regulating school disciplinary practices. The Justices have declined invitations to reconsider *Ingraham v. Wright*. Lower courts have found that corporal punishment in public schools can violate due process if it goes too far, but it has to go *very* far. The leading decision says that physical punishment of schoolchildren violates the Constitution only when it causes such severe injuries, is so grossly disproportionate, or is so malicious or sadistic that it amounts to "a brutal and inhumane abuse of official power literally shocking to the conscience."[54]

Before leaving the topic of corporal punishment in schools, it is worth noting that the practice disproportionately impacts particular subpopulations of students in troubling ways. That is notably true of minority students. James Wright was African American, as were all the other students at his school, which was notorious for its harsh physical discipline. Today African American children constitute roughly 15 percent of the students in public schools but 38 percent of the students who are paddled, spanked, or struck. Some of this is because Black children are more likely to live in states where the practice is permitted, but even within those states, and even adjusting for frequency and severity of misbehavior, African American children are disproportionately singled out for physical punishment. Corporal punishment is also visited disproportionately on children with disabilities, particularly in some places. Analyzing data collected by the US Department of Education, researchers found that in one-third to one-half of all school districts in Alabama, Arkansas, Georgia, Louisiana, and Mississippi, children with disabilities were more than 50 percent more likely to receive corporal punishment. Statistics of this kind convinced lawmakers in Tennessee and Louisiana to ban corporal punishment for children with disabilities, but not for other children. Boys are spanked, paddled, or struck at school four times as often as girls, but there may be particular reasons to be concerned about the manner in which corporal punishment against girls is carried out, and the way it may appeal to conscious or unconscious sexual fantasies.[55]

Public schools are virtually the only governmental agencies still licensed to mete out corporal punishment. Correctional facilities do not have this authority. Neither do police departments. Strictly speaking, however, this means only that correctional agencies and police departments cannot use force on a person *for the sake of inflicting punishment;* it is far from a ban on violence. We examined the legal rules about police uses of force in Chapter 3, and Chapter 6 will explore how the law thinks about violence in prisons, jails, and other penal and detention facilities. What is worth noting here, though, is that almost none of those rules are specifically targeted at the use of violence against juveniles. There are no special restrictions, for example, on when the police may use force against children or adolescents, or what kinds of force they can employ.

The law sometimes pays a good deal of attention to the way that violence can beget more violence, particularly among children and adolescents. In family and dependency court, parents can lose custody of their children—to their former partners or to the state—not just for treating their children violently, but for allowing their children to *witness* violence, including violence directed at the partner whose custody is at issue. Advocates for abused women have complained that the desire to protect children from exposure to violence, however well meaning, can be carried too far, with the result that abused women can be unfairly punished with the loss of their children, something that often winds up harming the children as well. Some states now specifically bar taking a child away from a domestic violence victim solely on the ground that the child was exposed to the parent's victimization. The consensus view of child welfare professionals is now that the developmental consequences of being exposed to violence vary widely; some children are impacted much less than others. But guarding children against exposure to violence, not just violence itself, remains a central goal of family law and child welfare, in part because of the widespread recognition that being around violence, let alone experiencing violence, can damage young people in a range of ways, including by making them more prone to violence themselves.[56]

That connection often seems lost, though, when the criminal legal system addresses the intersections of violence and youth. There is a set of rules for responding to violence committed by juveniles, and there is a set of rules that govern violence against juveniles, and by and large these two sets of rules are mutually independent, shaped by discourses that do not overlap. This itself may reflect certain assumptions about violence, about where it comes from and how it should be understood, and certain assumptions, too, about youth. When it banned capital punishment for juvenile offenses, and later did the same for life without possibility of parole, the Supreme Court stressed the impulsivity of adolescents, their susceptibility to peer pressure and outside influences, and their unfinished maturation. The Court said that the law has to treat these differences as though they matter. If the Court is right about that, it may mean that the law will need to stop treating violence against juveniles and violence by juveniles as two separate problems. It may mean that the intergenerational cycle of violence—the ways in which children subjected to violent abuse can themselves become violently abusive—should play a larger role in assessing appropriate sanctions for youthful offenders, and in formulating rules about corporal punishment of children in schools and at home.

6 | Prison Violence

One obstacle to thinking clearly about violence is the way violence can crowd out or compete with other dimensions of our shared experience: the idea, for example, that rape is either sex or violence but not both, or the sense that serious violence is incompatible with genuine youth, and that therefore children or adolescents who carry out violent offenses should not be treated as juveniles. Prison violence presents the opposite challenge. Violence in carceral institutions can seem so natural that it can lose its ability to shock. It can seem normal. Prisons become arenas of tolerated violence.

There are other arenas of tolerated violence. Popular entertainment is one of those areas, although the violence in movies, television shows, and video games usually is fictional. As discussed in Chapter 1, many competitive sports also provide, quite literally, arenas of permissible violence, and the violence in a sport like boxing, football, or hockey is real, not imaginary. But the violence in sports is constrained by rules: even in "mixed martial arts," knives and guns are off-limits. And sports violence is at least nominally consensual for the participants. The violence that is tolerated behind bars goes much further.

This chapter will explore the complicated roles that violence plays in the legal regulation of prisons and jails, as well as the more general idea of arenas of permissible violence. Formally, violence against persons in custody is categorically off-limits. As an official matter, corporal punishment doesn't exist in the United States, leaving aside the gaping exception of the death penalty. Outside the context of capital punishment, the constitutional ban on "cruel and unusual punishments" is understood, almost universally, to disallow striking or otherwise physically assaulting someone as a criminal sanction. The same constitutional ban, imposed by the Eighth Amendment, can also be violated by failures to protect people locked up in jails and prisons from assaults by their fellow inmates, at least when those failures manifest "deliberate indifference." We punish people for crimes by removing them from society and depriving them of liberty, not by causing them physical injury or corporal pain. That is the theory.

In practice, though, jails and prisons are notoriously violent. Moreover, the violence often seems tacitly accepted, if not actively encouraged. Vulnerability to assault has long seemed an almost ordinary component of incarceration—part of how a prison sentence works, and what it has come to mean. This is particularly true of sexual assault. The cultural understanding of prison rape has changed in recent years; it is not quite the object of mirth in popular culture that it used to be. Nonetheless, the social response to sexual assault in prison remains ambivalent. It is formally condemned but often, in practice, treated as being far less serious than sexual assault outside of carceral institutions. To some extent this is true more generally of violence behind bars. Officially, physical assault is as serious a crime in prison as it is in the outside world. Unofficially, though, violent crimes in prison are often treated as though they do not entirely count.

The ambiguous legal treatment of violence in jails and prisons is linked to a debate about the nature and origins of that violence: what it is that makes carceral institutions so dangerous. One well-established view is that prisons are brutal and sanguinary because of the people who are sentenced to serve time in them. In a frequently quoted opinion, Judge Frank Easterbrook of the United States Court of Appeals for the Seventh Circuit wrote that "prisons are dangerous places" because "they place violent people in close quarters." He explained that "those who have difficulty conforming to society's norms outside prison may find obedience no more attractive inside—and the threat of punishment is diminished for one already serving a long term."[1]

The reality of prison violence, we will see, is more complicated. Many prisons are horrifically violent, but many others are not. Nonetheless, the *idea* of prisons as dangerous places, and of prisoners as inherently violent, plays a pervasive, outsized role in how prisons and prisoners are understood, both by the public and by courts and legislatures. If prisons are dangerous because the people sent to prison are dangerous, then to a great extent prison violence seems unavoidable. "Some level of brutality and sexual aggression," Judge Easterbrook explained, ". . . is inevitable no matter what the guards do."[2] Moreover, if the violence in a prison is the fault of the people locked up there, their victimization can seem less serious: they are not "innocents." And violence in prisons can validate the need not just for restrictive conditions of incarceration, but for punitive criminal justice policies more generally: aggressive policing, for example, and long mandatory sentences. If crimes are committed by people who are, by their nature, violent, the violence of the law seems more justified. Tit for tat.

There is a different way to understand carceral violence, though—another long-standing explanation for why jails and prisons are dangerous. Perhaps prisons make prisoners violent, as opposed to the other way around. This theory finds some support in how widely rates of violence vary from one prison or jail to another, and how they have fluctuated over time. And if this theory is accepted, it carries different implications for how the legal system should respond to violence behind bars.

The word "prison" usually refers to an institution for long-term incarceration; a "jail" typically is used to lock someone up for a shorter period—pending trial, or to serve a sentence of a year or less. Most prisons are run by states; most jails, by local governments. But the lines can be blurred. Since 2011, for example, jails in California have held many people serving long, multiyear sentences. In this chapter I will sometimes use the words "prison" and "imprisonment" to refer to incarceration more generally.

More than 100,000 people in the United States are locked up in facilities *other than* prisons or jails: immigration detention centers, juvenile halls and "camps," and psychiatric hospitals. Immigration detention centers hold more than juvenile and psychiatric facilities combined. I will focus here on violence experienced by the more than two million people incarcerated in American prisons and jails, but much of what I will say also applies to other locked institutions.[3]

Prison Violence: In Theory

The Supreme Court has never actually held that striking or otherwise assaulting a prisoner violates the Eighth Amendment's ban on "cruel and unusual punishments," but for the past half century lawyers and judges, including the Justices of the US Supreme Court, have largely assumed this is the case. The leading authority for this proposition is a frequently cited Court of Appeals decision, authored in 1968 by then-Judge Harry Blackmun, which banned the use of the strap as a disciplinary tool in Arkansas prisons. The decision has come to stand for the broader rule that prisoners cannot be punished corporally, or at least for the "general abandonment" of that practice. The one, glaring exception is capital punishment, which remains constitutional. It is noteworthy, though, that the primary means of execution today is lethal injection, a method designed to downplay the violence of the death penalty. The use of lethal injection is one part of the dramatic, centuries-long shift away from punishments that make a spectacle of violence toward punishments that consist, at least in theory, of deprivations of liberty, not bodily assaults.[4]

The death penalty has long been deeply controversial. But no one defends corporal punishments for criminal offenses, or for violations of prison rules. As we saw in Chapter 5, corporal punishment of schoolchildren remains constitutional and is practiced in some parts of the United States. Outside the school context, however, the use of bodily violence for official disciplinary purposes is not simply assumed to be unconstitutional; it has become virtually unthinkable. Here is an exception that proves the rule: In 2009, Stephanos Bibas—then a law professor, now a federal appellate judge—wrote a paper with the title "Corporal Punishment, not Imprisonment." He argued that transitory, "nondisfiguring" physical punishments would actually be more humane and less permanently damaging than our current practices of incarceration. Bibas circulated the paper to other scholars and presented it publicly. But he never published it, and he later repudiated the whole idea. During his judicial confirmation process, he told the Senate that corporal punishment of prisoners is never permissible. He renounced it even as a thought experiment, in a disavowal to end all disavowals: "It is wrong and deeply offensive.... [I]t is cruel, and it is un-American.... It is degrading, inhumane, and an affront to human dignity. I categorically, emphatically, and unequivocally reject it."[5]

Violence against prisoners can violate the Constitution even when it is not officially sanctioned. So can other excessively cruel conditions of confinement, such as overcrowding or denial of adequate medical care. For the most part the Supreme Court has said that conditions of confinement violate the Eighth Amendment only if they cause "serious" harm and reflect "deliberate indifference" by prison officials. But when correctional officials use force against inmates, the standard is different: an "unnecessary and wanton infliction of pain" violates the Eighth Amendment even if it does not cause serious harm. Guards responding to a prison disturbance, for example, violate the Eighth Amendment if they use force "maliciously or sadistically," as opposed to "a good-faith effort to maintain or restore discipline." In 2015 the Supreme Court held that any "objectively unreasonable" use of force by jail guards against a pretrial detainee violates the due process clause of the Fourteenth Amendment.[6]

Failing to protect people behind bars from attacks by other inmates can also violate the Constitution. Endorsing the reasoning of lower courts, the Supreme Court has said that "prison officials have a duty ... to protect prisoners from violence at the hands of other prisoners"— especially because prisoners have "demonstrated proclivities for antisocial ... and often violent conduct," and because the state deprives them "of virtually every means of self-protection and foreclose[s] their access to outside aid." Consequently, failing to protect incarcerated people from physical attacks is one of the conditions of confinement that can constitute "cruel and unusual punishment" in contravention of the Eighth Amendment. Like other conditions of confinement, though, it is treated as a violation of the Constitution only if it satisfies two tests: it must be the result of the deliberate indifference of prison officials, and it must have caused serious harm.[7]

Regarding sexual assault in prison, the official legal response is more emphatic, albeit at the statutory rather than the constitutional level. The Prison Rape Elimination Act of 2003—often referred to by its acronym,

"PREA"—was signed into law by President George W. Bush after receiving unanimous approval from both houses of Congress. PREA declares "a zero-tolerance standard for the incidence of rape in prisons in the United States" and expressly aims to "make the prevention of rape a top priority in each prison system." Almost two decades after the statute's passage, its practical effects remain uncertain, for reasons we will explore below. But PREA cannot be faulted for equivocating about the evil of sexual assault in prison. Prison rape, the statutory findings explain, is an "epidemic" and a "day-to-day horror."[8]

Prison Violence: In Practice

Formally, then, the law treats violence in prison as being no less violent, and no less criminal, than violence in the outside world. At the level of practice, though, things are different. Prison violence is notoriously common, and it often seems to be officially tolerated, if not encouraged.

Reliable statistics are difficult to come by, in part because prison violence is drastically underreported. Correctional officials have strong incentives to underreport violence, and prisoners fear retaliation for reporting attacks—retaliation from prison officials for reporting violence by guards, and retaliation from other prisoners for reporting violence by prisoners. Even homicide rates in prison are subject to manipulation; there is reason to believe that a significant but unknown number of prison homicides are erroneously classified as suicides or accidents. For example, a 2019 report by the US Department of Justice on Alabama's state prisons for men found "numerous instances" of deaths that were likely caused by prisoner-on-prisoner violence but were classified by state correctional officials as being due to "natural" causes.[9]

Still, homicide statistics are almost certainly more reliable than statistics on other violent crimes among prisoners, just as they are for the US population more generally. And statistics on prison homicides do not tell a simple story. As American prison populations began to skyrocket in the 1980s, the homicide rate for people behind bars plummeted, from close to 60 per 100,000 before 1980 to between 3 and 4 per 100,000 in the early 2000s. Then the rate began to rise again, reaching 7 per

100,000 in 2012, 2013, and 2014, the most recent years for which national statistics are available. (All of these numbers are for state prisons; federal prisons appear on the whole to have been comparably violent, but they hold vastly fewer people, and as a consequence the number of reported homicides each year is too low to allow calculating a meaningful rate.) The prison homicide rate thus appears to have roughly doubled in recent years, but it remains about 90 percent lower than it was a quarter century ago. Moreover, it is not dramatically different from the general homicide rate in the United States, which has hovered between 4.5 and 5.5 per 100,000 since the year 2000.[10]

These figures, though, obscure as much as they reveal. Although rates of nonfatal physical attacks in prison are much harder to determine than homicide rates, violence in prison appears to be much more commonplace than in society more generally. A landmark survey of more than 7,000 prisoners in 2005 concluded that more than 20 percent had been physically assaulted by other prisoners within the previous six months. This was true for female as well as male prisoners, although most of the attacks on male prisoners involved a weapon and most of the attacks on female prisoners did not. Nearly a quarter of male prisoners reported experiencing physical violence from correctional staff within the previous six months; for female prisoners the figure was slightly over 8 percent. Even adjusting for the socioeconomic characteristics of the victims, physical assaults are more than ten times more common in prison than in the outside world.[11]

Moreover, rates of prison violence—both fatal and nonfatal—vary widely, not just over time but between institutions. Alabama men's prisons provide a chilling example: their homicide rate went from close to zero in 2007 to 35 per 100,000 inmates in 2018—roughly five times the national average in 2012, 2013, and 2014. In 2017 a reporter who toured the St. Clair Correctional Facility in Springville, Alabama, and interviewed current and former inmates, described the facility as "virtually ungoverned." He wrote that "corrections officers disappeared from cellblocks for long periods. Those who were present were often disregarded. With officers absent or ignored, vulnerable inmates, including those who were wounded and bleeding, often pleaded in vain for help, several inmates said. Violence—robberies in dark tunnels, assaults in crowded dormitories, stabbings in cramped cells—was virtually unavoidable." The federal Department of Justice concluded in 2019 that violence was pervasive in Alabama's entire system of men's prisons, comprising thirteen separate institutions, and that there was reason to believe that the state was violating the Eighth Amendment by its deliberate indifference to the problem. The *New York Times* summarized some of what the DOJ found: "One prisoner had been dead for so long that when he was discovered lying face down, his face was flattened. Another was tied up and tortured for two days while no one noticed. Bloody inmates screamed for help from cells whose doors did not lock." During a single week in 2017, the federal investigators reported, Alabama men's prisons were the site of four stabbings, one of which was fatal; five beatings, one with a sock full of metal locks; three sexual assaults; and an arson involving setting fire to a prisoner's bed while he slept. A follow-up report by the Department of Justice in 2020 found that instances of excessive force by guards in Alabama prisons were so common that some officers appeared to view them as unremarkable. Supervisors and other guards would watch guards brutally attacking prisoners and not intervene. Often the attacks were carried out on prisoners who were handcuffed or compliant. The 2020 report linked the pattern of unconstitutional force in Alabama prisons to the same overcrowding and understaffing that contributed to high levels of violence between prisoners. Indeed the DOJ noted that violence between prisoners often led directly to uses of force by guards.[12]

Alabama's prisons are an extreme case, but they are not entirely atypical. Five prisoners were killed in Mississippi in just the first week of 2020. And vulnerability to physical attack is a defining feature of daily life in many, if not most, American correctional institutions. Sexual assault plays a special role here, despite the fact that it constitutes, numerically, a small fraction of prison violence. For decades the danger of being raped by fellow inmates has seemed an implicit, if unofficial, part of what it means to be imprisoned in the United States, particularly for men. Politicians and entertainers joke about it. For especially reviled defendants, the public sometimes seems to rejoice in, or at least to take solace in, the danger of prison rape. And for many incarcerated men, the threat of rape feels ever present. Craig Haney, a psychologist who has spent decades studying incarceration and its effects, says that for many men behind bars the threat of rape operates as a "primordial fear" demanding "hyper-vigilance" and, often, preemptive aggression. Women behind bars—a growing percentage of the prison population—tend to experience a different source of sexual abuse: they are more likely to be victimized by guards than by fellow prisoners. For women as well as for men, though, sexual abuse often seems to be an implied, informal component of prison sentences. The formerly incarcerated writer Chandra Bozelko calls prison rape, of men and of women, "the cultural wallpaper of American correctional facilities."[13]

Most of the sexual abuse of women in prison involves verbal harassment, groping, voyeurism, or "consensual" sex, but rape by force or the threat of force occurs as well. For male prisoners, too, sexual assault appears to be accomplished more often by threats and harassment than by the actual exercise of force, but the threats operate against the background of the "primordial fear" of physical sexual violence.[14]

The actual prevalence of rape and other forms of sexual abuse in prisons and jails is difficult to assess, because much of it goes unreported. This may be particularly true when the victims are men, given the stigma and sense of emasculation associated with being the victim of male-on-male rape. Estimates of the percentage of prisoners experiencing sexual threats or assaults range from a low of 1 percent to upward of 20 percent. When it enacted the Prison Rape Elimination Act of 2003, Congress concluded that at least 13 percent of prison and jail inmates had been sexually assaulted while incarcerated. Certain subpopulations are at elevated risk of sexual assault in prison; these include juveniles, sex offenders, and inmates who are physically slight, mentally ill, or gay or gender nonconforming.[15]

The chief significance of PREA may have been symbolic rather than practical. The statute provided no new rights to prisoners. Instead it directed the Department of Justice to collect statistics on prison rape; it created a National Prison Rape Elimination Commission and directed it to recommend standards for addressing the problem; and it threatened a 5 percent reduction in federal funding to state prison systems that failed to comply with the standards or work toward compliance. Congress further mandated that the standards promulgated by the commission could not impose "substantial additional costs" on prison systems that adopted them. The standards were promulgated in 2009; they address training and supervision of staff; reporting, investigation, and prosecution of abuse; and a wide range of other procedures. A decade later only two states—New Hampshire and New Jersey—had certified full compliance with the standards. Forty-six other states had committed to working toward compliance.[16]

Even where they have been adopted, the effectiveness of the PREA standards in reducing rates of sexual assault remains uncertain. At the symbolic level, the passage of PREA did signify a shift in public attitudes toward the offense. It is not as common as it once was to treat prison rape as risible, or to welcome it as a form of retribution. Still, old attitudes die hard. Jokes about prison rape are still common. So is the sense—drawing on the tit-for-tat logic often found in discussions about violence—that prison rape can function as a kind of rough justice. When Larry Nassar, the former team doctor for USA Gymnastics, was sentenced in 2017 to 175 years in prison for sexually assaulting many of the athletes under his care, the judge told him that she was signing his "death warrant," and that if the Constitution allowed it, she would allow "other or many people to do to him what he did to others." Her comments were criticized, but they were also applauded.[17]

Nassar was assaulted by other prisoners hours after being released into the general population of a high-security correctional facility.[18] As a notorious sex offender, Nassar was at high risk for such an attack; it is unclear why he nevertheless was released into the general population or whether any special precautions were taken for his safety. Prison officials may well have been blameless with regard to Nassar. It is hard to be confident of that, however, precisely because correctional staff are so frequently accused of acquiescing in or even encouraging violence between inmates.

Prisoners and former prisoners routinely charge that correctional staff knowingly tolerate sexual assaults and other violence among inmates, partly as a strategy for pacifying prisoners, and partly out of a sense, shared by many members of the public, that prison violence is part of how we punish convicted criminals for their offenses. Scholars studying prisons, and judges presiding over lawsuits brought on behalf of prisoners, have often reached the same conclusion, and correctional staff themselves sometimes acknowledge having looked the other way. At times prison officials appear to do more than turn a blind eye to violence within their institutions; some actively promote it, stage it, or carry it out themselves.[19]

In Alabama and Mississippi, inmates and officers have blamed the startling high rate of prison violence on a correctional culture that tacitly accepts it.[20] In Texas a federal judge found that prison officials "deliberately resist providing reasonable safety to inmates," turning a blind eye to beatings and rapes.[21] In a separate federal lawsuit, California prison officials were found to have staged "gladiator fights" between prisoners in what are officially known as "Special Housing Units" and unofficially called "supermaxes"—ultra-high-security facilities supposedly reserved for the "worst of the worst." (We will return to these orchestrated fights below.) The supermax guards also beat prisoners, hog-tied them, and used excessive force in removing them from their cells; this happened so frequently that the trial court judge concluded that guards were using force, not just to maintain discipline, but "for the very purpose of inflicting punishment and pain."[22]

How Law Thinks about—and Tolerates—Prison Violence

The Supreme Court ruled in 1994 that failing to protect prisoners from violent attacks violates the constitutional ban on "cruel and unusual punishments"—but only if (a) prisoners face a "substantial risk of serious harm," and (b) correctional officials are aware of that risk and consciously disregard it by failing to take reasonable steps to reduce it. In order to prevail in court, prisoners raising a constitutional challenge to unsafe prison conditions must therefore prove that officials have culpable mental states, not just that they have tolerated or even fostered high rates of violence within their institutions. Showing that prison officials had this kind of culpable mental state—that their hearts as well as their hands were unclean—is notoriously difficult. Most legal scholars who write about prisons view this requirement as the single most significant doctrinal obstacle faced by prisoners challenging unsafe conditions.[23]

Part of the reason it is so difficult for prisoners to prove that officials had a culpable mental state is that judges often assume that a good deal of prison violence is beyond the control of state officials—"inevitable no matter what the guards do," in Judge Easterbrook's frequently quoted words.[24] Judges assume that prisons are dangerous because the people sent there are dangerous. This understanding of prison violence—that prison violence is largely characterological, not situational—is also part of the reason the Supreme Court required a showing of conscious disregard in the first place. The Justices reasoned in 1994 that the Eighth Amendment bars only cruel and unusual *punishment,* and punishment is partly a matter of mind-set. But lying behind that semantic argument was an understanding of what prison officials, as well as prisoners, were up against: the fundamental fact that prisons grouped together "persons who have a demonstrated proclivity for antisocial criminal, and often violent, conduct." Concurring separately, Justice Thomas was even blunter. "Prisons are necessarily dangerous places," he wrote, because "they house society's most antisocial and violent people in close proximity with one another."[25]

This idea—that prisons are inevitably violent because the people who are sent there are violent—might be thought to have gained explanatory power over the past several decades because the percentage of prisoners serving time for offenses classified as "violent" has grown. Beginning in the 1990s, the increasing focus of criminal prosecutions on violent offenders, and the proliferation of long mandatory minimum sentences for violent offenses—the trends discussed in Chapter 2 of this book—resulted in a dramatic increase in the proportion of prison inmates who had been convicted of violent offenses. Today most state prisoners fall into this category. (Federal prisoners are different: half are serving time for drug offenses, and less than 10 percent have been convicted of violent crimes. But state prisoners outnumber federal prisoners by more than five to one.) But the spread of mandatory minimum sentences has also meant that prisoners today are significantly older on average, and older prisoners are less violent. Moreover, prison homicide rates *dropped* during the 1990s and remain far lower today than they were in the 1980s, when a significantly smaller share of prisoners were serving time for violent offenses.[26]

The dramatic drop in prison homicide rates since the 1980s—a fall of roughly 90 percent—is one reason to view prison violence as situational rather than dispositional. Another reason is how widely rates of violence vary from prison to prison and from state to state, even leaving aside the nightmarish figures from Alabama. In the first decade and a half of the twenty-first century, the homicide rate per 100,000 in state prison systems ranged from zero in several states and between 2 and 3 in Illinois, Pennsylvania, New York, and Texas, to 9 in California, 12 in Maryland, and 13 in Oklahoma. Similar disparities can be observed in prison violence statistics from other countries. The wide variations in rates of prison homicides and prison assaults suggest that the level of violence behind bars is a function more of how prisons are operated than of who is incarcerated.[27]

A well-run institution can guard against violence even among inmates who come to prison with histories of violence or with mental illnesses that make them dangerous. A poorly run prison is likely not just to fail at that task but to make prisoners more violent and more dangerous than when they arrived. The psychologist Craig Haney points out that "homosexual rape in men's prison is often committed by persons who have no experience with rape or with homosexuality. The environment of jail and prison renders them capable of both." Poorly run prisons may also have a culture that tolerates violence, both by prisoners and by guards—the kind of culture that federal judges found in California and Texas prisons in the 1990s, and that inmates and prison officials have reported more recently in Alabama.[28]

The toleration of prison violence reflects ideas not just about the origins of that violence, that it is dispositional rather than situational, but also about what counts as violence in the first place. The legal scholar Bennett Capers argues, "We treat prisons as invisible zones, as lawless zones, as zones that need not concern us."[29] Partly because prisons are

out of sight, and partly because the people sent there have been convicted of crimes, there can be a tendency to write off what happens inside prisons, not to treat it as a true violent offense—similar to how violence inside marriages used to be treated, and how violence toward
children still is sometimes treated. In debates about penal policies, for
example, it is common to hear suggestions that, however else prison fails,
it at least is fully effective at preventing people who are incarcerated from
committing further crimes while they serve their sentences—as though
crimes committed against other prisoners do not really count.[30]

The legal test for when prison officials responsible for violence
between inmates—the rule requiring prisoners to show that officials
knew about a particular risk of violence and intentionally disregarded
it—may itself reflect a willingness to tolerate prison violence, or at least
a sense that it need not distress us greatly. Some Justices on the US Supreme Court have argued that officials should be responsible for violence
(or, for that matter, other unacceptable prison conditions) that they
should have known about and taken steps to prevent, even if simple care-
lessness or a callous lack of concern made them unaware of the danger.
In the language of the law, prison officials could be made responsible for
negligent failures to protect prisoners, not just *reckless* failures. Legal
scholars who study prisons have made the same recommendation, as
have some lower-court judges. A longtime federal magistrate judge suggested some years ago that if the courts actually were serious about reducing prison violence, they would require officials to have more than a
"clean heart" and an "empty head."[31]

The doctrinal basis for a more demanding standard would not be hard
to find. The Supreme Court has said for decades that police officers violate the Constitution—specifically the Fourth Amendment—when they
use force that is "objectively unreasonable," even if the officers are well
intentioned. In 2015 the Justices said the same is true for guards in pretrial detention facilities, although there the rule is based on the constitutional guarantee of due process of law, rather than on the Fourth
Amendment. In prisons, though, the Supreme Court reasons that the
use of force by officials violates the Constitution only if it is used "maliciously and sadistically for the very purpose of causing harm," in which

case it amounts to "cruel and unusual punishment." The legal scholar Margo Schlanger has pointed out that there is no principled reason the due process standard—whether force is "objectively unreasonable"— could not also be applied to prison guards; nor would there be any obvious logical problem with applying the same standard to a failure to protect prisoners, whether before or after a criminal conviction, from attacks by other inmates. No lower court has pursued either of these possibilities, however.[32]

Violence as Spectacle

Over the past three decades guards in various correctional facilities, ranging from "supermax" prisons to local jails, have been accused of staging "gladiator style" fights between prisoners.[33] The most notorious of these abuses occurred in Corcoran State Prison, in California's Central Valley, in the 1990s, where, by one estimate, guards staged some 8,000 fights between inmates between 1988 and 1998. Surveillance cameras at Corcoran recorded guards releasing prisoners from rival gangs two at a time into small exercise yards, in the hopes that they would attack each other. Guards watched the fights from a distance, sometimes bringing along girlfriends or other prison employees as guests. The guards also wagered on the outcomes, and they used rifles to break up fights that spiraled out of control. At least five prisoners were shot to death in these circumstances. Corcoran guards were also alleged to have orchestrated the rape of prisoners for disciplinary purposes.[34]

In 2000, eight Corcoran guards were prosecuted in federal court on civil rights charges arising from the gladiator fights, but their trial ended in acquittals.[35] Despite that verdict, even some prison reformers believed that Corcoran-style gladiator fights were fading into history. Recent years, though, have seen new complaints of guards staging fights between prisoners, at Corcoran and at other prisons and jails.[36]

Prisoners, prison reformers, and scholars who study prisons have all suggested that American carceral institutions unofficially tolerate violence because it serves a range of purposes. Prison violence functions as a tacit part of criminal penalties, and a disciplinary tool, a way of keeping order and retaliating against prisoners who are insufficiently compliant. Gladiator fights orchestrated by guards show that prison violence, like violence more generally, also serves as entertainment, as spectacle—not just a necessary evil, but something enjoyed by onlookers. The fights are a kind of morbid parody of combat sports like football or boxing, minus the rules and even a veneer of consent.

Punishment itself used to serve as spectacle, quite overtly. Open-air executions, pillories, public floggings: all of these drew crowds in search of diversion. Public punishment was supposed to edify spectators and deter them from wrongdoing, but there is no question that it also functioned as entertainment.[37] Prisons moved punishment out of sight and, in theory, substituted deprivations of liberty for physical chastisement. Today the spectacle of violence is found chiefly in movies, television shows, and video games—including, of course, the hundreds of movies and television shows set in prisons.[38] But the idea of places or times marked off as zones of violence is not limited to stories set behind bars.

The 2013 horror movie *The Purge* imagines that in the near future a totalitarian political party takes over the United States, and the government establishes an annual "holiday"—the Purge—during which all crimes including murder are legal for twelve hours. The official purpose of the holiday is to allow for a "country-wide catharsis . . . letting us release the aggression we all have inside of us." The Purge is what sociologists call a "moral holiday"—a temporary suspension of normal constraints on behavior—but with the official sanction of the government.[39] So far the movie has spun off three sequels plus a television show, with yet another theatrical version in the works.

The Purge and its offshoots are plainly dystopian; the audience is not supposed to think that the annual spree of violence is actually a good idea. The filmmakers behind the franchise say they wanted to make a "cautionary tale" about the dangers of gun culture and the need for gun control. The business about "social catharsis" is supposed to be understood as a cynical pretense put forward by an ultra-right-wing, homicidal government. But of course the movies themselves offer their own version of violent catharsis. As one critic put it, "the stated moral may be that violence is terrible," but "the visceral message is that it's a lot of fun."[40]

Prisons themselves are such a frequent setting for on-screen story-telling that a small scholarly literature has emerged debating the reasons for it. The explanations likely are several. Part of it is that prisons are exotic, precisely because they are walled off from public view. Some of it is the stripped-down iconography of prisons, which lends itself to movies and television. Much of it, no doubt, has to do with the stark and elemental oppositions that prison stories can so easily draw upon: good and evil, captivity and freedom, power and abasement, sin and redemption. Some of it pertains to the frisson of physical danger.[41]

Beyond all of this, though, movies and television shows set in prisons may provide some of what public punishment used to provide: the spectacle of violence, especially when visited on those who can be thought to deserve it. (Movies and television shows about police—"cop shows"—often do the same. So do vigilante fantasies of the kind that proliferated on-screen in the 1970s and 1980s.) The stock prison movie involves a sympathetic hero, usually one whose incarceration is unjustified. Moreover, most prison movies cast prisons themselves in an unflattering light; the guards are often portrayed as incompetent, corrupt, or sadistic. On the whole, prison movies therefore might be said to have a reformist subtext. Nonetheless, the standard prison movie portrays most prisoners as brutal and dangerous, suggesting not only that prisons are necessary institutions but that the violence visited on *them*, like the violence visited on corrupt or sadistic guards, is justified. It is a version of the tit-for-tat logic explored in Chapter 1 and a pervasive trope in discussions of violence.[42]

But prison violence is not just a trope of video entertainment. In the real world, hundreds of thousands of people locked up in prisons and jails in the United States are subjected to daily risks of violence that would be deemed intolerable in the outside world, but that the correctional facilities often seem tacitly to tolerate or even to encourage. Prison violence—like violence by police officers, or like violence against children by parents and teachers—seems often to be viewed through a different lens than "ordinary" violence, the kind of violence that the criminal law, increasingly, takes as its principal concern.

7 | Speech and Guns

Early in the afternoon of March 15, 2019, during the time Muslims set aside for Friday prayer, a 28-year-old white supremacist entered two mosques in Christchurch, New Zealand, and shot fifty-one worshipers to death. He was armed with five guns, including a military-style assault rifle; he used a strobe light mounted on one of the weapons to disorient his victims. The gunman live-streamed the massacre on Facebook. Hours earlier he had posted a hate-filled manifesto on white nationalist websites, and he announced the attacks online minutes before entering the first mosque. It was a mass shooting performed for an internet audience.

Several weeks later, on April 27, 2019, a 20-year-old right-wing extremist carrying a military-style assault rifle and wearing a tactical vest entered a synagogue in a San Diego suburb on the last day of Passover, which fell that year on the Jewish Sabbath. He shot and killed a 60-year-old woman and wounded the congregation's rabbi, and then opened fire into the sanctuary and an adjoining banquet hall. When his gun malfunctioned, he fled. He had tried but failed to live-stream the shooting. Earlier in the day he had posted a racist, anti-Semitic manifesto online, crediting the inspiration of the Christchurch massacre as well as a mass shooting in October 2018 at a Pittsburgh synagogue, in which eleven congregants had been killed.[1]

The murders in the Christchurch mosques sparked two significant reform initiatives. First, New Zealand tightened its firearms laws. Weeks after the massacre, the country banned most military-style assault rifles, and it subsequently moved to register all guns in the country. Second, in May 2019 New Zealand helped convene an international summit in Paris to address online violence. The summit culminated with the issuance of the "Christchurch Call," a commitment by governments and online service providers to curtail the propagation of "terrorist and violent extremist content." Seventeen countries signed the Christchurch Call at the conclusion of the Paris summit, and another thirty-one joined in September.[2]

The United States did not participate in the Paris summit and did not join the Christchurch Call. Nor has the United States moved to tighten the regulation of firearms—not after the Christchurch massacre; not after the synagogue shooting near San Diego; not after thirteen people were shot to death in a municipal building in Virginia Beach on May 31, 2019; not after a gunman killed twenty-two people in a Walmart in El Paso, Texas, on August 3 of that year; not after ten people were shot to death outside a bar in Dayton on August 4; not after eight people were killed by a gunman in Odessa, Texas, on August 31; not after California had three mass shootings over just four days in November of the same year, leaving ten people dead. (There were 417 shooting incidents in the United States during 2019 with four or more victims, not counting the shooter, which is to say the country as a whole averaged more than one mass shooting a day.)[3]

Restrictions on "violent extremist content" are nonstarters in the United States. They are viewed as inconsistent with the nation's strong commitment to free expression, reflected in the First Amendment to the Constitution. For this reason even many critics of the Trump administration agreed with its refusal to join the Christchurch Call.[4] Gun control, meanwhile, is restricted by the Second Amendment to the Constitution, which the Supreme Court reinterpreted in 2008 to safeguard the right of individuals to possess and carry firearms, regardless of whether they are part of any "well regulated militia."[5] Moreover, most states have adopted statutes in recent decades aimed at encouraging individuals to "stand their ground" and use the threat of lethal violence to protect themselves and their property.

The First and Second Amendments—the principal focus of this chapter—are not the only constitutional provisions that have helped shape the legal response to violence in the United States. As discussed in Chapter 3, the Fourth Amendment bar against "unreasonable searches and seizures" regulates, albeit quite loosely, the violence that police officers are allowed to employ. And the Eighth Amendment ban on "cruel and unusual punishments," as discussed in Chapter 6, limits the kinds of violence to which prisoners may be subjected.

As we have seen, interpretation of the Fourth and Eighth Amendments has been shaped by tacit ideas about violence: ideas about how much it should matter whether particular police conduct, or particular instances of punishment, are violent or nonviolent; ideas about what should count as violent; and ideas about how violence originates. This is true of the First and Second Amendments as well. Here, too, the law relies upon and reinforces ideas about violence, ideas that often are left unarticulated. And here, too, it is worth surfacing those ideas and holding them up for inspection, in part because they often differ markedly from the ideas about violence reflected elsewhere in the law.

Criminal law treats violence as highly significant and categorically worthy of especially strong condemnation. In First Amendment law, though, violence has low significance: the danger of violence isn't treated as a special kind of threat. And the legal rules built on or inspired by the Second Amendment—the constitutional right to have and use guns, and the statutes encouraging gun owners to "stand their ground"—embody a view that private violence, including lethal violence, is often to be welcomed. One important point of continuity, though, is that Second Amendment law, like criminal law, increasingly views violence as characterological rather than situational—as the result of individual dispositions rather than the circumstances in which people find themselves.

Violence and Free Expression

The First Amendment protection for freedom of speech has never been thought absolute. It is a commonplace of American constitutional law that certain kinds of expression can be restricted—obscenity, for example, or libel. What is striking is how little *violence* matters in determining whether speech is protected. Violence has little or no salience in First Amendment law.

There are free speech doctrines that might be thought to remove protection for violent expression, doctrines that might be thought to allow space for the kinds of restrictions contemplated by the Christchurch Call. The Supreme Court has long said that "incitement" may be prohibited and punished, and the same is true for "fighting words" and "true threats." Moreover, gruesome representations of violence are often, quite literally, obscene. They fall within the most common definition of "obscene": "disgusting to the senses" or "repulsive."[6] But none of these doctrines give much significance to violence. Doctrines regarding incitement, "fighting words," and "true threats" come closest to doing so, but each of these has developed in a way that provides little opening for something like the Christchurch Call.

The incitement doctrine allows the government to penalize speech that seems calculated to produce "imminent" unlawful action; at times the Court has said there needs to be a "clear and present danger." The doctrine emerged out of cases involving the danger of illegal force: riots or other mob action. The opinion often credited with inspiring the modern test for incitement—Justice Brandeis's dissent in *Whitney v. California*—said in passing that the doctrine should apply only where there was a likelihood of, or advocacy for, "immediate serious violence." But elsewhere in the opinion Brandeis suggested that what needed to be "imminent" was "serious crime" or a "substantive evil," not necessarily *violence*. What Brandeis stressed was that the danger needed to be "imminent."[7]

And this was true as well of the later cases where the Supreme Court Justices took Brandeis's opinion in *Whitney* as their North Star. The leading modern authority on incitement, the Supreme Court's 1969 decision in *Brandenburg v. Ohio*, strips First Amendment protection from speech calculated to produce "imminent lawless action," and that formulation has been repeated in subsequent cases. In 1971, in *Cohen v. California*, the Supreme Court ruled that a jacket with the words "Fuck the Draft" was constitutionally protected speech, in part because there was no proof that the wearer intended "to incite disobedience to or disruption of the draft." What the Justices did not say, evidently because the thought did not occur to them, was that intentional incitement of draft resistance would still be protected speech, as long as the draft resistance was nonviolent.[8]

Partly because the "imminence" requirement is so demanding, the Supreme Court has never squarely addressed whether inciting *nonviolent* crimes is constitutionally protected even when the crimes *are* imminent. Technically this remains an open question.[9] But the language of *Brandenburg* and the decisions following it, and the reasoning in cases like *Cohen,* place little or no weight on the line between violence and nonviolence; virtually all of the emphasis is on imminence. (In his celebrated dissent in *Whitney v. California,* Justice Brandeis did argue that "relatively trivial" dangers could not justify restricting speech even if they were imminent. The danger needed to be "relatively serious" in addition to imminent. But Brandeis also made it clear that "serious" didn't mean "violent." Neither the likelihood of "violence" nor the prospect of "destruction of property" sufficed, only "the probability of serious injury to the state.")[10]

The "fighting words" doctrine, on the other hand, seems directly focused on violence, and if anything, that focus has strengthened over the decades. The Supreme Court first applied this doctrine in *Chaplinsky v. New Hampshire,* a 1942 decision that declared the First Amendment inapplicable to words "which, by their very utterance, inflict injury or tend to incite an immediate breach of the peace." But by the time the Court decided *Cohen v. California,* it had narrowed the category. *Cohen* defines fighting words as "those personally abusive epithets which, when addressed to the ordinary citizen, are, as a matter of common knowledge, inherently likely to provoke violent reaction."

The jacket inscription in *Cohen* did not constitute fighting words, the Justices explained, because "no individual actually or likely to be present could reasonably have regarded the words on appellant's jacket as a direct personal insult." That gave an indication of how demanding the doctrine had become. A year later the Supreme Court made this even plainer, limiting the category of fighting words to utterances likely to elicit "an immediate violent response" from an individual being directly addressed. This reinterpretation of the doctrine, coupled with the fact that for well over half a century the Supreme Court has not found a set of facts satisfying the fighting-words doctrine, has led most First Amendment scholars to conclude that the doctrine is now moribund, or at best no more than a particular application of the incitement doctrine. Unlike the broader incitement doctrine, the fighting-words doctrine does focus on the danger of violence, at least on its face. But it has little vitality today.[11]

Moreover, the rare cases that *have* applied the fighting-words doctrine in recent decades generally have not involved any real danger of violence. Instead, they involve defendants who taunted police officers in ways that courts found too juvenile and vulgar for constitutional protection. Some courts have treated the fighting-words doctrine as even more limited when the words in question were directed to a law enforcement officer; these courts have reasoned that because police officers are trained to respond calmly and with restraint, taunts that come their way are less likely to cause violence than is abuse hurled at other people. But other courts disagree. As a result, there are scattered cases in which defendants have been convicted for spouting "fighting words" at police officers, even when there was never any significant possibility of a violent response.[12]

Just as violence is nominally central to the fighting-words doctrine, it is also, in theory, at the heart of the exception to the relatively new doctrine removing First Amendment protection from "true threats." The Supreme Court declared in 2003 that the Constitution allows the prohibition of a "true threat," which it defined as a "serious expression of an intent to commit an act of unlawful violence to a particular individual or group of individuals." The Justices ruled that cross burnings for the purpose of intimidation fell within this exception.[13]

Threats to commit a property offense, or to reveal compromising information, do not fall within this exception. But if those kinds of threats are accompanied with an express or implied demand—for money, for a favor, or for any other action—they will generally constitute extortion or blackmail, and the criminal laws against extortion and blackmail have never been thought to raise serious problems under the First Amendment. At least this is true when physical injury or property destruction is threatened in order to coerce someone to do something. Credible claims *have* been made that the First Amendment should bar the expanded use of extortion statutes to penalize, for example, social or economic protests that interfere with business operations. But those arguments, too, do not draw the line at violence; they draw the line between protest activity and more classic forms of extortion.[14]

Just as laws against extortion and blackmail have long been assumed to be fully consistent with the First Amendment, so too have laws against soliciting a crime, or "abetting" a crime by encouraging someone to commit it. Courts have sometimes struggled to draw the line between punishable solicitation or abetting, and protected advocacy. But distinctions have rarely been drawn in this regard between violent and nonviolent offenses. Soliciting or abetting any kind of crime is itself a crime.[15]

There is one famous, frequently cited Supreme Court opinion that *does* call for violent speech to receive significantly less protection under the First Amendment. But it is a dissent. The case was *Terminiello v. City of Chicago,* and it warrants a brief detour.

In 1946 Arthur Terminiello was the main speaker at a far-right, anti-Semitic rally held in Chicago. Terminiello was a defrocked Catholic priest praised by his allies as the "Father Coughlin of the South." In 1945 he had called for a "march of death" in Washington, DC, to demand that those who had led the United States into World War II be hanged as traitors. Days before speaking in Chicago, Terminiello had warned an audience in Detroit that "brazen" Jews were out to "dilute Christianity with their paganism," to "democratize our Republic," to "Sovietize our Christian home," and to "fertilize with American boys the Zionist empire." He had also told the crowd that former president Franklin Roosevelt, who had died the previous year, might actually still be alive: "Some people do not think he's dead. Some think he's in Palestine!" Following a speech in Cleveland, Terminiello had punched a protester.

Terminiello's speech in Chicago struck predictable notes. (It also anticipated some of the rhetorical tactics Donald Trump would later favor.) Hundreds of anti-Fascist protesters had gathered outside the rally hall; Terminiello called them "scum" and warned they were trying "to destroy America by revolution." He railed against the Jews, while denying he was anti-Semitic:

> I am going to talk about—I almost said, about the Jews. Of course, I would not want to say that. However, I am going to

talk about some Jews. I hope that—I am a Christian minister.
We must take a Christian attitude. I don't want you to go
from this hall with hatred in your heart for any person, for no
person. . . . [T]his danger which we face—let us call them
Zionist Jews if you will, let's call them atheistic, communistic
Jewish or Zionist Jews, then let us not fear to condemn them.

Terminiello charged that former Treasury secretary Henry Morgen-
thau had convinced Roosevelt to starve "little babies and pregnant
women in Germany," and he suggested that doctors of a certain "kind"
serving in the American military during the war had "made it a practice
to amputate the limbs of every German they came in contact with whenever they could get away with it; so, that they could never carry a gun."
When a rock flew through the window, Terminiello asked his audience,
"Do you wonder they were persecuted in other countries in the world?"
He said that the "mobs" outside were joining in a "caveman's chant," that
they had been "trained this afternoon," that they were "being led," and
that "there will be violence." He compared the protesters to bedbugs or
snakes, and encouraged his listeners to "walk out of here dignified." "We
will not be tolerant of that mob out there," he explained: "We are not
going to be tolerant any longer. We are strong enough. We are not going
to be tolerant of their smears any longer. We are going to stand up and
dare them to smear us." Terminiello concluded: "We must all be like the
Apostles before the coming of the Holy Ghost. We must not lock ourselves in an upper room for fear of the Jews. I speak of the Communistic
Zionistic Jew, and those are not American Jews. We don't want them
here; we want them to go back where they came from."

Following the rally, rioting broke out between Terminiello's audience
and the protesters who had surrounded the hall. Terminiello was arrested, charged with breach of the peace, convicted by a jury, and fined
$100. On a 5–4 vote the Supreme Court reversed the judgment. The
problem, Justice William Douglas explained for the majority, was that
the jury instructions permitted a conviction on proof merely that Terminiello's speech had "stirred people to anger, invited public dispute, or
brought about a condition of unrest." Chief Justice Vinson and Justice

Frankfurter both argued in dissent that Terminiello had waived any objection to the jury instructions by failing to raise the point at trial. Justice Jackson, though, filed a longer and more substantive dissent, also signed by Justice Burton.

Jackson, who had served as the chief American prosecutor at the Nuremberg trials, noted that Terminiello's speech had followed, "with fidelity that is more than coincidental, the pattern of European fascist leaders," and he pointed out the key role that violent demonstrations had played in the rise of Nazism. Jackson argued that democracies needed to be able to protect themselves against violent extremism, that "the ways in which mob violence may be worked up are subtle and various," and that the problem cannot be "solved merely by going through a transcript of the speech to pick out 'fighting words.'" Free discussion itself depended on a degree of public order. Jackson acknowledged that the line drawing could be difficult, and that "courts must beware lest they become mere organs of popular intolerance." But he insisted that "in the long run, maintenance of free speech will be more endangered if the population can have no protection from the abuses that lead to violence." In conclusion, he warned that the Bill of Rights should not be turned "into a suicide pact."[16]

Jackson's dissent in *Terminiello* is often quoted, but generally only for that concluding line, divorced from its context. Jackson's dissent in *Terminiello* is not like Brandeis's dissent in *Whitney:* the Court has never suggested that Jackson might have been right. Neither have legal scholars, for that matter. Aside from Jackson's memorable turn of phrase about not converting the Constitution into a suicide pact, *Terminiello* is remembered today as an admirable example of the First Amendment in action, and of the principle that even unpopular and upsetting advocacy deserves protection unless it presents a serious, immediate danger.[17] Jackson thought that First Amendment law needed to take account of the special dangers that appeals to mob violence pose to democratic discourse. But he lost. Whether the danger is violent or nonviolent plays relatively little role in First Amendment analysis.

Also playing little role in such analysis is the question whether the speech *describes* or *depicts* violence, and if so, how, to whom, and under what circumstances. Sexual content can make speech constitutionally unprotected. This is the import of the obscenity doctrine, which allows the government to ban expression that has "prurient" appeal, includes "patently offensive" depictions of sexual conduct, and lacks serious cultural, political, or scientific value.[18] Material that does not satisfy this standard for adults may still be "obscene as to youths," and therefore may be restricted if it is addressed to or distributed to children.[19] Furthermore, sexual material involving children as models or actors can be restricted even when directed to or possessed only by adults; the Supreme Court has reasoned that the harm of involving children in the production of pornography is so grave that it is permissible to ban the materials themselves, in order to dry up the market.[20]

There are no comparable rules for depictions of violence. The Supreme Court made that clear in 2011, when it struck down a California statute that barred the sale or rental of violent video games to minors. The case was *Brown v. Entertainment Merchants Association.* California had modeled its statute on obscenity laws, defining "violent video games" as those that appealed "to a deviant or morbid interest in minors," included "patently offensive" depictions of violence, and lacked serious cultural, political, or scientific value for minors. But the Supreme Court said violence differed from sex. There was a long-standing legal tradition of allowing censorship of obscene depictions of sex, but not of depictions of violence, no matter how lurid or offensive. Writing for the Court, Justice Scalia explained that the obscenity doctrine applies only to "sexual content": for purposes of the First Amendment, "speech about violence is not obscene."

In the Supreme Court's view, violent video games were just a new form of speech about violence. They were not fundamentally different from violent movies, violent comic books, or "true crime" magazines. It is a staple of First Amendment law that even constitutionally protected speech can be restricted by a law that passes "strict scrutiny," which means a law that the Justices find to be narrowly tailored to serve a "compelling government interest." But it is also well known that almost every law subjected to this test is found to fail it, and the California video game statute was no exception. Justice Scalia said in *Brown v. Entertainment*

Merchants Association that there was no convincing proof that playing violent video games made children more violent, any more than watching Warner Brothers cartoons would do. California's law was just "the latest episode in a long series of failed attempts to censor violent entertainment for minors."

Writing separately, Justice Breyer and Justice Alito each found the evidence of harmful effects of video games on children more troubling than did the majority of the Court, and each thought it indefensible to give depictions of violence more constitutional protection than depictions of sex or nudity. Justice Breyer dissented from the Court's decision. He would have upheld the California statute. Breyer pointed out that many researchers, and many associations of health professionals, had concluded that violent video games increased physical aggression in children, and that they were more dangerous in this regard than movies, television, or print media, because they were much more immersive and interactive:

> What sense does it make to forbid selling to a 13-year-old boy a magazine with an image of a nude woman, while protecting a sale to that 13-year-old of an interactive video game in which he actively, but virtually, binds and gags the woman, then tortures and kills her? What kind of First Amendment would permit the government to protect children by restricting sales of that extremely violent video game only when the woman— bound, gagged, tortured, and killed—is also topless?

Justice Alito, too, thought it ridiculous that states could ban the sale of "'girlie magazines'" to children, but could not ban "the most violent and depraved video games imaginable." Alito was shocked by the level and the nature of violence in some video games:

> Victims are dismembered, decapitated, disemboweled, set on fire, and chopped into little pieces. They cry out in agony and beg for mercy. Blood gushes, splatters, and pools. Severed body parts and gobs of human remains are graphically shown. In some games, points are awarded based, not only on the

number of victims killed, but on the killing technique
employed. . . .

There are games in which a player can take on the identity
and reenact the killings carried out by the perpetrators of the
murders at Columbine High School and Virginia Tech. The
objective of one game is to rape a mother and her daughters; in
another, the goal is to rape Native American women. There is
a game in which players engage in "ethnic cleansing" and can
choose to gun down African-Americans, Latinos, or Jews. In
still another game, players attempt to fire a rifle shot into the
head of President Kennedy as his motorcade passes by the
Texas School Book Depository.

Like Justice Breyer, Justice Alito also thought it was important that
video games allowed players to *act out* violence, not just see it depicted.
And Justice Alito pointed out that the rapidly emerging technology of
virtual reality would soon make video games even more immersive and
even more lifelike, with high-definition, three-dimensional graphics
and sensory feedback, allowing players "to experience in an extraordinarily personal and vivid way what it would be like to carry out un-
speakable acts of violence." Justice Alito concurred in the judgment
invalidating California's video game statute, because he thought the
law was not drafted with enough precision. But he strongly objected
to the Court's sweeping conclusion that violent video games, even
when sold to children, should receive the full protection of the First
Amendment.

Still, Justices Alito and Breyer were the only members of the Court
who appeared to think that violence should matter as much as sex under
the First Amendment, or even at all. Justice Thomas also dissented from
the judgment in *Brown v. Entertainment Merchants,* but on the broader
and more idiosyncratic ground that the First Amendment was completely inapplicable to speech that is directed at children and bypasses
their parents. Ultimately, Justice Breyer's dissent in this case, and Justice Alito's concurrence, were like Justice Jackson's dissent in *Terminiello:* they represented a path not taken in First Amendment law, a path

in which violence would matter. The path actually taken by First Amendment law has been very different.[21]

In one sense, then, *Terminiello* and *Entertainment Merchants* stand for the low significance of violence in First Amendment law. From another perspective, though, violence *could* be said to matter in First Amendment law, just not in the way the dissenters in these cases thought it should. The expansive protection given to free expression in the United States—even to forms of speech that glorify or encourage violence—is an application, in a way, of the idea that expression and violence are alternatives or even opposites, and that speech should be unrestricted precisely because it isn't violence. It is a truism of our constitutional culture that speech may be most valuable precisely when it is distressful. Writing for a majority of the Supreme Court in *Terminiello,* Justice Douglas explained that free expression may "best serve its high purpose" when it makes people uncomfortable or angry. This was why advocacy could be restricted only when it created "a clear and present danger of a serious substantive evil that rises far above public inconvenience, annoyance, or unrest." The First Amendment exception for fighting words initially included not just language likely to provoke a violent response but also words that *themselves,* "by their very utterance, inflict injury." But the Supreme Court has jettisoned this part of the doctrine—rejecting, in effect, the idea that words themselves can be violent.[22]

So First Amendment law could be said to incorporate a particular *definition* of violence, rather than an idea about the *significance* of violence. It could be said to reflect the notion that "verbal violence" is a contradiction in terms. Here as elsewhere, a set of ideas about the significance of violence can be rephrased as ideas about the definition of violence, and vice versa. Frequently these are just different, equivalent ways of expressing the same point.

Still, with regard to the First Amendment it seems more accurate to say that violence has low significance, not that violence is being defined in a particular way. What seems most important is that the exceptions carved out to the First Amendment do not give much weight to whether the speech the government wants to restrict depicts, describes, or encourages violence, as opposed to depicting, describing, or encouraging anything else.

Lurking in the background of First Amendment law, there may also be ideas about the *nature* of violence, about how it works. First Amendment law often appears to draw on a dispositional or characterological view of violence: speech doesn't cause violence; violent people cause violence. The dissenters in *Terminiello* and *Entertainment Merchants* spent much of their time arguing against this premise. In *Terminiello,* Justice Jackson argued that speech often is the *sine qua non* of violence: "No serious outbreak of mob violence, race rioting, lynching or public disorder is likely to get going without help of some speech-making. . . . Unity of purpose, passion and hatred, which merges the many minds of a crowd into the mindlessness of a mob, almost invariably is supplied by speeches."[23] In *Brown v. Entertainment Merchants,* Justice Breyer devoted a large part of his dissent to a review of scientific evidence supporting the conclusion that when children play violent video games, it changes their behavior in the actual, physical world. Justice Alito—whose concurring opinion in that case was effectively a dissent from the majority's central conclusions—also underscored the reasons to think that the effects of violent video games on young players might be very different from the effects of reading about or watching depictions of violence.

In both cases, though, the majority dismissed these concerns as speculative. The Court did not deny, in either case, that speech could make violence more likely, but in both cases the Court viewed the causal connection as loose and relatively untroubling. What the Court actually said in *Terminiello* wasn't that the threat from speech was minimal. It was that the threat for allowing speech to be suppressed was greater, because "the vitality of civil and political institutions in our society depends on free discussion." But that argument itself reflected a belief about how violence works: that responsible members of society wouldn't be driven to violence by inflammatory rhetoric. Justice Scalia was more explicit when writing for the Court in *Brown v. Entertainment Merchants;* he argued that the studies cited by Justice Breyer show, at most, "a correlation between exposure to violent entertainment and minuscule real-world effects."[24]

Violence and Gun Rights

The Second Amendment to the United States Constitution protects "the right of the people to keep and bear arms." That guarantee is prefaced, though, by language declaring that a "well regulated militia" is "necessary to the security of a free state," and throughout the twentieth century the prevailing view of courts, including the Supreme Court, was that the Second Amendment applied only to weapons connected with militia service. In 1939 the Supreme Court rejected, without dissent, a constitutional challenge to the federal ban on sawed-off shotguns. The Justices reasoned that weapons of this kind had no "reasonable relationship to the preservation or efficiency of a well regulated militia."[25]

But in a 2008 decision, *District of Columbia v. Heller,* the Supreme Court dramatically changed its reading of the Second Amendment. A bare majority of the Justices in *Heller* concluded that the Constitution provides individuals with the right to possess and carry weapons for self-defense. Two years later the Supreme Court reiterated that understanding of the Second Amendment in *McDonald v. City of Chicago,* and held that it applied to the states as well as to the federal government. *Heller* and *McDonald* called individual self-defense "the central component" of the right protected by the Second Amendment. Neither decision suggested that the right was absolute; both recognized that some restrictions on gun ownership and use were permissible. Writing for the majority in *Heller,* Justice Scalia took pains not to question the constitutionality of "longstanding prohibitions on the possession of firearms by felons and the mentally ill, or laws forbidding the carrying of firearms in sensitive places such as schools and government buildings, or laws imposing conditions and qualifications on the commercial sale of arms." Furthermore, the Court made it clear that the Second Amendment protected only the possession and use of weapons "in common use at the time"; it did not apply to "dangerous and unusual weapons." The firearms laws challenged in *Heller* and in *McDonald* essentially prohibited the private ownership and use of handguns. This went too far, the Supreme Court said, because "the American people have considered the handgun to be the quintessential self-defense weapon."[26]

The basic reasoning of *Heller* and *McDonald* is that there was a pre-constitutional, common-law right to own and use firearms for self-protection, and that the Constitution codified this right because it was connected to the idea of the citizen militia, which the drafters and adopters of the Bill of Rights thought was an important protection against tyranny. Even though the purpose of codifying the right was to protect the institution of the militia—an institution that *Heller* and *McDonald* recognized might be obsolete in the modern world of professional armies and police departments—a majority of the Court concluded that the underlying right protected by the Second Amendment was itself far from obsolete, because its core rationale was individual self-defense. Because eighteenth-century militias were composed of men who brought their own weapons from home, it made sense, the Supreme Court thought, to limit the Second Amendment right to weapons in common use. But not weapons in common use at the time the amendment was adopted: common use today.

Justice Scalia's opinion for the Court in *Heller* and Justice Alito's majority opinion in *McDonald* both were, in form, heavily historicist. Both stressed the importance of following the "original understanding" of the Second Amendment. But both also reflected, as constitutional historian Adam Winkler has noted, "a thoroughly modern understanding of gun rights." Winkler points out that eighteenth-century America did not have the restrictions on gun rights that *Heller* took pains to avoid questioning, and laws of that kind probably would not have been thought legitimate at the time. That is partly because the kinds of guns in existence today did not exist in the eighteenth century, and neither did professional police forces or the modern military.[27]

Heller and *McDonald* were the culmination of a decades-long campaign by gun rights advocates and the National Rifle Association, beginning in the 1960s, to secure constitutional protection for an individual right to own and use firearms. That campaign succeeded in part because it tapped into a broader cultural change: the rising salience of violent crime. Legal scholar Jonathan Simon has suggested that beginning in the 1960s, American politics were reshaped by growing fears of private violence, which placed new demands not just on elected leaders but also on constitutional law. Inevitably this influenced how courts thought about the Second Amendment.[28]

The Supreme Court's decisions in *Heller* and *McDonald* did not just reflect heightened concerns about violent crime. They reflected particular ideas about where violence comes from and how it operates. The majority and dissenting Justices in these cases, like the opposing sides in the bitter public arguments about gun control, had different views about the relationship between guns and violence. In a sense the disagreements were ultimately about whether gun violence is fundamentally situational or dispositional. The question was whether guns themselves are part of the problem of violence in the United States, or whether gun violence, like other forms of violence, arises from the violent character of assailants—whether, as the NRA's executive director has repeatedly insisted, "the only thing that stops a bad guy with a gun is a good guy with a gun." Dissenting in *McDonald,* Justice Stevens argued that although firearms might assist in self-defense, they had "a unique potential to facilitate death and destruction and thereby to destabilize ordered liberty." There was a tight "link between handgun ownership and public safety," Justice Stevens thought: "The handgun's bullets *are* the violence."[29]

But the majority in *Heller* and in *McDonald* shared the NRA's view that guns are essentially neutral: that in violent hands, guns are tools of violence, but in law-abiding hands, they are ways to *stop* violence. Justice Alito's majority opinion in *McDonald* viewed gun rights as part and parcel of the "ancient" and fundamental right to "individual self-defense," and suggested that guns were particularly valuable for "women and members of other groups that may be especially vulnerable to violent crime." It made sense to Justice Scalia, writing for the Court in *Heller,* that Americans would value handguns as a tool of self-defense. There is a long-running debate about whether handguns kept in the home actually make people safer. A good deal of evidence suggests, on the contrary, that people with firearms in their homes are far more likely to be killed by those weapons—or to kill themselves with them—than to use them successfully in self-defense. But Justice Scalia noted that a handgun is easier than a rifle to keep "readily accessible," that a handgun takes less strength than a rifle to lift and aim, and that a handgun, unlike a rifle, "can be pointed at a burglar with one hand while the other hand dials the police."[30]

A characterological understanding of gun violence is thus bound up with the Supreme Court's new view of the Second Amendment as safeguarding an individual right to keep and use firearms. It may also shape the resolution of new tensions between the Second Amendment and the treatment of firearms in substantive criminal law and in the Fourth Amendment. Gun violations typically are treated as violent crimes, which means that they serve as predicates for additional terms of imprisonment, make it harder for defendants to avoid prison or secure early release, and lead to all the other forms of especially harsh treatment that criminal law increasingly reserves for violent offenders. This strikes many people as common sense. Justice Stevens is not alone in thinking that guns are linked with violence almost by definition. In 2019 the New York Police Department criticized Brooklyn district attorney Eric Garcia for opening his pretrial diversion program to certain youthful offenders who pleaded guilty to weapons possession charges. New York mayor Bill de Blasio joined in the complaints. Diversion was fine "for nonviolent offenses," de Blasio said, but "when a gun is in the equation . . . it's a whole different ballgame." Larry Krasner, the reform-minded district attorney of Philadelphia, has also been criticized for authorizing diversion for some defendants arrested for illegal gun possession; an official with the Pennsylvania Attorney General's Office called this putting "violent offenders" back on the street. But when guns are viewed the way the Supreme Court viewed them in *Heller* and *McDonald*—as treasured instruments of self-defense, central to the American ideal of liberty—it becomes harder to think of gun possession as a violent crime, especially when violent crimes are understood as a category apart, the worst and most blameworthy of transgressions.[31]

Guns are also at the heart of the constitutional framework that has governed investigatory stops by the police for half a century. The Supreme Court's 1968 decision in *Terry v. Ohio* allows the police to pull over a car, or briefly detain a pedestrian, based on reasonable suspicion of criminality, which can be short of the "probable cause" needed for an arrest. Once detained, suspects can be "patted down" or "frisked" if there is reason to suspect they are "armed and dangerous." As the Supreme Court itself recognized, the term "frisk" is a euphemism; the tactile searches permitted by *Terry* can be invasive and humiliating. And the grounds for suspecting that an individual stopped by the police is armed and dangerous, like the grounds for suspecting criminal activity in the first place, need not rise to the level of "probable cause"—the standard for arrests and also for search warrants.[32]

The "stop and frisk" tactic has become highly controversial, and debates about policing often are framed in terms of whether the tactic should be employed at all.[33] But every police department uses the powers granted by *Terry v. Ohio;* the real questions are how aggressively and under what circumstances. In the 1990s and early 2000s many police departments across the United States—most famously the NYPD—used stop and frisk *very* aggressively. Often, as in New York City, the tactic was explicitly framed as an effort to get guns off the streets. Therefore, many stops, and not just the frisks that accompanied them, were based on grounds for thinking the suspect was armed. Fully a quarter of all investigative stops carried out by the NYPD in the early 2000s were based on suspicion of "criminal possession of a weapon," more than any other offense category.[34] And people stopped for this reason were automatically searched, because by definition there was reason to believe that they were armed. This entire strategy was predicated, however, on the understanding that anyone carrying a weapon was probably doing so illegally, or engaging in some other criminal activity, or both. In New York and many other cities, this was generally a safe assumption, because carrying a weapon in public usually required a permit, and the permits were hard to obtain. Some licensing schemes restricted only carrying a concealed weapon, and some restricted only "open carry." But most law-abiding people didn't walk around with guns, anyway, so the fact that someone was carrying a gun could itself be thought suspicious, like carrying burglary tools.

Those assumptions are now in doubt due to changes in how guns and gun rights are understood in the United States. The challenge arises not so much because of the legal holdings in *Heller* and *McDonald,* but more because of the ideas about firearms that motivated those decisions. The gun control laws invalidated by the Supreme Court in *Heller* and *McDonald* were unusually restrictive, essentially banning the ownership of handguns. The Supreme Court said explicitly in *Heller* that the Second Amendment right was not "unlimited," and it spoke approvingly of traditional laws that, for example, banned guns in "sensitive places such as schools and government buildings," placed "conditions and qualifications on the commercial sale of arms," or kept guns from people convicted of felonies or suffering from mental illnesses. That could mean it is also constitutional to require permits for open or concealed carrying of weapons, and to grant those permits only when there is a showing of special need. Most gun control laws challenged in court since *Heller* and *McDonald* have in fact been upheld, contributing to complaints—including by some members of the Supreme Court—that "the Second Amendment is a disfavored right." But part of the reason Second Amendment challenges have tended to fail in the lower courts is that state and local governments have themselves become more solicitous of gun rights.[35]

One way this new solicitude has manifested itself is in the loosening of licensing regimes for the open or concealed carrying of firearms in public. The trend was apparent within a few years after the Supreme Court's decisions in *Heller* and *McDonald*. Writing in 2015, law professor Jeffrey Bellin noted that states were "steadily migrating from 'no-issue' (i.e., no concealed carry permits) to 'may-issue' (i.e., permits issued at the discretion of a police chief); from 'may-issue' to 'shall-issue' (i.e., permits must be issued to any qualified applicant); and from 'shall-issue' to not requiring a permit at all."

"The emerging reality," Bellin observed, ". . . is that carrying a concealed handgun is a perfectly 'lawful act,'" and "courts will be hard-pressed to accept, as constituting 'reasonable suspicion' of a crime, an observation of an increasingly common activity that is not only lawful, but specifically protected by the Second Amendment." In theory, police could try to stop only people they suspect lack the necessary permit to carry a concealed weapon, but it is hard to determine whether individuals have permits without stopping them—and that requires some reasonable suspicion at the outset. Increasingly, courts are invalidating *Terry* stops that are based solely on suspicion that someone is carrying a weapon, regardless of whether the weapon is concealed or openly displayed.[36]

Even if the police can lawfully stop someone they suspect is carrying a weapon, changing ideas about guns and gun rights create an additional problem. The Supreme Court's decision in *Terry v. Ohio* allows someone who is lawfully stopped to be frisked for a weapon if there are reasonable grounds for thinking the suspect may be armed and dangerous. For decades, "armed and dangerous" meant, essentially, "armed and therefore dangerous." Armed was necessarily dangerous. So if the police had reasonable grounds to suspect that someone was carrying a concealed weapon, they generally could stop the individual and then carry out a frisk. That is still the assumption made by most judges, but the assumption is increasingly questioned.[37] And if the police cannot be confident of their entitlement to frisk someone they suspect may be armed, they may be more wary of stopping the individual to begin with.

The expanding right to own and carry guns in the United States may therefore be on a collision course with the stop-and-frisk powers the Supreme Court has given to the police, at least as those powers have traditionally been exercised. The Second Amendment and the *Terry* doctrine do not mix well. One strategy to make them compatible is to treat them as applying to different groups of people: gun rights for the law abiding, stop and frisk for the lawless. But that requires distinguishing the two groups of people, and in practice this kind of bifurcation tends to rely on racial stereotypes.

For example, during his presidential campaign Donald Trump championed both a strong Second Amendment and the aggressive use of stop and frisk. The great thing about stop and frisk, he said, is that it allowed the police to take guns away from people they see on the street. When pressed about his support for what sounded like gun confiscation, he said that he had been "really referring to Chicago." As law professor Mary Anne Franks observes, this amounted to "a barely coded reference to race," with "Chicago" standing in for "black men and black crime."[38]

Ideas about guns, like ideas about violence, have long been heavily racialized: white extremists with guns are "patriots"; Black extremists with guns are "thugs." As a result, gun rights also wind up being racialized. In theory, Americans of all races have the same rights to own and to carry firearms. In practice, though, an African American or Latino with a gun is perceived and treated differently than a white person with a gun. The difference shows up dramatically in laboratory experiments, and the real-life consequences can be deadly. In 2014, police near Dayton, Ohio, shot and killed a Black man after he picked up an air rifle on display in a Walmart store, and several months later a Cleveland police officer shot dead a 12-year-old African American boy carrying a pellet gun in a public park. In 2016 a Black motorist was pulled over by police in a suburb of Saint Paul, Minnesota; he was fatally shot after telling the police he had an open-carry permit and a gun in the car. The New York stop-and-frisk program became notorious because it was applied disproportionately to members of racial minorities, especially young Black men. Complaints about racial targeting ultimately caused the NYPD to roll back the program and led to a judicial finding that the department had violated the equal protection clause of the federal Constitution. But if police officers cannot stop and frisk someone who appears to be carrying a concealed weapon—if a stop is legal only when the police have special reason to suspect that the weapon is being carried illegally, and a frisk is legal only when the police are confronting someone they have particular reason to think cannot be trusted with a gun—the police will need to look for signs that an individual has a violent disposition. And to expect that inquiry to be carried out in a race-neutral way is to ignore everything we know about the history and psychology of prejudice.[39]

The idea that gun possession, by itself, does not make a person dangerous has implications beyond stop and frisk. One increasingly popular strategy for addressing gun violence in the United States has been the use of "red flag laws"—statutes authorizing judges to take away the guns of individuals who have been shown to be an extreme danger to themselves or to others, and to ban those individuals from purchasing additional guns. The orders are temporary but can be extended. Seventeen states now have red flag laws, and there are ongoing efforts to enact a federal version. But concerns about both the First Amendment and the Second Amendment often limit the application of the laws, particularly when the signs of danger are mainly what the gun owner has said or written. Judges often conclude that menacing language doesn't satisfy the statutory language of red flag laws, or doesn't rise to the level of a "true threat" under the First Amendment, if the language can't be shown to have been aimed at intimating particular individuals or groups. For example, Washington State's red flag law was found inapplicable to a man who had said online that he would "shoot any woman any time for any reason," had posted about his fantasies of hurting women, and had talked about threatening his mother with a gun. A judge in Florida refused to extend an order banning a college student from purchasing guns, even though the student had praised mass shooters online and had suggested to investigators he might carry out a school shooting himself if something pushed him over the edge. The student's lawyer stressed to reporters that "if it's not a true or credible threat, it's constitutionally protected speech."[40]

The First and Second Amendments can both be invoked to oppose taking guns from people based on what they have said. With regard to red flag laws, therefore, free speech rights and gun rights often work in concert. On the broader question of how to respond to deadly violence, though, the two sets of rights can be at cross-purposes. Many zealous defenders of the First Amendment are staunchly opposed to gun rights, and Second Amendment activists often favor restrictions on free expression. This is because each side rejects certain situational explanations for violence that members of the other side find plausible. First Amendment law downplays the possibility that speech causes violence, and Second Amendment law downplays the risk that the availability of guns leads to violence. But rejecting either of these situational theories of violence does not necessarily entail rejecting the other. That is why the makers of the "Purge" movies, who necessarily reject the idea that on-screen violence leads to real-world violence, can see their movies as advertisements for gun control. And that is why the National Rifle Association can blame movies and video games for mass shootings—

even though gun manufacturers, who provide much of the funding for the NRA, pay the makers of the video games to help them market their weapons.[41] One situational theory of violence can be wrong but the other can still be right. In fact, the theories are often in competition: blaming violent entertainment can be a way of absolving guns, and vice versa.

Lethal Force and Personal Sovereignty

The Supreme Court's reinterpretation of the Second Amendment is not the only way in which gun rights in the United States have significantly expanded over the past quarter century. Equally important has been the rise of "make my day" and "stand your ground" laws. These statutes, which have been widely adopted over the past several decades and are now on the books in a majority of states, strengthen the right to use lethal force in self-defense or, in some cases, in defense of property. Collectively they constitute a significant change in the legal treatment of lethal force in the United States. But these statutes are even more important for what they symbolize. Their largest impacts have not been on the technical legal standards applied by judges and juries, but instead on American beliefs about violence and when it can legitimately be invoked. The story of make-my-day and stand-your-ground laws is not a story about how the law, standing alone, thinks about violence; it is a story about how legal and popular ideas about violence feed on each other. Popular ideas about violence can take their lead from legal changes, and vice versa.

It is telling in this regard that the earliest of these statutes were called "make my day" laws, borrowing from a catchphrase spoken by "Dirty Harry" Callahan, the trigger-happy, vigilante police officer played by Clint Eastwood in a series of five movies in the 1970s and 1980s. Harry is the hero of the movies. He uses the phrase when a gunman is threatening to kill a hostage and Harry has his own, large-caliber revolver pointed at the gunman's face. "Go ahead," Harry says, "make my day."

The provisions of make-my-day and stand-your-ground laws vary widely from state to state, but collectively they curtail two traditional rules regarding the use of deadly force as legal self-help. The first of these is the rule of proportionality, which generally allows deadly force only in response to the use or threatened use of deadly force. The second is what is sometimes called the "duty to retreat": the legal doctrine that makes it illegal to use lethal force in self-defense when it is possible to avoid or end the confrontation by withdrawing to safety.

This duty to retreat is a centuries-old doctrine in criminal law; the American colonies inherited it from England. It has long been limited by the so-called castle doctrine, which generally eliminates the duty to retreat within one's own home. In the late 1800s, though, many jurisdictions in the United States pushed back much further against the duty to retreat. They reasoned, in the words of an influential opinion by the Ohio Supreme Court, that "a true man, who is without fault, is not obliged to fly from an assailant." The Mississippi Supreme Court explained that when a person "is in a place where he has a right to be," he "is not bound to retreat" from an unprovoked attack but "may stand his ground and resist force with force." This new American doctrine eventually became known as the "true man" rule. It was thought to reflect distinctively American (and gendered) ideals of personal sovereignty and rugged individualism.

The true-man rule always had its critics. They thought it licensed needless killings. The Model Penal Code, promulgated by the American Law Institute in 1961, rejects the true-man rule and revives the duty to retreat. The Code forbids the use of deadly force in self-defense by someone who "knows that he can avoid the necessity of using such force with complete safety by retreating or by surrendering possession of a thing to a person asserting a claim of right thereto or by complying with a demand that he abstain from any action which he has no duty to take." There is an exception codifying a slightly expanded version of the castle doctrine: the duty to retreat does not apply to someone attacked at home or at work, unless he was the first aggressor or is attacked at work by a co-worker.[42] By the middle decades of the twentieth century, some American jurisdictions were returning to stronger versions of the duty to retreat.

Make-my-day and stand-your-ground statutes push back in the opposite direction, in effect codifying versions of the true-man rule—and also, in the bargain, limiting the rule of proportionality. The two most influential of these statutes were adopted by Colorado in 1985 and by Florida, twenty years later, in 2005. The Colorado measure was the first to be called "Make My Day." It authorized deadly force against anyone who entered a home illegally, if the occupant reasonably believed both that the intruder had committed or would commit a crime inside the residence, and that the intruder might use physical force "no matter how slight" against any occupant of the home. The Colorado statute was passed at a time when fear of violent crime was becoming an increasingly prominent theme in American politics, and it inspired similar legislative initiatives in many other states, often nicknamed "Make My Day," "Shoot the Burglar," or "Shoot the Carjacker" laws. The common denominator of these statutes was that they licensed private individuals to use deadly force to protect some forms of property—homes, or in some cases vehicles—without any requirement that the defender was himself or herself facing a clear threat of death or grave physical harm.[43]

The second wave of these statutes, initiated by Florida's "Stand Your Ground" law in 2005, differed from the first, both in their genesis and in their emphasis. Regarding their genesis: unlike the 1980s, the first decade of the twenty-first century was not a time of escalating violent crime. On the contrary, it followed the dramatic drop in crime rates during the 1990s. The Florida law and the measures it helped inspire in many other states therefore were not responses to rising public fears. They were instead the result of statehouse lobbying by the NRA and the American Legislative Exchange Council, a libertarian-leaning advocacy group. The second-wave self-defense laws were less about crime than about gun rights. Just as their genesis differed from those of the first wave, so did their emphasis. The Florida law applied everywhere, not just in homes and vehicles. It focused on protection against physical assault, wherever it occurred, rather than protection against burglars and carjackers. And it was framed squarely in opposition to the duty to retreat. Hence the shift in vernacular shorthand, from "Make My Day" to "Stand Your Ground."[44]

Make-my-day and stand-your-ground laws have generated lots of litigation, but it is unclear how many criminal cases have come out differently because of the substantive legal changes made by these stat-utes. It is rare for anyone to be prosecuted, let alone convicted, for using deadly force against a burglar encountered inside the home, or a carjacker encountered inside a vehicle. It is rare today, and it was rare forty years ago. Moreover, the duty to retreat has always been re-stricted to situations in which it is obvious both that withdrawing would be safe and that it would completely defuse the situation, conditions that are typically unsatisfied in violent encounters. Backers of Florida's stand-your-ground law have argued that the legislation was necessary so that the law would not require, for example, "an elderly woman in a dimly lit parking lot" or "a college girl walking back to her dorm at night" to "turn her back and try to flee" if attacked, putting her at risk of being overcome, raped, and killed. But the duty to retreat would not apply to either of these victims, precisely because trying to escape could be dan-gerous. A task force impaneled by the American Bar Association in 2013 to assess stand-your-ground laws could not find actual cases where indi-viduals acting in genuine self-defense were unprotected by traditional criminal law doctrines. Testifying before the task force, Pennsylvania district attorney Edward Marcisco Jr. called stand-your-ground laws "a solution looking for a problem."[45]

But if make-my-day and stand-your-ground laws altered little, prac-tically speaking, in the legal requirements for using lethal force, the pro-cedural innovations in these laws have proven more consequential. Many of these measures, including the law Colorado enacted in 1995 and the statute Florida adopted in 2005, do more than create defenses that can be asserted at trial; they create immunities that prevent a criminal case, or even a civil tort suit for damages, from going forward in the first place. A defendant who claims his actions were lawful under these stat-utes is entitled to a hearing at the outset of the case, and—if a prepon-derance of the evidence supports the defense—to an immediate dis-missal. There is anecdotal evidence that the prospect of these hearings, and of having to "try the case twice," can deter prosecutors from pur-suing cases in which make-my-day or stand-your-ground defenses are raised, even when prosecutors believe the defenses are ill-founded. Proving that the defenses are ill-founded, and doing it twice, can seem too daunting.[46]

The defenses allowed under make-my-day and stand-your-ground laws therefore may have their greatest effects on prosecutions, not by being proven in court, but simply by being available. The point can be made more broadly: these statutes are more significant for how they change people's thinking than for how they change legal analysis. They are understood to valorize the use of lethal force—and, more specifically, the use of guns—as a privatized and decentralized response to crime. Cultural historian Carolyn Light sees these state laws as helping to construct a new civic ideal, "DIY-security citizenship," framed around the responsibility to stand and fight rather than retreat.[47]

Because make-my-day and stand-your-ground laws have carried such heavy cultural baggage, they are often invoked in situations where, strictly speaking, they do not apply. In November 2007, two months after Texas adopted a stand-your-ground law modeled on Florida's, a 61-year-old man named Joe Horn called 911 to report that two men were burglarizing his neighbor's house in a Houston suburb. Horn told the dispatcher that he had a shotgun, and he offered to use it to stop the burglars. He described the men as Black. (It turned out they were undocumented Colombian nationals.) The dispatcher told Horn to stay in his house, because there was "no property worth shooting somebody over." But Horn said he was "not going to let them get away" with it, that a shotgun was "a legal weapon," and—referencing the new Texas statute—that the laws had "been changed in this country since September the first, and you know it and I know it." When the two burglars left the house, Horn went outside and shot them in the back as they fled, killing both of them. Horn was not arrested, and a grand jury refused to charge him.[48]

Four years later, in February 2012, a neighborhood watch coordinator named George Zimmerman shot and killed an unarmed teenager named Trayvon Martin in a gated community in Florida. Martin was walking home from a 7-Eleven after buying candy; Zimmerman thought he looked suspicious. Zimmerman called 911 and was advised not to follow Martin, but he confronted him anyway. Following the shooting he claimed that Martin had tackled him and tried to wrestle away his gun. Zimmerman was arrested but released hours later. The local police chief said that the stand-your-ground law did not allow Zimmerman's arrest.

Zimmerman was subsequently charged with second-degree murder but acquitted after a jury trial.[49]

The stand-your-ground statutes in Texas and Florida do not appear to have altered any important legal principles in either the Horn case or the Zimmerman case. Horn's victims were outside when he shot them, and they were running away: they were not in his residence or vehicle, and they were not threatening him. Horn, though, thought the law mattered. He made that clear when talking to the police dispatcher. Horn appeared to view the law as endorsing the new ideal of "DIY-security citizenship" that Carolyn Light has described.[50] He saw it as recognizing not just the right but the responsibility of private citizens to use lethal violence to preserve order, instead of staying in their houses, waiting for the police to arrive, and letting criminals escape. The grand jury's refusal to indict Horn suggests that they may have understood the law this way, too.

Trayvon Martin also was outside when he died, not in a residence or a vehicle. He was an unarmed African American teenager in a hoodie, and his killing led to protests throughout the country, in part because Zimmerman's initial decision to confront him looked like the worst kind of racial profiling. President Barack Obama said, "If I had a son, he'd look like Trayvon."[51] If Martin had in fact tackled Zimmerman and tried to take his weapon, Zimmerman may have had a valid claim of self-defense. But if so, the claim was valid with or without the stand-your-ground law, because Zimmerman would not have had the option of safely retreating.

Zimmerman, in fact, did not seek a finding of immunity under Florida's stand-your-ground law. He did ask the judge to instruct the jury about the provisions of that law, though, and the judge complied. The issue of immunity would have been decided by the judge, not the jury, so Zimmerman's lawyers appear to have calculated that they had little likelihood of convincing a *judge* that the stand-your-ground statute applied to their client, but the statute might be useful in convincing a *jury* that he had acted appropriately. The selective invocation of stand-your-ground by Zimmerman's lawyers was a tacit recognition that the statute did not help their client legally but might well help him symbolically. Legally, Zimmerman's self-defense claim depended entirely on whether the jury believed his story that Martin had attacked him and tried to wrestle away his gun, and that Zimmerman himself was not the initial aggressor. The stand-your-ground law had nothing to say about any of that. Symbolically, though, the law meant a lot. By valorizing "lethal self-defense as a core responsibility of the ideal citizen who stands his ground in the face of perceived threat rather than retreating from a fight," the statute made it easier to paint Zimmerman as a hero rather than a public danger. The same was true of Joe Horn, who was lionized by the Tea Party and conservative media.[52]

The symbolic meaning of make-my-day and stand-your-ground laws helps to explain why they seem to have had real, tangible impacts in the states that have adopted them, notwithstanding the limited number of cases in which the doctrinal changes they make are truly material. Stand-your-ground laws, in particular, appear to have increased homicide rates in the states that have adopted them, without having any observable effects on other crimes. They also seem to have affected the legal treatment of homicides, in a manner that exacerbates racial disparities. Shootings are more often found legally justifiable in states with stand-your-ground statutes, and the effect is particularly dramatic in cases with white perpetrators and Black victims. Even in states without stand-your-ground laws, fatal shootings are most likely to be found justifiable when the shooters are white and the victims are Black. But the disparity is strikingly larger in states that have passed stand-your-ground laws, a fact that lends some support to the suggestion that standing one's ground is largely a white man's privilege.[53]

For this reason and others, Mary Anne Franks argues that the expansive protections provided to free speech and gun rights in the United States reflect a kind of constitutional fundamentalism: a selective reading of the Constitution aimed at entrenching white male supremacy. There is no doubt that First and Second Amendment law has been shaped in part by assumptions about race and gender, nor that those assumptions skew in favor of long-standing social hierarchies. But interpretations of the First and Second Amendments have also reflected and reinforced particular ideas about violence. These include not only views about how violence should be defined and where it comes from, but also understandings of the moral significance of violence. Gun rights, in particular, are increasingly associated with the idea that the command of legal violence is not just the prerogative of free citizens; it is part of what it *means* to be a free, sovereign individual.

In December 2019 a report commissioned by the House of Representatives of Washington State concluded that a member of that body, State Representative Matt Shea, had participated in and promoted three episodes of "armed . . . political violence"—"domestic terrorism"—against the government of the United States, including the six-week armed takeover in 2015 of the Malheur National Wildlife Refuge in eastern Oregon. Shea belonged to and helped to lead a network of right-wing extremists dedicated to violent defense of their conception of American liberty. He had written and distributed a document calling for the creation of a theocracy in the United States and for "killing all males" who did not agree to end abortion, abolish same-sex marriage, and establish biblical law. "Liberty must be kept by force," Shea had told his followers.[54]

Shea's extensive involvement with the right-wing militia movement made him an outlier among elected politicians, even on the far right. He also had a history of domestic violence, and he had once drawn a gun on another driver in a road rage incident, so his participation in domestic terrorism could be understood as part of a larger, personal embrace of violence. But his ideology fits easily with a long-standing tradition in American political thought, the tradition that includes, for example, Thomas Jefferson's famous observation that the "tree of liberty must be refreshed from time to time with the blood of patriots and tyrants." Gun rights rhetoric is drenched in this tradition. It is emphatically not a tradition of nonviolence. It is a tradition that sees violence as not only justified but praiseworthy, as long as it is in the service of what is right—"liberty," or "security," or a particular vision of America. That is why many Americans could sympathize with Ammon Bundy, the cowboy-hat-wearing rancher's son who led the armed takeover of the Malheur National Wildlife Refuge, and why, even if they disapproved of the "occupation," they would not have described it as a violent crime. (The Malheur "occupation" turned deadly when police shot and killed one of Bundy's confederates.) Introducing Joe Horn to a cheering crowd in

2009, the broadcaster Glenn Beck noted approvingly that "it's a different world in Texas," and Horn agreed. "Yes it is," he said, "and thank God for it!" They meant that Texas was different, and better, because it welcomed the use of lethal force by private citizens defending personal security and property rights.[55]

You do not need to squint very hard to see lots of "ordinary" violent crime as motivated by an analogous sense of righteousness, however perverted that sense may be. This is true not just of the atrocities carried out by someone like Timothy McVeigh, whose bombing of the Oklahoma City Federal Building in 1995 killed 168 people, and who liked to quote Jefferson's line about the tree of liberty. The sociologist Donald Black, who taught law at Yale and Harvard in the 1970s, pointed out that *most* violent crimes, including most murders, are typically "moralistic." They are understood by their perpetrators as efforts at getting justice through self-help. The offenders seek to impose punishment, express disapproval, or obtain recompense, "whether applied reflectively or impulsively, with coolness or in the heat of passion." Most violent crime and a good deal of other crime, Black argued, is a decentralized, privatized form of "social control."[56]

Black wasn't excusing violent crime, just trying to explain it. And an armed takeover of a wildlife refuge, even if it ends in a fatality, is not the same as a premeditated murder, a rape, a home invasion, or a carjacking. Nonetheless it is worth seeing how the ideas about violence invoked when discussing the problem of "violent crime" differ from many of the ideas about violence embedded in discussions of free expression, gun rights, and some protest movements—mainly the ones associated with white, politically conservative men. The point is not that one set of beliefs is obviously correct and the other obviously wrong. The point is that the beliefs are different, that they get applied to different kinds of people, and that all of these differences should be noticed and interrogated. Otherwise how the law thinks about violence can wind up justifying the unjustifiable.

CONCLUSION

Violence presents the law with profound challenges. The most obvious challenges are practical: to reduce violence and to obtain a measure of justice for the victims of violence. Violent crime is less common in the United States than it was twenty years ago, but it still takes a horrible toll. Homicide is the third leading cause of death among Americans aged 15 to 34; it is the leading cause of death among Black males under 45 and the second leading cause of death among Latino males under 45. Every year, some five million Americans are victims of criminal assaults and more than 700,000 are raped. Police officers in the United States kill roughly a thousand people each year. Ten percent of all men and 20 percent of all women in the United States have experienced intimate partner violence. Violence is pervasive in many American prisons: in Mississippi, for example, six prisoners were killed in just the first week of 2020. How the law responds or fails to respond to these ongoing calamities helps to define us as a society.[1]

Beyond these practical problems, though, violence also presents the law with a more basic, conceptual challenge. The challenge is to think clearly about violence: to define it sensibly, to accord it the right kind of significance, to understand how it functions, and to appreciate the different forms it takes. This is the challenge that has been the focus of this book. It is a critical challenge. When our ideas about violence are muddled, our responses to violence are muddled. The problem is not only that bad ideas make it harder to reduce violence and to seek justice for its victims. Confused thinking about violence does not just make the legal system less effective; it can make the system harmful. The way the law thinks about violence can determine whether the law itself becomes an engine of inequality and a factory of needless suffering.

Violence can seem easy to identify and easy to condemn, no matter how hard it is to understand and control it. But violence is surprisingly tricky to define, and moral judgments about violence often prove slippery. Sometimes the label "violence" is reserved for acts involving physical force against other people, but at other times the category is extended to physical force against property, or to *threats* of physical force, or to acts that create the *danger* of physical force being used. Often the category is stretched even further and we speak of "symbolic," "verbal," or "emotional" violence. Sometimes the category of violence is restricted to acts that are illegal or illegitimate, so that "justified violence" becomes a contradiction in terms, but sometimes the term "violence" is used more broadly, without a built-in judgment that the acts in question are wrongful. The Supreme Court's efforts to interpret the terms "violent crime" and "crime of violence" in the federal criminal code have been spectacularly unsuccessful, and the Justices have repeatedly concluded that significant parts of the statutory definitions are unconstitutionally vague. As with definitions of violence, so also with moral assessments of violence. Sometimes violence is treated as beyond the pale: a category of behavior so unacceptable that people who engage in it should be condemned in the strongest possible terms and subjected to the heaviest possible penalties. Sometimes violence is celebrated and treated as heroic. And sometimes the line between violent and nonviolent conduct is given little significance of any kind.

These ambiguities, and others, pervade the law's treatment of violence. The ideas about violence incorporated within the law are glaringly inconsistent. This is true not only of ideas about how violence should be defined and ideas about the moral significance of violence—how much it matters whether something is violent, and in what ways. It is true as well of theories about how violence operates: how it originates, how it progresses, and how it can be stopped.

Ideas about the significance of violence and the definition of violence are closely related: one way to make violence matter less is to define it so broadly that almost everything counts as violent, or conversely to define it so narrowly that very little qualifies. The law is remarkably inconsistent about both the significance of violence and its definition. Over the past half century, criminal law has made violence increasingly consequential. The line between "violent" and "nonviolent" offenses has become the most important dividing line in criminal law. Whether an offense counts as violent often determines whether a defendant will be subjected to draconian sentencing "enhancements"; whether he or she will be ineligible for diversion programs or for drug court, veteran's court, or mental health court; whether the defendant will be eligible for early parole; and whether he or she will face a host of collateral consequences of conviction—from deportation to removal of voting rights. What counts as a "violent" crime, though, is often unpredictable and counterintuitive, and it can vary from state to state and depending on the context.

In stark contrast, the line between violent and nonviolent conduct plays almost no role in criminal procedure, the set of constitutional, legislative, and administrative rules that govern the police. The constitutional rules the Supreme Court has crafted for law enforcement draw little distinction between violent and nonviolent tactics, and the internal rules adopted by police departments generally employ a "use of force continuum" that largely abolishes any sharp distinction between violence and nonviolence. Controversy continues regarding how narrowly responses to sexual assault and domestic abuse should focus on *violent* forms of victimization, even as advocates for victims of sexual assault and domestic abuse argue that the main issue is control, not physical violence. In the area of juvenile justice, there has been a retreat from the idea that violent offenses are, almost by definition, not appropriate for resolution in juvenile court, and in the area of child welfare the argument is increasingly heard that emotional abuse can be worse than physical abuse. But in these areas, too, the category of violence retains significant purchase, and violence often is treated as a category apart—both violence by juveniles and violence against juveniles. The idea that violence is a category apart lies behind the move away from corporal punishment of children, but that move is very far from complete. A significant number of jurisdictions continue to allow corporal punishment in public schools, and no jurisdiction has banned or even significantly restricted corporal punishment carried out by parents or guardians.

In carceral institutions, corporal punishment *is* formally banned. For the purposes of the Eighth Amendment, violence is very much a category apart—except when it comes to the death penalty, and even there, modern methods of execution seem designed to downplay the use of physical force and to avoid the spectacle of violence. In the actual operation of jails and prisons, however, violence is often so openly tolerated that it seems an informal part of the punishment imposed on prisoners. Public discussions of criminal violence, moreover, often ignore violence within jails or prisons, treating it—sometimes implicitly, sometimes explicitly—as not raising the same kinds of concerns as violence outside the walls of correctional institutions.

Meanwhile the interpretation and application of the First Amendment downplays the distinction between violence and nonviolence, and Second Amendment doctrine increasingly reflects the view that the important line is not the one between violence and nonviolence, but the one between justified and unjustified uses of violence. Gun offenses—including possession of a gun by someone who has lost the privilege—are typically treated as violent offenses for purposes of the many, often draconian distinctions that criminal law draws between violent and nonviolent offenses. But lawful possession of a gun, and lawful use of a gun in self-defense or in defense of property, is valorized, not only in much popular discourse, but increasingly in the law as well, in constitutional doctrine and in stand-your-ground laws.

The law also incorporates and reinforces ideas about how violence works: what drives it, how it starts and stops. Here, too, the law is inconsistent. Contemporary sentencing statutes, especially "Three Strikes" laws and other provisions aimed at "habitual" offenders, are strongly shaped by the view that violence is dispositional rather than situational. They are shaped, that is to say, by the belief that violence is driven by the character of particular, dangerous individuals rather than by the circumstances in which people find themselves. This same idea lies behind the law of free expression under the First Amendment and the expansive understanding of gun rights the Supreme Court has recently brought to its interpretation and application of the Second Amendment.

Why does constitutional law so rarely allow speech to be restricted in the interest of preventing violence? Partly because freedom of speech is so highly valued, but partly, too, because the Supreme Court has been highly skeptical of claims that speech of any kind—even the "speech" of ultraviolent video games—is likely to result in actual bloodshed unless people are already inclined to violence, in which case the speech is unnecessary to spur them on. So too with firearms: guns don't kill people, the National Rifle Association repeatedly says, people kill people. The same skepticism about gun control laws is reflected in the Supreme Court's recent Second Amendment decisions, although the Court has refrained from carrying that skepticism as far as gun rights activists would like. Likewise, a dispositional theory of violence underlies the complacency that courts often show toward violence in jails and prison. If what makes carceral institutions violent is the nature of the people confined in them, then violence behind bars is inevitable: prisons are dangerous places because prisoners are dangerous people.

But violence is not always understood as a matter of character. Legal regulation of the police reflects a long-standing tension between two different ways of thinking about police violence: one is dispositional, focusing on "bad apples," and the other is situational, focusing on the dangers faced by officers and the split-second decisions they sometimes have to make. Thinking about sexual assault, and about domestic violence, is similarly marked by long-standing debates about whether these problems stem from the pathologies of individual offenders or instead from a pervasive culture of male domination. Prison reformers have long pointed to evidence that violence behind bars is not, in fact, inevitable: that it results from the way particular carceral institutions are operated. Similarly, recent changes in the treatment of juvenile violence reflect a renewed belief that young offenders are distinguished in part by their suggestibility and impetuosity—which is to say, their susceptibility to situational drivers of violence.

Recognizing the wide difference in how the law thinks about violence does not tell us how the law *should* think about violence. It does not tell us how violence can best be defined, what moral significance it has, or how it can best be understood. But it does teach some lessons about how *not* to think about violence. It warns us about mistakes the law should avoid.

The most important of these mistakes is the assumption that violence is a thing apart: an easily recognizable, objectively distinguishable, superlatively condemnable set of behaviors, engaged in by an easily recognizable, objectively distinguishable, superlatively condemnable category of people. Stated in this manner, the mistake seems easy to avoid—a straw man, even. Nearly everyone recognizes that the line between violence and nonviolence is sometimes blurry, that a normally nonviolent person can sometimes become violent, and that nonviolent wrongdoing can be worse than relatively minor forms of violence. On the last night of 2019, Pope Francis angrily slapped away the hand of a woman who had grabbed his own hand and would not let go. He apologized the next day.[2] No one suggested that his transgression—if it was a transgression—had crossed some kind of a line, that whatever other complaints people might have about the Vatican, this was an entirely different, and worse, category of ecclesiastical misconduct. Most of us recognize that the moral universe can't be navigated simply by distinguishing between violent and nonviolent behavior, or violent and nonviolent people. A scam artist who cheats hundreds of elderly victims out of their life savings seems at least as bad as a music producer who angrily swings a kettlebell during an argument at a college gym—or even a waitress who, when provoked, slams a customer's head into the bar.

The legal system, too, recognizes the folly of trying to use the presence or absence of violence to draw a bright line between serious and less serious violations. At least it does sometimes. That is why simple assault is not a felony, but bank fraud is. It is why constitutional law makes little distinction between violent and nonviolent police misconduct, and why the internal regulations of law enforcement agencies talk about a "use of force continuum." It is why many domestic violence intervention programs now focus less on violence per se than on "coercive control," and why advocates for abused children increasingly argue that the worst forms of household "violence" can be verbal or emotional, rather than physical.

At other times, though, the law does try to use violence as a master category, dividing grave transgressions from minor ones, and serious offenders from those who deserve understanding and mercy. Over the past half century this simplistic approach has been employed most dramatically, and with especially ruinous results, in substantive criminal law, especially in laws shaping the penalties and collateral consequences for criminal violations. Even as the country has begun to retreat from the draconian criminal justice policies adopted in the 1980s and 1990s, the new leniency has typically not been extended to "violent" offenders. The overreliance on violence as a legal category helped to create mass incarceration and now helps to sustain it. Simplistic ideas about violence also helped to fuel the "superpredator" scare in the 1980s, which shrank the role of the juvenile justice system and wound up sending thousands of young offenders to long terms in adult prisons. Today those ideas continue to slow efforts to restore the juvenile justice system to its historic role.

Because some crimes we would ordinarily call violent do not seem serious, and some crimes that are not obviously violent can seem very serious, the category of "violent" crimes winds up being a legal construction, a kind of conceptual gerrymander. The boundaries of the category are set arbitrarily, depending on which offenses, and which offenders, seem to warrant the harshest sanctions. That kind of subjective line-drawing is an open invitation to racial bias, and the category of violent criminals inevitably winds up disproportionately comprised of minority defendants. But because the category remains nominally defined by violence—and violence in the abstract seems so threatening to our safety, security, and civilized society—penal policies that otherwise would seem too heartless and destructive can become acceptable. For the same reason, the fact that so many of the defendants subjected to these policies are Black or Latino can seem an unfortunate by-product of the way things are, rather than the consequence of social choices. In fact, racial prejudice can make the lopsided impact of antiviolence policies look like a confirmation that the targeting is working, that the defendants being locked away for decades really are violent and dangerous. It now seems obvious that this dynamic was part of the reason the "superpredator" theory could gain hold in the 1980s with so little evidence to back it up: when young men of color committed violent crimes, racial prejudice made it easier to label them as monsters.

Criminal law is an effort to respond in principled ways to wrongdoing. The great dilemma of criminal law, faced in virtually every case, is how to reconcile the conflict between two powerful instincts: on the one hand, the pull toward sympathy and understanding, the sense of "there but for the grace of God go I"; on the other hand, the desire for justice, the belief that people are moral agents and should be held accountable for what they do. There is always a temptation to cut the knot by dividing defendants into two categories: those who have erred but remain redeemable, and those who are beyond the pale. But the world is messier, and offenders can't be so neatly sorted.

Janet Reno, when she was US attorney general in the 1990s, sometimes told federal prosecutors that they needed to distinguish between defendants who needed help getting back on the right path, and the "bad baddies." When it came to the bad baddies, there was no alternative to locking them up and throwing away the key. I was one of the federal prosecutors who received this advice from Reno. I have always felt fortunate to have worked in the Justice Department when Janet Reno led it. She was an exemplary public servant: wise, skillful, and thoroughly decent. But she was wrong to think that the great dilemma of criminal law—the choice between understanding and judgment—can be addressed by dividing defendants into two fundamentally different groups, one deserving understanding and the other needing condemnation. The overreliance on violence to identify the defendants least deserving of mercy has been a ruinous, decades-long example of that mistake.

If the first lesson of this book is not to oversimplify violence—not to treat the category of violence as having sharp and uncontroversial boundaries—a closely related and equally important lesson is not to ignore or downplay violence because it doesn't match a stereotyped preconception of what "violence" means. When violence is imagined to be an entirely separate realm of human activity, stemming from the distinctive, fundamentally violent nature of the perpetrators, then a fair bit of what we otherwise might call violence drops out of sight. Violence by police officers becomes "use of force" or "response to resistance"—unless the police, too, are thought to be pathologically inclined to violence, in which case their tactics are described not just as violence but as "brutality." Either way, we lose the ability to see, simultaneously, the particular concerns raised by violent forms of policing, and the tactical choices that are likely to create circumstances in which the police feel the need to use violence. The simplistic view of violence as a category apart, engaged in by people who are themselves in a category apart, makes it easier to write off the violence in prisons and jails as inevitable, given the violent nature of the people housed in these institutions, and easier not to even count it as "violence," because the victims are not themselves innocent.

Through a similar process of exclusion, the term "violence" begins to seem inapplicable to the brandishing and use of guns by people imagined to be generally "law-abiding." Corporal punishment of children gets read out of the category of violence, as well, especially when that punishment is meted out by parents. The danger that violence can be fomented by online incitement or gruesome video games also becomes easier to dismiss if the problem of real-world violence is understood to be principally a problem of people who are fundamentally violent: "bad baddies." It is a mistake to rely too heavily on the category of violence, to think we can use that category to distinguish easily between truly bad people and people who have merely done bad things. It is a mistake both because it can blind us to the humanity of the people we categorize as violent, and because it can lead us to overlook or to minimize the violence carried out by other people. Making too much of violence has fueled mass incarceration; making too little of violence has discredited police reform.

Simplistic ideas about violence can lead the law astray in yet another way. The category of violence can occlude other categories. Calling something violent can seem inconsistent with characterizing it in other, important ways. But responding intelligently to youth violence requires understanding both that it matters that the perpetrators are young and that it matters that they have acted violently. Juvenile justice went wrong in the 1980s and 1990s partly because of the idea that violent offenses should not be treated as juvenile offenses—that the categories of "juvenile" and "violent" were somehow inconsistent. Responses to rape and domestic violence have sometimes been hindered by an unstated premise that emphasizing the violence in a sexual assault, or in a pattern of intimate-partner abuse, means not seeing the significance of the gender dynamics at play, or the exercise of power and control. The violence in police tactics like stop and frisk can be hard to see, let alone to understand and rectify, without paying attention to how those tactics function as mechanisms of racial subjugation. Violence is not a separate world. It exists alongside and often works in combination with other dimensions of domination, persecution, and victimization.

Violence has always been a particular challenge for the law: not just particularly important to address, but particularly difficult to think sensibly about. The law tries to respond in principled and deliberate ways to violence, but that requires pondering the unfathomable, reasoning about the unreasonable. The Hebrew Bible told the adjudicators of ancient Israel what to do when the task became too difficult. "If there arise a matter too hard for thee in judgment, between blood and blood, between plea and plea, and between stroke and stroke," Deuteronomy instructs, ". . . then shalt thou arise, and get thee up into the place which the Lord thy God shall choose." There, in the Lord's place, the priests would provide a judgment.[3] But we do not have recourse to that expedient today. We have only the tools of our heads and our hearts. It is incumbent on us to use those tools to the best of our abilities: to think as clearly as we can about violence and how to respond to it, and to be ever vigilant lest our ideas blind us to injustice or harden us against mercy.

APPENDIX

REFERENCES TO "VIOLENT" CRIMES AND "CRIMES OF VIOLENCE" IN TITLE 18 OF THE UNITED STATES CODE

	Citation	Brief Description	Date
1	18 U.S.C. § 1952, Interstate and foreign travel or transportation in aid of racketeering enterprises	Criminalizing interstate travel or use of mail to commit crime of violence in furtherance of unlawful activity	1961
2	18 U.S.C. § 929, Use of restricted ammunition	Criminalizing use of firearm in commission of crime of violence	1984
3	18 U.S.C. § 3521, Witness relocation and protection	Authorizing witness protection where there is a likelihood of crime of violence against witness	1984
4	18 U.S.C. § 5038, Use of juvenile records	Requiring fingerprinting and photographing of juveniles who commit acts that if committed by adults would be felony crimes of violence	1984
5	18 U.S.C. § 924, Penalties	Mandating extra prison time for carrying or using weapon during crime of violence	1984
6	18 U.S.C. § 1959, Violent crimes in aid of racketeering activity	Criminalizing threats of crimes of violence in aid of racketeering	1984
7	18 U.S.C. § 3156, Definitions	Defining "crime of violence"	1984
8	18 U.S.C. § 5032, Delinquency proceedings in district courts; transfer for criminal prosecution	Special provisions for juveniles charged with crimes of violence	1984

	Citation	Brief Description	Date
9	18 U.S.C. § 3142, Release or detention of a defendant pending trial	Authorizing pretrial detention in cases involving crimes of violence	1984
10	18 U.S.C. § 16, Crime of violence defined	Defining "crime of violence"	1984
11	18 U.S.C. § 2516, Authorization for interception of wire, oral, or electronic communications	Authorizing electronic interception in cases involving violent crimes in aid of racketeering activity	1986
12	18 U.S.C. § 3559, Sentencing classification of offenses	Mandating imprisonment for violent crimes against children	1994
13	18 U.S.C. § 521, Criminal street gangs	Addressing federal felony "crime of violence"	1994
14	18 U.S.C. § 2261, Interstate domestic violence	Criminalizing interstate travel to commit crime of violence against spouse, intimate partner, or dating partner	1994
15	18 U.S.C. § 3561, Sentence of probation	Defining "domestic violence crime"	1994
16	18 U.S.C. § 4042, Duties of Bureau of Prisons	Requiring notice of release of prisoners convicted of crimes of violence	1994
17	18 U.S.C. § 922, Unlawful acts	Addressing crimes of violence with firearms	1994
18	18 U.S.C. § 3181, Scope and limitation of chapter	Permitting surrender of persons who have committed crimes of violence against US nationals in foreign countries	1996
19	18 U.S.C. § 844, Penalties	Criminalizing transfer of explosives to commit crimes of violence	1996
20	18 U.S.C. § 3663A, Mandatory restitution to victims of certain crimes	Providing for restitution to victims of crimes of violence	1996

	Citation	Brief Description	Date
21	18 U.S.C. § 1028, Fraud and related activity in connection with identification documents, authentication features, and information	Prescribing punishment for fraudulent use of documents in connection with crime of violence	1998
22	18 U.S.C. § 842, Unlawful acts	Criminalizing assistance in use of explosives and other devices to commit crimes of violence	1999
23	18 U.S.C. § 1956, Laundering of monetary instruments	Criminalizing money laundering in connection with crime of violence	2001
24	18 U.S.C. § 931, Prohibition on purchase, ownership, or possession of body armor by violent felons	Prohibiting possession of body armor by person convicted of crime of violence	2002
25	18 U.S.C. § 25, Use of minors in crimes of violence	Prescribing penalties for using minor to commit crime of violence	2003
26	18 U.S.C. § 2250, Failure to register	Mandating enhanced sentence for defendants who commit crimes of violence	2006
27	18 U.S.C. § 1039, Fraud and related activity in connection with obtaining confidential phone records information of a covered entity	Providing enhanced penalties for use of information in connection with crimes of violence	2007
28	18 U.S.C. § 119, Protection of individuals performing certain official duties	Criminalizing use of information to incite crime of violence	2008
29	18 U.S.C. § 3553, Imposition of sentence	Limiting applicability of statutory minimum sentence for nonviolent offenses	2018
30	18 U.S.C. § 2523, Executive agreements on access to data by foreign governments	Allowing dissemination of information relating to "significant violent crime"	2018

NOTES

INTRODUCTION

1.   On mass incarceration, its drivers, and its costs, see Rachel Elise Barkow, *Prisoners of Politics: Breaking the Cycle of Mass Incarceration* (Cambridge, MA: Harvard University Press, 2019), 17–102; James Forman Jr., *Locking Up Our Own: Crime and Punishment in Black America* (New York: Farrar, Straus and Giroux, 2017); National Research Council, *The Growth of Incarceration in the United States: Exploring Causes and Consequences* (Washington, DC: National Academies Press, 2014); Franklin E. Zimring, "Imprisonment Rates and the New Politics of Criminal Justice," *Punishment & Society* 3 (2001): 161–166.

2.   William J. Stuntz, "Privacy's Problem and the Law of Criminal Procedure," *Michigan Law Review* 93 (1995): 1016–1078, at 1066. Regarding the promise and the limits of community policing, see David Alan Sklansky, *Democracy and the Police* (Stanford, CA: Stanford University Press, 2008); James Forman Jr., "Community Policing and Youth as Assets," *Journal of Criminal Law and Criminology* 95 (2004): 1–48; Debra Livingston, "Police Discretion and the Quality of Life in Public Places: Courts, Communities, and the New Policing," *Columbia Law Review* 97 (1997): 551–672; Tracey L. Meares and Dan M. Kahan, "The Coming Crisis of Criminal Procedure," *Georgetown Law Journal* 86 (1998): 1153–1185, at 1160–1166; Kami Chavis Simmons, "New Governance and the 'New Paradigm' of Police Accountability: A Democratic Approach to Police Reform," *Catholic University Law Review* 59 (2010): 373–426.

3.   Mary Douglas, *How Institutions Think* (Syracuse, NY: Syracuse University Press, 1986), 7–8.

1. VIOLENCE AS A LEGAL PROBLEM

1.   Christophe Menke, "Law and Violence," *Law and Literature* 22 (2010): 1–17, at 1; Robert M. Cover, "Violence and the Word," *Yale Law Journal* 95 (1986): 1601–1629, at 1601.

2.   See, for example, Austin Sarat and Thomas R. Kearns, eds., *Law, Violence and the Possibility of Justice* (Princeton, NJ: Princeton University Press, 1992);

Austin Sarat, ed., *Law, Violence and the Possibility of Justice* (Princeton, NJ: Princeton University Press, 2001).

3. Steven Pinker, *The Better Angels of Our Nature: Why Violence Has Declined* (New York: Viking, 2011).

4. Raymond Williams, *Keywords: A Vocabulary of Culture and Society,* rev. ed. (1983; London: Fourth Estate, 2014), 325; Jerome H. Skolnick, *The Politics of Protest* (New York: Ballantine, 1969), 6; Merriam-Webster, s.v. "violence," accessed August 24, 2020, https://www.merriam-webster.com/dictionary/violence.

5. Andrew Verstein, "Violent White-Collar Crime," *Wake Forest Law Review* 49 (2014): 873–887, at 879; Cover, "Violence and the Word," 1607; Rob Nixon, *Slow Violence and the Environmentalism of the Poor* (Cambridge, MA: Harvard University Press, 2011), 2.

6. Lisa Feldman Barrett, "When Is Speech Violence?," *New York Times,* Sunday Review, July 16, 2017, p. 9; Williams, *Keywords,* 325; William C. Gay, "Supplanting Linguistic Violence," in *Gender Violence: Interdisciplinary Perspectives,* ed. Laura O'Toole, Jessica Schiffman, and Margie L. Edwards, 2nd ed. (New York: NYU Press, 2007), 435–442; Kathleen Ho, "Structural Violence as a Human Rights Violation," *Essex Human Rights Review* 4, no. 2 (September 2007); Pierre Bourdieu, *The Logic of Practice,* trans. Richard Nice (Stanford, CA: Stanford University Press 1980), 125–134; Newton Garver, "What Violence Is," *Nation,* June 24, 1968, 819–822, at 820–821. Pierre Bourdieu used the term "symbolic violence" to refer to social practices that reinforce patterns of domination by making them seem legitimate and natural to the people being subordinated. The communications scholar George Gerbner used the phrase differently; by "symbolic violence" he meant the depiction of violence in the media, particularly in television dramas. Gerbner, "Violence in Television Drama: Trends and Symbolic Functions," in *Television and Social Behavior: Media Content and Control,* ed. George A. Comstock and Eli A. Rubinstein (Washington, DC: US Government Printing Office, 1972), 28–187. Gerbner argued that "symbolic violence" is a social tool "for achieving the aims of real violence without having to commit any" (44). Bourdieu, of course, thought something similar about the practices that *he* called "symbolic violence": they were a "soft" form of domination that substituted for physical force. Bourdieu, *Logic of Practice,* 125–134; Keith Topper, "Not So Trifling Nuances: Pierre Bourdieu, Symbolic Violence, and the Perversions of Democracy," *Constellations* 8, no. 1 (March 2001), 30–56.

7. Thomas Fuller, "Berkeley Cancelation Won't Deter Some Right-Wing Speakers," *New York Times,* September 24, 2017, p. A16 (quoting Nancy Scheper-Hughes); Barrett, "When Is Speech Violence?"; Amanda Hess, "Battle Cry," *New*

York Times Magazine, August 20, 2017, 11; Peter Holley, "The NRA Recruitment Video That Is Even Upsetting Gun Owners," *Washington Post,* June 29, 2019.

8.   Joanne B. Freeman, *The Field of Blood: Violence in Congress and the Road to Civil War* (New York: Farrar, Straus and Giroux, 2018), 233–234.

9.   Paul Ricoeur, "Violence and Language," in *Political and Social Essays,* ed. David Stewart and Joseph Bien (Athens, OH: Ohio University Press, 1974), 88–101, at 89–90; Gay, "Supplanting Linguistic Violence," 436 ("violence of sexist language").

10.   C. A. Coady, "The Idea of Violence," *Journal of Applied Philosophy* 3 (1986): 3–19; Randall Collins, *Violence: A Micro-Sociological Theory* (Princeton, NJ: Princeton University Press, 2008), 25; Alice Ristroph, "Criminal Law in the Shadow of Violence," *Alabama Law Review* 62 (2011): 571–621, at 575.

11.   Garver, "What Violence Is," 819.

12.   Gerald Runkle, "Is Violence Always Wrong?," *Journal of Politics* 38 (1976): 367–389, at 368; Coady, "The Idea of Violence," 14–15; Justin A. Joyce, "The Warp, Woof, and Weave of This Story's Tapestry Would Foster the Illusion of Further Progress: *Justified* and the Evolution of Western Violence," *Western American Literature* 47 (2012): 174–199.

13.   Ristroph, "Criminal Law in the Shadow of Violence," 582.

14.   18 U.S.C. § 924(e); Johnson v. United States, 135 S. Ct. 2551 (2015).

15.   18 U.S.C. § 924(e)(2)(B). Regarding the history of this clause, see Taylor v. United States, 495 U.S. 575, 581–589 (1990).

16.   Johnson v. United States, 2559.

17.   Johnson v. United States, 2561; Stokeling v. United States, 139 S. Ct. 544 (2019) ("overcoming resistance"); Quarles v. United States, 139 S. Ct. 1872 (2019) ("burglary").

18.   Sessions v. Dimaya, 138 S. Ct. 1204 (2018); United States v. Davis, 139 S. Ct. 2319 (2019).

19.   See, for example, Amanda Cawston, "What Is Violence?," in *Women and Violence: The Agency of Victims and Perpetrators,* ed. Herjeet Marway and Heather Widdows (London: Palgrave Macmillan, 2015), 217–225.

20.   Jeffrey Standen, "The Manly Sports: The Problematic Use of Criminal Law to Regulate Sports Violence," *Journal of Criminal Law and Criminology* 99 (2009): 619–642; Cheryl Hanna, "Sex Is Not a Sport: Consent and Violence in Criminal Law," *Boston College Law Review* 42 (2001): 239–290; Carolyn E. Light, *Stand Your Ground: A History of America's Love Affair with Lethal Self-Defense* (Boston: Beacon, 2017); Mary Anne Franks, "Men, Women, and Optimal Violence," *University of Illinois Law Review* 2016: 929–968.

21. Jefferson to William Stephens Smith, November 13, 1878, in *Letters and Addresses of Thomas Jefferson,* ed. William B. Parker and Jonas Viles (New York: Unit Book, 1905), 65; Paul Butler, *Chokehold: Policing Black Men* (New York: New Press, 2017), 242; Andrew Delbanco, *The War before the War: Fugitive Slaves and the Struggle for America's Soul from the Revolution to the Civil War* (New York: Penguin Books, 2018), 337–338.

22. James Forman Jr., *Locking Up Our Own: Crime and Punishment in Black America* (New York: Farrar, Straus and Giroux, 2017); Peter H. Rossi et al., "The Seriousness of Crimes: Normative Structure and Individual Differences," *American Sociological Review* 29 (1974): 224–237; Douglas Hay, "Property, Authority, and Criminal Law," in *Albion's Fatal Tree: Crime and Society in Eighteenth-Century England* (New York: Pantheon, 1975), 18.

23. Coady, "The Idea of Violence," 10; Ristroph, "Criminal Law in the Shadow of Violence," 621; Dante Alighieri, *The Inferno,* Canto 11, 25–27 ("Ma perché frode è l'uom proprio male, / più spiace a Dio; e però stan di sotto / li frodolenti, e più dolo li assale").

24. Runkle, "Is Violence Always Wrong?," 375.

25. Margaret T. Gordon and Stephanie Riger, *The Female Fear: The Social Cost of Rape* (New York: Free Press, 1991).

26. James Miller, *Democracy Is in the Streets: From Port Huron to the Siege of Chicago* (Cambridge, MA: Harvard University Press, 1994); Robert Paul Wolff, "On Violence," *Journal of Philosophy* 66 (1969): 601–616, at 610.

27. J. D. Vance, *Hillbilly Elegy: A Memoir of a Family and a Culture in Crisis* (New York: HarperCollins, 2016), 17, 255.

28. Government's Supplemental and Amended Sentencing Memorandum, United States v. Stone, Crim. No. 19-cr-18-ABJ (D.D.C. February 11, 2020).

29. Butler, *Chokehold,* 43; Mary Anne Franks, *The Cult of the Constitution: Our Deadly Devotion to Guns and Free Speech* (Stanford, CA: Stanford University Press, 2019), 90–91.

30. See the tweets by Clarke (@SheriffClarke) on October 15, November 9, and November 11, 2016: https://twitter.com/SheriffClarke/status/787314656641712128; https://twitter.com/SheriffClarke/status/796574545243148288; https://twitter.com /SheriffClarke/status/797275978691026944.

31. Michael E. Miller, "Donald Trump on a Protester: 'I'd Like to Punch Him in the Face,'" *Washington Post,* February 23, 2016; Sam Reisman, "Trump Tells Crowd to 'Knock the Crap Out' of Protesters, Offers to Pay Legal Fees," Mediaite, February 1, 2016, https://www.mediaite.com/online/trump-tells-crowd-to -knock-the-crap-out-of-protesters-offers-to-pay-legal-fees/; Maggie Haberman and Liz Robbins, "Trump, on Long Island, Vows an End to Gang Violence," *New*

York Times, July 29, 2017, p. A14; Jess Bravin, "Acting DEA Chief Rebuts Trump's Remarks on Police Use of Force," *Wall Street Journal,* August 1, 2017; Brian M. Rosenthal, "Police Criticize Trump for Urging Officers Not to Be 'Too Nice' with Suspects," *New York Times,* July 30, 2017, p. A16.

32. Peter King, "Trump Calls on NFL Owners to Fire Players Who Protest, and Mocks Efforts to Make the Game Safer," *Sports Illustrated,* September 23, 2017.

33. David Leonhardt, "Trump Encourages Violence," *New York Times,* March 18, 2019, p. A21; Philip Bump, "With a Wink, Trump Asks that Supporters Not Hurt Protesters Criticizing His Rhetoric," *Washington Post,* October 24, 2019.

34. Ben Collins and Brandy Zadrozny, "In Trump's 'LIBERATE' Tweets, Extremists See a Call to Arms," NBC News, April 17, 2020, https://www.nbcnews.com/tech/security/trump-s-liberate-tweets-extremists-see-call-arms-n1186561; Adam Gabbat, "Thousands of Americans Backed by Rightwing Donors Gear Up for Protests," *Guardian,* April 18, 2020; Davey Alba, Kate Conger, and Raymond Zhong, "Twitter Attaches Warnings to Posts, Escalating Feud with the White House," *New York Times,* May 30, 2020, p. A16.

35. Michael R. Ebner, *Ordinary Violence in Mussolini's Italy* (New York: Cambridge University Press, 2011), 3–8, 262, 267; Federico Finchelstein, *From Fascism to Populism in History* (Oakland: University of California Press, paperback ed. 2019), xviii, xxi, 73–81; Steven Levitsky and Daniel Ziblatt, *How Democracies Die* (New York: Crown, 2018), 21–24, 62–64; Jelani Cobb, "Donald Trump Is Serious when He 'Jokes' about Police Brutality," *New Yorker,* August 1, 2017; Michael Scherer, "Trump Employs Images of Violence as Political Fuel for Reelection Fight," *Washington Post,* September 8, 2020.

36. James Hamblin, "How a Man Takes a Body Slam," *Atlantic,* May 25, 2017; Christopher Mele, "Montana Republican Greg Gianforte Is Sentenced in Assault on Reporter," *New York Times,* June 13, 2017; Matt Pearce, "Some Conservatives Justify 'Manly' Montana Candidate's Alleged Body-Slam of 'Snowflake' Reporter," *Los Angeles Times,* May 25, 2017; David Weigel, "Montana's Familiar Story: A Wealthy Candidate Became a Warrior against the 'Establishment,'" *Washington Post,* May 26, 2017; Scherer, "Trump Employs Images of Violence."

37. Tauriq Moosa, "The 'Punch a Nazi' Meme: What Are the Ethics of Punching Nazis?," *Guardian,* January 31, 2017; Liam Stack, "Attack on Alt-Right Leader Has Internet Asking: Is It O.K. to Punch a Nazi?," *New York Times,* January 21, 2017; Abby Ohlheiser, "How a GOP Candidate's Alleged Body Slam of a Reporter Played Out on the Trump Internet," *Washington Post,* May 25, 2017. There was an echo of the "punch a Nazi" controversy fourteen months later, when former vice president Joseph Biden said that if he were in high school he would

"beat the hell out of" President Trump for boasting about sexually assaulting women. Predictably, Trump responded with his own threat, tweeting that Biden "would go down fast and hard, crying all the way." Eileen Sullivan, "Trump Threatens Joe Biden, Saying He Would 'Go Down Fast and Hard' if They Fought," *New York Times,* March 22, 2018.

38. Philip Bump, "Trump's Speech Encouraging Police to Be 'Rough,' Annotated," *Washington Post,* July 28, 2017 (italics added).

39. Miller, *Democracy Is in the Streets.*

40. Angela Davis, interview by Bo Holmström, in *The Black Power Mixtape 1967–1975,* directed by Göran Hugo Olsson (New York: IFC Films, 2011), 56:20–59:57.

41. Lydia O'Connor, "Fox News Host Compares Charlottesville White Supremacists to Black Lives Matter," Huffpost, August 13, 2017, https://www.huffpost.com/entry/fox-news-charlottesville_n_59907720e4b090964297b9d3. Several days after the violence in Charlottesville in 2017, Trump's personal lawyer John Dowd distributed an email declaring that the Black Lives Matter movement had been "totally infiltrated by terrorist groups," and blaming the movement for deadly attacks on police officers. Michael S. Schmidt and Matt Apuzzo, "Trump Lawyer Spreads Email with Secessionist Rhetoric," *New York Times,* August 17, 2017, p. A16. Regarding Trump's own statements on Charlottesville, see Jackie Calmes, "Trump Says Blame Belongs 'on Many Sides' amid White Supremacist Violence in Virginia," *Chicago Tribune,* August 12, 2017; Michael D. Shear and Maggie Haberman, "Trump Again Says Two Sides at Fault in Rally Violence," August 16, 2017, p. A1; Glenn Thrush, "Trump Condemns Racists but Creates Fresh Uproar," *New York Times,* August 15, 2017, p. A1; David Weigel, "Fear of 'Violent Left' Preceded Events in Charlottesville," *Washington Post,* August 13, 2017; Linda Qiu, "On Spectrum of Extremism, Far Left Takes Relatively Little Space," *New York Times,* August 16, 2017, p. A13. A year after Charlottesville, as midterm elections approached, Trump returned to the theme of left-wing violence, warning a group of evangelical leaders that if Democrats won, they would "overturn everything we've done and . . . do it quickly and violently. . . . When you look at antifa, and look at some of these groups, these are violent people." Michael Shear, "Trump Has a Stark Warning for Pastors," *New York Times,* August 29, 2018, p. A12. In the summer of 2020, when protests against police violence and conservative counterprotests across the country themselves sometimes turned violent, Trump defended his supporters by arguing they were simply reacting to "tremendous violence" by those on the other side. Ashley Parker, Robert Klemko, and Mark Guarino, "Trump Blames 'Far-Left' Politicians for Violence in Wake of Police Shooting on Visit to Wisconsin," *Washington Post,* September 1, 2020; Aaron

Blake, "Trump's Illuminating Defense of Aaron Rittenhouse," *Washington Post,* September 1, 2020; Scherer, "Trump Employs Images of Violence."

42. Yoav Fromer, "Why the American Left Gave Up on Political Violence," *Washington Post,* August 18, 2017; Qiu, "On Spectrum of Extremism."

43. Thomas Fuller, Alan Feuer, and Serge F. Kovaleski, "A Left-Wing Faction Ready to Swing Its Fists at the Far Right," *New York Times,* August 18, 2017, p. A1.

44. Freeman, *The Field of Blood,* 259.

45. American Law Institute, Model Penal Code § 3.04; Tennessee v. Garner, 471 U.S. 1 (1985); Franklin E. Zimring and Gordon Hawkins, *Crime Is Not the Problem: Lethal Violence in America* (New York: Oxford University Press, 1997), 11.

46. State v. Shelley, 929 P.2d 489 (Wash. App. 1997); Collins, *Violence,* 285–295; Standen, "The Manly Sports."

47. Standen, "The Manly Sports," 622–630, 635 (quoting People v. Schacker, 670 N.Y.S. 2d 834 (N.Y. Dist. 1998)); Hanna, "Sex Is Not a Sport."

48. George Orwell, "The Sporting Spirit" (December 14, 1945), in *The Collected Essays, Journalism, and Letters of George Orwell,* ed. Sonia Orwell and Ian Angus, vol. 4, *In Front of Your Nose, 1945–1950* (New York: Harcourt Brace Jovanovich, 1968), 40–44; Brendan Gallagher, "How Orwell Misread the Sporting Spirit," *Telegraph,* July 30, 2004; Collins, *Violence,* 282–334, 465. Law professor Mary Anne Franks has argued that it would be good for more women to participate in sports like martial arts that teach "violence literacy," so that they could defend themselves against and deter attacks from men. Franks, "Men, Women, and Optimal Violence," 959–962.

49. Gregg Easterbrook, "Tuesday Morning Quarterback: Trump's War against the NFL," *Washington Examiner,* September 26, 2017 ("more violence against black bodies"); Tom Kertscher, "Amid Anthem Protests, Checking if 'NFL Family' Is Diverse," Politifact, September 28, 2017, https://www.politifact .com/article/2017/sep/28/amid-anthem-protests-checking-if-nfl-family-divers; Ken Belson, "Banished for 5 Years, Youth Football Roars Back in a Texas Town," *New York Times,* November 17, 2019, pp. A1, A18.

50. Collins, *Violence,* 1–3; David T. Courtright, *Violent Land: Single Men and Social Disorder from the Frontier to the Inner City* (Cambridge, MA: Harvard University Press, 1996), 9–25; Matthew R. Durose et al., *Recidivism of Prisoners Released in 30 States in 2005: Patterns from 2005 to 2010* (Washington, DC: United States Department of Justice, 2014); Pinker, *Better Angels of Our Nature;* Adrian Raine, "From Genes to Brain to Antisocial Behavior," *Current Directions in Psychological Science* 17 (2008): 323–338.

51. See, for example, Robinson v. California, 370 U.S. 660 (1962); People v. Zackowitz, 172 N.E. 466 (N.Y. 1930).

52.   District of Columbia v. Heller, 554 U.S. 570 (2008); Franks, "Men, Women, and Optimal Violence," 931; Randolph Roth, *American Homicide* (Cambridge, MA: Harvard University Press, 2009), 17; Donald Black, "Crime as Social Control," *American Sociological Review* 48 (1983): 34–45; Mark Cooney, "The Decline of Elite Homicide," *Criminology* 35 (1997): 381–407.

53.   James Gilligan, "Punishment and Violence: Is the Criminal Law Based on One Huge Mistake?," *Social Research* 67 (2000): 745–772; Nikki Jones, remarks at Stanford Medical School Symposium on Race, Policing, and Public Health, Stanford, CA, March 6, 2017; Butler, *Chokehold,* 118. Regarding corporal punishment, see Pinker, *Better Angels of Our Nature,* 435–437; Elizabeth Gershoff and Andrew Grogan-Kaylor, "Spanking and Child Outcomes: Old Controversies and New Meta-Analysis," *Journal of Family Psychology* 30 (2016): 453–469. Regarding capital punishment, see, for example, Gilligan, "Punishment and Violence," 751, 754.

54.   José María Gómez et al., "The Phylogenetic Roots of Lethal Human Violence," *Nature* 538 (2016): 233–237; Collins, *Violence,* 2, 8, 20, 466.

55.   Courtright, *Violent Land,* 1.

56.   Zimring and Hawkins, *Crime Is Not the Problem;* Roth, *American Homicide,* 14; Courtright, *Violent Land,* 1–3.

57.   Jens Ludwig and Philip Cook, eds., *Evaluating Gun Policy: Effects on Crime and Violence* (Washington, DC: Brookings Institution Press, 2003); John J. Donohue, Abhay Aneja, and Kyle D. Weber, "Right-to-Carry Laws and Violent Crime: A Comprehensive Assessment Using Panel Data and a State-Level Synthetic Controls Analysis," *Journal of Empirical Legal Studies* 16 (2019): 198–247; Melinda Wenner Moyer, "More Guns Do Not Stop More Crimes, Evidence Shows," *Scientific American,* October 1, 2017.

58.   Light, *Stand Your Ground;* Richard Slotkin, *Regeneration through Violence: The Mythology of the American Frontier, 1600–1860* (Middletown, CT: Wesleyan University Press, 1973); Slotkin, *The Fatal Environment: The Myth of the Frontier in the Age of Industrialization, 1800–1890* (New York: Atheneum, 1985); Richard Slotkin, *Gunfighter Nation: The Myth of the Frontier in Twentieth-Century America* (New York: Atheneum, 1992).

59.   Pinker, *Better Angels of Our Nature,* 508.

2. VIOLENT CRIME AND VIOLENT CRIMINALS

1.   Michael O'Hear, "Third-Class Citizenship: The Escalating Legal Consequences of Committing a 'Violent' Crime," *Journal of Criminal Law and Criminology* 109 (2019): 165–236, at 168, 212–217; Julian V. Roberts, "The Role of Criminal Record in the Sentencing Process," *Crime and Justice* 22 (1997): 303–362, at 330;

Ohio Rev. Code 2953.36(A)(3); Neb. R. Evid. 505(3)(a), Neb. Rev. Stat. § 27-505(3)
(a); State v. Palmer, 224 Neb. 282, 294–295 (1986).

2.   Danielle Sered, *Until We Reckon: Violence, Mass Incarceration, and a Road to
Repair* (New York: New Press, 2019), 5–6, 11; Josie Duffy Rice, "My Brother, the
Violent Offender," Slate, August 14, 2017, https://slate.com/news-and-politics
/2017/08/the-criminal-justice-system-treats-violent-offenders-as-irredeemable
-theyre-not.html ("separated rhetorically"); *An Analysis of Non-Violent Drug Offenders with Minimal Criminal History* (Washington, DC: United States Department of Justice, 1994), 6, 13–14; Kamala Harris with Joan O'C. Hamilton, *Smart
on Crime: A Career Prosecutor's Plan to Make Us Safer* (San Francisco: Chronicle
Books, 2009), 99, 124; Alexi Jones, "Reforms without Results: Why States
Should Stop Excluding Violent Offenses from Criminal Justice Reforms"
(Prison Policy Initiative, April 2020), https://www.prisonpolicy.org/reports
/violence.html. Regarding the focus of recidivist enhancements, see, for example, Franklin E. Zimring, Gordon Hawkins, and Sam Kamin, *Punishment
and Democracy: Three Strikes and You're Out in California* (New York: Oxford
University Press, 2001), 7, 46–50; Michael G. Turner et al., "'Three Strikes and
You're Out' Legislation: A National Assessment," *Federal Probation,* September 1995,
16, 25, 34. On sentencing reform in 2015, see *Defining Violence: Reducing Incarceration by Rethinking America's Approach to Violence* (Washington, DC: Justice Policy
Institute, 2016), 16.

3.   California General Election, Official Voter Information Guide, November 8,
2016; John Myers, "Why Gov. Jerry Brown Is Staking So Much on Overhauling
Prison Parole," *Los Angeles Times,* October 27, 2016.

4.   15 Cal. Code of Regulations § 3490(a) (2017); Tracy Kaplan and Robert Sa-
longa, "Debate Rages On about Which Inmates Should Be Released Early," *San
Jose Mercury News,* September 4, 2017; Anne Marie Schubert, "Concerns about Parole Measure Are Coming True," *Sacramento Bee,* July 28, 2017; Maria Cramer,
"Californians Ready to Vote on Changes to Strengthen Parts of Three Strikes
Law," *New York Times,* May 13, 2020, p. A23. California's determinate sentencing
law imposes a one-year sentence enhancement for a felony term of incarceration
previously served by a defendant subsequently convicted of a felony, and a three-
year sentence enhancement for every prison term previously served for a violent
felony by a defendant subsequently convicted of a violent felony. Cal. Penal Code
§ 667.5(a)-(c).

5.   Michael Wines, "Kentucky Restores Vote to 14,000 Ex-Felons," *New York
Times,* December 13, 2019, p. A21; Sydney Ember and Matt Stevens, "Sanders Backs
Voting Rights for All Prisoners," *New York Times,* April 28, 2019, p. A25; Rocco
Parascandola and Leonard Green, "'It's Supposed to Mean Something'—Mayor

and Top Cops Say Second-Chance Sentencing Program Undermines Gun Arrests," *New York Daily News,* July 8, 2019; Alexei Koseff, "Will Coronavirus Pandemic Free California Prisoners? Gavin Newsom Says No," *San Francisco Chronicle,* March 30, 2020; Timothy Williams et al., "Social Distancing Isn't an Option, so Prisons Free Inmates to Try to Slow Infection," *New York Times,* March 31, 2020, p. A9; "A State-by-State Look at Coronavirus in Prisons," The Marshall Project, updated October 23, 2020, https://www.themarshallproject.org/2020/05/01/a-state-by-state-look-at-coronavirus-in-prisons; "Coronavirus in the U.S.: Latest Map and Case Count," *New York Times,* updated October 25, 2020, https://www.nytimes.com/interactive/2020/us/coronavirus-us-cases.html. Regarding the negligible decline in prison populations during the first three months of 2020, see Jacob Kang-Brown, Chase Montagnet, Eital Schattner-Elmaleh, and Oliver Hinds, *People in Prison in 2019* (New York: Vera Institute of Justice, 2020).

6.   See, for example, Don Thompson, "California Bill Seeks to Ease Hiring of Ex-Convicts," AP News, April 23, 2018, https://apnews.com/37d1fbb4e1c5446d86a7411f75033dde; Eli Haber, "Redemption and Rejection: From Prison to Ph.D.," *New York Times,* September 13, 2017, p. A1.

7.   See, for example, W. David Ball, "Tough on Crime (on the State's Dime): How Violent Crime Does Not Drive California Counties' Incarceration Rates—and Why It Should," *Georgia State University Law Review* 28 (2012): 987–1083, at 997.

8.   Regarding the Google Books Ngram Viewer, see Jean-Baptiste Michel et al., "Quantitative Analysis of Culture Using Millions of Digitized Books," *Science* 331 (2011): 176–182; Google Books Ngram Viewer, http://books.google.com/ngrams/info. Years after 2000 have been excluded from Figure 1 as well as from Figure 4 in Chapter 3, because Google Ngram data for that period is less reliable and not readily comparable with data from earlier years. Stephen Chrisomalis, "Conservative Skewing in Google N-Gram Frequencies," Glossographia (blog), July 14, 2013, https://glossographia.wordpress.com/2013/07/14/conservative-ngram-skew/. The lines in both charts show seven-year trailing averages: the value plotted for the frequency of "violent crime" in the year 2000, for example, is the average of the frequencies reported by Google Books Ngram Viewer for that phrase in the years 1994–2000.

9.   William Blackstone, *Commentaries on the Laws of England* (Oxford: Clarendon Press, 1765–1769), 2: *15, *242; Karl Llewellyn, introduction to *Theft, Law and Society,* by Jerome Hall (Boston: Little, Brown, 1935): xv (italics in original). Regarding Blackstone's influence in the United States, see Harry W. Jones, "The Common Law in the United States: English Themes and American Variations,"

in *Political Separation and Legal Continuity,* ed. Harry W. Jones (Chicago: American Bar Association, 1976), 91–137, at 96–97; Dennis R. Nolan, "Sir William Blackstone and the New American Republic: A Study of Intellectual Impact," *New York University Law Review* 51 (1976): 731–768, at 737–738.

10. James FitzJames Stephen, *A History of the Common Law of England* (London: Macmillan, 1883), 2:192–193; Blackstone, *Commentaries,* 4: *5, *7, *95; Francis Wharton, *Treatise on the Criminal Law of the United States* (Philadelphia: Kay, 1846), 1:1; Commissioners of the Code, *Draft of a Penal Code for the State of New York* (Albany: Weed, Parsons, 1864), § 5, at 5.

11. Stephen, *History of the Common Law,* 194 ("antiquated and unmeaning"); J. H. Baker, *An Introduction to English Legal History,* 5th ed. (Oxford: Oxford University Press, 2019); Tennessee v. Garner, 471 U.S. 1, 14, 20 (1985).

12. Wharton, *Treatise on the Criminal Law,* 1:1; Alice Ristroph, "Farewell to the Felonry," *Harvard Civil Rights-Civil Liberties Law Review* 53 (2018): 563–618; *Defining Violence,* 5, 9–10.

13. Lawrence M. Friedman, *Crime and Punishment in American History* (New York: Basic Books, 1993), 43–44; Hall, *Theft, Law and Society,* 114–115.

14. Charles E. Torcia et al., *Wharton's Criminal Law,* 15th ed. (Deerfield, IL: Clark Boardman Callaghan 1996), 1: § 22.

15. Julia Ann Simon-Kerr, "Moral Turpitude," *Utah Law Review* (2012): 1001–1070, at 1010; Brooker v. Coffin, 5 Johns. 188, 188–189 (N.Y. Sup. Ct. 1809); Jordan v. De George, 341 U.S. 223, 227 (1951). For examples of professional codes disqualifying individuals convicted of crimes of moral turpitude, see Rules of the State Bar of California, Rule 2.15 (2015) (attorneys); Vernon's Tex. Code Ann. § 143.1017 (2017) (firefighters and police officers); S.D. Codified Laws § 36-21C-13 (home inspectors).

16. Letter from John W. Spiegel to Martin D. Singer regarding Charlie Sheen / *Two and a Half Men,* March 7, 2011, quoted in Stephen M. Gallagher, "Who's Really 'Winning'?: The Tension of Morals Clauses in Film and Television," *Virginia Sports and Entertainment Law Journal* 12 (2016): 88–119, at 107–110.

17. When the Supreme Court held in 1951 that, for purposes of immigration law, conspiracy to defraud the United States was a crime of moral turpitude, the Justices noted that federal and state courts had held "[w]ithout exception . . . that a crime in which fraud is an ingredient involves moral turpitude." Jordan v. De George, 227.

18. Simon-Kerr, "Moral Turpitude," 1018; Burton v. Burton, 3 Greene 316, 318 (Iowa 1851). For more recent decisions defining "moral turpitude," see also Jean-Louis v. Attorney General, 582 F.3d 462 (3d Cir. 2009); Kapnik v. Ashcroft, 384 F.3d 84, 89 (3d Cir. 2004).

19.   Simon-Kerr, "Moral Turpitude," 1051; Ciambelli *ex rel.* Maranci v. Johnson, 12 F.2d 465, 466 (D. Mass. 1926); Partyka v. Attorney General, 417 F.3d 408, 414 (3d Cir. 2005).

20.   Leon Radzinowicz, *A History of English Criminal Law and Its Administration from 1750* (London: Stevens and Sons, 1948), 1:268–396; Sanford H. Kadish, "Codifiers of the Criminal Law: Wechsler's Predecessors," *Columbia Law Review* 78 (1978): 1098–1144.

21.   Charles de Montesquieu, *The Spirit of the Laws* (1748), trans. Anne M. Cohler, Basia C. Miller, and Harold S. Stone (Cambridge: Cambridge University Press, 1989), 189–191. Regarding Montesquieu's influence in America, see Bernard Bailyn, *The Ideological Origins of the American Revolution* (Cambridge, MA: Harvard University Press, 1967); Paul Merrill Spurlin, *Montesquieu in America, 1760–1801* (Baton Rouge: LSU Press, 1940); Gordon S. Wood, *The Creation of the American Republic, 1766–1787* (Chapel Hill: University of North Carolina Press, 1969).

22.   Jeremy Bentham, *An Introduction to the Principles of Morals and Legislation* (1789; Oxford: Clarendon Press, 1879), 302–308.

23.   Kadish, "Codifiers of the Criminal Law"; Edward Livingston, *A Code of Crime and Punishments,* in *The Complete Works of Edward Livingston on Criminal Jurisprudence,* vol. 2 (New York: National Prison Association, 1873), arts. 79–80, 209–225, 406–568, 586–689.

24.   Thomas Macaulay, *A Penal Code Prepared by the Indian Law Commissioners* (London, 1838), §§ 125–137, 294–362, 375–382 (1838); Commissioners of the Code, *Draft of a Penal Code for the State of New York* (Albany, NY: Weed, Parsons, 1864), §§ 228–403, 473–478, 485–486; Criminal Code (Indictable Offences) Bill (42 Vict. 170) §§ 84–98, 165–243, §§ 244–426 (1879).

25.   *Model Penal Code and Commentaries,* vol. 3 (Philadelphia: American Law Institute, 1985), 38–40.

26.   United States v. Davis, 139 S. Ct. 2319, 2330 (2019). See the Appendix, this volume, for a list of federal statutes referring to "violent crimes" or "crimes of violence."

27.   Charles E. Silberman, *Criminal Violence, Criminal Justice* (New York: Random House, 1978), ix, 3; William J. Clinton, Address before a Joint Session of the Congress on the State of the Union, January 25, 1994; Jeremy Travis, Bruce Western, and Steve Redburn, eds., *The Growth of Incarceration in the United States: Exploring Causes and Consequences* (Washington, DC: National Academies Press, 2014), 70; Jonathan Simon, *Governing through Crime: How the War on Crime Transformed American Democracy and Created a Culture of Fear* (New York: Oxford University Press, 2007), 4–5.

28. Alice Ristroph, "Criminal Law in the Shadow of Violence," *Alabama Law Review* 62 (2011): 571–622, at 572–573, 612; Sered, *Until We Reckon*, 2, 10–11. Sered thinks it obvious that even the late twentieth-century "war on drugs" was "largely about violence"—that "the line of argument that buttressed it" had to do with protection from "an imagined monstrous other."

29. Federal Bureau of Investigation, Uniform Crime Reporting Statistics, https://www.ucrdatatool.gov; William J. Stuntz, *The Collapse of American Criminal Justice* (Cambridge, MA: Harvard University Press, 2011), 19. The FBI groups murders together with incidents of "nonnegligent manslaughter"; the figures in the text are for this combined category.

30. John J. Donohue, "Comey, Trump, and the Puzzling Pattern of Crime in 2015 and Beyond," *Columbia Law Review* 117 (2017): 1297–1354, at 1303; Franklin E. Zimring, *The Great American Crime Decline* (New York: Oxford University Press, 2007), 4.

31. Eric H. Monkkonen, *Murder in New York City* (Berkeley: University of California Press, 2001), 21; Roger Lane, "Urbanization and Criminal Violence in the 19th Century: Massachusetts as a Test Case," in *Violence in America: Historical and Comparative Perspectives,* ed. Hugh Davis Graham and Ted Robert Gurr (New York: F. A. Praeger, 1969), 2:359–370, at 365–366; Robert M. Fogelson, *Big-City Police* (Cambridge, MA: Harvard University Press, 1977); Khalil Gibran Muhammad, *The Condemnation of Blackness: Race, Crime and the Making of Modern Urban America* (Cambridge, MA: Harvard University Press, 2010).

32. Norbert Elias, *The Civilizing Process: Sociogenetic and Psychogenetic Investigations* (1939), trans. Edmund Jephcott, rev. ed. (Oxford: Blackwell, 2000); Steven Pinker, *The Better Angels of Our Nature: Why Violence Has Declined* (New York: Viking, 2011). For discussions of the "civilizing project" and its effects on English criminal law since the early nineteenth century, see Lindsay Farmer, *Making the Modern Criminal Law* (Oxford: Oxford University Press, 2016), 48–59, 261–263; Martin J. Wiener, *Men of Blood: Violence, Manliness and Criminal Justice in Victorian England* (Cambridge: Cambridge University Press, 2004), 9–29.

33. Lane, "Urbanization and Criminal Violence," 368.

34. Silberman, *Criminal Violence, Criminal Justice,* 19–20.

35. Elaine Tyler May, *Fortress America: How We Embraced Fear and Abandoned Democracy* (New York: Basic Books, 2017), 61; Ristroph, "Criminal Law in the Shadow of Violence," 585–586. On the sense of unraveling, see, for example, Joan Didion, *The White Album* (New York: Simon and Schuster, 1979); David Talbot, *Season of the Witch: Enchantment, Terror, and Deliverance in the City of Love* (New York: Free Press, 2012). On prison riots and uprisings, see Keramet Reiter, *23/7: Pelican Bay Prison and the Rise of Long Term Solitary Confinement* (New Haven, CT:

Yale University Press, 2016), 38–58; Heather Ann Thompson, *Blood in the Water: The Attica Prison Uprising of 1971 and Its Legacy* (New York: Pantheon Books, 2016).

36.   Niall Ferguson, *The War of the World: Twentieth-Century Conflict and the Descent of the West* (New York: Penguin Press, 2006), xxxiv ("The hundred years after 1900 were without question the bloodiest in modern history, far more violent in relative and absolute terms than any previous era"); James Gilligan, "Punishment and Violence: Is the Criminal Law Based on One Huge Mistake?," *Social Research* 67 (2000): 745–772, at 745; Pinker, *Better Angels of Our Nature.*

37.   Kyle Swenson, "Black-Clad Antifa Members Attack Peaceful Right-Wing Demonstrators in Berkeley," *Washington Post,* August 28, 2017; John Eligon, Matt Furber, and Campbell Robertson, "Spreading Unrest Leaves a Nation on Edge," *New York Times,* May 31, 2020, p. A1; Mark Rudd, "Political Passion Turned Violent," *New York Times,* March 6, 2020, p. A23.

38.   James Forman Jr., "Racial Critiques of Mass Incarceration: Beyond the New Jim Crow," *New York University Law Review* 87 (2012): 21–69, at 49.

39.   Stuntz, *Collapse of American Criminal Justice,* 15–40; Muhammad, *The Condemnation of Blackness,* 1; Paul Butler, *Chokehold: Policing Black Men* (New York: New Press, 2017), 17; Elizabeth Hinton, *From the War on Poverty to the War on Crime: The Making of Mass Incarceration in America* (Cambridge, MA: Harvard University Press, 2016); May, *Fortress America.* A large-scale statistical study in the early 2000s found that violent crime, much more so than property crime, remains concentrated in minority neighborhoods, even controlling for the economic characteristics of communities. Ruth D. Peterson and Lauren J. Krivo, *Divergent Social Worlds: Neighborhood Crime and the Racial-Spatial Divide* (New York: Russell Sage Foundation, 2010), 17–19.

40.   Muhammad, *The Condemnation of Blackness,* 80–84, 136, 207, 210.

41.   *Lynching in America: Confronting the Legacy of Racial Terror,* 3rd ed. (Montgomery, AL: Equal Justice Initiative, 2017), 30–31; *Reconstruction in America: Racial Violence after the Civil War, 1865–1876* (Montgomery, AL: Equal Justice Initiative, 2020), 7, 68–69, 72. See also Richard Maxwell Brown, *Strain of Violence: Historical Studies of American Violence and Vigilantism* (New York: Oxford University Press, 1975), 217–218; Philip Dray, *At the Hands of Persons Unknown: The Lynching of Black America* (New York: Random House, 2002); Estelle B. Freedman, *Redefining Rape: Sexual Violence in the Era of Suffrage and Segregation* (Cambridge, MA: Harvard University Press, 2013), 8, 89–103, 189–192; James Goodman, *Stories of Scottsboro* (New York: Pantheon Books, 1994); Gilbert King, *Devil in the Grove: Thurgood Marshall, the Groveland Boys, and the Dawn of a New America* (New York: HarperCollins, 2012); Timothy B. Tyson, *The Blood of Emmett Till* (New York: Simon and Schuster, 2017). Paul Butler notes that "for centuries, many white

men, sanctioned by the law of the land, enslaved, tortured, raped, and lynched black people, but we've conveniently started our narrative about who's dangerous with the spike in violent crime in the 1960s, a move that puts the focus on African American men." Butler, *Chokehold,* 126.

42. Butler, *Chokehold,* 25–28; May, *Fortress America,* 60–61. For examples of "jungle" rhetoric in late twentieth-century discussions of urban crime, see William J. Stuntz, "Unequal Justice," *Harvard Law Review* 121 (2008): 1969–2040, at 2005 (quoting Ronald Reagan's lament that "our city streets are jungle paths after dark"); Jeremy Travis and Bruce Western, "Poverty, Violence, and Black Incarceration," in *Policing the Black Man,* ed. Angela J. Davis (New York: Pantheon Books, 2017), 294–321, at 299 (quoting Barry Goldwater's 1964 rhetoric about "the license of the mob and the jungle," and Richard Nixon's 1968 warning that "the city jungle will cease to be a metaphor" and "will become a barbaric reality"). Language like this was not used only by politicians. The political scientist James Q. Wilson, for example, writing about urban policing in 1963, spoke of the need to "bend the law of the Yankee to suit the conditions of the jungle." Wilson, "The Police and Their Problems: A Theory," *Public Policy* 12 (1963): 189–216, at 216.

43. Hinton, *From the War on Poverty,* 307–332; David A. Sklansky, "Cocaine, Race, and Equal Protection," *Stanford Law Review* 47 (1985): 1283–1322, at 1285–1290. Regarding the history of American drug policy, see David F. Musto, *The American Disease: Origins of Narcotic Control,* 3rd ed. (New York: Oxford University Press, 1999).

44. They learned the lesson quickly. Elaine Tyler May notes that Dukakis responded to the "Willie Horton" ad "not with a condemnation of Bush's race-baiting and fear-mongering but with a 'Willie Horton' ad of his own, featuring a Latino parolee from a federal prison who had raped and murdered a woman during Bush's years at the helm of the Central Intelligence Agency." May, *Fortress America,* 86.

45. Simon, *Governing through Crime,* 69; Stuntz, *Collapse of American Criminal Justice,* 240; Joseph E. Kennedy, "Monstrous Offenders and the Search for Solidarity through Modern Punishment," *Hastings Law Journal* 51 (2000): 829–908, at 887–897; "Death for the Mentally Disabled," *Economist,* March 8, 2014.

46. *An Analysis of Non-Violent Drug Offenders with Minimal Criminal History,* 6.

47. Reginald Fluellen and Jennifer Trone, *Do Drug Courts Save Jail and Prison Beds?* (New York: Vera Institute of Justice, 2000); Ryan S. King and Jill Pasquarella, *Drug Courts: A Review of the Evidence* (Washington, DC: Sentencing Project, 2009), 3; *Drug Courts: Overview of Growth, Characteristics, and Results* (Washington, DC: United States General Accounting Office, 1997), 53; Claudia Arno, "Proportional Response: The Need for More—and More Standardized—Veterans'

Courts," *University of Michigan Journal of Law Reform* 48 (2015): 1039–1072, at 1044; Mangeh Duggal, "Long May You Run: Drug Courts in the Twenty-First Century," *Berkeley Journal of Criminal Law* (2016): 126–186, at 155; Michael M. O'Hear, "Rethinking Drug Courts: Restorative Justice as a Response to Racial Injustice," *Stanford Law and Policy Review* 20 (2009): 463–499, at 465, 479.

48. John Baker, "We Need Veterans Courts in Minnesota," Twincities.com, August 29, 2010, https://www.twincities.com/2010/08/28/john-baker-we-need -veterans-courts-in-minnesota-heres-why/ ("a veteran's court without veterans"); Harris, *Smart on Crime,* 125; Mark A. McCormick-Goodhart, "Leaving No Veteran Behind: Policies and Perspectives on Combat Trauma, Veterans Court, and the Rehabilitative Approach to Criminal Behavior," *Pennsylvania State Law Review* 117 (2013): 895–926, at 910; O'Hear, "Third-Class Citizenship," 193; Michael L. Perlin, "'John Brown Went Off to War': Considering Veterans Courts as Problem-Solving Courts," *Nova Law Review* 37 (2013): 445–477, at 458.

49. Norval Morris, *The Habitual Criminal* (Cambridge, MA: Harvard University Press, 1951); Zimring, Hawkins, and Kamin, *Punishment and Democracy,* 49n2.

50. 18 U.S.C. § 3559(c); Simon, *Governing through Crime,* 155–156; Daniel W. Stiller, "Initiative 593: Washington's Voters Go Down Swinging," *Gonzaga Law Review* 30 (1994): 433–465; Travis, Western, and Redburn, *The Growth of Incarceration,* 70; Zimring, Hawkins, and Kamin, *Punishment and Democracy,* 8.

51. Ewing v. California, 538 U.S. 11, 15 (2003); *A Primer: Three Strikes—The Impact after More than a Decade* (California Legislative Analyst's Office, October 2005), https://lao.ca.gov/2005/3_strikes/3_strikes_102005.htm; Sarah French Russell, "Rethinking Recidivist Enhancements: The Role of Prior Drug Convictions in Federal Sentencing," *UC Davis Law Review* 43 (2010): 1135–1233, at 1149; Simon, *Governing through Crime,* 155–156; Robert Weisberg, Debbie A. Mukamal, and Jordan D. Segall, *Life in Limbo: An Examination of Parole Release for Prisoners Serving Life Sentences with the Possibility of Parole in California* (Stanford, CA: Stanford Criminal Justice Center, 2011), 6; Zimring, Hawkins, and Kamin, *Punishment and Democracy,* 8.

52. Simon, *Governing through Crime,* 89; Turner et al., "'Three Strikes and You're Out' Legislation," 25, 34; Zimring, Hawkins, and Kamin, *Punishment and Democracy,* 46.

53. United States v. Davis, 139 S. Ct. 2319, 2337 (2019) (Kavanaugh, J., dissenting).

54. O'Hear, "Third-Class Citizenship," 171–176; 11 Del. Code Ann. § 4201(c); La. Stat. Ann. § 142.2; Miss. Code Ann. § 97-3-2(1); N.H. Rev. Stat. Ann. § 651:5; 57 Okla. Stat. Ann. § 571(2).

55.   First Step Act, Pub. L. No. 115-391, 132 Stat. 5194, § 403 (2018); Florida Amendment 4, Voting Rights Restoration for Felons Initiative (2018); Erik Faust and Mark Motivans, "Sex Offenders in the Federal Correctional System: The Consequences of Heightened Attention on Increased Certainty and Severity of Punishment," *Justice Research and Policy* 16 (2015): 81–98; Carissa Byrne Hessick, "Disentangling Child Pornography from Child Sex Abuse," *Washington University Law Review* 88 (2011): 853–902; Michael Winerip, "Crime Fiction," *New York Times Magazine,* August 30, 2020, p. 36; Matthew Clarke, "Due to Steps Taken by New Mexico Prison Officials, Only Sex Offenders Present When Prison Overwhelmed by COVID-19," *Prison Legal News,* August 2020, p. 48; Tamara Rice Lave and Franklin E. Zimring, "Assessing the *Real* Risk of Sexually Violent Predators: Doctor Padilla's Dangerous Data," *American Criminal Law Review* 55 (2018): 705–787.

56.   For rare exceptions, see Colo. Rev. Stat. Ann. §§ 18-1.3-406(2), -4-202 (treating burglary as a "crime of violence" only if the burglar or an accomplice "assaults or menaces any person," "is armed with explosives," or "uses" or "possesses and threatens the use of a deadly weapon"); Tenn. Code Ann. §§ 39-14-404, 40-35-120(b)(1)(L) (treating burglary as a "violent offense" only if it is residential and "the victim suffers serious bodily injury").

57.   Wyo. Stat. Ann. §§ 6–104(xii), 6-2-501 to -502, 6-10-201; State v. Janisch, 290 N.W.2d 473, 476 (S.D. 1980).

58.   Fla. Stat. Ann. § 784.045; *2019 National Incident-Based Reporting System User Manual* (Washington, DC: United States Department of Justice, 2018), 22.

59.   Michael R. Romeo, "A Puncher's Chance: Assessing the Classification of Martial Artists' Hands as Deadly Weapons," *Jeffrey S. Moorad Sports Law Journal* 24 (2017): 23–47; Tracy Bateman Farell, "Parts of Human Body, Other than Feet, as Deadly or Dangerous Weapons or Instrumentalities for Purposes of Statutes Aggravating Offenses Such as Assault and Robbery," *American Law Reports 6th* (Westlaw, originally published 2011), 67:103; Fern J. Kletter, "Dog as Deadly or Dangerous Weapon for Purposes of Statutes Aggravating Offenses Such as Assault and Robbery," *American Law Reports 5th* (Westlaw, originally published 2004), 124:657; Vitauts M. Gulbis, "Walking Cane as Deadly or Dangerous Weapon for Purpose of Statutes Aggravating Offenses Such as Assault and Robbery," *American Law Reports 4th* (Westlaw, originally published 1981), 8:842; John Kimpflen and Karl Oakes, "Character of Weapon Required for Assault with a Dangerous or Deadly Weapon," *Corpus Juris Secundum* (Westlaw, originally published 2018), 6A: § 95; Jack K. Levin, "Other Objects as Deadly or Dangerous Weapons," *American Jurisprudence 2nd* (Westlaw, originally published 2018), 6: § 41; Butler, *Chokehold,* 31; "Sean 'Diddy' Combs Not Charged with Assault over

Kettlebell Encounter," *Guardian,* July 2, 2015; Arthur v. United States, 602 A.2d 174, 177 (D.C. 1992) (explaining that "'shoes on feet' are dangerous weapons, 'at least when they inflict serious injuries'") (quoting Medlin v. United States, 207 F.3d 33, 33 (D.C. Cir. 1953).

60. *2019 National Incident-Based Reporting System User Manual,* 22; State v. Mc-Daniels, 16 N.W.2d 164, 167 (Neb. 1944) ("graver and more serious"); People v. Ybarra, 543 P.2d 529 (Colo. App. 1975) ("substantial risk of death"); Janisch, 290 N.W.2d, at 476 ("apprehension of danger to life, health, or limb"); Minnix v. State, 282 P.2d 772, 777 (Okla. Cr. App. 1955) (same); Wyo. Stat. Ann. § 6-1-104(a)(x).

61. Kelly v. State, 153 P.3d 926 (Wyo. 2007).

62. State v. Kane, 762 A.2d 677, 681 (N.J. App. 2000).

63. Martinez v. State, 199 P.3d 526 (Wyo. 2009).

64. See, for example, Rivers v. State, 565 S.E.2d 596, 597 (Ga. App. 2002); State v. Bogenreif, 465 N.W.2d 777, 781 (S.D. 1991); Commonwealth v. Kinney, 157 A.3d 968, 972 (Pa. Super. 2017).

65. Martinez v. State, 535.

66. Wyo. Stat. Ann. §§ 6-1-104(xii), -3-301; 11 Del. Code Ann. 4201(c); D.C. Code Ann. §§ 22-1804a(b)(2), 23-1331(4); Miss. Code Ann. § 97-3-2; N.Y. Penal L. § 70.02(1), Utah Code Ann. §§ 76-3-203.5(1)(c).

67. Franklin E. Zimring, *American Youth Violence* (New York: Oxford University Press, 1998), 19, 38–46. Regarding South Bend, see Jeff Asher, "How Reporting Practices Can Skew Crime Statistics," *New York Times,* December 18, 2019, p. A27.

68. S. 1688, 97th Cong., 1st Sess. (1981); Violent Crime and Drug Enforcement Improvement Act, 128 Cong. Rec. 32767, 32778 (daily ed. December 20, 1982); Ronald Reagan, *H.R. 3963—Memorandum of Disapproval,* January 14, 1983, reprinted in 128 Cong. Rec. H 33442 (daily ed. December 21, 1982); H.R. Rep. 1073, 98th Cong., 2d Sess. 3–6 (1984).

69. H.R. Rep. 1073, 98th Cong., 2d Sess. 3 (1984) (quoting Specter's remarks in January 1983); *Career Criminal Life Sentence Act of 1981: Hearings before the Subcomm. on Juvenile Justice of the Senate Comm. on the Judiciary,* 97th Cong., 1st Sess. 1 (1981) (remarks of Sen. Specter).

70. *Career Criminal Life Sentence Act of 1981: Hearings before the Subcomm. on Juvenile Justice of the Senate Comm. on the Judiciary,* 97th Cong., 1st Sess. 1, 16 (1981) (remarks of Sen. Specter); ibid., 19 (testimony of D. Lowell Jensen); *Armed Robbery and Burglary Prevention Act: Hearings before the Subcomm. on Crime of the House Comm. of the Judiciary,* 97th Cong., 2d Sess. 1 (1982) (remarks of Rep. Hughes).

71. S. 1688, 97th Cong., 1st Sess. (1981) ("violent and major crime," italics added); *Hearings on Career Criminal Life Sentence Act of 1981*, 1.

72. Gerald Ford, *Special Message to the Congress on Crime,* June 19, 1975; *Hearings on Career Criminal Life Sentence Act of 1981,* 19 (testimony of D. Lowell Jensen); *Hearings on Armed Robbery and Burglary Prevention Act,* 27 (testimony of Alexander D. Lehrer); ibid., 76, 144 (reprinting James Dimm, Phil Pacheco, and Cindy Noe, *Report of the Survey of Local Career Criminal Programs* [1981]).

73. *Hearings on Armed Robbery and Burglary Prevention Act,* 46 (testimony of Adjoa Aiyetoro).

74. Comprehensive Crime Control Act of 1984, H.J. Res. 648, Tit. II, 98th Cong., 2d Sess. (1984). The definition of "crime of violence," now found in 18 U.S.C. § 16, was set forth in section 1001 of the CCCA.

75. *Armed Career Criminal Legislation: Hearings before the Subcomm. on Crime of the House Comm. of the Judiciary,* 99th Cong., 2d Sess. 1–2 (1986) (remarks of Rep. Hughes); ibid., 8 (remarks of Rep. Wyden).

76. Ibid., 3–6, 8–9, 11.

77. Tennessee v. Garner, 471 U.S. 1, 11, 21 (1985); ibid., 27 (O'Connor, J., dissenting). Chief Justice Burger and Justice Rehnquist joined Justice O'Connor's dissent.

78. *Hearings on Armed Career Criminal Legislation,* 11–12, 26 (remarks of Rep. Hughes); ibid., 12 (testimony of Rep. Wyden); ibid., 46 (testimony of Sen. Specter); ibid., 26 (testimony of Deputy Assistant Attorney General James Knapp); ibid., 49–50 (testimony of Ronald Castille); ibid., 28, 38 (testimony of Bruce Lyons).

79. 18 U.S.C. § 924(e)(2)(B).

80. H.R. Rep. 849, 99th Cong., 2d Sess. 3 (1986); Quarles v. United States, 139 S. Ct. 1872, 1879 (2019); Taylor v. United States, 495 U.S. 575, 588 (1990); United States v. Parson, 955 F.2d 858, 868 (3d Cir. 1992).

81. U.S.S.G. § 4B1.2(1); Parson, 955 F.2d at 862–66.

82. United States v. Booker, 543 U.S. 220 (2005) ("effectively advisory"); United States v. Molina-Martinez, 136 S. Ct. 1338, 1346 (2016) ("lodestar"); Peugh v. United States, 569 U.S. 530, 543 (2013).

83. Beckles v. United States, 137 S. Ct. 886 (2017).

84. *Supplement to the 2015 Guidelines Manual* (Washington, DC: United States Sentencing Commission, 2016), Amendment 798.

85. *Report to the Congress: Career Offender Sentencing Enhancements* (Washington, DC: United States Sentencing Commission, 2016), 3.

86. 18 U.S. Code § 924(e)(2)(B); Ristroph, *Criminal Law in the Shadow of Violence,* 603–605.

87.   Randall Collins, *Violence: A Micro-Sociological Theory* (Princeton, NJ: Princeton University Press, 2008).

88.   Michelson v. United States, 335 U.S. 469 (1948); People v. Zackowitz, 172 N.E. 466 (N.Y. 1930); Fed. R. Evid. 404. The English legal scholar Nicola Lacey argues persuasively that eighteenth-century criminal law often used an offender's *actus reus* to draw conclusions about his moral temperament—whether, for example, he was "malicious" or had an "abandoned heart." But she shows that this tendency was in retreat by the middle of the nineteenth century, and that the retreat continued through most of the twentieth century. Today, Lacey notes, criminal law increasingly emphasizes "a new sense of bad character, not as religiously inflected sinfulness but rather as the status of presenting risk or being 'dangerous.'" Nicola Lacey, *In Search of Criminal Responsibility: Ideas, Interests, and Institutions* (Oxford: Oxford University Press, 2016), 137–138, 147–148.

89.   Blackstone, *Commentaries* 2: *15.

90.   Muhammad, *The Condemnation of Blackness;* "Whites Commit Crimes, but Black Males Are Criminals," Harvard University Press Blog, January 5, 2010, https://harvardpress.typepad.com/hup_publicity/2010/01/whites-commit-crimes-but-black-males-are-criminals.html (quoting Lewis).

3. POLICE VIOLENCE

1.   Mapp v. Ohio, 367 U.S. 643 (1961); J. Michael Martinez, *The Greatest Criminal Cases: Changing the Course of American Law* (Santa Barbara: Praeger, 2014), 75–98; Priscilla H. Machado Zotti, *Injustice for All:* Mapp v. Ohio *and the Fourth Amendment* (New York: Peter Lang, 2005); Yale Kamisar, "*Mapp v. Ohio:* The First Shot Fired in the Warren Court's Criminal Procedure 'Revolution,'" in *Criminal Procedure Stories,* ed. Carol S. Steiker (New York: Foundation Press, 2006), 45–100.

2.   Wesley M. Oliver, *The Prohibition Era and Policing: A Legacy of Misregulation* (Nashville: Vanderbilt University Press, 2018), 127.

3.   Marilynn S. Johnson, *Street Justice: A History of Police Violence in New York City* (Boston: Beacon Press, 2003).

4.   The Google Books Ngram Viewer and the derivation of Figure 4 are discussed in note 8 to Chapter 2. The line for "warrantless" or "without a warrant" tracks the sum of the frequency of "warrantless" among all 1-grams and the frequency of "without a warrant" among all 3-grams.

5.   "President Trump's Call with US Governors over Protests," CNN, June 1, 2020, https://www.cnn.com/2020/06/01/politics/wh-governors-call-protests/index.html.

6.   Philip Bump, "Trump's Speech Encouraging Police to Be 'Rough,' Annotated," *Washington Post,* July 28, 2017; Johnson, *Street Justice,* 140.

7.   Johnson, *Street Justice,* 140.

8.   See, for example, William Ker Muir, *Police: Streetcorner Politicians* (Chicago: University of Chicago Press, 1977). "The role of the police," wrote the criminologist Egon Bittner in a widely quoted passage, "is best understood as a mechanism for the distribution of non-negotiably coercive force employed in accordance with the dictates of an intuitive grasp of the situational emergencies." Egon Bittner, "The Capacity to Use Force as the Core of the Police Role," in *Moral Issues in Police Work,* ed. Frederick Elliston and Michael Feldberg (Totowa, NJ: Rowman and Allanheld, 1985), 15–25, at 23.

9.   United States Commission on Civil Rights, *Report 5: Justice* (1961), 5; William Westley, "Violence and the Police," *American Journal of Sociology* 59 (1953): 34–41, at 37–38; Wilbur Miller, *Cops and Bobbies: Police Authority in New York and London, 1830–1870* (Chicago: University of Chicago Press, 1977), 20; Johnson, *Street Justice,* 101, 121, 202, 211.

10.   Brandon Garrett and Seth Stoughton, "A Tactical Fourth Amendment," *Virginia Law Review* 103 (2017): 211–307, at 246–249, 265–266, 367–368; Tom Dart, "'Verbal Judo': The Police Tactic That Teaches Cops to Talk before They Shoot," *Guardian,* July 21, 2016; Max Lewontin, "Could 'Verbal Judo' Help Cops Defuse Tense Situations?," *Christian Science Monitor,* July 21, 2016. It is hard to say with confidence whether police, on the whole, are less violent today than they used to be, partly because advances in this respect have been at least somewhat offset by increases in the use of military equipment and tactics, and partly because the available statistics on uses of force by the police are fragmentary and often unreliable—far more fragmentary and far less reliable than statistics on violent crimes. Garrett and Stoughton, "A Tactical Fourth Amendment," 245, 249; Franklin E. Zimring, *When Police Kill* (Cambridge, MA: Harvard University Press, 2017), 23–40.

11.   Nikki Jones, remarks at Stanford Medical School Symposium on Race, Policing, and Public Health, Stanford, CA, March 6, 2017; Johnson, *Street Justice,* 140, 141, 211; John Byrne and Rick Pearson, "Donald Trump Says Cops Should Be Tougher on Chicago Crime," *Chicago Tribune,* June 29, 2015; Paul Butler, *Chokehold: Policing Black Men* (New York: New Press, 2017), 118.

12.   Perry Miller, *The Life of the Mind in America: From the Revolution to the Civil War* (New York: Harcourt, Brace and World, 1965), 121; David A. Sklansky, "The Fourth Amendment and Common Law," *Columbia Law Review* 100 (2000): 1739–1814, at 1794–1807.

13.   See Helen A. Anderson, "From the Thief in the Night to the Guest Who Stayed Too Long: The Evolution of Burglary in the Shadow of Common Law," *Indiana Law Review* 45 (2012): 629–668, at 633–634; Minturn T. Wright III, "Statutory Burglary—The Magic of Four Walls and a Roof," *University of Pennsylvania Law Review* 100 (1951): 411–445, at 411–412; Note, "A Rationale of the Law of Burglary," *Columbia Law Review* 51 (1951): 1009–1029, at 1012–1013; Wright, *Statutory Burglary,* 412, 412n3 (citing Coke, Hale, Blackstone, and East); Joseph Chitty, *A Practical Treatise on the Criminal Law* (London: A. J. Valpy, 1816), 1:54, 56.

14.   Richards v. Wisconsin, 520 U.S. 385, 391 (1997); Wilson v. Arkansas, 514 U.S. 927, 936–937 (1995); Hudson v. Michigan, 547 U.S. 586, 594 (2006).

15.   Rochin v. California, 342 U.S. 165, 171–174 (1952), reversing People v. Rochin, 225 P.2d 1 (1950).

16.   297 U.S. 278, 282–284, 286 (1936).

17.   Wickersham Commission, *Report on Lawlessness in Law Enforcement* (1931), 46; Oliver, *Prohibition Era and Policing,* 7, 52, 64–81; Johnson, *Street Justice,* 133–142.

18.   Spano v. New York, 360 U.S. 315, 323 (1959); Miranda v. Arizona, 384 U.S. 436, 445, 448, 458, 467; Oliver, *Prohibition Era and Policing,* 86.

19.   Johnson, *Street Justice,* 148; William J. Stuntz, "Privacy's Problem and the Law of Criminal Procedure," *Michigan Law Review* 93 (1995): 1016–1078, at 1077.

20.   Stuntz, "Privacy's Problem," 1007–1018; Boyd v. United States, 116 U.S. 616, 630 (1886).

21.   Olmstead v. United States, 277 U.S. 438, 478 (1928) (Brandeis, J., dissenting); Katz v. United States, 389 U.S. 347, 351 (1967); Alderman v. United States, 394 U.S. 165, 179n11 (1969).

22.   Warden v. Hayden, 387 U.S. 294 (1967); Silverman v. United States, 365 U.S. 505 (1961); Oliver, *Prohibition Era and Policing,* 127.

23.   Westley, "Violence and the Police," 37–38; David Alan Sklansky, "'One Train May Hide Another': *Katz,* Stonewall, and the Secret Subtext of Criminal Procedure," *UC Davis Law Review* 41 (2008): 875–934, at 900–902.

24.   Olmstead v. United States, 277 U.S. 438 (1928); Jones v. United States, 565 U.S. 400, 409 (2012) (*"added to"*) (italics in the original); Florida v. Jardines, 569 U.S. 1, 5 (2013).

25.   Tracey L. Meares, "Programming Errors: Understanding the Constitutionality of Stop and Frisk as a Program, Not an Incident," *University of Chicago Law Review* 82 (2015): 159–179, at 161.

26.   Butler, *Chokehold,* 82–83, 114; Kami Chavis Simmons, "The Legacy of Stop and Frisk: Addressing the Vestiges of a Violent Police Culture," *Wake Forest Law Review* 49 (2014): 849–872, 860–863.

27. Butler, *Chokehold,* 97–98, 105–106; Simmons, "Legacy of Stop and Frisk," 860; Bernard E. Harcourt, "Unconstitutional Police Searches and Collective Responsibility," *Criminology & Public Policy* 3 (2004): 363–378; Josephine Ross, "What the #MeToo Campaign Teaches about Stop and Frisk," *Idaho Law Review* 54 (2018): 543–561, at 549–555; Seth Stoughton, "*Terry v. Ohio* and the (Un)forgettable Frisk," *Ohio State Journal of Criminal Law* 15 (2015): 19–34, at 29.

28. Dunaway v. New York, 442 U.S. 200, 212 (1979) ("brief" and "narrowly circumscribed"); Buie v. Maryland, 550 A.2d 79, 83 (1988) ("slight"), quoted with approval and reversed on other grounds, 494 U.S. 325, 329 (1990); Terry v. Ohio, 392 U.S. 1, 10, 16–18 (1968); People v. Rivera, 14 N.Y.2d 441, 464 (1964).

29. Terry v. Ohio, 392 U.S. 7 at 16–17; Mapp v. Ohio, 367 U.S. at 645; Stuntz, "Privacy's Problem," 1065.

30. People v. Batista, 88 N.Y.2d 650, 654 (1996) (the "answer . . . may be a bullet") (quoting People v. Rivera, 14 N.Y.2d 441, 446 (1964)); Terry v. Ohio, 392 U.S. at 8.

31. Tennessee v. Garner, 471 U.S. 1 (1985); Graham v. Connor, 490 U.S. 386, 396 (1989) ("reasonableness"); Scott v. Harris, 550 U.S. 372, 382 (2007) ("rigid preconditions"); Yates v. Terry, 817 F.3d 877, 886 (4th Cir. 2016) ("immediate safety risk"); Young v. County of Los Angeles, 655 F.3d 1156, 1158 (9th Cir. 2011) ("minor infraction" and "no risk to . . . safety").

32. Escondido v. Emmons, 139 S. Ct. 500, 503 (2019) ("particularly important"); Kisela v. Hughes, 138 S. Ct. 1148, 1152–1153 (2018) ("squarely governs") (quoting Mullenix v. Luna, 136 S. Ct. 305, 309 (2015)).

33. "One constitutional word—seizures—encompasses a wide range of police activity, from the brief investigative stop short of a full arrest, all the way to the killing of a suspect. And one other word—unreasonable—is all that the constitutional text itself offers to distinguish licit from illicit seizures." Alice Ristroph, "The Constitution of Police Violence," *UCLA Law Review* 64 (2017): 1182–1245, at 1184. In practice, Ristroph notes, "the constitutional law of police force is not indeterminate, but determinately permissive" (1189).

34. Ristroph, "Constitution of Police Violence," 1212; Butler, *Chokehold,* 49–51; Garrett and Stoughton, "A Tactical Fourth Amendment," 279.

35. Garrett and Stoughton, "A Tactical Fourth Amendment," 291; Ristroph, "Constitution of Police Violence," 1214.

36. Ristroph, "Constitution of Police Violence"; Devon W. Carbado, "From Stopping Black People to Killing Black People: The Fourth Amendment Pathways to Violence," *California Law Review* 105 (2017): 125–164.

37. Johnson, *Street Justice,* 35, 88–93.

38. Oliver, *Prohibition Era and Policing,* 24–25, 80; Johnson, *Street Justice,* 121–133; Westley, "Violence and the Police."

39. James Baldwin, "Fifth Avenue, Uptown," in James Baldwin, *Nobody Knows My Name: More Notes of a Native Son* (New York: Dial Press, 1961), 56–71; see also James Baldwin, "A Report from Occupied Territory," *Nation* (New York), July 11, 1966.

40. David Alan Sklansky, *Democracy and the Police* (Stanford, CA: Stanford University Press, 2008); Baldwin, "Fifth Avenue, Uptown" ("the gun in the holster, and the swinging club"); Baldwin, "Report from Occupied Territory" ("thunder and fire"); James Miller, *Democracy Is in the Streets: From Port Huron to the Siege of Chicago* (Cambridge, MA: Harvard University Press, 1994), 298–306; Giovanni Russonello, "The Nation Seethes, and Trump's Response Follows a Pattern," *New York Times,* June 1, 2020, https://nyti.ms/3dooY6C (updated June 2, 2020); Michael Wilson, "Inside a Huge Brooklyn Protest: 'The World Is Watching,'" *New York Times,* June 1, 2020.

41. Johnson, *Street Justice,* 232–233, 237–251; Samuel Walker, *Police Accountability: The Role of Citizen Oversight* (Belmont, CA: Wadsworth Thompson Learning, 2001), 25–45; Jerome H. Skolnick, *Justice without Trial: Law Enforcement in Democratic Society* (New York: Wiley, 1966); Jerome H. Skolnick and James J. Fyfe, *Above the Law: Police and the Excessive Use of Force* (New York: Free Press, 1993); Muir, *Police: Streetcorner Politicians,* 3–4, 37–43; Hans Toch et al., *Agents of Change: A Study in Police Reform* (New York: Halsted Press, 1975).

42. Elaine Tyler May, *Fortress America: How We Embraced Fear and Abandoned Democracy* (New York: Basic Books, 2017), 104–109; Brian T. Tochterman, *The Dying City: Postwar New York and the Ideology of Fear* (Chapel Hill: University of North Carolina Press, 2017), 145–171.

43. Sklansky, *Democracy and the Police,* 74–105; Dorothy Guyot, *Policing as though People Matter* (Philadelphia: Temple University Press, 1991); Susan L. Miller, *Gender and Community Policing: Walking the Talk* (Boston: Northeastern University Press, 1999); James Forman Jr., "Community Policing and Youth as Assets," *Journal of Criminal Law and Criminology* 95 (2004): 1–48; David Alan Sklansky, "Not Your Father's Police Department: Making Sense of the New Demographics of Law Enforcement," *Journal of Criminal Law and Criminology* 96 (2006): 1209–1244.

44. Radley Balko, *Rise of the Warrior Cop: The Militarization of America's Police Forces* (New York: Public Affairs, 2013); Jonathan Mummolo, "Militarization Fails to Enhance Police Safety or Reduce Crime but May Harm Police Reputation," *Proceedings of the National Academy of Sciences* 115 (2018): 9181–9186; Callum Borchers, "BearCat Truck Maker Unruffled by Obama's Order," *Boston Globe,* May 21, 2015; Adam Goldman, "Trump Reverses Restrictions on Military Hardware for Police," *New York Times,* August 28, 2017; Catie Edmonson, "Lawmakers

Push to Stop Sending Military Gear to Police," *New York Times,* June 2, 2020, p. A26; Peter Baker et al., "How Trump's Idea for a Photo Op Led to Havoc in a Park," *New York Times,* June 3, 2020, p. A1.

45. American Civil Liberties Union, *War Comes Home: The Excessive Militarization of American Policing* (2014), https://www.aclu.org/report/war-comes-home-excessive-militarization-american-police; Mummolo, "Militarization Fails"; Paul Chevigny, *Edge of the Knife: Police Violence in the Americas* (New York: New Press, 1995), 138; Zimring, *When Police Kill,* 4–9, 23–40, 75–76.

46. Zimring, *When Police Kill,* 4–12, 46; David Crary, "AP Poll: Police Killings of Blacks Voted Top Story of 2014," AP News, December 22, 2014, https://apnews.com/ad250438af4e4fae95d7e41f537661ef.

47. Ta-Nehisi Coates, *Between the World and Me* (New York: Spiegel and Grau, 2015), 10; Butler, *Chokehold,* 97; Nikki Jones, remarks at Stanford Medical School Symposium.

48. Johnson, *Street Justice,* 37; United States Commission on Civil Rights, *Report 5: Justice,* 5.

49. Sklansky, "Fourth Amendment and Common Law," 1805.

50. Davis v. United States, 564 U.S. 229, 241 (2011); see also, for example, Utah v. Strieff, 136 S. Ct. 2056, 2063 (2016).

51. Scott v. Harris, 550 U.S. 32 (2007); Escondido v. Emmons, 139 S. Ct. 500, 503 (2019).

52. Monell v. Department of Social Services, 436 U.S. 658 (1978).

53. 34 U.S.C. § 12601 (2018).

54. See, for example, Barbara E. Armacost, "Organizational Culture and Police Misconduct," *George Washington Law Review* 72 (2004): 453–546; Seth W. Stoughton, "Principled Policing: Warrior Cops and Guardian Officers," *Wake Forest Law Review* 51 (2016): 611–676. For further discussion of the link between professional norms and police misconduct, see Sklansky, *Democracy and the Police,* 39–41; David Alan Sklansky, "Seeing Blue: Police Reform, Occupational Culture, and Cognitive Burn-In," in *Police Occupational Culture: New Debates and Directions,* ed. Megan O'Neill et al. (Amsterdam: JAI Press, 2007), 19–45.

55. Zimring, *When Police Kill,* 86, 99–100, 107–108. Most uses of force by the police are proactive, not defensive; see Seth W. Stoughton, "Policing Facts," *Tulane Law Review* 88 (2014): 847–898, 868. But that might not be true of deadly force; see Zimring, *When Police Kill,* 61–63.

56. Garrett and Stoughton, "A Tactical Fourth Amendment."

57. Graham v. Connor, 490 U.S. 386, 397 (1989). Lower courts quoted this language more than 2,300 times in the twenty-five years following the Supreme Court's decision in *Graham.* Stoughton, "Policing Facts," 865.

58. Monell v. Department of Social Services, 691–692, 701; City of Los Angeles v. Heller, 475 U.S. 796 (1986); Garrett and Stoughton, "A Tactical Fourth Amendment," 216, 237–240. Not all courts employ the "split-second theory of policing"; Garrett and Stoughton note with approval that some lower courts consider whether the officer's conduct was reasonable during each part of the encounter. Garrett and Stoughton, "A Tactical Fourth Amendment," 291–293.

59. Regarding police shootings of suspects armed with knives, see Zimring, *When Police Kill,* 57–63, 100–102; Police Executive Research Forum, *Re-Engineering Training on Police Use of Force* (2015), 7–8, https://www.policeforum.org/assets /reengineeringtraining1.pdf; *Guiding Principles on Use of Force* (Washington, DC: Police Executive Research Forum, 2016), 54, https://www.policeforum.org/assets /30%20guiding%20principles.pdf; Ron Martinelli, "Revisiting the '21-Foot Rule,'" *Police Magazine,* September 18, 2014; Norton v. City of South Portland, 831 F. Supp. 2d 340 (D. Me. 2011); Samuel v. City of Broken Arrow, No. 10-CV-683, 2011 WL 6029677 (N.D. Okla. December 5, 2011); Estate of Larsen v. Murr, No. 03 CV 02589, 2006 WL 322602 (D. Colo. February 10, 2006); Porter v. City of Muncie, No. IP 98-1491-C, 2000 WL 682660 (S.D. Ind. February 16, 2000).

60. Rich Morin et al., *Behind the Badge* (Washington, DC: Pew Research Center, 2017), 38.

4. RAPE AND DOMESTIC ASSAULT

1. George MacDonald Fraser, *Flashman* (London: Barrie and Jenkins, 1969; New York: HarperCollins, 2015), 13, 20–21, 80 (citations refer to the HarperCollins edition); Christopher Hitchens, "Fraser's Flashman: Scoundrel Time," in *Arguably* (Ontario: Signal, 2011), 358–364, at 360 ("anti-hero"); Saul David, "Flash Man," *Telegraph* (London), April 16, 2006 ("marvelously funny," "caddish"); Stanley Reynolds, "George MacDonald Fraser," *Guardian,* January 3, 2008 ("bright gems"); Tom Harper, "Flashman by George MacDonald Fraser: Book of a Lifetime," *Independent* (London), September 5, 2015; John Updike, "Flashy to the Rescue: George MacDonald Fraser's Latest Flashman Novel," *New Yorker,* November 21, 2005. Michael Dirda, the Pulitzer-winning book critic for the *Washington Post,* wrote fondly in 2018 of the "breezy, cheeky manner" of the Flashman series. Michael Dirda, "The Timely Message in Christopher Buckley's Historical Novel," *Washington Post,* May 2, 2018. Fraser borrowed his main character from Thomas Hughes's 1857 novel, *Tom Brown's School Days,* in which Flashman plays a bit part as an adolescent bully.

2. Hitchens, "Fraser's Flashman," 360.

3.   William Blackstone, *Commentaries on the Law of England* (Oxford: Clarendon Press, 1765–1769), 4:210; Coker v. Georgia, 433 U.S. 584 (1977).

4.   Estelle B. Freedman, *Redefining Rape: Sexual Violence in the Era of Suffrage and Segregation* (Cambridge, MA: Harvard University Press, 2013); Jill Elaine Hasday, "Contest and Consent: A Legal History of Marital Rape," *California Law Review* 88 (2000): 1373–1506; Lisa R. Eskow, "The Ultimate Weapon? Demythologizing Spousal Rape and Reconceptualizing Its Prosecution," *Stanford Law Review* 48 (1996): 677–709; Julia Simon-Kerr, "Unchaste and Incredible: The Use of Gendered Conceptions of Honor in Impeachment," *Yale Law Journal* 117 (2008): 1854–1899; William Westley, "Violence and the Police," *American Journal of Sociology* 59 (1953): 34–41, at 37.

5.   Freedman, *Redefining Rape,* 276–282; Maria Bevacqua, *Rape on the Public Agenda: Feminism and the Politics of Sexual Assault* (Boston: Northeastern University Press, 2000).

6.   Bevacqua, *Rape on the Public Agenda;* Rose Corrigan, *Up Against a Wall: Rape Reform and the Failure of Success* (New York: NYU Press, 2013), 7, 28–29; Robert O. Self, *All in the Family: The Realignment of American Democracy since the 1960s* (New York: Farrar, Straus and Giroux, 2012), 210–213; Susan Griffin, "Rape: The All-American Crime," *Ramparts* (San Francisco), September 1971, pp. 26, 27, 30, 35; Susan Brownmiller, "On Goosing," *Village Voice* (New York), April 15, 1971, p. 5; Susan Brownmiller, *Against Our Will: Men, Women and Rape* (New York: Bantam, 1975). In calling rape "a metaphor for all male-female relations," Brownmiller was quoting Diana Crothers. Regarding "rape culture," see Corrigan, *Up Against a Wall,* 28; Kate Manne, *Down Girl: The Logic of Misogyny* (New York: Oxford University Press, 2018), 196–205; Joyce E. Williams, "Rape Culture," in *Blackwell Encyclopedia of Sociology,* ed. George Ritzer (Hoboken, NJ: Wiley-Blackwell, 2007), 8:3783; Kate Millett, *Sexual Politics* (Garden City, NY: Doubleday, 1970), 44. On the significance of *Sexual Politics* and *Against Our Will,* see, respectively, Sheila Jeffreys, "Kate Millett's *Sexual Politics:* 40 Years On," *Women's Studies International Forum* 34 (2011): 76–84, and Sascha Cohen, "How a Book Changed the Way We Talk about Rape," *Time,* October 7, 2015.

7.   Griffin, "Rape," 29; Self, *All in the Family,* 213; Corrigan, *Up Against a Wall,* 41; Freedman, *Redefining Rape,* 278; Susan Estrich, "Rape," *Yale Law Journal* 95 (1986): 1087–1184, at 1150; Christine A. Littleton, "Feminist Jurisprudence: The Difference Method Makes," *Stanford Law Review* 41 (1989): 751–784, at 776.

8.   Steven Pinker, *The Better Angels of Our Nature: Why Violence Has Declined* (New York: Viking, 2011), 403.

9.   Griffin, "Rape," 27; Alice Ristroph, "Criminal Law in the Shadow of Violence," *Alabama Law Review* 62 (2011): 571 621, at 595.

10.   Robin Morgan, "Theory and Practice: Pornography and Rape," in *Going Too Far: The Personal Chronicle of a Feminist* (New York: Random House, 1977), 163–169, at 169; Self, *All in the Family,* 208; Catharine A. MacKinnon, *Feminism Unmodified: Discourses on Life and Law* (Cambridge, MA: Harvard University Press, 1987), 85; Charlotte L. Bynum, "Feminism and Pornography: A New Zealand Perspective," *Tulane Law Review* 65 (1991): 1131–1182, at 1170; Susan Griffin, *Pornography and Silence: Culture's Revenge against Nature* (New York: Harper and Row, 1981), 93–119.

11.   Corrigan, *Up Against a Wall,* 34–36, 53–55; Freedman, *Redefining Rape,* 278, 284; Self, *All in the Family,* 209; Clifford S. Fishman, "Consent, Credibility, and the Constitution: Evidence Relating to a Sex Offense Complainant's Past Sexual Behavior," *Catholic University Law Review* 44 (1995): 709–820; Marie Gottschalk, *The Prison and the Gallows: The Politics of Mass Incarceration in America* (Cambridge: Cambridge University Press, 2006), 121–133; Aya Gruber, "Rape, Feminism, and the War on Crime," *Washington Law Review* 84 (2009): 581–660, at 587–595; Hasday, "Contest and Consent"; Patricia Yancey Martin, *Rape Work: Victims, Gender, and Emotions in Organization and Community Context* (New York: Routledge, 2005), 96–100; Barbara G. Collins and Mary B. Whalen, "The Rape Crisis Movement: Radical or Reformist?," *Social Work* 34 (1989): 61–63, at 61; Pub. L. No. 103-322, 108 Stat. 1902. The Supreme Court invalidated a provision of the Violence Against Women Act that allowed victims of gender-motivated crimes of violence to sue their attackers in federal court; the Justices concluded that the creation of the remedy exceeded the powers that the Constitution gave to the federal government. United States v. Morrison, 529 U.S. 598 (2000). But the lawsuits authorized by the statute were never numerically significant, even before the Supreme Court's decision; the principal importance of the civil rights remedy was symbolic. Judith Resnik, "Drafting, Lobbying, and Litigating VAWA: National, Local, and Transnational Interventions on Behalf of Women's Equality," *Georgetown Journal of Gender and the Law* 11 (2010): 557–570, at 563; "Welcoming Remarks and Panel One: Present at the Creation: Drafting and Passing the Violence Against Women Act (VAWA)," *Georgetown Journal of Gender and the Law* 11 (2010): 511–532, at 519 (remarks of Sally Goldfarb); Carolyn S. Schmidt, "What Killed the Violence Against Women Act's Civil Rights Remedy before the Supreme Court Did?," *Virginia Law Review* 101 (2015): 501–558, at 506–509, 524.

12.   Rachel E. Morgan and Jennifer L. Truman, *Criminal Victimization, 2017* (Washington, DC: United States Department of Justice, 2018), 7; Susan Milligan, "Sexual Assault Reports Spike in #MeToo Era," *U.S. News & World Report,* December 27, 2018; Ashley Southall, "Rape Reports Are Up Sharply, and Mayor Points to #MeToo," *New York Times,* January 6, 2019, p. A19. Even in the notoriously sexist and violent universe of video games, it appears that rape is taboo, at

least in the West. The legal scholar Francis X. Shen, who has studied the contents of these games, reports that "rape may be the one thing you can't put into a video game. . . . [A]llowing someone to press the X-button to rape another character is off-limits." Pinker, *Better Angels of Our Nature,* 401 (quoting Shen). The exceptions generate such fierce, across-the-board outrage that they tend to prove the rule. See, for example, Jennifer Graham, "Custer May Be Shot Down Again in a Battle of the Sexes over X-Rated Video Games," *People,* November 15, 1982; Latoya Peterson, "A Vicious Reflection of Society," *Guardian,* March 2, 2009.

13.   Candace Kruttschnitt, William D. Kalsbeek, and Carol C. House, eds., *Estimating the Incidence of Rape and Sexual Assault* (Washington, DC: National Academies Press, 2014), 49–69, 153–158; Pinker, *Better Angels of Our Nature,* 402; Michael R. Rand, James P. Lynch, and David Cantor, *Criminal Victimization, 1973–95* (Washington, DC: United States Department of Justice, 1997), 3. Regarding changes in the National Crime Victimization Survey, see Ronet Bachman and Linda E. Saltzman, *Violence against Women: Estimates from the Redesigned Survey* (Washington, DC: United States Department of Justice, 1995), 8; Rand, Lynch, and Cantor, *Criminal Victimization,* 3, 7n5; Marianne W. Zawitz et al., *Highlights from 20 Years of Surveying Crime Victims: The National Crime Victimization Survey, 1973–92* (Washington, DC: United States Department of Justice, 1993), 37. Regarding undercounting, see Ronet Bachman and Bruce M. Taylor, "The Measurement of Family Violence and Rape by the Redesigned National Crime Victimization Survey," *Justice Quarterly* 11 (1994): 499–512, at 505–506; Emily Bazelon, "We've Been Measuring Rape All Wrong," Slate, November 19, 2013, https://slate.com/human-interest/2013/11/national-crime -victimization-survey-a-new-report-finds-that-the-justice-department-has -been-undercounting-instances-of-rape-and-sexual-assault.html.

14.   Corrigan, *Up Against a Wall,* 5, 65–116; Benjamin Weiser, Ali Watkins, and Joseph Goldstein, "Attitudes Are Changing in Sex Assault Cases," *New York Times,* July 26, 2019, p. A24; Barbara Bradley Hagerty, "An Epidemic of Disbelief," *Atlantic,* August 2019. In many jurisdictions, even allegations of "stereotypical" rape are still treated skeptically by police and prosecutors, especially if the victim has a criminal record, has been involved in sex work, or had been drinking or using drugs before she was attacked. Hagerty, "Epidemic of Disbelief." On the limited success of rape law reforms, see also, for example, Francis X. Shen, "How We Still Fail Rape Victims: Reflecting on Responsibility and Legal Reform," *Columbia Journal of Gender and Law* 22 (2012): 1–80.

15.   Freedman, *Redefining Rape,* 1 (italics added); John Eligon and Michael Schwirtz, "In Rapes, Candidate Says, Body Can Block Pregnancy," *New York Times,* August 20, 2012, p. A13.

16. Estrich, "Rape," 7, 1150.

17. Estrich, "Rape," 1088, 1092, 1105, 1150, 1183.

18. Catharine A. MacKinnon, *Butterfly Politics: Changing the World for Women* (Cambridge, MA: Harvard University Press, 2017, paperback edition 2019), 290.

19. Regarding date rape, see Freedman, *Redefining Rape,* 284 ("passive victims"); Bevacqua, *Rape on the Public Agenda,* 183–190. On the creation and limited success of sexual harassment laws, see Carrie N. Baker, *The Women's Movement against Sexual Harassment* (New York: Cambridge University Press, 2008); Lauren B. Edelman, *Working Law: Courts, Corporations, and Symbolic Civil Rights* (Chicago: University of Chicago Press, 2016); Anna-Maria Marshall, "Idle Rights: Employees' Rights Consciousness and the Construction of Sexual Harassment Policies," *Law & Society Review* 39 (2005): 83–124; Kate Roiphe, *The Morning After: Sex, Fear, and Feminism on Campus* (Boston: Back Bay Books, 1994); Self, *All in the Family,* 216–217. Regarding rape as "abuse" and the focus on coercion, see Estrich, "Rape," 1183; *Model Penal Code: Sexual Assault and Related Offenses, Council Draft No. 8* (Philadelphia: American Law Institute, 2018), § 213.0 comment 6, at 25, § 213.6, at 186; Robert Chiarito and Elizabeth A. Harris, "At R. Kelly's Bond Hearing, Prosecutors Reveal Details of Sex Abuse Charges," *New York Times,* February 24, 2019, p. A20; Jason Horowitz and Elizabeth Diaz, "Francis Invokes 'All-Out Battle' on Sexual Abuse," *New York Times,* February 25, 2019, p. A1.

20. Andrea Dworkin, *Our Blood: Prophecies and Discourses on Sexual Politics* (New York: Harper and Row, 1976), 29, 33, 45–46 ("our primary model," "*any* forced sexual act," "presumptive rape") (italics in original); Andrea Dworkin, *Intercourse,* 20th anniv. ed. (New York: Basic Books, 2006), 154; Andrea Dworkin, *Last Days at Hot Slit: The Radical Feminism of Andrea Dworkin,* ed. Johanna Fateman and Amy Scholder (Los Angeles: Semiotext(e), 2019); Michelle Goldberg, "Not the Fun Kind of Feminist," *New York Times,* February 24, 2019, p. SR4; Jeremy Lybarger, "Finally Seeing Andrea," *Boston Review,* February 23, 2019; Lauren Oyler, "The Radical Style of Andrea Dworkin," *New Yorker,* April 1, 2019; Katherine Viner, "'She Never Hated Men,'" *Guardian,* April 12, 2005.

21. See, for example, Ala. Code § 15-22-36(e)(1); Alaska Stat. Ann. §§ 12.55.125(i), 33.16.089-.090; Ark. Code Ann. § 16-93-609; D.C. Code Ann. § 22-1804a(a)(2); 11 Del. Code Ann. § 4201(c); Ky. Rev. Stat. Ann. § 532.080; La. Stat. Ann. § 15:529.1; Miss. Code Ann. § 97-3-2; 57; Okla. Stat. Ann. § 571; Wash. Rev. Code Ann. § 9.94A.030(33).

22. Corrigan, *Up Against a Wall,* 27–51; Donna Coker, "Crime Logic, Campus Sexual Assault, and Restorative Justice," *Texas Tech Law Review* 49 (2016): 147–210, at 158–159; Gruber, "Rape, Feminism, and the War on Crime"; Erin Murphy, "Grading Sex" (unpublished manuscript, February 13, 2017), 20–23.

23. Gottschalk, *Prison and the Gallows,* 124–133; Gruber, "Rape, Feminism, and the War on Crime."

24. Michelle Alexander, *The New Jim Crow: Mass Incarceration in the Age of Color-blindness* (New York: New Press, 2010); Freedman, *Redefining Rape,* 1, 12, 27, 32, 288; "Crime in the United States 2017, Table 43," Federal Bureau of Investigation, accessed June 17, 2020, https://ucr.fbi.gov/crime-in-the-u.s/2017/crime-in-the-u.s.-2017/tables/table-43.

25. Self, *All in the Family,* 212–215; *Reconstruction in America: Racial Violence after the Civil War, 1865–1876* (Montgomery, AL: Equal Justice Initiative, 2020), 70–71. Regarding the problem of race in second-wave feminism more generally, see, for example, bell hooks, *Feminist Theory: From Margin to Center* (Boston: South End Press, 1984; New York: Routledge, 2015), 1–17. Citations refer to the Routledge edition.

26. Brownmiller, *Against Our Will,* 247, 251–255 (italics in original); Eldridge Cleaver, *Soul on Ice* (New York: McGraw-Hill, 1968), 33, 34; Eldridge Cleaver, interview by Nat Hentoff, *Playboy,* October 1968, p. 89 (quoted in Brownmiller, *Against Our Will,* 251); Angela Y. Davis, *Women, Race and Class* (New York: Random House, 1981; New York: Vintage, 1983), 178–179; Kimberle Crenshaw, "Demarginalizing the Intersection of Race and Sex: A Black Feminist Critique of Antidiscrimination Doctrine, Feminist Theory and Antiracist Politics," *University of Chicago Legal Forum* 1989 (1989): 139–167, at 158–160, 158n50, 159n54; Nathan Hare, "Revolution without a Revolution: The Psychology of Sex and Race," *Black Scholar* 9 (1978): 14–19, at 15, 18; Alice Walker, "Letter to the Editor," *New York Times Book Review,* November 30, 1975, p. 65.

27. Griffin, "Rape: The All-American Crime," 27; Dworkin, *Our Blood,* 33; Corrigan, *Up Against a Wall,* 35–36; Freedman, *Redefining Rape,* 277; Self, *All in the Family,* 213; Kate Manne, *Down Girl,* 199 ("all too human"); Peggy Orenstein, "It's Not that Men Don't Know What Consent Is," *New York Times,* February 24, 2019, p. SR4.

28. Regarding evidence rules in sexual assault cases, see Fed. R. Evid. 413–415; Calif. Evid. Code § 1108; United States v. LeCompte, 131 F.3d 767 (8th Cir. 1997); United States v. Cunningham, 103 F.3d 553 (7th Cir. 1996); Aviva Orenstein, "No Bad Men! A Feminist Analysis of Character Evidence in Rape Trials," *Hastings Law Journal* 49 (1998): 663–716; Roger C. Park, "The Crime Bill of 1994 and the Law of Character Evidence: Congress Was Right about Consent Defense Cases," *Fordham Urban Law Journal* 22 (1995): 271–283. Regarding registration and notification statutes, see Corrigan, *Up Against a Wall,* 205–217; Kristen M. Zgoba et al., "The Adam Walsh Act: An Examination of Sex Offender Risk Classification Systems," *Sexual Abuse* 28 (2016): 722–740; Adam Walsh Child Protection and Safety

Act of 2006, Pub. L. 109-248, §§ 111–113, 125, codified as amended at 34 U.S.C. § 20911–20913, 20927.

29. Corrigan, *Up Against a Wall,* 217–248.

30. Susan Schechter, *Women and Male Violence: The Visions and Struggles of the Battered Women's Movement* (Boston: South End Press, 1982), 34–43.

31. Erin R. Collins, "The Evidentiary Rules of Engagement in the War against Domestic Violence," *New York University Law Review* 90 (2015): 397–459; Leigh Goodmark, "Should Domestic Violence Be Decriminalized?," *Harvard Journal of Law and Gender* 40 (2017): 53–114, at 61–63; Emily J. Sack, "Battered Women and the State: The Struggle for the Future of Domestic Violence Policy," *Wisconsin Law Review* 2004 (2004): 1657–1740, at 1662–1665; Elizabeth M. Schneider, "Domestic Violence Law Reform in the Twenty-First Century: Looking Back and Looking Forward," *Family Law Quarterly* 42 (2008): 353–364; Ristroph, "Criminal Law."

32. Schechter, *Women and Male Violence,* 11 ("to name the hidden and private violence"); Collins, "Evidentiary Rules of Engagement," 404; Margaret B. Drew, "Collaboration and Coercion," *Hastings Women's Law Journal* 24 (2013): 79–106, at 83; Larissa MacFarquhar, "A House of Their Own," *New Yorker,* August 19, 2019, p. 36. Regarding the traditional use of the term "domestic violence" to refer to unrest within the national borders, see Elizabeth Pleck, *Domestic Tyranny: The Making of American Social Policy against Family Violence from Colonial Times to the Present* (New York: Oxford University Press, 1987), 194. This is how the term is used in Article IV of the United States Constitution, a point often remarked upon by advocates of "originalism" in constitutional interpretation. See, for example, Lawrence B. Solum, "The Fixation Thesis: The Role of Historical Fact in Original Meaning," *Notre Dame Law Review* 91 (2015): 1–78, at 16–18, 71–73; Mark S. Stein, "The Domestic Violence Clause in 'New Originalist' Theory," *Hastings Constitutional Law Quarterly* 37 (2009): 129–140.

33. Kimberly D. Bailey, "Lost in Translation: Domestic Violence, 'The Personal Is Political,' and the Criminal Justice System," *Journal of Criminal Law & Criminology* 100 (2010): 1255–1300, at 1268; Collins, "Evidentiary Rules of Engagement," 404–412; Richard D. Friedman and Bridget McCormack, "Dial-in Testimony," *University of Pennsylvania Law Review* 150 (2002): 1171–1254; Goodmark, "Should Domestic Violence Be Decriminalized?," 63–65; Aya Gruber, "The Feminist War on Crime," *Iowa Law Review* 92 (2007): 741–834, at 792–800; Kit Kinports, "So Much Activity, So Little Change: A Reply to Critics of Battered Women's Self-Defense," *Saint Louis University Public Law Review* 23 (2004): 155–192, at 156–157; Sack, "Battered Women," 1668–1676.

34. Sack, "Battered Women," 1667–1668; Jeannie Suk, "Criminal Law Comes Home," *Yale Law Journal* 116 (2006): 2–71, at 13–16.

35. Gottschalk, *Prison and the Gallows,* 139–164; Lisa N. Sacco, *The Violence Against Women Act: Overview, Legislation, and Federal Funding* (Washington, DC: Congressional Research Service, 2015); Emily S. Rueb and Niraj Chokshi, "The Violence Against Women Act Is Turning 25: Here's How It Has Ignited Debate," *New York Times,* April 4, 2019.

36. Amy Farmer and Jill Tiefenthaler, "Explaining the Recent Decline in Domestic Violence," *Contemporary Economic Policy* 21 (2003): 158–172; Julie Bosman, "When Staying Home, or Trying to Leave, Carries Its Own Risk," *New York Times,* May 17, 2020, p. A10; Goodmark, "Should Domestic Violence Be Decriminalized?," 55–56. Even before COVID-19, there was evidence of an uptick in the number of women killed by domestic partners, for reasons that are poorly understood. Violence Policy Center, *When Men Murder Women: An Analysis of 2017 Homicide Data* (2019), 2, https://vpc.org/studies/wmmw2019.pdf; Nicole Santa Cruz and Iris Lee, "As Homicides Drop in L.A. County, More Women Are Being Killed—Often by Intimate Partners," *Los Angeles Times,* September 9, 2019; Emma E. Fridel and James A. Fox, "Gender Differences in Patterns and Trends in U.S. Homicide, 1976–2017," *Violence and Gender* 6 (2019): 27–36.

37. Bailey, "Lost in Translation"; Goodmark, "Should Domestic Violence Be Decriminalized?," 67–74; Gruber, "Feminist War on Crime"; Sack, "Battered Women"; Suk, "Criminal Law Comes Home," 8 ("state-imposed de facto divorce"). Regarding mandatory arrest and "no drop" policies, see Richard A. Berk et al., "The Deterrent Effect of Arrest in Incidents of Domestic Violence: A Bayesian Analysis of Four Field Experiments," *American Sociological Review* 57 (1992): 698–708; Alexandra Pavlidakis, Comment, "Mandatory Arrest: Past Its Prime," *Santa Clara Law Review* 49 (2009): 1201–1236, at 1208–1210.

38. Katherine T. Bartlett, Deborah L. Rhode, and Joanna L. Grossman, *Gender and Law: Theory and Commentary,* 8th ed. (New York: Wolters Kluwer, 2020), chap. 3; Jennifer Mascia, "The Untold Story of Gun Violence," *Cosmopolitan,* September 12, 2018; Ristroph, "Criminal Law," 602.

39. Serious Crime Act 2015, c. 9, § 76 (Eng. & Wales); Domestic Violence Act 2018 (Act. No. 6 / 2018), § 39 (Ir.), http://www.irishstatutebook.ie/eli/2018/act/6/enacted/en/print; Domestic Abuse (Scotland) Act 2018, (ASP 5) §§ 1–2 (Scot.); Marilyn McMahon and Paul McGorrery, "Criminalising Controlling and Coercive Behaviour: The Next Step in the Prosecution of Family Violence," *Alternative Law Journal* 41 (2006): 98–101. For calls for similar legislation in the United States, see, for example, Alafair S. Burke, "Domestic Violence as a Crime of Pattern and Intent: An Alternative Reconceptualization," *George Washington Law Review* 75 (2007): 552–612, at 601–602; Deborah Tuerkheimer, "Recognizing and Remedying the Harm of Battering: A Call to Criminalize Domestic Violence,"

Journal of Criminal Law & Criminology 94 (2004): 959–1032, at 1019–1020. For calls to broaden the category of domestic violence to include "emotional violence," see Margaret E. Johnson, "Redefining Harm, Reimagining Remedies, and Reclaiming Domestic Violence Law," *UC Davis Law Review* 42 (2009): 1107–1164, at 1110, 1110n4; Joy M. Bingham, Note, "Protecting Victims by Working around the System and within the System: Statutory Protection for Emotional Abuse in the Domestic Violence Context," *North Dakota Law Review* 81 (2005): 837–858, at 843. Since 2020, California and Hawaii have authorized protection orders against coercive control, but no state has made it a stand-alone offense. Cal. Family Code § 6320; Hawaii Rev. Stat. § 581–1.

40. "Domestic Violence," Office on Violence Against Women, United States Department of Justice, accessed May 1, 2020, https://www.justice.gov/ovw/domestic-violence; Natalie Nanasi, "The Trump Administration Quietly Changed the Definition of Domestic Violence and We Have No Idea What For," Slate, January 21, 2019, https://slate.com/news-and-politics/2019/01/trump-domestic-violence-definition-change.html; Rebecca R. Ruiz, "Attorney General Orders Tougher Sentences, Rolling Back Obama Policy," *New York Times*, May 12, 2017.

41. Lenore Walker, *The Battered Woman* (New York: Harper and Row, 1979); see also Lenore E. A. Walker, *The Battered Woman Syndrome*, 4th ed. (New York: Springer, 2016).

42. Collins, "Evidentiary Rules of Engagement," 406–408; Kinports, "So Much Activity," at 161–162; Beth Rothenberg, "The Success of Battered Woman Syndrome: An Analysis of How Cultural Arguments Succeed," *Sociological Forum* 17 (2002): 81–103.

43. Collins, "Evidentiary Rules of Engagement," 448–449; Rothenberg, "The Success of Battered Woman Syndrome," 85–86. For evidence supporting the theory, see Walker, *The Battered Woman Syndrome*, 94–98.

44. Carolyn B. Ramsey, "The Stereotyped Offender: Domestic Violence and the Failure of Intervention," *Penn State Law Review* 120 (2015): 337–420, at 363–367; Lauren Justice, "'What Would I Have Done if I Would Have Killed Her That Night?,'" *New York Times*, March 3, 2019, p. SR6.

45. "Wheels," Domestic Abuse Intervention Programs, accessed May 1, 2020, https://www.theduluthmodel.org/wheels/.

46. Ramsey, "The Stereotyped Offender," 367–373. Regarding evidence rules in domestic violence cases, see Collins, "Evidentiary Rules of Engagement," 420–421.

47. See, for example, MacFarquhar, "A House of Their Own," 42, 48–49.

48. Rachel Louise Snyder, *No Visible Bruises: What We Don't Know about Domestic Violence Can Kill Us* (New York: Bloomsbury, 2019); Nicholas Bogel-Burroughs, "Estranged Husband Kills Wife and Three Children," *New York*

Times, November 17, 2019, p. A27. Regarding domestic violence among police officers, see Bailey, "Lost in Translation," at 1279.

49. hooks, *Feminist Theory,* 117–132; bell hooks, *Feminism Is For Everybody: Passionate Politics* (Cambridge, MA: South End Books, 2000), 61–64; "Trump, Illinois Governor Spar during Call over Get-Tough Talk," *New York Times,* June 2, 2020; "Trump Suggests Governors Call in National Guard to 'Dominate the Streets,'" *New York Times,* June 5, 2020; Gail Collins, "What We Have Here Is a Failure to Dominate," *New York Times,* June 4, 2020, p. A26; Paul Krugman, "Donald Trump Is No Richard Nixon," *New York Times,* June 5, 2020, p. A26. On rape culture as a dimension of patriarchal dominance, see Manne, *Down Girl.*

50. Snyder, *No Visible Bruises;* Jacquelyn C. Campbell, Daniel W. Webster, and Nancy Glass, "The Danger Assessment: Validation of a Lethality Risk Assessment Instrument for Intimate Partner Femicide," *Journal of Interpersonal Violence* 24 (2009): 653–674; Jacquelyn C. Campbell, "Danger Assessment," updated 2019, https://www.dangerassessment.org/uploads/DA_NewScoring_2019.pdf.

51. Ramsey, "The Stereotyped Offender"; Snyder, *No Visible Bruises.*

5. VIOLENCE AND YOUTH

1. William Golding, *Lord of the Flies* (New York: Penguin Putnam, 1954), 202.

2. Barry C. Feld, *The Evolution of the Juvenile Court: Race, Politics, and the Criminalizing of Juvenile Justice* (New York: NYU Press, 2017), 71–191; Cara H. Drinan, *The War on Kids: How American Juvenile Justice Lost Its Way* (New York: Oxford University Press, 2018), 16–24, 45–65; Franklin E. Zimring and Máximo Langer, "The Central Mission of Separate Juvenile Courts," in *American Juvenile Justice,* 2nd ed., by Franklin E. Zimring (New York: Oxford University Press, 2019), 73; David S. Tanenhaus and Steven A. Drizin, "'Owing to the Extreme Youth of the Accused': The Changing Legal Response to Juvenile Homicide," *Journal of Criminal Law and Criminology* 92 (2003): 641–705. For predictions that "superpredators" would cause a "bloodbath of violence," see Kathleen M. Heide, "Juvenile Violence," in *The Cambridge Handbook of Social Problems,* ed. A. Javier Treviño (Cambridge: Cambridge University Press, 2018), 2:346 (quoting James Fox); William J. Bennett, John J. DiIulio Jr., and John P. Walters, *Body Count: Moral Poverty . . . and How to Win America's War against Crime and Drugs* (New York: Simon and Schuster, 1996), 21–38; James Alan Fox, *Trends in Juvenile Justice: A Report to the United States Attorney General on Current and Future Rates of Juvenile Offending* (Washington, DC: United States Department of Justice, 1996).

3. Feld, *Evolution of the Juvenile Court,* 141–144, 185–190, 195–223; Drinan, *War on Kids,* 51–52, 84–96, 132–133. On declining rates of juvenile violence, see

Zimring, *American Juvenile Justice,* 145–171. Regarding advances in brain science and the Supreme Court's reaction, see Terry A. Maroney, "The Once and Future Juvenile Brain," in *Choosing the Future for American Juvenile Justice,* ed. Franklin E. Zimring and David S. Tanenhaus (New York: NYU Press, 2014), 189–215; Miller v. Alabama, 567 U.S. 460 (2012); Graham v. Florida, 560 U.S. 53 (2010); Roper v. Simmons, 543 U.S. 551 (2005).

4. Karen J. Renner, *Evil Children in the Popular Imagination* (New York: Palgrave Macmillan, 2016); Transcript of Oral Argument, Roper v. Simmons (No. 03-633), October 13, 2004, p. 40. Regarding the resonance between new developments in brain science and common understandings of adolescence, see Maroney, "Once and Future Juvenile Brain," 191, 203; Franklin E. Zimring and David S. Tanenhaus, "On Strategy and Tactics in Juvenile Justice Reform," in Zimring, *American Juvenile Justice,* 290–294.

5. Linda Collier, "Adult Crime, Adult Time: Outdated Juvenile Laws Thwart Justice," *Washington Post,* March 29, 1998, p. C1 ("violent juvenile offenders of today"); Tanenhaus and Drizen, "'Owing to the Extreme Youth,'" 641–642, 683 (quoting Chicago prosecutor); Blair Stenvick, "Oregon Prosecutors Continue to Fight Criminal Justice Reform with Fearmongering," Portland Mercury Blogtown, April 29, 2019, https://www.portlandmercury.com/blogtown/2019/04/29/26401524/oregon-prosecutors-continue-to-fight-criminal-justice-reform-the-with-fearmongering (quoting Oregon district attorney).

6. Zimring, *American Juvenile Justice,* 107–124, 290–294.

7. Anders Walker, "When Gangs Were White: Race, Riots, and Youth Crime in New York City, 1954–1964," *Saint Louis University Law Journal* 55 (2011): 1369–1378.

8. Justin Driver, *The Schoolhouse Gate: Public Education, the Supreme Court, and the Battle for the American Mind* (New York: Pantheon, 2018), 141–183; Steven Pinker, *The Better Angels of Our Nature: Why Violence Has Declined* (New York: Viking, 2011), 428–441; Elizabeth T. Gershoff and Sarah A. Font, "Corporal Punishment in U.S. Public Schools: Prevalence, Disparities in Use, and Status in State and Federal Policies," *Social Science Policy Report* 30 (2016): 1; Lekha Menon, "Spare the Rod, Save a Child: Why the Supreme Court Should Revisit *Ingraham v. Wright* and Protect the Substantive Due Process Rights of Students Subjected to Corporal Punishment," *Cardozo Law Review* 39 (2017): 313–343; Christina Caron, "In 19 States, It's Still Legal to Spank Children in Public Schools," *New York Times,* December 13, 2018; "Global Progress toward Prohibiting All Corporal Punishment," Global Initiative to End All Corporal Punishment of Children, accessed June 15, 2020, https://endcorporalpunishment.org/wp-content/uploads/legality-tables/Global-progress-table-commitment.pdf.

9. See, for example, Elizabeth T. Gershoff and Andrew Grogan-Kaylor, "Spanking and Child Outcomes: Old Controversies and New Meta-Analyses," *Journal of Family Psychology* 30 (2016): 453–469; Paul Butler, *Chokehold: Policing Black Men* (New York: New Press, 2017), 118.

10. Graham Parker, "The Juvenile Court Movement: The Illinois Experiment," *University of Toronto Law Review* 26 (1976): 253–306, at 257; "Juvenile Court Committee Flyer, n.d.," Encyclopedia of Chicago, accessed June 23, 2020, http://www.encyclopedia.chicagohistory.org/pages/11146.html ("saving" children and "making them honest citizens"); Julian Mack, "The Juvenile Court," *Harvard Law Review* 23 (1909): 104–122, at 107; Zimring, *American Juvenile Justice*, 33–48, 73–95.

11. Zimring, *American Juvenile Justice*, xi; Zimring and Langer, "Central Mission," 73.

12. Zimring, *American Juvenile Justice*, 195; Drinan, *War on Kids*, 20; Tanenhaus and Drizin, "'Owing to the Extreme Youth,'" 648–649.

13. Drinan, *War on Kids*, 21; Patrick Griffin et al., *Trying Juveniles as Adults: An Analysis of State Transfer Laws and Reporting* (Washington, DC: United States Department of Justice, 2011), 8–9; Kevin J. Strom, *Profile of State Prisoners under Age 18, 1985–97* (Washington, DC: United States Department of Justice, 2000), 1.

14. John DiIulio, "The Coming of the Super-Predators," *Weekly Standard,* November 27, 1995, p. 23; Fox, *Trends in Juvenile Justice;* Zimring, *American Juvenile Justice,* 154; Heide, "Juvenile Justice," 346.

15. Tanenhaus and Drizin, "'Owing to the Extreme Youth,'" 643 (quoting McCollum); *Hearing on the Juvenile Justice and Delinquency Prevention Act before the House Subcommittee on Early Childhood, Youth and Families,* 104th Cong., 2d Sess. 90, 93 (1996) (testimony by Rep. McCollum about "the coming generation of 'super-predators'"); Hillary Clinton, "Hillary Clinton Campaign Speech," C-SPAN, recorded January 25, 1996, YouTube video, 26:05, http://cs.pn/1nVtFW3.

16. Zimring, *American Juvenile Justice*, 157, fig. 9.7; *Youth Violence: A Report of the Surgeon General* (Rockville, MD: United States Department of Health and Human Services, 2001), 5; Clyde Halberman, "Retro Report: When Youth Violence Spurred 'Superpredator' Fear," *New York Times,* April 6, 2014 (quoting DiIulio); Elizabeth Becker, "As Ex-Theorist on Young 'Superpredators,' Bush Aide Has Regrets," *New York Times,* February 9, 2001, p. A19.

17. Alfred Blumstein, Frederick P. Rivara, and Richard Rosenfeld, "The Rise and Decline of Homicide—And Why," *Annual Review of Public Health* 21 (2000): 505–541; John J. Donohue and Steven D. Levitt, "The Impact of Legalized Abortion on Crime," *Quarterly Journal of Economics* 117 (2001): 379–420; Kevin Drum,

"Lead: America's Real Criminal Element," *Mother Jones,* January / February 2013; Zimring, *American Juvenile Justice,* 158–168; Franklin E. Zimring, *American Youth Violence* (New York: Oxford University Press, 1998), 31–47.

18. DiIulio, "Coming of the Super-Predators"; Fox, *Trends in Juvenile Justice,* 2; John H. Laub, "A Century of Delinquency Research and Delinquency Theory," in *A Century of Juvenile Justice,* ed. Margaret K. Rosenheim et al. (Chicago: University of Chicago Press, 2002), 179–205, at 186; Zimring, *American Juvenile Justice,* 292 ("essentially nonadolescent"); Zimring, *American Youth Violence,* 37 ("new, more vicious type").

19. Neil Steinberg, "Judge Convicts Boy, 11, in Woman's Slaying," *Chicago Sun-Times,* October 7, 1994, p. 14 ("whole new breed"); Pete Wilson, Veto Message for SB 668, August 25, 1997, http://leginfo.ca.gov/pub/97-98/bill/sen/sb_0651 -0700/sb_668_vt_19970825.html.

20. Feld, *Evolution of the Juvenile Court,* 122; Megan C. Kurlychek and Brian D. Johnson, "The Juvenile Penalty: A Comparison of Juvenile and Young Adult Sentencing Outcomes in Criminal Court," *Criminology* 42 (2004): 485–517, at 486; Kurt Streeter, "A W.B.N.A. Star Leaves the Game to Court Justice," *New York Times,* June 30, 2019, p. SP1 (regarding Irons); Brian Hansen, "Kids in Prison: Are States Too Tough on Young Offenders?," *Congressional Quarterly Researcher* 16 (2001): 345–376, at 347, 355 (regarding Laster).

21. Douglas Kalajian, "Adult Crime, Adult Time: State Leads Nation in Prosecuting Teens as Adults," *Palm Beach Post,* June 4, 2000, p. 1A ("murder is an adult crime"); Griffin et al., *Trying Juveniles as Adults,* 4–6, 12; Barry Feld, "Juvenile Court Meets the Principal of the Offense: Legislative Changes in Juvenile Waiver Statutes," *Journal of Criminal Law and Criminology* 78 (1987): 471–533 (1987). The charges against Laster were dropped when *60 Minutes* began to prepare a story on the case. By then he had spent a month behind bars. Hansen, "Kids in Prison," 347.

22. Tanenhaus and Drizin, "'Owing to the Extreme Youth,'" 665, 689 ("ceased to be a mitigating factor"); Feld, *Evolution of the Juvenile Court,* 121; Hansen, "Kids in Prison," 360; Kurlychek and Johnson, "Juvenile Penalty," 500–506; Megan C. Kurlychek and Brian D. Johnson, "Juvenility and Punishment: Sentencing Juveniles in Adult Criminal Courts," *Criminology* 48 (2010): 725–758, at 746–747.

23. Kurlychek and Johnson, "Juvenility and Punishment," 731; Michael Tonry, "Predictions of Dangerousness in Sentencing: Déjà Vu All Over Again," *Crime and Justice* 48 (2019): 439–482, at 454–455.

24. Zimring, *American Juvenile Justice,* 107–129; Jack Katz, "Metropolitan Crime Myths," in *New York and Los Angeles: Politics, Society and Culture,* ed. David

Halle (Chicago: University of Chicago Press, 2003), 195–224; Michael Welch, Eric A. Price, and Nana Yankey, "Moral Panic over Youth Violence: Wilding and the Manufacture of Menace in the Media," *Youth & Society* 34 (2002): 3–30 (2002); Kamala Harris with Joan O'C. Hamilton, *Smart on Crime: A Career Prosecutor's Plan to Make Us Safer* (San Francisco: Chronicle Books, 2009), 184–185.

25. Katz, "Metropolitan Crime Myths"; H. Mitchell Caldwell, "Reeling In Gang Prosecution: Seeking a Balance in Gang Prosecution," *University of Pennsylvania Journal of Law and Social Change* 18 (2015): 341–375, at 346–351; Gary R. Brown, "Less Bark, More Bite: Fixing the Criminal Street Gang Enhancement," *Federal Sentencing Reporter* 16 (2003): 148–152; Erin Yoshino, "California's Criminal Gang Enhancements: Lessons from Interviews with Practitioners," *Southern California Review of Law and Social Justice* 18 (2008): 117–152, at 118–121; Mitchell Eisen, Brenna Dotson, and Gregory Dohi, "Probative or Prejudicial: Can Gang Evidence Trump Reasonable Doubt?," *UCLA Law Review Discourse* 62 (2014): 2–18; James M. Binnall, "Divided We Fall: Parole Supervision Conditions Prohibiting 'Inter-Offender' Associations," *University of Pennsylvania Journal of Law and Social Change* 22 (2019): 25–69.

26. Wilson, Veto Message for SB 668; Roper v. Simmons, 543 U.S. 551, 558 (2005).

27. Michael Rocque, "Exploring School Rampage Shootings: Research, Theory, and Policy," *Social Science Journal* 49 (2012): 304–313; Wendy Cai and Jugal K. Patel, "A Half-Century of School Shootings Like Columbine, Sandy Hook and Parkland," *New York Times*, May 11, 2019; "K–12 School Shooting Database: Active Shooter Graphs," Naval Postgraduate School Center for Homeland Defense and Security, accessed June 16, 2020, https://www.chds.us/ssdb/category/active-shooter/; Christopher A. Mallett, "The School-to-Prison Pipeline: A Critical Review of the Punitive Paradigm Shift," *Child and Adolescent Social Work Journal* 33 (2016): 15–24, 17–18.

28. Zimring, *American Juvenile Justice*, 164, 235; Hansen, "Kids in Prison," 346–347, 360, 362–363; Mallett, "School-to-Prison Pipeline," 17; Rocque, "Exploring School Rampage Shootings," 306.

29. Feld, *Evolution of the Juvenile Court*, 179–182; Mallett, "School-to-Prison Pipeline," 18; Ronnie Casella, "School Security and Its Corporate Offerings," in *Palgrave International Handbook of School Discipline, Surveillance, and Social Control*, ed. Jo Deakin, Emmeline Taylor, and Aaron Kupchik (New York: Palgrave Macmillan, 2018); Thomas Mowen and John Brent, "School Discipline as a Turning Point: The Cumulative Effect of Suspension on Arrest," *Journal of Research in Crime and Delinquency* 53 (2016): 628–653, at 632–633 (2016).

30. This event is discussed in Chapter 1.

31.   Pinker, *Better Angels of Our Nature,* 441–442; Sandra Graham, "Victims of Bullying in Schools," *Theory into Practice* 55 (2016): 136–144, at 137–138 (2016); David C. Rettew and Sara Pawlowski, "Bullying," *Child and Adolescent Psychiatric Clinics of North America* 25 (2016): 235–242; Peter K. Smith and Paul Brain, "Bullying in Schools: Lessons from Two Decades of Research," *Aggressive Behavior* 26 (2000): 1–9, at 3–5; Shelley Hymel and Susan M. Swearer, "Four Decades of Research on Bullying: An Introduction," *American Psychologist* 70 (2015): 293–299; Maria Konnikova, "How the Internet Has Changed Bullying," *New Yorker,* October 21, 2015; Dave Cullen, "The Depressive and the Psychopath," Slate, April 20, 2004, https://slate.com/news-and-politics/2004/04/at-last-we-know-why-the-columbine-killers-did-it.html.

32.   Pinker, *Better Angels of Our Nature,* 442–443, fig. 7–22; Graham, "Victims of Bullying," 137; Chad A. Rose, Amanda B. Nickerson, and Melissa Stormont, "Advancing Bullying Research from a Social-Ecological Lens," *School Psychology Review* 44 (2015): 339–352, at 339–340; Catherine P. Bradshaw, "Translating Research into Practice in Bullying Prevention," *American Psychologist* 70 (2015): 322–332; Antti Kärnä et al., "A Large-Scale Evaluation of the KiVa Antibullying Program: Grades 4–6," *Child Development* 82 (2011): 311–330; Rettew and Pawlowski, "Bullying," 239–240; Anne Williford, "Effects of the KiVa Anti-Bullying Program on Adolescents' Depression, Anxiety, and Perception of Peers," *Journal of Abnormal Child Psychology* 40 (2012): 289–300.

33.   Drinan, *War on Kids,* 48–49; Feld, *Evolution of the Juvenile Court,* 182–184; Kelly Welch and Allison Ann Payne, "Zero Tolerance School Policies," in Deakin, Taylor, and Kupchik, *Palgrave International Handbook,* 215–234, at 216–217.

34.   Paul J. Hirschfield, "Trends in School Social Control in the United States: Explaining Patterns of Decriminalization," in Deakin, Taylor, and Kupchik, *Palgrave International Handbook,* 43–64; American Psychological Association Zero Tolerance Task Force, "Are Zero Tolerance Polices Effective in the Schools? An Evidentiary Review and Recommendations," *American Psychologist* 63 (2008): 852–862; Daniel Losen et al., *Are We Closing the School Discipline Gap?* (Los Angeles: UCLA Center for Civil Rights Remedies, 2015); Aaron Kupchik, "The School-to-Prison Pipeline: Rhetoric and Reality," in Zimring and Tanenhaus, *Choosing the Future for American Juvenile Justice,* 94–119; Mowen and Brent, "School Discipline as a Turning Point"; Jason Nance, "Students, Police, and the School-to-Prison Pipeline," *Washington University Law Review* 93 (2016): 919–987; Catherine Winter, "Spare the Rod," *APM Reports,* August 25, 2016, https://www.apmreports.org/story/2016/08/25/reforming-school-discipline.

35.   "News Release: Attorney General Holder, Secretary Duncan Announce Effort to Respond to School-to-Prison Pipeline by Supporting Good Discipline

Practice," United States Department of Justice, July 21, 2011, https://www.justice
.gov/opa/pr/attorney-general-holder-secretary-duncan-announce-effort
-respond-school-prison-pipeline; "White House Report: The Continuing Need
to Rethink Discipline," Executive Office of the President, December 9, 2016,
https://obamawhitehouse.archives.gov/the-press-office/2016/12/09/white-house
-report-continuing-need-rethink-discipline; Hirschfield, "Trends," 45, 48, 57;
Eliza Shapiro, "Reckoning on Charters, from Within," *New York Times,* July 6,
2019, p. A1.

36. Erica L. Green, "Trump Points to Culprit in School Shootings, and It Isn't
Guns," *New York Times,* March 13, 2018, p. A10; Erica L. Green and Katie Benner,
"Trump Parkland Inquiry Attacks Protections for Minority Students," *New York
Times,* December 17, 2018, p. A1; Laura Meckler, "Trump Administration Revokes
Effort to Reduce Racial Bias in School Discipline," *Washington Post,* December 21,
2018; *Final Report of the Federal Commission on School Safety* (2018): 67.

37. "K–12 School Shooting Database: Active Shooter Graphs"; Feld, *Evolution of
the Juvenile Court,* 161–163; Margaret A. Zahn et al., *Violence by Teenage Girls: Trends
and Context* (Washington, DC: United States Department of Justice, 2008): 3–5;
Samantha Ehrmann, Nina Hyland, and Charles Puzzanchera, *Girls in the Juvenile
Justice System* (Washington, DC: United States Department of Justice, 2019).

38. Feld, *Evolution of the Juvenile Court,* 159–170; Zahn et al., *Violence by Teenage
Girls,* 3–9, 15; Meda Chesney-Lind and Vickie V. Paramore, "Are Girls Getting
More Violent? Exploring Juvenile Robbery Trends," *Journal of Contemporary
Criminal Justice* 17 (2001): 142–166, at 162–163; Meda Chesney-Lind, "Girls and
Violence: Is the Gender Gap Closing?," National Resource Center on Domestic
Violence, 2004.

39. Julie Scelfo, "Bad Girls Go Wild," *Newsweek,* June 12, 2015 (quoting
Howard Spivak, "not what people think they are"); Jerry Sandler, "How to Defuse 'Girl on Girl' Violence," *Christian Science Monitor,* June 23, 2005; Karol Mar-
kowicz, "America's Girls Have a Violence Problem," *New York Post,* September 7,
2015 ("something wrong").

40. Roper v. Simmons, 543 U.S. 551 (2005); Graham v. Florida, 560 U.S. 53
(2010); Miller v. Alabama, 567 U.S. 460 (2012). Even Justice O'Connor, who dissented in *Simmons,* was troubled by the prosecutor's suggestion that the defendant's youth was an aggravating circumstance. Roper v. Simmons, 603.

41. Death Penalty Information Center, "The Juvenile Death Penalty Prior to
Roper v. Simmons," accessed June 16, 2020, https://deathpenaltyinfo.org/policy
-issues/juveniles/prior-to-roper-v-simmons; Graham v. Florida, 75; Feld, *Evolution
of the Juvenile Court,* 212; Reginald Dwayne Betts, "What Break Do Children
Deserve? Juveniles, Crime, and Justice Kennedy's Influence on the Supreme

Court's Eighth Amendment Jurisprudence," *Yale Law Journal Forum* 128 (2019): 743–758, at 751–752.

42. Miller v. Alabama, 471–472, 481; Roper v. Simmons, 569–570; Graham v. Florida, 68, 73 (quoting Workman v. Commonwealth, 429 S.W.2d 374, 378 (Ky. App. 1968) ("inconsistent with youth")).

43. Roper v. Simmons, 599–600 (O'Connor, J., dissenting); ibid., 618–619 (Scalia, J., dissenting); Graham v. Florida, 118 (Thomas, J., dissenting); Miller v. Alabama, 509–510 (Alito, J., dissenting). The dissents in *Simmons, Miller,* and *Graham* also took issue with some of the tools the majority used to interpret the constitutional ban on "cruel and unusual punishments." They objected, for example, to taking guidance from legal developments in other countries. See, for example, Roper v. Simmons, 622–628 (Scalia, J., dissenting); Graham v. Florida, 114n12 (Thomas, J., dissenting).

44. Drinan, *War on Kids,* 91–94.

45. Roper v. Simmons, 600 (O'Connor, J., dissenting); ibid., 619 (Scalia, J., dissenting); Miller v. Alabama, 510, 513 (Alito, J., dissenting).

46. Regarding age patterns in offending, see Alex R. Piquero, J. David Hawkins, and Lila Kazemian, "Career Criminal Patterns," in *From Juvenile Delinquency to Adult Crime: Criminal Careers, Justice Policy, and Prevention,* ed. David P. Farrington and Rolf Loeber (New York: Oxford University Press, 2012): 14–46, at 20–25, 28–35; Franklin E. Zimring and Jeffrey Fagan, "Two Patterns of Age Progression in Adolescent Crime," in Zimring, *American Juvenile Justice,* 91–103; Rolf Loeber, Magda Stouthamer-Loeber, and Lia Ahonen, "Key Behavioral Aspects of Desistance from Conduct Problem and Delinquency," in *Global Perspectives on Desistance: Reviewing What We Know and Looking to the Future,* ed. Joanna Shaplund, Stephen Farrall, and Anthony Bottoms (Abingdon, UK: Routledge, 2016), 85–98, at 91–92; Arjan Blokland and Niek De Schipper, "How Important Are Life-Course Transitions in Explaining Desistance? Examining the Extent to Which Marriage, Divorce and Parenthood Account for the Age-Crime Relationship in Former Juvenile Delinquents," in Shaplund, Farrall, and Bottoms, *Global Perspectives on Desistance,* 144–169, at 159. For the specialization argument, see Rolf Loeber et al., *Violence and Serious Theft: Development and Prediction from Childhood to Adulthood* (New York: Routledge, 2008), 317. Regarding group offending, see Feld, *Evolution of the Juvenile Court,* 205; Zimring, *American Juvenile Justice,* 107–112. Rape appears to be an exception to the normal pattern of juveniles offending with others: a study of delinquency cases in New York City in the early 1980s found that half of juvenile rapes involved only one offender. Zimring, *American Juvenile Justice,* 110, fig. 7.3.

47. Frank J. Elgar et al., "Corporal Punishment Bans and Physical Fighting in Adolescents: An Ecological Study of 88 Countries," *BMJ Open* (2018), http://dx .doi.org/10.1136/bmjopen-2018-021616; Jeff R. Temple et al., "Childhood Corporal Punishment and Future Perpetration of Dating Violence," *Journal of Pediatrics* 194 (2018): 233–237; Prov. 13:24 (King James Version).

48. Driver, *Schoolhouse Gate,* 168; Pinker, *Better Angels of Our Nature,* 435–437; Gershoff and Grogan-Kaylor, "Spanking and Child Outcomes"; Cynthia Godsoe, "Redefining Parental Rights: The Case of Corporal Punishment," *Constitutional Commentary* 32 (2017): 281–305, at 296; Robert D. Sege et al., "Effective Discipline to Raise Healthy Children," *Pediatrics* 142 (2018); "Global Progress toward Prohibiting All Corporal Punishment."

49. *Model Penal Code and Commentaries* (Philadelphia: American Law Institute, 1985), § 3.08(1); Cynthia Godsoe, "Redefining Parental Rights."

50. Scott Clement, "Millennials Like to Spank Their Kids Just as Much as Their Parents Did," *Washington Post,* March 5, 2015; "Favor Spanking to Discipline Child," GSS Data Explorer, https://gssdataexplorer.norc.org/variables/646 /vshow, accessed June 16, 2020; *Parenting in America* (Washington, DC: Pew Research Center, 2015), 12, 45–46; "Few Consider Spanking Child Abuse," Rasmussen Reports, November 15, 2018, https://www.rasmussenreports.com/public _content/lifestyle/general_lifestyle/november_2018/few_consider_spanking _child_abuse; Stacey Patton, "Stop Beating Black Children," *New York Times,* March 20, 2017; Ta-Nehisi Coates, *Between the World and Me* (New York: Penguin Random House, 2015), 82–83; Coates, *The Beautiful Struggle* (New York: Penguin Random House, 2008), 141; Coates, "Spanking and 'Middle-Class Acculturation,'" *Atlantic,* January 22, 2010; "Transcript: Obama at the NAACP Convention," CBS News, July 17, 2009, https://www.cbsnews.com/news/transcript -obama-at-the-naacp-convention/.

51. Driver, *Schoolhouse Gate,* 183–184; Gershoff and Font, "Corporal Punishment," 5, 16; Caron, "In 19 States."

52. Gershoff and Font, "Corporal Punishment," 8; Caron, "In 19 States"; "Civil Rights Data Collection, 2013–2014," United States Department of Education, accessed June 17, 2020, https://ocrdata.ed.gov/StateNationalEstimations /Estimations_2013_14.

53. Ingraham v. Wright, 430 U.S. 651, 660–661, 669–672 (1977); Driver, *Schoolhouse Gate,* 165–169, 178, 183.

54. Driver, *Schoolhouse Gate,* 178, 473n141; Hall v. Tawney, 621 F.2d 607, 613 (4th Cir. 1987) ("literally shocking to the conscience"); Menon, "Spare the Rod, Save a Child," 332–340.

55.   Driver, *Schoolhouse Gate,* 169, 176–177; Gershoff and Font, "Corporal Punishment," 10, 12; Caron, "In 19 States"; "Civil Rights Data Collection, 2013–2014."

56.   Leslie Joan Harris, "Failure to Protect from Exposure to Domestic Violence in Private Custody Contests," *Family Law Quarterly* 44 (2010): 169–195; Megan Shipley, "Revile Mothers: Custody Modification Cases Involving Domestic Violence," *Indiana Law Journal* 86 (2011): 1587–1615; Jessica Dixon Weaver, "The Principle of Subsidiarity Applied: Reforming the Legal Framework to Capture the Psychological Abuse of Children," *Virginia Journal of Society Policy & the Law* 18 (2001): 247–318.

6. PRISON VIOLENCE

1.   McGill v. Duckworth, 944 F.2d 344, 345 (7th Cir. 1991), cert. denied, 503 U.S. 907 (1992).

2.   Ibid., 348.

3.   For population figures for various categories of carceral institutions, see Wendy Sawyer and Peter Wagner, "Mass Incarceration: The Whole Pie 2020," Prison Policy Initiative, March 24, 2020, https://www.prisonpolicy.org/reports/pie2019.html.

4.   Margo Schlanger, "The Constitutional Law of Incarceration, Reconfigured," *Cornell Law Review* 103 (2018): 357–436, at 431–432; Jackson v. Bishop, 404 F.2d 581 (8th Cir. 1968) (opinion for the court by Blackmun, J.); Ingraham v. Wright, 430 U.S. 651, 661n15 (1977); Furman v. Georgia, 408 U.S. 238, 287–288 (1972) (Brennan, J., dissenting); Baze v. Rees, 553 U.S. 35, 40–43 (2008) (opinion of Roberts, C. J.); Stuart Banner, *The Death Penalty: An American History* (Cambridge, MA: Harvard University Press, 2002), 297–299; Carol S. Steiker and Jordan M. Steiker, *Courting Death: The Supreme Court and Capital Punishment* (Cambridge, MA: Harvard University Press, 2016), 13–15. The classic discussion of the move away from spectacles of punishment is Michel Foucault, *Discipline and Punish: The Birth of the Prison,* trans. Alan Sheridan (New York: Pantheon, 1977).

5.   "Nomination of Stephanos Bibas to the U.S. Court of Appeals for the Third Circuit, Questions for the Record, Submitted October 11, 2017: Questions from Senator Feinstein," https://www.judiciary.senate.gov/imo/media/doc/Bibas Responses to QFRs.pdf. Bibas's 2012 book, *The Machinery of Criminal Justice* (New York: Oxford University Press), also rejected the idea of corporal punishment of prisoners, albeit more equivocally. Bibas argued that prisons should "force all able-bodied prisoners to work," but that "returning to chain gangs, corporal punishment, or similar hallmarks of slavery would deeply divide public opinion" (135).

6.   Estelle v. Gamble, 429 U.S. 97 (1976) ("deliberate indifference"); Hudson v. McMillian, 503 U.S. 1, 5–7 (1992) ("unnecessary and wanton infliction of pain"); Kingsley v. Hendrickson, 135 S. Ct. 2466 (2015). The Justices expressly declined to decide in *Kingsley* whether the standard of objective unreasonableness should apply to a due process claim brought by a convicted prisoner. Lower courts generally have assumed that the answer is no, largely on the grounds that—as the Supreme Court itself emphasized in *Kingsley*—"pretrial detainees (unlike convicted prisoners) cannot be punished at all, much less 'maliciously and sadistically.'" For criticism of this reasoning, see Schlanger, "Constitutional Law of Incarceration," 431–432.

7.   Farmer v. Brennan, 511 U.S. 825, 833, 834 (1994).

8.   Pub. L. 108-79, §§ 2–3, 117 Stat. 972, 973–974 (September 4, 2003); Valerie Jenness and Michael Smyth, "The Passage and Implementation of the Prison Rape Elimination Act: Legal Endogeneity and the Uncertain Road from Symbolic to Instrumental Effects," *Stanford Law and Policy Review* 22 (2011): 489–527, at 490–491.

9.   Nancy Wolff et al., "Physical Violence inside Prisons: Rates of Victimization," *Criminal Justice and Behavior* 34 (2007): 588–599, at 589 (incentives to underreport prison violence); James M. Byrne and Don Hummer, "The Nature and Extent of Prison Violence," in *The Culture of Prison Violence* (Boston: Pearson, 2007) 12–26, at 14 (misclassification of prison homicides); *Investigation of Alabama's State Prisons for Men* (Washington, DC: United States Department of Justice, 2019), 11–12.

10.   Derek A. Kreager and Candace Kruttschnitt, "Inmate Society in the Era of Mass Incarceration," *Annual Review of Criminology* 1 (2018): 261–283 (2018); Margaret E. Noonan, *Mortality in State Prisons, 2001–2014: Statistical Tables* (Washington, DC: United States Department of Justice, 2016), 4, tables 1 and 2; Nathan James, *Recent Violent Crime Trends in the United States* (Washington, DC: Congressional Research Service, 2018), 3, fig. 2.

11.   Wolff et al., "Physical Violence inside Prisons," 593, table 1, 595.

12.   Noonan, "Mortality in State Prisons, 2001–2014"; Wolff et al., "Physical Violence inside Prisons," 595; "Alabama's Prisons Are Deadliest in the Nation," Equal Justice Initiative, December 3, 2018, https://eji.org/news/alabamas-prisons-are-deadliest-in-nation/; Campbell Robertson, "An Alabama Prison's Grim Slide into Violence," *New York Times,* March 29, 2017, p. A1; *Investigation of Alabama's State Prisons for Men* (2019), 1–3; Katie Brenner and Shaila Dewan, "'Common, Cruel' Violence Met by Indifference," *New York Times,* April 4, 2019, p. A1 (summary of DOJ findings); *Investigation of Alabama's State Prisons for Men* (Washington, DC: United States Department of Justice, 2020), 1–3, 10, 21–22.

13.   Rick Rojas and Richard Fasset, "Gangs, Riots, Killings: 'Undeniable Crisis' in Mississippi Prisons," *New York Times,* January 10, 2020, p. A21; Craig Haney, "The Perversions of Prison: On the Origins of Hypermasculinity and Sexual Violence in Confinement," *American Criminal Law Review* 48 (2011): 121–141, at 129; James E. Robertson, "A Clean Heart and an Empty Head: The Supreme Court and Sexual Terrorism in Prison," *North Carolina Law Review* 81 (2003): 434–481, at 476; Kim Shayo Buchanan, "Impunity: Sexual Abuse in Women's Prisons," *Harvard Civil Rights-Civil Liberties Law Review* 42 (2007): 45–87, at 45–47, 51–57 (2007); Angela Y. Davis, *Are Prisons Obsolete?* (New York: Seven Stories Press, 2003), 77–79; Chandra Bozelko, "Why We Let Prison Rape Go On," *New York Times,* April 18, 2015, p. A19.

14.   Buchanan, "Impunity," 55; Alice Ristroph, "Sexual Punishments," *Columbia Journal of Gender and Law* 15 (2006): 139–184, at 154.

15.   Tess M. S. Neal and Carl B. Clements, "Prison Rape and Psychological Sequelae: A Call for Research," *Psychology, Public Policy, and Law* 16 (2010): 284–299, at 285–287; Pub. L. 108-79, § 2, 117 Stat. at 972.

16.   Jenness and Smyth, "Passage and Implementation"; Robert Weisberg and David Mills, "Violence Silence: Why No One Really Cares about Prison Rape," Slate, October 1, 2003, https://slate.com/news-and-politics/2003/10/why-no-one -really-cares-about-prison-violence.html; Michael B. Mushlin, *Rights of Prisoners,* 5th ed., vol. 1 (Saint Paul, MN: Thompson Reuters, 2017), § 3.48; 42 U.S.C.A. § 15606(e)(3).

17.   Derek Gilna, "Five Years after Implementation, PREA Standards Remain Inadequate," *Prison Legal News,* November, 2017, https://www.prisonlegalnews .org/news/2017/nov/8/five-years-after-implementation-prea-standards-remain -inadequate/; Tina Vasquez, "In Search of Justice: How DHS PREA Standards Don't Necessarily Protect Immigrants from Assault," Rewire.News, March 13, 2019; Ristroph, "Sexual Punishments," 148; Katharina Jehle, "Legislating 'Legitimate' Victims: How the 'Jailhouse Exclusion' Denies Inmates the Protection of California's Rape Shield Statute," *Stanford Journal of Criminal Law and Policy* 3 (2016): 56–116, at 88–89; Scott Cacciola and Victor Mather, "Gymnasts' Abuse Draws Sentence Likely to Be Life," *New York Times,* January 24, 2018, p. A1; Lovisa Stannow, "No One Deserves to Be Raped—Not Even Larry Nassar," *Los Angeles Times,* January 28, 2018; Diana Moskovitz, "Even Larry Nassar Does Not Deserve to Be Raped in Prison," Deadspin, January 26, 2018, https://deadspin.com/even -larry-nassar-does-not-deserve-to-be-raped-in-priso-1822427894; Rachel Marshall, "The Moment the Judge in the Larry Nassar Case Crossed a Line," Vox, January 25, 2018, https://www.vox.com/the-big-idea/2018/1/25/16932656/judge -aquilina-larry-nassar-line-between-judge-advocate-sentencing; Eric Levenson

and Ellie Kaufman, "She's the Judge These Larry Nassar Victims Needed," CNN, January 18, 2018, https://www.cnn.com/2018/01/17/us/larry-nassar-judge -sentencing/index.html. One of the victims who spoke at Nassar's sentencing hearing concluded by telling him to "have fun in prison," because "now it's your turn to be abused." "Latest: Victim Says 'Have Fun in Prison Larry, Now It's Your Turn to Be Abused,'" Fox 47 News, January 31, 2018, https://www.fox47news .com/news/local-news/latest-victim-says-have-fun-in-prison-larry-now-its-your -turn-to-be-abused.

18. Kim Kozlowski, "Nassar Assaulted in Prison; Court Filing Blames Judge," *Detroit News,* July 25, 2018.

19. Bozelko, "Why We Let Prison Rape Go On"; Robertson, "Clean Heart and Empty Head," 446; Anders Kaye, "Dangerous Places: The Right to Self-Defense in Prison and Prison Conditions Jurisprudence," *University of Chicago Law Review* 63 (1996): 693–726; Ristroph, "Sexual Punishments," 182; Weisberg and Mills, "Violence Silence"; Ahmed A. White, "The Concept of 'Less Eligibility' and the Social Function of Prison Violence in Class Society," *Buffalo Law Review* 56 (2008): 737–820.

20. Robertson, "Alabama Prison's Grim Slide"; Rojas and Faucett, "Gangs, Riots, Killings"; Joseph Neff and Alysia Santo, "Corporate Confession: Gangs Ran This Private Prison," Marshall Project, June 26, 2019, https://www .themarshallproject.org/2019/06/26/corporate-confession-gangs-ran-this -private-prison.

21. Ruiz v. Johnson, 37 F. Supp. 2d 855, 928, 940 (S.D. Tex. 1999), reversed on other grounds, 243 F.3d 941 (5th Cir. 2001).

22. Madrid v. Gomez, 889 F. Supp. 1146 (N.D. Cal. 1995) ("for the very purpose"); Keramet Reiter, *23/7: Pelican Bay and the Rise of Long-Term Solitary Confinement* (New Haven, CT: Yale University Press, 2016); Donald Specter, "Making Prisons Safe: Strategies for Reducing Violence," *Washington University Journal of Law & Policy* 22 (2006): 125–134, at 129.

23. Farmer v. Brennan, 511 U.S. 835 (1994); Sharon Dolovich, "Cruelty, Prison Conditions, and the Eighth Amendment," *New York University Law Review* 84 (2009): 881–979, at 890; Robertson, "Clean Heart and Empty Head," 437–438; Schlanger, "Constitutional Law of Incarceration," 360.

24. McGill v. Duckworth, 348.

25. Farmer v. Brennan, 833, 837–838; ibid., 858 (Thomas, J., concurring). The language about prisoners' "demonstrated proclivity" was quoted from the Court's earlier decision in Hudson v. Palmer, 468 U.S. 517, 526 (1984).

26. Todd R. Clear and Natasha A. Frost, *The Punishment Imperative: The Rise and Failure of Mass Incarceration in America* (New York: NYU Press, 2014), 22–23;

John F. Pfaff, *Locked In: The True Cause of Mass Incarceration—and How to Achieve Real Reform* (New York: Basic Books, 2017), 32–33, table 1.2 (2017); Kreager and Kruttschnitt, "Inmate Society"; Sawyer and Wagner, "Mass Incarceration"; Byrne and Hummer, "Nature and Extent of Prison Violence."

27. Noonan, "Mortality in State Prisons, 2001–2014," 13, table 14; Steffen Bieneck and Dirk Baier, "Victimization and Perpetration among Prison Inmates," in *Representative Studies on Victimization: Research Findings from Germany,* ed. Dirk Baier and Christian Pfeiffer (Baden-Baden: Nomos, 2016), 185–202, at 199; Specter, "Making Prisons Safe," 126, 131.

28. Haney, "Perversions of Prison," 128; see also Ristroph, "Sexual Punishments," 148.

29. Bennett Capers, "Real Rape, Too," *California Law Review* 99 (2011): 1259–1308, at 1263.

30. For example, law professor Andrew Leipold writes that "it is hard to dispute the efficacy of imprisonment," because "those in prison don't commit any new crimes except against guards and other inmates, and so by extending the periods of imprisonment . . . we extend the period where the inmate cannot re-offend. . . . [A]s long as they are in prison, we worry far less about the downsides of the failures of rehabilitative efforts." Andrew D. Leipold, "Recidivism, Incapacitation, and Criminal Sentencing Policy," *University of St. Thomas Law Journal,* 3 (2006): 536–558, at 542.

31. Farmer v. Brennan, 851 (Blackmun, J., concurring); ibid., 858 (Stevens, J., concurring); Dolovich, "Cruelty"; Robertson, "Clean Heart and Empty Head"; Schlanger, "Constitutional Law of Incarceration"; Smith v. Ullman, 874 F. Supp. 979 (D. Neb. 1994) ("clean heart" and "empty head"); Cory Matteson, "Magistrate Judge to Retire after 28 Years on Bench," *Lincoln Journal Star,* July 24, 2009.

32. Graham v. Connor, 490 U.S. 386 (1989) (Fourth Amendment); Kingsley v. Hendrickson, 135 S. Ct. 2466 (2015) (pretrial detention); Hudson v. McMillian, 503 U.S. 1 (1991); Schlanger, "Constitutional Law of Incarceration."

33. See, for example, Harris v. May, No. 19-CV-0196, 2019 WL 1172013 (E.D. Pa. March 13, 2019); Randle v. Alexander, 170 F. Supp. 3d 580 (S.D.N.Y. 2016); Carranza v. Brown, No. 3:14-CV-0773-GPC-BLM, 2016 WL 4376852 (S.D. Cal. 2016); Crow v. Severs, No. 12-CV-2216 PJS/FLN, 2014 WL 468219 (D. Minn. February 6, 2014); Johnson v. Felker, No. 2:12-CV-02719, 2013 WL 6243280 (E.D. Cal. December 3, 2013); Schoppe-Rico v. Horel, No. C 11-1089 YGR, 2013 WL 3829470 (N.D. Cal. July 23, 2013); Anderson v. Zika, No. C 11-04276, 2013 WL 132546 (N.D. Cal. January 9, 2013); Roettgen v. Arnold, No. 11-2562, 2012 WL 3060816 (S.D. Cal. 2012); Dillon v. Dickhaut, No. 12-10713-GAO, 2012 WL 1852506 (D. Mass. May 12, 2012); Roman v. Knowles, No. 07CV1343 JLS, 2009 WL 1675863

(S.D. Cal. June 15, 2009); Anderson v. Tilton, No. C 08-3204 MMC, 2009 WL 210451 (N.D. Cal. January 26, 2009); Gaston v. Caden, No. CIVS031707-LKK-CMKP, 2007 WL 2727142 (E.D. Cal. September 17, 2007).

34. Regarding Corcoran State Prison, see Corey Weinstein, "Even Dogs Confined to Cages for Long Periods of Time Go Berserk," in *Building Violence: How America's Rush to Incarcerate Creates More Violence,* ed. John P. May and Khalid R. Pitts (Thousand Oaks, CA: Sage, 2000): 118–124, at 122; Reiter, *23/7,* 21; Craig Haney, "Riding the Punishment Wave: On the Origins of Our Developing Standards of Decency," *Hastings Women's Law Journal* 9 (1998): 27–78, at 36–37; J. C. Oleson, "The Punitive Coma," *California Law Review* 90 (2002): 829–901, at 855.

35. Mark Arax, "8 Prison Guards Are Acquitted in Corcoran Battles," *Los Angeles Times,* June 10, 2000; Keramet Reiter, "Supermax Administration and the Eighth Amendment: Deference, Discretion, and Double Bunking, 1986–2010," *UC Irvine Law Review* 5 (2015): 89–151, at 126.

36. Reiter, *23/7,* 21, 156; Max Cherney, "When Prison Guards Force Inmates to Fight," Vice, April 3, 2015, https://www.vice.com/en_us/article/av45x5/when-prison-guards-force-inmates-to-fight-403; Erik Ortiz, "More Inmates Say Guards at St. Louis Jail Forced Them to Fight 'Gladiator-Style,'" *New York Daily News,* July 3, 2013; Sheyanne N. Romero, "California Inmates Accuse Prison Guards of Orchestrating 'Gladiator Fights,'" *Visalia Times-Delta,* February 25, 2019; Brian Sonenstein, "California Prisoners Say Videos Show 'Gladiator Fights' at Soledad Prison," Shadowproof, February 18, 2019, https://shadowproof.com/2019/02/18/california-prisoners-say-videos-show-gladiator-fights-at-soledad-state-prison/.

37. Banner, *Death Penalty,* 5–23; Foucault, *Discipline and Punish;* Michael Meranze, *Laboratories of Virtue: Punishment, Revolution, and Authority in Philadelphia, 1760–1835* (Chapel Hill: University of North Carolina Press, 1996), 19–54; Steven Pinker, *The Better Angels of Our Nature: Why Violence Has Declined* (New York: Viking, 2011), 145–149.

38. Kevin Kehrwald, *Prison Movies: Cinema behind Bars* (New York: Columbia University Press, 2017), 4–5.

39. Randall Collins, *Violence: A Micro-Sociological Theory* (Princeton, NJ: Princeton University Press, 2008), 243.

40. Alex Godfrey, "Making America Gory Again: How the Purge Films Troll Trumpism," *Guardian,* July 4, 2018 (quoting producer Jason Blum); Sonaiya Kelley, "An Oral History of 'The Purge' Franchise: From Micro-Horror Breakout to Trump-Era Cautionary Tale," *Los Angeles Times,* July 4, 2018 (quoting writer-director James DeMonaco); A. O. Scott, "A Campaign Platform of Blood Lust," *New York Times,* June 30, 2016, p. C7 ("visceral message").

41. Katherine A. Foss, "Introduction: Uniting Media, Prison, and Experience," in *Demystifying the Big House: Exploring Prison Experience and Media Representations,* ed. Katherine A. Foss, vol. 1 (Carbondale: Southern Illinois University Press, 2018); Dawn K. Cecil, "Prisons in Popular Culture," *Oxford Research Encyclopedia, Criminology and Criminal Justice* (March 2017), https://oxfordre.com/criminology/view/10.1093/acrefore/9780190264079.001.0001/acrefore-9780190264079-e-194; Kehrwald, *Prison Movies.*

42. Richard Sparks, *Television and the Drama of Crime: Moral Tales and Place of Crime in Public Life* (Buckingham, UK: Open University Press, 1992); David Wilson and Sean O'Sullivan, "Re-Theorizing the Penal Reform Functions of the Prison Film," *Theoretical Criminology* 9 (2005): 471–491; Cecil, "Prisons in Popular Culture"; Paul Mason, "The Screen Machine: Cinematic Representations of Prison," in *Criminal Visions: Media Representations of Crime and Justice,* ed. Paul Mason (Cullompton, UK: Willan, 2003), 278, 281, 294–295.

7. SPEECH AND GUNS

1. Charlotte Graham-McLay, Austin Ramzy, and Daniel Victor, "New Zealand Left in Shock as 2 Mosques Are Attacked," *New York Times,* March 15, 2019, p. A4; Charlotte Graham-McLay, "51st Death from Attack on Mosques," *New York Times,* May 3, 2019, p. A10; Kevin Roose, "A Shooting Disturbingly Rooted in the Internet," *New York Times,* March 16, 2019, p. A1; Ben Collins and Andrew Blankstein, "Anti-Semitic Open Letter Posted Online under Name of Chabad Synagogue Shooting Suspect," NBC News, April 27, 2019, https://www.nbcnews.com/us-news/anti-semitic=posted-online-under-chabad-synagogue-n999211; Kristina Davis, "Not Guilty Plea Entered for Alleged Synagogue Shooter on 109 Federal Charges," *San Diego Union-Tribune,* May 14, 2019; Campbell Robertson, Christopher Mele, and Sabrina Tavernise, "Rampage Kills 11 at a Synagogue in Pittsburgh," *New York Times,* October 28, 2018, p. A1; Charlie Warzel, "Mass Shootings Have Become a Sickening Meme," *New York Times,* April 28, 2019.

2. Charlotte Graham-McLay, "New Zealand Makes Plans for 2nd Batch of Gun Laws," *New York Times,* July 23, 2019, p. A9; Shibani Mahtani, "New Zealand Passes Law Banning Most Semiautomatic Weapons, Less than a Month after Mosque Massacres," *Washington Post,* April 10, 2019; "Christchurch Call," accessed June 21, 2020, https://www.christchurchcall.com/; Charlotte Graham-McLay and Adam Satarino, "New Zealand Asks World to Tackle Online Extremism," *New York Times,* May 13, 2019, p. B1.

3. Tony Romm and Drew Harwell, "White House Declines to Back Christchurch Call to Stamp Out Online Extremism amid Free Speech Concerns," *Wash-*

ington Post, May 15, 2019; Sam Levin, "Ten Dead after California Sees Three Mass Shootings in Four Days," *Guardian,* November 19, 2019; Gun Violence Archive, Mass Shootings in 2019, accessed June 21, 2020, https://www.gunviolencearchive .org/reports/mass-shooting?year=2019.

4. See, for example, Graeme Wood, "Trump Was Right Not to Sign the Christchurch Call," *Atlantic,* May 22, 2019.

5. District of Columbia v. Heller, 554 U.S. 570, 592 (2008); see also McDonald v. City of Chicago, 561 U.S. 742, 767, 780 (2010).

6. The first definition of "obscene" provided by Merriam-Webster's online dictionary is "disgusting to the senses: repulsive." Merriam-Webster, s.v. "obscene," accessed June 21, 2020, https://www.merriam-webster.com/dictionary/obscene.

7. Whitney v. California, 274 U.S. 357, 376–379 (1927) (Brandeis, J., dissenting); Ashutosh A. Bhagwat, "The Story of *Whitney v. California:* The Power of Ideas," in *Constitutional Law Stories,* ed. Michael C. Dorf (New York: Foundation Press, 2004), 407, 407–408, 422–423; Vincent Blasi, "The First Amendment and the Ideal of Civic Courage: The Brandeis Opinion in *Whitney v. California,*" *William and Mary Law Review* 29 (1988): 653–697.

8. Brandenburg v. Ohio, 395 U.S. 444 (1969); Cohen v. California, 403 U.S. 15, 18 (1971).

9. Goedert v. City of Ferndale, 596 F. Supp. 2d 1027, 1032 (E.D. Mich. 2008); Daniel A. Farber, *The First Amendment,* 4th ed. (Saint Paul, MN: Foundation Press, 2014), 77–78; Alan K. Chen, "Free Speech and the Confluence of National Security and Internet Exceptionalism," *Fordham Law Review* 86 (2017): 379–399, at 382n21; Margot E. Kaminski, "Incitement to Riot in the Age of Flash Mobs," *University of Cincinnati Law Review* 81 (2013): 1–84, at 44.

10. Whitney v. California, 377–378 (Brandeis, J., dissenting).

11. Chaplinsky v. New Hampshire, 315 U.S. 568, 572 (1942); Cohen v. California, 20; Gooding v. Wilson, 405 U.S. 518, 528 (1972); Texas v. Johnson, 491 U.S. 397, 409 (1989); Farber, *First Amendment,* 114; Rodney A. Smolla, *Smolla and Nimmer on Freedom of Speech,* 2019 update (Saint Paul, MN: Thompson Reuters, 2019), § 10:31; Frederick M. Lawrence, "Violent-Conducive Speech: Punishable Verbal Assault or Protected Political Speech?," in *Freedom of Speech and Incitement against Democracy,* ed. David Kretzmer and Francine Kershman (The Hague: Kluger Law International, 2000): 11–32, at 29; Michael J. Mannheimer, "The Fighting Words Doctrine," *Columbia Law Review* 93 (1993): 1527–1571; "The Demise of the *Chaplinsky* Fighting Words Doctrine: An Argument for Its Interment," *Harvard Law Review* 106 (1993): 1129–1146.

12. For examples of cases upholding "fighting words" convictions for speech directed at police officers, see State v. Robinson, 82 P.3d 27 (Mont. 2003); State v.

Read, 680 A.2d 944 (Vt. 1996). For judicial opinions finding the fighting-words doctrine especially narrow when applied to police officers, see, for example, Lewis v. City of New Orleans, 415 U.S. 130, 135 (1974) (Powell, J., concurring); United States v. Poocha, 259 F.3d 1077 (9th Cir. 2001); State v. John W., 418 A.2d 1097 (Me. 1980).

13.   Virginia v. Black, 538 U.S. 343 (2003).

14.   United States v. Larson, 807 F. Supp. 2d 142, 165 (W.D.N.Y. 2011); Smithfield Foods, Inc. v. United Food & Commercial Workers Int'l Union, 593 F. Supp. 2d 840, 844 (E.D. Va. 2008); Brian J. Murphy, "Protesters, Extortion, and Coercion: Preventing RICO from Chilling First Amendment Freedoms," *Notre Dame Law Review* 75 (1999): 691–760.

15.   American Law Institute, Model Penal Code §§ 2.06, 5.02; Kent Greenawalt, *Speech, Crime, and the Uses of Language* (New York: Oxford University Press, 1989), 83; United States v. Williams, 553 U.S. 285, 297–298 (2008); Eugene Volokh, "Crime-Facilitating Speech," *Stanford Law Review* 57 (2005): 1095–1222, at 1143n194 (2005); Eugene Volokh, "The 'Speech Integral to Criminal Conduct' Exception," *Cornell Law Review* 101 (2016): 981–1052, at 991.

16.   John Roy Carlson, *Under Cover: My Four Years in the Nazi Underworld of America* (New York: E. P. Dutton, 1943): 120–127; Dan J. Puckett, *In the Shadow of Hitler: Alabama's Jews, the Second World War, and the Holocaust* (Tuscaloosa: University of Alabama Press, 2013), 190–195; Terminiello v. City of Chicago, 337 U.S. 1, 5 (1949); ibid., 17–21, 31–27 (1949) (Jackson, J., dissenting).

17.   Farber, *First Amendment,* 70–71.

18.   Miller v. California, 413 U.S. 15 (1973); Farber, *First Amendment,* 143–146.

19.   Ernoznik v. City of Jacksonville, 422 U.S. 205, 213–214 (1975); see also Ginsberg v. New York, 390 U.S. 629, 646–647 (1968).

20.   New York v. Ferber, 458 U.S. 747 (1982).

21.   Brown v. Entertainment Merchants Association, 564 U.S. 786, 792–793, 799–804 (2011); ibid., 851–856 (Breyer, J., dissenting); ibid., 816, 818–819 (Alito, J., concurring); ibid., 821–839 (Thomas, J., dissenting).

22.   Terminiello v. City of Chicago, 4 ("clear and present danger"); Chaplinsky v. New Hampshire, 572 ("by their very utterance").

23.   Terminiello v. City of Chicago, 32 (Jackson, J., dissenting).

24.   Ibid., 4 (opinion of the Court) ("vitality of civil and political institutions"); Brown v. Entertainment Merchants Association, 800.

25.   United States v. Miller, 307 U.S. 174, 178 (1939).

26.   District of Columbia v. Heller, 554 U.S. 570, 626–627, 629 (2008); McDonald v. City of Chicago, 561 U.S. 742 (2010).

27.   District of Columbia v. Heller, 625; McDonald v. City of Chicago, 788; Adam Winkler, *Gun Fight: The Battle over the Right to Bear Arms in America* (New York: W. W. Norton, 2011), 287.

28. Michael Waldman, *The Second Amendment: A Biography* (New York: Simon and Schuster, 2014); Jonathan Simon, "Gun Rights and the Constitutional Significance of Violent Crime," *William and Mary Bill of Rights Journal* 12 (2004): 335–356.

29. Eric Lichtblau and Motoko Rich, "N.R.A. Envisions 'a Good Guy with a Gun' in Every School," *New York Times,* December 22, 2012, p. A1; McDonald v. City of Chicago, 891, 895 (Stevens, J., dissenting).

30. McDonald v. City of Chicago, 767, 789–790; District of Columbia v. Heller, 629; Aaron J. Kivisto et al., "Firearm Ownership and Domestic versus Nondomestic Homicide in the U.S.," *American Journal of Preventative Medicine* 57 (2019): 311–320; Paul S. Nestadt et al., "Urban-Rural Differences in Suicide in the State of Maryland: The Role of Firearms," *American Journal of Public Health* 107 (2017): 1548–1553; David Hemenway, "There's a Scientific Consensus on Guns—and the NRA Won't Like It," *Los Angeles Times,* April 22, 2015.

31. Aidan Graham, "District Attorney Spars with NYPD over Increase in Northern Brooklyn Shootings," *Brooklyn Paper,* July 12, 2019; Alex Yablon, "Larry Krasner's Lonely, Radical Crusade to Solve America's Gun Problem," *New Republic,* January 28, 2020 (quoting Brendan O'Malley, Pennsylvania's chief deputy attorney general for gun violence).

32. Terry v. Ohio, 392 U.S. 1, 10, 17 (1968); Illinois v. Wardlow, 528 U.S. 119 (2000); Brown v. Texas, 443 U.S. 47 (1979); Seth W. Stoughton, "*Terry v. Ohio* and the (Un)forgettable Frisk," *Ohio State Law Journal* 15 (2017): 19–33.

33. See, for example, Daniel Bergner, "Is Stop-and-Frisk Worth It?," *Atlantic,* April 2014.

34. Greg Ridgeway, *Analysis of Racial Disparities in the New York Police Department's Stop, Question, and Frisk Practices* (Santa Monica, CA: RAND, 2007), 8–11; Jeffrey Bellin, "The Right to Remain Armed," *Washington University Law Review* 93 (2015): 1–43, at 4; Sharad Goel, Justin M. Rao, and Ravi Shroff, "Precinct or Prejudice? Understanding Racial Disparities in New York City's Stop-and-Frisk Policy," *Annals of Applied Statistics* 10 (2016): 365–394, 366.

35. District of Columbia v. Heller, 626–627; Silvester v. Becerra, 138 S. Ct. 945 (2018) (Thomas, J., dissenting) ("disfavored right"); Peruta v. California, 137 S. Ct. 1995 (2017) (Thomas, J., dissenting, joined by Gorsuch, J.) (same); Joseph Blocher, "Gun Rights Talk," *Boston University Law Review* 94 (2014): 813–833, at 815 (2014).

36. Bellin, "Right to Remain Armed," 5, 17, 25–26, 40; Commonwealth v. Hicks, 208 A.3d 916 (Penn. 2019); Pinner v. State, 74 N.E.3d 226 (Ind. 2017); Northrup v. City of Toledo Police Department, 785 F.3d 1128 (6th Cir. 2015).

37. See, for example, Matthew J. Wilkins, "Armed and Not Dangerous? A Mistaken Treatment of Firearms in *Terry* Analysis," *Texas Law Review* 95 (2017): 1165–1188; Northrup v. City of Toledo Police Department, 1132.

38. Mary Anne Franks, *The Cult of the Constitution: Our Deadly Devotion to Guns and Free Speech* (Stanford, CA: Stanford University Press, 2019), 101–102.

39. Jennifer Eberhardt, *Biased: Uncovering the Hidden Prejudice That Shapes What We See, Think and Do* (New York: Viking, 2019); Paul Butler, *Chokehold: Policing Black Men* (New York: New Press, 2017), 91; Floyd v. City of New York, 959 F. Supp. 2d 540 (S.D.N.Y. 2013); Sharad Goel et al., "Combatting Police Discrimination in the Age of Big Data," *New Criminal Law Review* 20 (2017): 181–232, at 208–211, 215–217.

40. Mike Baker, "He Wrote, 'Kill All Women.' He Kept His Guns," *New York Times,* November 19, 2019, p. A1; Timothy Williams, "What Are 'Red Flag' Laws, and How Do They Work?," *New York Times,* August 7, 2019, p. A14.

41. Barry Meier and Andrew Martin, "Real and Virtual Firearms Nurture a Marketing Link," *New York Times,* December 25, 2012, p. A1; "NRA: Full Statement by Wayne LaPierre in Response to Newtown Shootings," *Guardian,* December 21, 2012.

42. American Law Institute, Model Penal Code § 3.04(2)(b)(ii).

43. Colo. Rev. Stat. § 18-1-704.5; Stuart P. Green, "Castles and Carjackers: Proportionality and the Use of Deadly Force in Defense of Dwellings and Vehicles," *University of Illinois Law Review* (1999): 1–41, at 3–4.

44. Franks, *Cult of the Constitution,* 93–94; Fla. Stat. § 776.032.

45. Franks, *Cult of the Constitution,* 94 (quoting arguments by Don and Matt Gaetz for Florida's stand-your-ground law); *National Task Force on Stand Your Ground Laws, Final Report and Recommendations* (American Bar Association, 2015), 19 (quoting Marcisco).

46. Bretherick v. State, 170 So.3d 766 (Fla. 2015); Wood v. People, 255 P.3d 1136 (Colo. 2011); *National Task Force on Stand Your Ground Laws, Final Report and Recommendations,* 23; Tamara F. Lawson, "A Fresh Cut in an Old Wound—A Critical Analysis of the Trayvon Martin Killing, the Prosecutors' Discretion, and the Stand Your Ground Law," *University of Florida Journal of Law and Public Policy* 23 (2012): 271–310, at 287–288.

47. Caroline E. Light, *Stand Your Ground: A History of America's Love Affair with Lethal Self-Defense* (Boston: Beacon Press, 2017), vii, ix.

48. Franks, *Cult of the Constitution,* 97; Tamara Rice Lave, "Shoot to Kill: A Critical Look at Stand Your Ground Laws," *University of Miami Law Review* 61 (2013): 827–860, at 827–831; Ralph Blumenthal, "Fatal Shootings Test Limits of New Self-Defense Law in Texas," *New York Times,* December 13, 2007, p. A32; Adam B. Ellick, "Grand Jury Clears Texan in the Killing of 2 Burglars," *New York Times,* July 1, 2008, p. A19.

49. Lizette Alvarez and Cara Buckley, "Zimmerman Is Acquitted in Trayvon Martin Killing," *New York Times,* July 14, 2013, p. A1.

50. Light, *Stand Your Ground*, viii.

51. Jackie Calmes and Helene Cooper, "A Personal Note as Obama Speaks on Death of Boy," *New York Times*, March 24, 2012, at A1.

52. Cynthia Lee, "(E)racing Trayvon Martin," *Ohio State Journal of Criminal Law* 12 (2014): 91–113, at 110–111; Light, *Stand Your Ground*, viii ("core responsibility of the ideal citizen"); Patrick Michels, "Joe Horn and Five Years with the Texas Castle Doctrine," *Texas Observer*, May 8, 2012.

53. Franks, *Cult of the Constitution*, 92–100; Light, *Stand Your Ground*, 1; *National Task Force on Stand Your Ground Laws, Final Report and Recommendations*, 12–14; John K. Roman, *Race, Justifiable Homicide, and Stand Your Ground Laws: Analysis of FBI Supplementary Homicide Report Data* (Washington, DC: Urban Institute, 2013); Andrew Morral and Rosanna Smart, "Study: 'Stand Your Ground' Laws Increase Violence," *Orlando Sentinel*, September 11, 2019; "Effects of Stand-Your-Ground Laws on Violent Crime," RAND, Gun Policy in America, March 2, 2018, https://www.rand.org/research/gun-policy/analysis/stand-your-ground/violent-crime.html.

54. Kathy Leodler and Paul Leodler, *Report of Investigation regarding Representative Matt Shea, Washington State House of Representatives* (Silverdale, WA: Rampart Group, 2019); Mike Baker, "A Legislator Rose in the G.O.P. while Preparing for a Civil War," *New York Times*, December 24, 2019, p. A1.

55. Jefferson to William Stephens Smith, November 13, 1878, in *Letters and Addresses of Thomas Jefferson*, ed. William B. Parker and Jonas Viles (New York: Unit Book, 1905), 65; Kirk Johnson and Jack Healy, "Armed Protesters Vow to Stay on Oregon Refuge Indefinitely," *New York Times*, January 4, 2016, p. A1; Julie Turkewitz and Eric Lichtblau, "Shooting of Occupier Is Called Justified; F. B. I. Faces Scrutiny," *New York Times*, March 9, 2016, p. A11; "Joe Horn at the Alamo Tea Party in San Antonio," Don Amato, YouTube video, April 17, 2009, https://youtu.be/UygmxerRfbU.

56. Jo Thomas, "Closing Arguments Made in Oklahoma Bomb Case," *New York Times*, December 16, 1997, p. A16; Donald Black, "Crime as Social Control," *American Sociological Review* 48 (1983): 34–45, at 34–36, 39.

CONCLUSION

1. "Leading Causes of Death in Males, United States," Centers for Disease Control and Prevention, accessed June 17, 2020, https://www.cdc.gov/healthequity/lcod/index.htm; "Violent Crime," United Health Foundation, America's Health Rankings, accessed June 17, 2020, https://www.americashealthrankings.org/explore/annual/measure/Crime/; *Criminal Victimization, 2018* (Washington, DC: United States Department of Justice, 2019), 4; Franklin E. Zimring, *When Police*

Kill (Cambridge, MA: Harvard University Press, 2017); "Factsheet: Preventing Intimate Partner Violence (2019)," Centers for Disease Control and Prevention, https://www.cdc.gov/violenceprevention/pdf/ipv-factsheet508.pdf; Rick Rojas and Richard Fasset, "Gangs, Riots, Killings: 'Undeniable Crisis' in Mississippi Prisons," *New York Times,* January 10, 2020, p. A21.

2.   Jason Horowitz, "Pope Says He Is Sorry over Slap on Hands," *New York Times,* January 2, 2020, p. A6.

3.   Deut. 17:8 (King James Version).

ACKNOWLEDGMENTS

Earlier versions of parts of this book were presented as the 2018 Kadish Lecture at the University of California, Berkeley; as the 2019 Criminal Justice Lecture at Goldsmiths, University of London; at law faculty workshops at Stanford, the University of California, Berkeley, the University of California, Davis, the University of San Diego, the University of Southern California, the University of Utah, and Vanderbilt University; at the Law of the Police Conference at the University of South Carolina in 2019; and at two sessions of the annual Criminal Justice Roundtable, one held at Harvard in 2018 and the other at Yale in 2019. I am grateful for the criticism and suggestions I received on these occasions, especially from Kathy Abrams, Scott Altman, Ashutosh Bhagwat, Paul Cassell, Sharon Dolovich, Trevor Garner, Dimitrios Giannoulopoulos, Rachel Harmon, Youngjae Lee, Katerina Linos, Sara Mayeux, Saira Mohamed, Daphna Renan, Dan Richman, Alice Ristroph, Andrea Roth, Jonathan Simon, Avani Sood, Seth Stoughton, and Aaron Tang. In between, many friends and colleagues read parts of the book and helped me strengthen it; I am particularly indebted to Michelle Anderson, Rick Banks, Ira Ellman, Todd Foglesong, James Forman, Barry Friedman, Emma Kaufman, Nicola Lacey, Máximo Langer, Bernadette Meyler, Deborah Rhode, Michael Wald, and Frank Zimring. As usual, my brother Jeff Sklansky paired perceptive criticism with warm encouragement. Once I finished the manuscript, James Forman, Jonathan Simon, Carol Steiker, and Frank Zimring all graciously read the whole thing, and the book is much better because of the feedback they provided.

Sharmila Sen, the editorial director of Harvard University Press, served as the book's principal editor and improved it in countless ways. I am deeply grateful for the faith Sharmila showed in the book and for her sage counsel and constructive criticism. Often she understood the book better than I did. The book's production editor at HUP, Louise Robbins, and Wendy Nelson, its copy editor at Westchester Publishing Services, sharpened my arguments and saved me from many embarrassing errors. Heather Hughes at HUP and Angela Piliouras at WPS kept the entire editorial process running smoothly, a remarkable feat in the pandemic year of 2020. I am indebted as well to Stephanie Vyce at HUP for helpful guidance and to David Luljak for preparing the index.

Stanford Law School has been a welcoming and sustaining home. I am grateful to my colleagues and students, to two wise and supportive deans, Liz Magill and Jenny Martinez, and to my superb administrative associate, Ginny Smith. I owe many thanks to the entire staff of the Robert Crown Law Library, and in particular to Richard Porter and to four current and former research librarians, Leizel Ching, Marion Miller, Katherine Siler, and George Wilson. Two law students at Stanford, Emma Schindler and Jennifer Teitell, also provided excellent research assistance, and in writing Chapter 3 I benefited from research presented in an insightful seminar paper by Clare Riva. Alain Kelder, in the law school's information technology department, helped me get the data for Figures 1 and 4.

I cannot express the extent of my debt to the executive director of the Stanford Criminal Justice Center, Debbie Mukamal, and to my fellow faculty co-directors at the center, Bob Weisberg and the late Joan Petersilia. Suffice it to say that their influence can be found on every page of this book. Joan's death in 2019 was a hard blow for Stanford and for the world of criminal justice scholarship. For Bob and Debbie and me it also meant losing a treasured friend.

My deepest thanks go to my wife, Deborah Lambe, and to our wonderful son, Joseph Edward Lambe Sklansky, to whom this book is dedicated.

INDEX

Note: Page numbers in italic type indicate figures.

ACCA. *See* Armed Career Criminal Act
ACLU (American Civil Liberties
　Union), 77
actus reus, 37, 86, 121, 264n88
affirmative action, 1
African Americans: and corporal
　punishment, 176, 178; mass
　incarceration of, 1, 135; as perpetrators
　and victims of crime, 61–62; police
　violence against, 113; and sexual vio-
　lence, 135–137, 139; situational vs.
　characterological explanations for
　crimes of, 87; in sports, 35; stop-and-
　frisk policing of, 103; war on drugs
　and, 64; whites' perception of
　criminality of, 61–63, 87; youth vio-
　lence committed by, 161–162
aggravated assault, 71–74
Alabama, 177, 178, 186–188, 191, 193
Alito, Samuel, 173–174, 208–209, 211,
　213, 214
American Academy of Pediatrics, 175
American Bar Association, 75, 224
American Civil Liberties Union
　(ACLU), 77
American exceptionalism, 39–40, 222
American Law Institute (ALI), 53, 133, 222
American Legislative Exchange Council,
　223

animals: violence associated with, 63, 94,
　115–116; whites' association of African
　Americans with, 63
Antifa, 60
anti-rape movement, 127–134, 139
anti-Semitism, 204–205
Arkansas, 69, 177, 178
armed and dangerous standard, 104, 105,
　216, 218
Armed Career Criminal Act (ACCA,
　1984), 20–22, 75–84
assault, 71–74
authoritarianism, 28–29

"bad apples," law-breaking police as, 94,
　116–117, 234
Bail Reform Act (1984), 78
Baldwin, James, 109
Barrett, Lisa Feldman, 17
battered woman syndrome, 144–145
Beck, Glenn, 229
Beckles, Travis, 83
Bellin, Jeffrey, 217
benefit of clergy, 48
Bentham, Jeremy, 52
Bibas, Stephanos, 184–185
Bible, 175, 239
Biden, Joe, 249n37
Bittner, Egon, 265n8